RESEARCHING AMERICAN-MADE TOY SOLDIERS

32 YEARS OF ARTICLES

RESEARCHING AMERICAN-MADE TOY SOLDIERS

32 YEARS OF ARTICLES

by

Richard O'Brien

RAMBLE HOUSE

ISBN 13: 978-1-60543-310-3

ISBN 10: 1-60543-310-1

Cover Design: Gavin L. O'Keefe

Preparation: Richard O'Brien and Fender Tucker
Cover photo by Richard O'Brien

INDEX

INTRODUCTION

I've loved toy soldiers virtually all my life. My mother believed I was fascinated by them before I was two. About the age of eleven or twelve I began wondering about the companies that made them; where they were located, how the figures were cast, how they were painted, and so on. I could find no information at all.

In the 1970s I worked on a project that required research in New York's mammoth Fifth Avenue Library. While awaiting the articles I'd requested to arrive from the stacks, I began checking the index cards for books on toys, and started ordering them as well as additional information for my original project. Bare mentions of toy soldiers, and no real information at all.

I made a few more stabs, with little effect, until my literary agent landed me a contract with a publisher for a book that eventually was called "Collecting Toys". The advance was small, but I used it as justification for pursuing my research with more intensity.

That was about 1977, I've been doing it ever since, and always with great joy, as one mystery after another fell away and inevitably other mysteries emerged that required solution. Eventually, all the major questions were answered, but the relatively minor remaining ones are intriguing enough, so I keep searching.

As the reader will find, I tried everything possible to get answers. The toy-trade magazines, bureaus of incorporation (tracking down the names found there), letters to the editors of newspapers where companies had been located to ask for information from former workers, even to stopping people in the streets in likely areas in the hope of finding further answers. I've spoken to former owners, former employees, to relatives and friends of both owners and sculptors, all of them helpful and gracious.

My original interest was just the dimestore toy soldiers of my childhood—all of them in the three-inch range—and basically bought by me between 1937 and 1942. But the late Hank Anton, a fellow collector, began pressing me to find out about all the companies that had produced toy soldiers in the United States, from the earliest days on. Those urgings eventually prevailed, and my subsequently-aroused curiosity about those firms kept me going. A huge help in this area was my finding a trove of Playthings Magazines in the offices of that ongoing publication, from its first issue in 1903. Toys & Novelties, a periodical that started about that early, was another rich source.

I don't know if this book will have many readers, but I know it will have one. As I've put these articles together for this book I've tried very hard to not get caught up in one piece after another that began to seize my interest, deciding to wait till I had this publication in hand. I love this stuff. Always have, and I assume I always will.

I've attempted to indicate the issue and date of each article. OTSN stands for Old Toy Soldier Newsletter, ATW for Antique Toy World, TSR is Toy Soldier Review and OTS Old Toy Soldier magazine.

Richard O'Brien
2009

RESEARCHING AMERICAN-MADE TOY SOLDIERS

32 YEARS OF ARTICLES

PART 1
by Richard O'Brien

AUBURN RUBBER CORP.

AUBURN INDIANA

★ ARMY DEFENSE SETS   ★ ANTI-AIRCRAFT GUNS
★ DREADNAUGHTS   ★ SEARCHLIGHT BATTERY
★ AIRPLANES   ★ AUTOMOBILES
★ MACHINE GUNNERS   ★ MANY OTHERS

Although four major companies manufactured toy soldiers in the United States prior to World War II, collectors, dealers and writers have concentrated almost entirely on Barclay, Manoil and Grey Iron, while ignoring the fourth, which is, of course, Auburn Rubber Corporation.

This is understandable to some extent. Certain of the solid rubber soldiers produced by Auburn had a tendency to look a little...well, silly. Unlike their unyielding metallic counterparts, Auburn's figures frequently had problems with maintaining their dignity, leaning this way and that, their bodies slanting outward from equally uncertain stands, giving them a precariously balanced, even drunken appearance. In addition, while Barclay's soldiers often appeared heroic and intelligent because of their curved eyelid-eyebrows with attached dot eyes, and Manoil's and Grey's figures get by to some extent with their straight line eyebrows and disattached dot eyes, Auburn's soldiers were given only a meager dot (no eyebrows or lids), investing them with a cartoony, simple-minded look. Judged by visage, Barclay's figures often were leaders, Auburn's always proles.

Also, probably due to their medium, Auburn's men were not as finely detailed as Barclay's or Manoil's, though in my opinion their later designs surpassed Grey's in both detail and imagination. Finally, there was the important matter of "feel". There is satisfactory weight to the three metal lines, while the lightness of rubber robs the Auburn soldiers of tactile pleasure.

Despite all these defects, I believe that Auburn deserves much more consideration than it has received till now, and hope through this article to stimulate more interest, and perhaps bring a greater number of the figures into the open.

Not much is known at present about the Auburn Rubber Corporation, which also used the name Aub-Rub'r. It appears to have begun operation around 1935 in Auburn, Indiana, and was the only American toy soldier company to stamp its geographical location on its product. As a child I envisioned Auburn as being a large manufacturing city, rather like Gary, Indiana, but in fact its 1940 census reveals a population of 5415.

A study of the magazines Playthings and Toys and Novelties shows the first Auburn ad in March, 1936 in Playthings Magazine. This is not a terribly reliable gauge, as Barclay appeared rarely in those magazines, and Manoil only twice (both times only as a maker of toy automobiles). However, in an extensive classified listing of toy soldier makers in the July 1934 issue of Toys and Novelties, Barclay and Grey are among the many listed while Auburn is not, which leads to the conclusion that Auburn (like Manoil) probably began around 1935, since its March 1936 ad has the look and feel of an already established company.

Although Auburn has been relatively neglected by those interested in American toy soldiers, anyone reading the pages of the toy trades from Auburn's era would have concluded that Auburn was the most successful manufacturer of all. Barclay would occasionally buy a small print ad, only once turning up with a fairly good-sized display ad, and was sporadically listed as a manufacturer of lead soldiers. Manoil was a total washout as far as advertising its soldiers went, and though Grey advertised more regularly than Auburn, most of its ads were one-inch institutional affairs, and the occasional large ads that it took as often as not concentrated on its other products. Auburn, however, ran a number of large display ads, at least once in a two-color process, and regularly employed drawings or (more frequently) photographs of its soldiers and other models.

OTSN 12/77

My impression, as a toy soldier-shopper beginning in the late 1930's, is that Auburn had more prestige than either Manoil or Grey, as, like Barclay, Auburn was found in the "class" five and tens, which were Woolworth's. Manoil was more likely to turn up at another good (but not as good) five and ten, Kresge's for example, while Grey, at least in the New York area, was generally to be found only in the shadows of dimly-lit, unprepossessing candy stores. (By 1941 this had changed - in the New York area at least - with Auburn no longer prominent, and Barclay and Manoil sharing the counter space at Woolworth's.)

While its competitors seem to have shrouded their modelmakers in obscurity, Auburn trumpeted the names of the designers of their soldiers and their boxes. In the April 1936 Playthings, the soldiers are advertised as "All designed by McCandlish" (or perhaps McCandish - my notes may be inaccurate on this), and five months later Auburn allowed "The molds are perfectly executed from excellent designs by Edward McCandish (definitely no "l" in McCandish in this ad).

Auburn had reason to trumpet that its boxes were designed by "Martin Ullman, Internationally famout package designer" (and New York-based), because in 1940 Auburn's packaged set of 18 baseball players won the Grand Prize at the 3rd National Toy Packaging Contest. This was no obscure, rigged affair; Auburn was competing with a number of heavyweights, with the games giant Parker Brothers having to settle for second place.

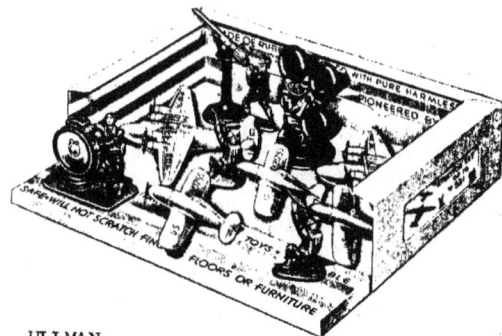

ULLMAN
1940 PACKAGING

Auburn's boxes, while prize-winning, were also models of how to advertise a product. Presumably, rubber soldiers had been introduced as an alternative for parents who worried about the effect lead soldiers might have on their offspring. The first edition of Consumers Union in May, 1936 warned against metal toys such as soldiers since they were found to be "of a soft metal alloy containing a high percentage of lead", which was considered dangerous not only to younger children "who enjoy their toys with their mouths as well as their hands", but also to elder children, since lead rubs off on the hands and can be "carried to the mouth."

In any event, over the years Auburn boxes contained such messages as: "Protect the Child While Playing," "Colored With Pure Vegetable Dyes", "Sanitary, Noiseless, Washable", "Will Not Scratch Fingers, Floors or Furniture", "Harmless, washable, unbreakable, and will not scratch or mar furniture", "Bounce 'em! Drop 'em! Squeeze 'em! Throw 'em! They just can't break!" and "Will Not Cut, Scratch, or Mar Furniture". (In 1935 Barr Rubber of Sandusky, Ohio advertised "Due to their rubber construction, these beautiful little cars cannot harm the child or mar the furniture." Since the phrase was similar, and the design of the cars remarkably like the ones done by Auburn, it's possible that Auburn was begun in 1935 by a defector, or defectors, from Barr.)

Auburn Rubber
Part 2

by Richard O'Brien

Auburn seems to have gone through three stages of figure development. The first were frail-looking, with long thin bodies and small heads. (The heads were small for a toy soldier - actually they were more in proportion than most.) These would include the first versions of the port arms infantryman, officer, bugler, machine gunner and tommy gunner, as well as a mounted officer in overcoat, and the "Foreign Legion." The latter consisted of an officer with sword and plumed headgear, and infantry at port arms; the headpiece was rather like a pith helmet and the uniform consisted of a hip-length belted tunic and trousers. The Foreign Legion, presumably when in another color, was also called some sort of "Guards" (perhaps "Imperial" or "Palace" - it's impossible to tell from the magazine ad reproduction of their boxtop). Though they did have their own offbeat charm, these figures were simple, with minimum detail.

At least as early as September 1936 the second version began to emerge, with some of the more respectable figures redesigned in a stockier and larger-headed size. Included were the redesigned running tommygunner, observer with binoculars, motorcycle with sidecar, and kneeling, firing AA gun upward. The third version seems to have been introduced in 1941, with this last edition incorporating many changes. These newly-designed soldiers were now more well-proportioned and realistic than any of their predecessors, were painted a medium brown, including helmets (as opposed to the silver-helmeted, light yellow-brown of the earlier military), and contained the largest proportion of dashing action figures.

My considerable thanks to Ed Poole, Jerry Zunker, and Don Pielin for helping me to compile the lists of soldiers and other pieces manufactured by Auburn that appear on page 9 and in Part 3 of this article. Where items are underlined, this is Auburn's own description.

All Auburn photographs by Ed Poole.

OTSN V2#3 2/78

AUBURN PRODUCTION

MILITARY

1. Marching at Port Arms — 1st version, smaller with rectangular base; came in
   several colors: light blue, navy, white, khaki, olive green with lighter green
   leggings. One of the blue versions was U.S. Marines.
2. Marching at Port Arms — 2nd version, larger, with oval base.
3. Bugler — 1st version, came in white, blue, yellow, khaki. Bugles in yellow and
   silver; helmets in silver, khaki, white, etc.
4. Bugler — later version, larger, with oval base.
5. "Foreign Legion" officer with plumed headgear, rectangular base; also known as
   "(?) Guards".
6. "Foreign Legion" infantryman, port arms. Also as "(?) Guards".
7. Officer — 1st version. Known in white with black trim.
8. Officer — 2nd version. White, khaki and blue uniforms.
9. Charging Soldier — Running with tommy gun at 45 degree angle — 1st version.
10. Charging Soldier — 2nd version.
11. Cavalry officer mounted on horse, long coat.
12. Machine Gunner — 1st version. Kneeling, firing machine gun.
13. Machine Gunner — 2nd version. Came in silver and khaki helmets.
14. Doctor.
15. Nurse — white and khaki uniforms.
16. Stretcher-Bearer in Overseas Cap.
17. Soldier lying wounded, feet in cast, head bandaged, arm in sling.
18. Kneeling with binoculars.
19. Signalman with semaphore flags.
20. Crawling, arm outstretched, rifle slung over shoulder.
21. Grenade thrower — holding rifle on ground in front. Came in yellow-brown and
    the later medium brown, with later version having medium brown helmet.
22. Aircraft Gunner — Kneeling, firing AA gun upward. Known in brown and grey.
    Note: The rest appear to be 1941 era.
23. Aircraft Defender — Standing, firing 50 cal. AA gun upward; water-cooled.
24. Color Bearer — carrying American flag.
25. Marching Soldier — Slope arms.

26. Firing Soldier - Kneeling, firing rifle.
27. Plane Shooter #272 - Kneeling, firing rifle upward.
28. Sound Detector - Standing with large sound detector, three "ears".
29. Searchlight - Standing with searchlight.
30. Trench Mortar #296 - Kneeling, placing shell in mortar.
31. Tank Defender - Firing submachine gun from shoulder; beret, jodphurs, goggles.
32. Tank Soldier (?) - Running with box, in beret, scarf and goggles.
33. Tank Soldier (?) - Running, looking skyward; pilot helmet and goggles.
34. Motor Scout - Pilot type helmet, goggles, rifle in sheath.
35. Motorcycle - With sidecar (pre-1941).
36. Motorcyclist - Looks like policeman, but in khaki uniform; presumably also came in blue - pre-1941.

Below: an example of what happens when a toy soldier fancier writes for comic strips. Richard O'Brien, the author of this Auburn series, is one of the writers for "Inside Woody Allen". His new book, tentatively titled AMERICANA TOY VALUE GUIDE NO. 1, is scheduled for publication this spring or summer by Books Americana. Cartoon reprinted by permission of King Features.

Auburn Rubber
Part 3

by Richard O'Brien

Unlike its competitors, Auburn
produced no cowboys, Indians,
sailors or civilians, except
for baseball and football
players. However, it did manufacture a
number of other toys. In 1940, Auburn
advertised "Autos, racers, airplanes,trucks, tractor (note the singular), farm animals,
farm implements, soldiers, ball players, fire engines, tanks, trains, sponge rubber
blocks, 5¢, 10¢, 25¢, 50¢ and $1.00 retail." Other products it advertised at one time
or another were: Streamlined Carry Car Trailer, quoits, hammers, hatchets, knives,
artillery, building bricks, circus sets (no indication of what they consisted), hop
bunnies, scotties, story book characters, and most intriguingly, in March, 1936,
"Ethiopians".

How big was Auburn, and how successful? Again, no one seems to know much of anything,
but in the August 1939 issue of Toys and Novelties, Auburn stated that it had made
"around 4 million of these tractors" (sold at 25¢), and as Toys and Novelties put it,
"claims to be the largest manufacturer of tractors in the U.S."

Auburn, like Barclay, Manoil and Grey, appears to have numbered its soldiers, but, like
Grey, did so only for its own purposes, never stamping the number on them. A paragraph
on Auburn's new toys in the March, 1941 issue of Toys and Novelties lists #272 Plane
Shooter (rifleman firing upward) and #296 Trench Mortar (soldier placing shell in mortar).

There have been several Auburn "mystery figures". These are among the most attractive
of Auburn's soldiers, and include a running "pilot", looking skyward; a running soldier in
beret and scarf carrying a box; and a soldier with goggles on his headgear, wearing
jodphur trousers and firing an automatic weapon from the shoulder. The speculation has
been that they were pilots, tank soldiers, dismounted motorcyclists (they resemble one
of Auburn's three motorcyclists, the Motor Scout), or even commandos. The mystery seems
to have been solved. A short paragraph in the April, 1941 Toys and Novelties discloses
that Auburn's "Defense Set" contained, among its 29 pieces, "three tank soldiers, two
tank defenders". Almost certainly the latter would be the man with automatic weapon,
and either or both (probably the latter) the running "pilot" and running soldier with box
would be the "tank soldiers", presumably one of them presented in duplicate in the set.

With the exception of its "Ethiopians"[1] and the rather inoffensive-looking "Foreign
Legion", there is no record of Auburn having manufactured any special enemy soldiers.
However, at least one of Auburn's standard soldiers has been seen in the grey uniform
that seems to have represented the "enemy" for several manufacturers. This was the
kneeling ack-ack gunner, so it can be presumed that at least a few of his fellows were
also turned out in grey.

Auburn's baseball players also made their appearance in penny arcades before the war,
imprisoned under glass in pinball-type games with a baseball motif. Little is known
about the football players, other than the fact that Don Pielin owns a set or two. They
appear in none of the periodicals I've researched, and thus it seems likely they were

---

[1]It has been established since this series began that Auburn did produce Ethiopians
in its toy soldier size.

first produced in late 1941 or early 1942, just before the Second World War caused Auburn to shut down production on its toys.

By April 1942 the toy trades ran the phrase, "Listing temporarily suspended" in the categories of soldiers and rubber toys, and the pressures of time have kept me from researching Auburn after the war. However, I have been told by someone associated with Sun Rubber, an Auburn competitor, that sometime after the war Auburn moved to one of the Carolinas, and Don Pielin has traced them to New Mexico (probably Deming), where they eventually expired in the early 1960's.

The listing of known Auburn figures begun in the February OTSN with military figures #1-36 continues on page 6. The list of boxed sets is no doubt incomplete, and represents only what I found in the ads and literature contained in the toy magazines I went through. I would be interested in hearing from anyone with more information on Auburn and its products: Richard O'Brien; 173 Midland Ave.; Montclair, NJ 07042.

Auburn's Complete Line of Molded RUBBER TOYS

37-41 ARE BASEBALL PLAYERS: Batter, fielder, runner, catcher, pitcher
42-46 ARE FOOTBALL PLAYERS: Center on the ball, Lineman on all fours, Crouching line backer, Running back with ball, Quarterback passing. Football players came in red and blue.

VEHICLES, SHIPS, PLANES
1. Turretless Tank - Soldier's head sticking up, large (4½") and small (3") versions. Large in brown; small in olive drab.
2. Small ambulance - khaki and white versions
3. Cannons: one 155 mm 7" long; one 75mm 7" long; third unknown dimensions.
4. Truck - large (5½") marked USA, khaki; small, green (4")
5. Battleship (8¼")
6. Freighter (approx. 8")
7. Submarine (6½")
8. Two engine transport plane.
9. 4-Engine Clipper plane, about 5" wingspan, USA on port wing, number on starboard.
10. Pursuit ship, P-40 type. Approx. 4" wingspan; US 21755 on wings.
11. Single-engine pursuit ship. Earlier version. No details.
12. Pursuit Ship, radial engine, low wing monoplane, open cockpit, 4" wingspan, marked across wings "Pursuit Ship", "25-P-75".
13. Ground attack or dive bomber. Low wing, closed cockpit monoplane, air-cooled engine, 4" wingspan, marked AUB-RUER under fuselage. (This may be #11.)
SEE BOXED SETS FOR OTHER VEHICLES, ETC.

POSSIBLE AUBURN:

14. Trainer; low wing monoplane with two staggered open cockpits.
15. Bomber - 4 engine.

NOTE: Items sometimes attributed to Auburn that are actually Sun Rubber include Large Medium Tank, Large Scout Car with 4 Machine Gunners in red and khaki versions, Medium Truck more streamlined than Auburn's.

BOXED SETS

Dates shown are from magazine ads and articles.
1V means first version.

1. Army Train - Engine, two flat cars with military loads, two tiny howitzers, two soldiers, and perhaps two trucks. (date unknown)
2. 9/36 - Bugler, mounted officer, 10 port arms (2V), machine gunner. $1.00
3. 10/36 - #231 Soldier Set - Mounted officer, 1V machine-gunner, 1V port arms, 1V bugler.

4. 4/37 - Tommy gun 1V, mounted officer, 9 port arms 1V, bugler 1V
5. 8/37 - Officer, machine gunner, 10 port arms 2V, officer on horse, one tommy gunner, $1.00. Also 9/38 - $1.00
6. 8/37 - Wheeled Set - 2 large airplanes, 2 small airplanes, 2 Cord cars, 2 Ford sedans, 2 Ford coupes. $1.00
7. 1937? - Pony, horse, two sheep, cow, calf
8. 10/37 - 10 port arms 1V, 2 tommy guns 1V, 1 machine gunner 1V, 1 mounted officer, 1 bugler 1V
9. 10/37 - Foreign Legion (also 2 Guards) - 1 officer, 7 port arms
10. 10/37 - Horse, colt, cow, two calves, 4 sheep, collie, 3 fences
11. 10/37 - Horse, colt, cow, two sheep, calf
12. 4/39 - 4 racers (racing cars), ambulance, motorcycle cop, nurse, doctor
13. 1940 - #105 Farm Animal - cow, calf, 3 sheep, 6 ducks and chickens, 2 pigs, 2 piglets, horse and colt
14. 4/40 - #105 Farm Animal - cow, calf, 2 sheep, 2 ducks, 3 chickens, fence, collie, 4 pigs, others
15. 1940 - #245, Ball Players - set of 5. Batter, pitcher, catcher, 3 fielders, 2 runners (also 4/39)
16. 1940 - #255, Baseball Set of 13 - 2 pitchers, 2 batters, 2 catchers, 6 runners, 6 fielders
17. 4/39 - Ack-ack sitting, officer, two signalmen, two tommy gun, motorcycle (cop type), motorcycle & sidecar, observer and cannon. $1.00
18. 1940 - #503 Farm Implement Set, 8 pieces. Tractor, truck, disc harrow, etc.
19. 1940 - #501 Wheel Set - 3 Plymouths, 1 large Oldsmobile, large truck, small milk truck, small truck, motorcycle cop, 2 planes.
20. 4/40 - #201 Soldier Set - contents unknown.
21. 4/40 - #101 Animal Set - contents unknown.
22. 4/40 - #325 Train set - contents unknown.
23. 4/40 - #577 Train Set - engine, tender, 3 gondolas, one dump car, caboose.
24. 4/40 - #207 Artillery Set - large truck, officer, two signalmen, kneeling with AA gun, 2 tommy guns, motorcycle with sidecar, cannon, tank
25. 4/40 & 1941 - #227 First Aid Set - 2 nurses, officer, doctor, two stretcher bearers, wounded soldier, stretcher (may have been gauze rather than canvas)
26. 1941 - #531 Aviation Set - two "Clipper" planes, 3 "P-40 type" planes, standing with AA gun, sound detector, searchlight, 2 rifle shooters
27. 4/41 - Defense Set - color bearer, aircraft defender, howitzer gun, officer, motor scout, sound detector, searchlight, 3 tank soldiers, 2 tank defenders, 3 plane shooters, 2 machine gunners, 3 firing soldiers, 3 marching soldiers, 2 trench mortars, 2 tanks.

NOTE: In 1941 Auburn issued a catalogue, the only one mentioned in its ads. Ed Poole has also had an Auburn farm with heavy board buildings, animals and equipment.

OLD TOY SOLDIER NEWSLETTER

Volume 2, #6   August, 1978

POPULAR IRON-1938

GREY IRON'S MOST WANTED LIST

by Richard O'Brien

In the course of researching the pre-World War II American toy soldier companies, I received photocopies of pages 2-8 of the 1938 Grey Iron Toys catalog from the very helpful Sandra Malik of Donsco, Inc. (which absorbed Grey on July 1, 1974). Not only did the pages illustrate what apparently was Grey's full line for that period, but the drawings of the soldiers were individually marked in order of volume of sales for 1938.

The soldiers were broken down into three categories: the usual single figures, duplex figures (which include the large cannon), and mounted figures. The latter two categories had their order of popularity preceded by a "T" to indicate that they sold for 10¢.

Following is a list I've assembled, starting from the figure highest in sales. In addition to establishing the relative popularity of each figure (at least for 1938), this listing would also seem to be a good indication of which figures should now be the most common.

The list may contain some surprises. It did for me. As a boy, I'd have had to be really desperate to buy a color bearer instead of some other more dynamic or interestingly-posed figure, and a cannon, too, would have been a rather low priority. All figures listed, by the way, are the later, larger-sized "Iron Men" which Grey introduced in July, 1936.

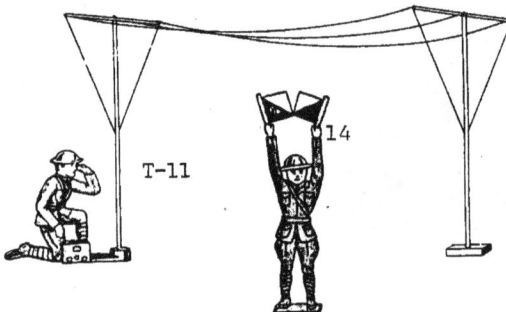

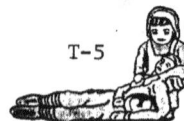

1. #24 Cannon, nickeled barrel, scarlet wheels, khaki carriage.
2. #13 U.S. Machine Gunner (seated)
3. #17/4 Legion Color Bearer
4. #6 U.S. Doughboy Shoulder Arms
5. #13/1 U.S. Machine Gunner (prone)
6. #11 Indian Chief, scarlet with black and white trim.
7. #4/6 U.S. Doughboy Combat Trooper (plunging rifle downward)
8. #21 Stretcher Bearer, khaki uniform, silver helmet, orange and brown trim
9. #4/2 U.S. Doughboy Combat Trooper (plunging rifle downward)
10. #12 Cowboy tan colored with scarlet and yellow trim (hands on hips)
11. #23 Red Cross Nurse, white uniform, blue cape lined with scarlet
12. #4/5 U.S. Doughboy Sharpshooter (kneeling with rifle)
13. #3 U.S. Infantry shoulder arms (cowboy hat)
14. #4/1 U.S. Doughboy signaling
15. #6/1 U.S. Doughboy charging
16. #4A U.S. Doughboy Officer with field glasses
17. #6/3 U.S. Doughboy Bomber (crawling with pistol)
18. #17/2 Legion Bugler
19. #20 Red Cross Doctor, white uniform, black trim
20. #17/3 Legion Drummer
21. #14/1 U.S. Sailor Signalman
22. #22 Stretcher with patient, khaki stretcher, white pillow
23. #14W U.S. Sailor
24. #3A U.S. Infantry Officer
25. #2 Cadet (with rifle)
26. #7/1 Legion Drum Major
27. #3/1 U.S. Infantry, port arms (campaign hat)
28. #22/2 Wounded on Crutches, khaki uniform, orange trim, white bandages
29. #6A U.S. Doughboy Officer
30. #6/2 U.S. Doughboy Sentry (in overcoat)
31. #25 Aviator, cream flying suit with orange trim
32. #11/1 Indian Brave copper colored, with blue, black & white trim
33. #22/1 Wounded sitting, khaki uniform, arm in white sling
34. #14W U.S. Naval Officer
35. #9 U.S. Marine, blue uniform, scarlet & white trim (rifle port arms)
36. #2A Cadet Officer
37. #6/4 U.S. Doughboy Grenade Thrower (rifle on slant)
38. #19 Knight in Armor
39. #3AR Red Cross Officer, khaki uniform, orange & brown trimmings, Red Cross arm band
40. #10 Royal Canadian Police (port arms)
41. #4/3 U.S. Doughboy with Range Finder
42. #14 U.S. Sailor (blue)
43. #4/4 U.S. Doughboy Ammunition Carrier
44. #6F Foreign Legion Shoulder Arms
45. #13F Foreign Legion Machine Gunner

46. #14A U.S. Naval Officer (blue, gold, black & white trim)
47. #3AP Traffic Officer, blue uniform, silver & black trimmings
48. #6/1F Foreign Legion Charging
49. #6/3F Foreign Legion Bomber (crawling)
50. #6AF Foreign Legion Officer
51. #15/1 Boy Scout Saluting
52. #15/2 Boy Scout Walking
53. #16/2 Pirate Chief
54. #16/4 Pirate with Hook
55. #16/3 Pirate with Dagger
56. #16/5 Pirate with Sword
57. #16/1 Pirate Boy

DUPLEX AND MOUNTED

T-1. #48 Large Shooting Cannon
T-2. #8M U.S. Cavalryman (mounted)
T-3. #8MA U.S. Cavalry Officer (mounted)
T-4. #12M Cowboy Mounted (horse bucking)
T-5. #D26 Nurse and wounded soldier
T-6. #D27 Doughboy supporting Wounded Soldier
T-7. #10M Royal Canadian Mounted
T-8. #11M Indian Mounted (lying on horse, firing rifle)
T-9. #8A/F Foreign Legion Cavalry Officer (mounted)
T-10. #8/F Foreign Legion Cavalryman (campaign hat, mounted)
T-11. #75 Radio Set, Operator and Aerial, Aerial, when erected, 7 inches high by 12 inches long.

(Note: all descriptions, except in parentheses, are Grey's.)

Richard O'Brien sent the photo of the hollowcast Indian marked
"Made in U.S.A." on the underside of the base. He's attached to
the ashtray by nut and bolt, with the bolt appearing to have
soldered onto the underside of the base. It's approximately
3½" high. Don Pielin has the same Indian and knows of
one other, but neither of these is attached to an ashtray
or has any indication that it was. Does anyone have any
information on this piece?

Mr. O'Brien also sent the photo of four Tommy Toys.
All are marked on the underside of the base with the
inscription 'Tommy Toy' and a description of the piece.
From left to right, they are 'Hand Grenade'; 'Wounded';
'Officer Gas Mask'; and 'Ground Arms'. The second
tallest, the 'Wounded', is 3" high. He knows they also
made a nurse and a man standing with a tommy gun marked
'Machine Gunner', but he has drawn a blank on
researching specifics about the company. Can
anyone help?

OTSN V2#7 10/78

Discovering Early **BARCLAY**

by Richard O'Brien

The Barclay Manufacturing Company was in business as early as 1924, quite probably starting in that year, under the aegis of a Frenchman named Donzé. Fortunately, several of the earliest employees are still around to tell their (and Barclay's) stories, and to identify some of the more obscure products of the company.

Louis Picco began at Barclay in 1924, George Fall in 1925, and Harry Bogaty, brother of the company's eventual owner, Michael Levy (Bogaty was the family's name in Poland) started as a summer worker in 1930, taking over as supervisor of soldier production in 1934. When I first questioned them, all three remembered Barclay as having made only three-inch soldiers, but the discovery of a piece that each had mentioned led to the refutation of that statement, and to the finding of a number of other arcane Barclay products of the 1920's and 1930's.

The figure recalled had been a mounted soldier with a moving arm, and when earlier this year I spotted a Britains-sized bugler on horseback in a New Jersey antiques barn, saw it had a movable arm and no identifying marks, I picked it up, just on the chance....

A photo of this piece, sent to the three men, led to a confirmation by all that, while it was not a 3" soldier, it was definitely a Barclay product, and furthermore, one of the men had more examples of early Barclays. I relayed the news on the first soldier to Ed Poole, who promptly fired back photos of other suspected Barclays, some of which the three men identified as the company's, and others which they, all three, agreed were not.

Since Picco began at the factory a year earlier than either of the others, and left in 1937, his memory of some toys and lack of knowledge of others has helped in at least tentative general dating of several. However, in all cases at least two (and generally three) identified the soldiers and other toys as Barclay-made.

The earliest shown here are probably the moving-arm figures, with Picco flatly stating "1924" on the photograph I sent him of the bugler on rearing horse (Figure 1). According to George Fall, who was in charge of the shipping department, the number on this was probably 87 or 187, and the same soldier also came with moving arm holding a pistol or a sword (Figure 1A). The soldier on non-charging horse (Figure 1B) would seem to be from the same era.

The mounted Indian (Figure 1) with movable rifle arm appears to be from this period. (According to Fall, its number was probably 89, with a mounted cowboy, also with movable arm, probably number 90.) The 2 3/4" cavalryman at the left in the same photo is "very early 1930's and probably late 1920's" according to Bogaty. There are no moving parts on this one.

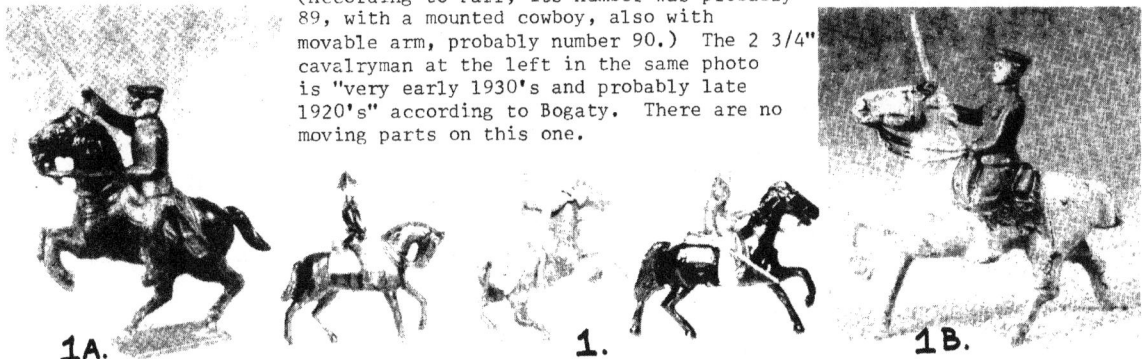

1A.   1.   1B.

The gracefully-sculpted ballplayers (Figure 2) are almost certainly from the 1920's, known by Picco and Fall who were at Barclay during that period, but not by Bogaty, who began in 1930. As with the aforementioned mounted men, the ballplayers have either no eyes at all, or a simple dot, not the unique eye normally associated with Barclay. The small (under 2¼") mounted soldier with steel helmet (Figure 3) is probably early 1930's, and also comes with no eye or a simple dot.

The monoplane (Figure 4) is middle 1930's and has metal wheels and propeller, both painted red; the plane is otherwise unpainted, with striations along wings and body. Since Picco remembers neither, the motorcycle rider and cart (Figure 5) and prairie schooner (Figure 6) are almost certainly 1937 or later, but judging by their look, are probably not very much younger than that. The motorcycle rider is two-dimensional and khaki-colored, while the cart is orange and three-dimensional. The motorcycle is approximately 2½" long; the prairie schooner with oxen under 6½" long.

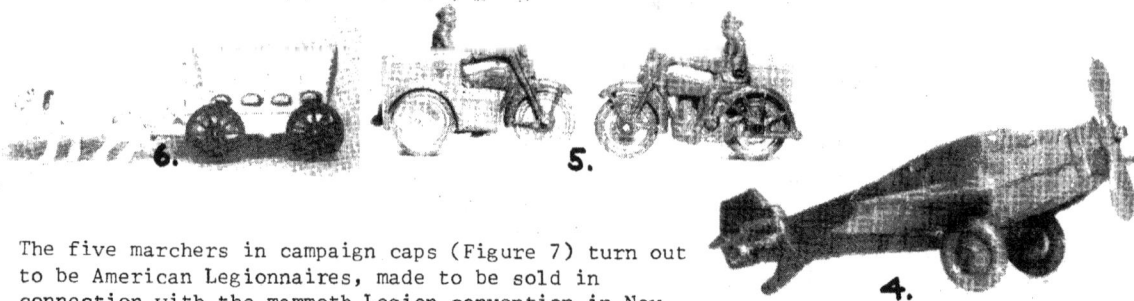

The five marchers in campaign caps (Figure 7) turn out to be American Legionnaires, made to be sold in connection with the mammoth Legion convention in New York in October, 1937, and assigned the number 953. These were produced in at least ten color combinations (there was also a flagbearer, not shown), with much detail, for Barclay, in the painting; the addition of an eyebrow above the standard Barclay eye reveals that the usual Barclay figure was graced with a dot eye attached to eyelashes or eyelid, rather than dot attached to eyebrow.

The Japanese pagoda, bridge, woman with umbrella (detachable from bridge), terii and bird (Figure 8) are almost certainly 1930's, probably fairly early, and seem to have been made to be used as a garden display. The pagoda is 2 3/4" high, including the pole above the roof. The eyes on the woman are two simple slanted lines, no dot attached.

The one mystery piece is the coach with two horses (Figure 9). According to Louis Picco, this is "not Barclay. I remember the mold in cast iron from Penn. If yours is lead it must be a copy." However, Fall and Bogaty remember it as being a Barclay product. Fall has no idea of the date and Bogaty responded "Barclay middle 30's (?)". Since the coach looks foreign and French to me, with no real tie to anything American of the 1920's or 30's, and since Donzé was French, my guess is that it would be one of

Barclay's earliest toys. Perhaps a design or mold
was brought over from Europe; possibly a few were
produced when Barclay began, and then a limited
run was done somewhere in the late 1930's, after
Picco had left. However, this is just conjecture,
and if anyone has more specific information, I'd
be glad to hear it.

P.S. What about the small Barclay-looking soldiers in Don Pielin's article in Volume 1,
Number 4 of OTSN? Harry Bogaty says, "All these figures look like Barclay products to
me", but George Fall says "definitely not", with Louis Picco echoing, "The small ones
are not Barclay."

Photos for Mr. O'Brien's article were supplied by Bill Kaufman, Norbert Schachter and
Ed Poole.

AUBURN RUBBER
by Richard O'Brien

While researching pre-WWII American toy soldier companies, I sent a letter to the Auburn Indiana Star, asking for information from their readers on the Auburn Rubber Corporation. I received two answers.

It's hard to conceive of coming up with two better informants. Charles (Mike) Hornett began with Auburn in 1919 and remained with the company until just a few years before its demise. Floyd Link, another long time emplyee, joined the company in 1930, participated in the production of Auburn's first toy, and lent me the catalog of photos (taken in 1938) which accompany this article.

Auburn was founded in 1910, as the Double Fabric Tire Corporation. Its product was auto tires and tubes, and about five years later the company changed its name to Auburn Rubber Crown Cord. By around 1928 it began molding rubber goods, making stick-on soles for shoes and various sizes of sport soles and heels, fly swatters, stair treads, can openers, etc.

However, it was not until 1935 that Auburn (also known as Aub-Rub'r) entered the toy business. Its president and chief stockholder, A. L. Murray, had gone to England and came back with a toy palace guard. Murray, who according to Floyd Link, was always trying to develop new items, came up with the idea of producing a soldier in rubber. The toy was taken to a local patternmaker who made patterns from it; original molds were then made from lead by Auburn and sample toys were molded for Murray. These samples were taken to an artist and decorated per Murray's instuctions. Presented to buyers, they immediately caught on, and Auburn quickly found itself very much in the toy business.

The first toys were five soldiers, which were molded in 24" rubber presses. Each mold contained 40 to 60 soldiers. Cure time was about 12 minutes. After removal from the mold, the excess rubber flash was trimmed off by hand, or later by "nipper" type dies.

ATW 1/79 V.9 #1

Freight cars approach the Auburn plant on the company's spur. Trucks are loaded at the shipping department exits. Four railroads intersect in Auburn, two trans-continental east-west federal highways are a few miles away and two main line north-south roads pass through the city.

Once trimmed, the soldiers were dipped in a base coat of laquer (advertised as "pure vegetable dyes"), and then sent down a conveyor belt for decorating, where women with small camel hair brushes added the finishing touches to uniforms, faces, belts, etc. After drying time, the soldiers, which sold for a nickel apiece, were individually wrapped in waxed paper and packed three dozen to a chipboard carton and 12 dozen chipboard cartons to a corrugated carton for shipment. Auburn's complete pre-war line of figures seems to have consisted of 37 military, five baseball players, and five football players.

Shortly after the soldiers went into production Auburn began producing wheeled toys. Its first car was a replica of the Cord, which was built in Auburn. (According to the Auburn-Cord-Duesenberg Museum in Auburn, other Auburn-built cars were the Auburn, Auburn Motor Buggy, DeKalb, DeSoto, DeSoto Majorette, Duesenberg, Eckhart, Handy Wagon, Imp, Imp-McIntyre, Kiblinger, McIntyre, McIntyre Special, Model, Union, and Zimmerman.) The cars were produced in much the same way as the soldiers, molded, trimmed, dipped with base coat laquer, and after the wheels were assembled, decorated by girls seated alongside a conveyor belt. The cars, like the soldiers, were designed outside the plant. Vehicles produced include Ford coupes and sedans, Plymouths, Oldsmobiles, racers, trucks, ambulances, and tractors. The tractor sold in the millions, and before the war ended toy production in 1942, Auburn was producing, among other things, trains, soldiers, vehicles, farm animals, airplanes, farm implements,

On this conveyor line assembling is continuous including dipping, assembly of wheels and axles, hand decorating, and, in the near foreground, inspection and sorting.

sponge rubber blocks, Streamlined Car Carry Trailer, quoits, hammers, hatchets, knives, circus sets, bunnies, scotties, and storybook characters.

During the war, Auburn was unable to use any rubber for toys. Although mostly involved in war production of soles, gaskets, soling sheets, etc., the company did experiment with non-critical products to produce toys. Used battery cases, sawdust and glue, excelsior and lime, and any other products that could possibly be molded into a toy were tried, but none worked out, and efforts were discontinued until the war ended and proper materials were again available.

For a time after the war, Auburn didn't have the space it wanted for toys, having added a great deal of new equipment to the plant, so the company bought a rubber plant in Connellsville, Pennsylvania, and set it up solely to produce rubber toys. After four years, buildings were added at Auburn and production of rubber toys resumed there in about 1950, continuing until 1952 when Auburn bought its first plastic injection molding machine. From then on all its toys were converted to vinyl plastic and were injection molded.

By 1959, Auburn had 16 molding machines, and a year later an offer from the city of Deming, New Mexico, to purchase its toy section only. Limited production began in Deming in February of 1960. By 1962 Auburn was producing 17 million toy items per year, as well as swim aids such as fins and masks.

However, by 1967 or 1968 the company went bankrupt. Today the largest single concentration of Auburn toys is probably at the Auburn-Cord-Duesenberg Museum, where several hundred toys, mostly autos, are on display in a 20' by 20' room.

Raw rubber is masticated in Banbury Mixers where compounding ingredients are added, and then milled through big rollers. Batches of stock are then put through extruding machines for heels and soles and other batches are calendered for soles, taps, and flyswatters. The rubber then goes to the PRESS ROOM above.

22

...of orders is assembled by responsible and capable clerks. Forms are checked and shipping instructions verified. The cartons are then sent to the trucks and freight cars.

These ... have the raised or overflow of rubber removed. Depending on the type of item they are either trimmed, buffed or die-trimmed. Proper ... at periods "humanize" labor conditions.

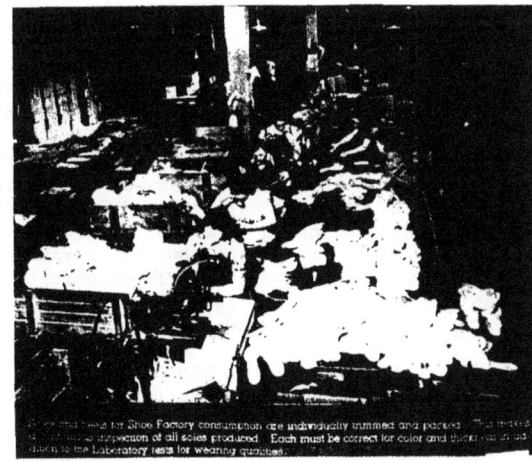

Soles and heels for Shoe Factory consumption are individually trimmed and packed. This trained ... is inspection of all soles produced. Each must be correct for color and thickness and ... check to the Laboratory tests for wearing qualities.

GENERAL OFFICE

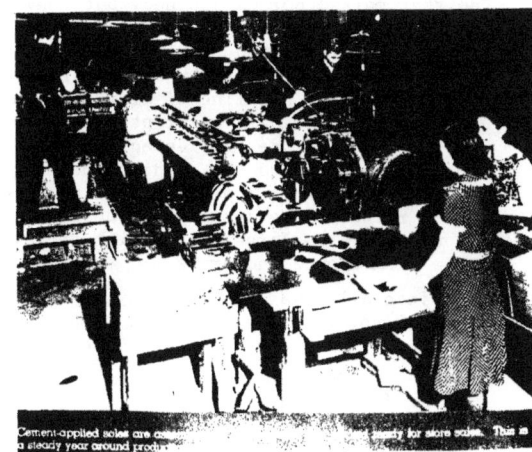

Cement-applied soles are ... ready for store sales. This is a steady year around prod...

SONS of BARCLAY
by Richard O'Brien

FERTILITY: The Barclay Mfg. Co. was not only the largest pre-WW II maker of American toy soldiers, it also appears to have spawned more offshoots than any of its competitors. Some sprang directly from Barclay's loins, while others, as we shall see, were considerably more illegitimate.

THE MYSTERIOUS DR. GREENE: In 1924 or earlier, Leon Donze, the head of Barclay, was in partnership with two brothers, Louis and Frank Castalluchi (spelling approximate). When the Castalluchis were unable to come up with needed capital, the three split, Donze then allying himself with Michael Levy, who later headed Barclay in its days of glory. The Castalluchis, who lived just a few blocks from Barclay on Chambers Street in West Hoboken, formed the Chambers Mfg. Co., which was financed by a local doctor named Greene.

The company was a sideline for the brothers, who manufactured the soldiers in a shed behind the house, occasionally assisted by Louis Picco, who was also working for Barclay at the time. Since Greene financed them, his name appeared on some of the toys, a bit of fame the Castalluchis seem to have denied themselves.

Their company may have lasted only a few years, and it's possible that Greene then continued with other associates. Greene's soldiers were said to greatly resemble those of Barclay, which might be an explanation for the "small Barclays" which longtime Barclay employees Louis Picco and George Fall say definitely were not Barclay's.

It was George Fall who recently turned up the airplane illustrated below. He had no idea how he got it, and it was the only lead non-Barclay toy in his possession. Since Greene was a known, and local, competitor of Fall's employer, it is probable that some of his toys found their way to Barclay, and thus into Fall's possession. At any rate, the plane is marked "Fred Green Toys" on the left wing and "Made in U.S.A." on the right; wingspan is 4-3/4". Unfortunately, none of my Barclay sources remember Dr. Greene's first name, but all agree he might have changed the spelling of his surname (dropping the "e") in an effort to prevent his patients from worrying about his association with anything other than medicine. From the look of the plane, Greene (if Greene it was) must have been in business at least into the 1930's.

AMERICAN ALLOY: Louis Picco, who had joined Barclay in July, 1924, working there as caster, mold repairman and foreman before he left in 1937, was President of American Alloy as well as one of its six partners. The company, which was located on Patterson Plank Road between 10th and 11th Streets in North Bergen, New Jersey, was in business for about a year in 1940-41.

American Alloy made only soldiers, which unfortunately were neither marked nor catalogued, but they should have a distinctive look to them, should any emerge. They were designed and sculpted by Olive Kooken (spelling phonetic), the sculptress employed by Barclay from the time they began producing their new line of civilians and cast helmet soldiers. Miss Kooken, from all descriptions a free spirit, charged from $100 to $150 per design, depending on its complexity and her whim. She sculpted the soldiers out of clay, then made a plaster mold, then a plaster casting which she would retouch. Patterns were subsequently made at a foundry in Jersey City, with the dies made from bronze and brass.

American Alloy was virtually a one-man operation, with Picco, who lived over the shop, doing the casting, some of the painting (two women also

painted) and the selling. The selling was often done directly with merchants on the lower East Side, orders being sought and placed under the shadow of the Manhattan Bridge, with the soldiers being sent C.O.D. to eliminate the need for bookkeeping personnel. Only a few thousand had been sold when the War broke out, and the government impounded 30 tons of lead that were waiting for American Alloy at a railroad siding.

Picco's memory is vague as to just how many different soldiers were produced. He does say they were similar to Barclay's in size, and in our first conversation thought they included a prone machine gunner, a stretcher bearer, a marcher, and a charging figure. In our more recent conversation, nine months later, he stated that he thought there were only four or five types, that perhaps there was a soldier standing and firing, perhaps one kneeling and firing, and he didn't mention the types he had described previously. Picco also rather doubts he could identify any now. However, if anyone out there has a photo of what might be American Alloy, I could try him, just on the chance...

The company was out of business during WW II. It was reorganized after the war as Toy Creations, which sold at least some of its products to Schranz and Bieber on 14th Street in New York, but Picco soon left the company.

COWBOY AND INDIAN PIRATES: George Fall remembers that at one time, probably shortly after the war, a company began producing duplicate copies of Barclay's mounted cowboy and Indian, the pre-war ones that were often painted to resemble the Lone Ranger and Tonto. Collector Al Rizzolo has a pair answering this description, and they are look-alikes, but the metal and paint is inferior to Barclay's. Fall does not remember whether this company produced any other Barclay rip-offs.

KNOCKED-OFF IN JAPAN: Finally, at least one Japanese toymaker produced copies of the early Barclay short stride soldiers, even to sometimes copying the Barclay "comma" eye. These figures are most easily recognized by the marking on the bottom of the base, stamped in some kind of dye, "Japan", and by the fact that the helmets are cast, rather than tin, as on the originals, and in some cases look somewhat more like WW II helmets than WW I. (When I first saw them I assumed they were clumsy post-war attempts by Barclay to produce pot helmet American soldiers.) At least four types have turned up: Rifle Across Waist, Port Arms, Drummer, and Naval Officer. (See above photograph: Japanese left, original Barclays on right.)

One last note on all of this. Some of the facts asserted here are based on memories going 40 or 50 years back. While the general outlines are probably right, some of the details could be wrong.

OLD TOY SOLDIER NEWSLETTER

Volume 3, Number 2   April, 1979

More SONS of BARCLAY

ALL-NU and TOMMY TOY

by Richard O'Brien

From the time I bought my first Tommy-Toy, "Officer Gas Mask", in a little shop in West 44th Street in Manhattan, I was puzzled. Something about the piece did not look American, and of course, the word "Tommy" suggested an English soldier. A few years later, when I lucked into "Wounded", "Hand Grenade", and "Ground Arms" in a Long Island antiquary, I was even more sure that they had been made in England or Canada. Their faces looked too pink, suggestive of Britains, and "Ground Arms" did not sound like an American military phrase. I discussed this with two other collectors, and they agreed it was possible--one of them even thinking he'd seen a Tommy Toy Beefeater (which would almost certainly have made them English). The other collector actually wrote to an English expert, but got no help there.

All-Nu puzzled me too. Those girls in the marching band looked like Barclay from the time I saw them in 1941 or so, and more recently, magazine photos I'd discovered of four All-Nu soldiers revealed them to be markedly similar to Barclay's style. But what to do? Information on both companies was virtually nil, augmented only by the three photographs, with captions, of All-Nu toys I'd found in a 1941 toy trade magazine.

The solution to the Tommy-Toy mystery, at least the first part of it, was simple. All three of us Tommy-Toy wonderers had seen Don Pielin's mention of the company in Volume 1, #2 of OTSN, but obviously it hadn't registered. There, when I reread it, in plain view were the words "This 10 piece group is marked Tommy Toy, Made in U.S.A.". So Tommy-Toy was American. But what then? None of the many former Barclay workers I'd spoken to knew anything about the company; most hadn't heard of it, but one thought vaguely that it "might have been located in Newark."

And then it dawned on me. Several of the pieces I owned had copyright marks. Now that they were established as American, it seemed likely the U.S. Copyright Office would have information on file. I'd been in touch with them before on a book I'd researched, so knew the procedures and promptly fired off a letter, listing the descriptions of two nursery rhyme figures I'd come up with. After a four month wait (due to a breakdown of some sort in the financial section),I got the word; and suddenly, I had found yet another company with a tie to Barclay.

In the meantime, there was one Barclay employee left whose name I'd been given that I hadn't been in touch with. His phone number was no longer in service, and for that reason I'd put off getting in touch with him. However, I finally wrote, and luckily, he was still at the same address. After a few weeks he called me; his call led to two other calls, and suddenly in addition to finding out much more about Barclay, I learned considerably more about All-Nu than I'd known, and again, this company too had its own particular link to Barclay--Barclay now rapidly becoming established as the Great Lead Father of them all!

Frank Krupp

Since this article, because of its length, will extend over more than one issue, and as I have virtually all of the All-Nu story, while hoping to discover yet more on Tommy-Toy, I shall concentrate at first on the former.

Why did so many of the All-Nu soldiers look so similar to Barclay? The answer is simple; All-Nu was owned by Frank Krupp, the man who originated and sculpted the tin-helmeted short and long stride Barclay figures. Claude Frank Krupp (he never used the Claude) was born on January 24, 1898 in New York City, moving when quite small to Eldred, New York; he died August 30, 1965. Creativity apparently ran in his family. His father, who'd been born in Essen, Germany, was a goldsmith. Krupp was a trained artist, studying modeling and design at New York's Beaux Art for three years, and architectural drafting at Cooper Union in Manhattan for four years. He worked for New York's Museum of Natural History around 1916, constructing toy soldier-like dioramas, some of which are undoubtedly still on display.

Krupp joined Barclay around 1930 or 1931, left in late 1937 or early 1938, and on February 16, 1938, incorporated All-Nu Products at 55-57 Main Street, Yonkers, New York. Eventually Krupp moved All-Nu to 67 Irving Place in Manhattan; his widow, Eva, believes it was because of rising rent and the deteriorating condition of the Yonkers building. Well-liked by virtually all who knew him, Krupp was tall (5'11"), slender, his hair snow-white by the age of 30, and in his younger years is said to have resembled actor Joseph Cotton. He was apparently able to fix anything, and although his first love was his creative work, he was known for his ability to improvise highly effective solutions to mechanical problems.

His family believes it was the War that prevented All-Nu from becoming a success, and all evidence points to this being true. I remember the marching girls' band being on sale in Woolworth's in 1941, and of course an outlet like that was a tremendous breakthrough for a small company. Unfortunately, shortly after December 7, 1941, the government impounded all shipments of lead. Krupp tried to surmount this by designing paper toys, drawing, painting and then producing 5" soldiers on heavy stock cardboard with an effective locking device to make them stand upright. He also manufactured one or more large cardboard weapons, but neither these nor the soldiers sold to any significant extent. All-Nu was not dissolved as a corporation until December 15, 1950, but in effect, it was out of business a year or two after the War began, with Krupp going into bankruptcy around 1944 or 1945.

Around 1946 Krupp continued in business as Faben Products, Inc. at 47 Walker Street in Manhattan; but from the evidence available, he no longer produced toy soldiers or the girls' band, even after the War was over and lead production was resumed. (Faben did continue the prewar horses, mounted hunters, jockeys and cowboy and cowgirl on bucking bronchos that All-Nu was producing in 1941.) Faben derived its name from two of the letters of Krupp's first name and the nickname of his partner (last name unknown). At All-Nu, Krupp had no partners, according to his family.

Recently I had the good fortune to meet Mrs. Krupp and the Krupp's only child, Evelyn Besser, at Mrs. Besser's home. His daughter had obviously spent a great deal of time with her father, knew much about his working techniques, and had strong sentimental attachments to the works he'd created. She remembers, as does Krupp's Barclay apprentice, Frank Cota, that Krupp never sculpted his toy soldiers from sketches (although he would occasionally refer to anatomy books). Instead he simply set up an armature of wire, and then employed red wax at Barclay, or green plasticene clay, the kind found in the toy section of dimestores, at All-Nu and after. Cota remembers it would take Krupp a day and a half to sculpt a figure. All-Nu's first product, incidentally, was a large souvenir horse.

Evelyn Besser seemed to have all the All-Nu products shown in the large display in a 1941 issue of Toys and Novelties. Unfortunately, she and her mother had far from all the toy soldiers All-Nu produced. She did not have, and doesn't remember having seen, the Newsreel Cameraman, Seated machinegunner, Standing, firing rifle, Signalman, Bugler, or Tommy-Gunner. She remembered, but did not have, a prone rifleman. On the other hand, she did have some soldiers and military equipment that I'd never seen or even heard of before, and the hasty sketches I made of them while visiting are reproduced on page 4. Sad to say, most of the military figures had their

original paint jobs covered over with a bronze or copper paint, possibly to see if they could be sold as souvenirs--or perhaps they were sold as souvenirs.

All-Nu was never a large company, with six or seven women doing the painting, five or six men pouring, and a few others assigned to the remaining necessary jobs. The New York location comprised one floor (the second) of an approximately 120' x 120' loft.

After Krupp's work with Faben, he seems to have given up any toy soldier-like activities. According to a resume he compiled, he worked from 1945-53 for Lee Mfg. Co. Inc. of River Edge, New Jersey, where as foreman he did original designs, modeling, plaster molds, plastic models, prototypes, and plastic molds for clock cases, lamp bases and coin-operated rides, and from 1953-56 did similar work for U.S. Fiber Glass of Norwood, New Jersey, for auto bodies, play pools, planter boxes and baby carriages. Like most resumes, however, Krupp's was written for a purpose, and is not wholly accurate. Barclay and All-Nu, for instance, are not even mentioned.

All-Nu soldiers are marked on the underside of the base with the company's name. Some have eyes painted like the early short stride Barclays; some like the long stride Barclays. Following is a listing of all known All-Nu soldiers and related items. I would appreciate hearing from anyone who knows of other All-Nu soldiers or products. I was lucky enough to buy a few duplicates from Mrs. Besser, among them a boxed set of the girls' band--consisting of the more common majorette and the five band members, in a plain red, totally unmarked box. On the cardboard on which the figures rest is rubber stamped "All-Nu Products, Inc. 55-57 Main St. Yonkers, N.Y.", and under each piece, a number, also rubber-stamped, running from 150 to 155. However, in Mrs. Besser's second box, some of the figures were placed under different numbers; hence my question mark after the numbers in the listing.

FIGURES

Newsreel cameraman in helmet
Seated Machine-Gunner
Advancing with Tommy-Gun
Grenade-thrower
Bugler
Signalman
Standing, firing rifle at shoulder
Marching, slope arms
Advancing, fixed bayonet
Officer kneeling with binoculars, drawing pistol
AA gunner in campaign cap (looks more like German cap)
Prone, firing rifle? (based on Evelyn Besser's memory; none have yet surfaced)
150? Majorette, baton in air
Majorette, baton held backward, cape-like cloth trailing behind her
151? Girl flagbearer
152? Girl fifist
153? Girl bugler
154? Girl saxophonist
155? Girl drummer

Mounted Cowboy masked, firing pistol straight ahead
Football player throwing ball (probably All-Nu)
Football player running with ball (probably All-Nu)
501 (Faben's number) Cowboy on Bucking Broncho
502 (Faben's number) Cowgirl on Bucking Broncho (these last two are really more souvenirs, particularly the girl, who is semi-barechested)

MILITARY EQUIPMENT

Tank, approximately 2" long
"Field Kitchen", approximately 2" long
Sound Detector, with 3 soldiers on it, approximately 1-3/4" high
Searchlight, one figure on it, approximately 1-3/4" high

PAPER SOLDIERS

These came in a cardboard box with no drawings on the box, simply the words "MILITARY TOYS - Two Dozen Made in U.S.A. All-Nu Products, Inc., New York, N.Y." and consisted of soldiers (and at least one nurse) in both WWI and WWII helmets.

UPDATE

And Richard O'Brien sent the following information:
"After my 'Early Barclay' article ran, I was told
by a collector that the mounted soldier in illustration '1' had originally been produced in
France. Barclay veteran Louis Picco informally
confirms this, saying that a 'Mr. Thompson' of Woolworth's would go to
Europe, buy soldiers there, and bring them back to Barclay, where they
would be made in a cheaper version. Picco further clarifies his remarks
on the Barclay coach in the same article (illustration 9), saying he is
sure the original was made by Grey Iron. Is it possible both companies were pirating
a European version? And Ed Poole has sent me a photo which vividly demonstrates how
Barclay copied European pieces. The motorcycle with sidecar at right (photo below)
is French-made. How do we know it was Barclay who swiped, rather than the French?
Because, as Ed points out, the machine-gun on both versions is French. Incidentally,
this establishes that the Auburn Rubber
version was a rip-off of Barclay's, since
it modifies Barclay's own modifications
of the original.

Also, I've just learned those American
Legionnaires pictured in my 'Early
Barclay' article were rescued from the
melting pot by Barclay employee George
Fall after the 1937 convention was over
and further sales unlikely. Although he
managed to save a few, the rest were
melted down, the paint scooped off,
and the lead used all over again on
other toys."

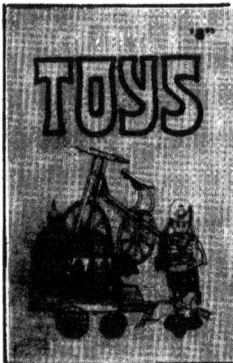

SONS of BARCLAY
Tommy Toy

by Richard O'Brien

Editor's Note: After months of false leads and dead ends, Richard O'Brien has uncovered the history of Tommy Toy and its relation to the companies of Barclay and American Alloy. Beginning with a few names, addresses and dates in 1936 drawn from copyright records on Tommy Toy nursery rhyme figures, Mr. O'Brien has pieced together the story which identifies Olive Kooken, the woman who sculpted figures for Barclay after Frank Krupp left to set up All-Nu, as a principal Tommy Toy sculptress, along with another woman, Margaret P. Cloninger; and proved that the connection between Barclay and Tommy Toy was not Dr. Greene (mentioned in Sons of Barclay, Vol. 3, #1), but Leon Donze, once Barclay's head. The whole fascinating Tommy Toy detective story will be told in a later OTSN, but here are the results of Mr. O'Brien's search.

Tommy Toy was owned, as a sideline, by Dr. Albert Greene and Charles E. Weldon, who back in the 1930's owned Towne Cabs, a fleet of 250 cabs, in New York City. John Zeman, who was in the holly berries business in Union City, was either a third partner or was involved in the actual operation of the business. And another name emerged - Leon Donze, the elderly, one-eyed Frenchman who had once been the head of Barclay. Donze had been edged out of Barclay and apparently, as one of Dr. Greene's patients, had become acquainted with the doctor, and, it seems likely, convinced him it would be financially worthwhile to get into the business of slush-mold lead toys.

Tommy Toy had its first sale on November 13, 1935, to Alphonso Greene, Dr. Greene's father, of 43 Center Street, Fort Plain, New York. This was recorded on a card marked "First Money Taken in Payment - one gross assorted toys - $6.30." The company was located on the second story of a two-story building (owned by Dr. Greene) which housed a parking garage on its ground floor, and was located at 131 Palisade Avenue in Union City, New Jersey. It was a small company, short-lived (only 2-3 years), with no more than 30-35 employees, and quite possibly not even that. Dr. Greene's son Robert, who was about 15 at the time, remembers three or four pourers and three or four motorized assembly lines along which the toys were trimmed, sprayed with a base coat, and hand-painted.

Tommy Toy made more than soldiers and its 10 nursery rhyme pieces. It turned out about 30, and possibly more, vehicles, none of them marked Tommy Toy. In addition, it made promotional banks for the Green River liquor company. No one I contacted thinks the company had catalogs or even order sheets. There also seems to be no question that the company was a financial failure, quite possibly because the two owners weren't closely enough involved. (Tommy Toy's product looks saleable, being generally attractive, and with an originality of its own.)

Those I spoke to doubted that Tommy Toy had ever made it into the chainstores such as Woolworth's or Grant's. No one was sure what the company's biggest seller was, though Marjorie Ross, Dr. Greene's daughter, believes it was the nursery rhyme toys. Robert Greene remembers his father wishing that the company had "held on" until the War. Presumably, since the actual advent of America's entry into the War ended all lead toy production, Dr. Greene was talking about the period before the War when toy soldiers suddenly began to sell, but whether he meant 1937, 38, 39, or 40 is not known. My own guess is that the company went out of business sometime in 1938. (Frank Terminini of Barclay remembers a man from Barclay leaving for Tommy Toy to work as foreman, and he believes the year was 1938.)

I had another question on Tommy Toy: the Tommy Toy soldiers that have turned up with an unmarked base. No one I spoke with knew anything about them, but during my visit to Union City I had noticed Paterson Plank Road was in the same area Tommy Toy and Barclay had been in, and Paterson Plank Road was where American Alloy had been located in 1940-41 (see "Sons of Barclay"). I called Louis Picco, onetime head of American Alloy, and asked him to check the picture of the four Tommy Toy soldiers in my book. He did, and confirmed that these figures were produced by American Alloy without base markings during its short business life.

Shortly after I received all this information, I drove out to the home of Charles E. Weldon, Jr., the son of the recently deceased Tommy Toy partner I had located. Quite possibly he owns the largest array of Tommy Toys in the world, about thirty different vehicles and 13 different soldiers, many in duplicate (67 soldiers, for instance). Earlier, I had made a list of known Tommy Toy soldiers, and others (now known to be American Alloy) that were suspected to be Tommy Toy - an officer with sword and doctor with stethoscope which had no markings. The number of pieces came to nine. Weldon had all of these, plus four more, which makes it seem mathematically likely that 13 different soldiers were all that Tommy Toy produced. I made quick sketches of the four soldiers I'd not previously known about, plus the Tommy Toy nurse, the lone military vehicle present (which I later found appears, unidentified, in Don Pielin's American Dimestore Soldiers, Volume 1), and an oil tanker because it was painted olive drab. However, it's unlikely that it was meant to be military, as I later noted several vehicles which could only be civilian that were also painted olive drab.

Many of the Tommy Toy soldiers had underbases that varied; some were issued with just the company markings, while others of the same type had a description (such as "Ground Arms") added. The nurse definitely had a variation. (See list) Possibly the other soldiers vary somewhat, aside from the underbase changes, but it wasn't apparent to my eye or to Weldon's as we examined them. There were also paint variations on the same figure, and all of this will be noted in the listing at the end of this article.

As for the vehicles, there were 3 or 4 different fire trucks, beer trucks with wooden barrels, a Chevy four-door sedan and a trailer marked "Tourist" on the side of the trailer, a paddy wagon marked "Police Patrol", an open double-decker bus with stairs in the back, two racing cars identical in everything but size, a "General Trucking" van truck, a "Delivery Deluxe" small panel truck, a "Milk Truck" with barrels, an open convertible roadster, a vehicle which looks like a trailer tractor but reads on its side "Motor

1. "Nurse" - marked this way, she has a fine-grained partition between her legs;
        marked only "Tommy Toy" the same area has a more vinelike decoration.
        Comes in white or olive drab. Some have their hair painted in; on
        others the hair looks like part of the uniform.

2. "Soldier Charging" - issued both with and without this description.

3. "Officer" - all seen were marked this way, but some were painted with orange
        leggings, and some with dark brown.

4. "Hand Grenade" - has orange leggings; the ones without description were painted
        olive drab, like the rest of the uniform.

5. "Port Arms" - has orange leggings; the ones without description were painted olive
        drab, like the rest of the uniform.

6. "Doctor" - all were marked this way, but some were painted brown with orange
        leggings, and some white with orange leggings.

7. "Officer Gas Mask" - all were marked this way; all had orange leggings.

8. "Stretcher-Bearer" - all were marked this way; some had orange leggings, and some
        had olive drab.

9. "Soldier Marching" - described this way, it had orange leggings; without
        description the leggings were olive drab.

10. "Wounded" - Somehow, I neglected to check out variations on this and the
        following soldiers.

11. "Ground Arms"

12. "Machine Gunner", standing upright, firing Tommy Gun.

13. "Soldier Firing", kneeling with rifle.

MILITARY EQUIPMENT

1. Cannon Car (or should it be considered a truck?)

NURSERY RHYME FIGURES

1. OLD MOTHER HUBBARD by Olive Kooken, copyright G23155, June 25, 1936.
2. TOM, TOM, THE PIPERS SON by Kooken, G23156, June 25, 1936.
3. HUMPTY-DUMPTY by Margaret R. Cloninger, copyright G23157, June 25, 1936.
4. LITTLE BO PEEP by Cloninger, G23158, June 25, 1936.
5. JACK & JILL by Kooken, G23159, June 25, 1936.
6. PUSS IN BOOTS by Cloninger, G23160, June 25, 1936.
7. JACK AND THE BEAN STALK by Cloninger, G23439, August 10, 1936.
8. OLD KING COLE by Cloninger, G23440, August 10, 1936.
9. LITTLE MISS MUFFET by Kooken, G23441, August 10, 1936.
10. OLD MOTHER WITCH by Kooken, G23442, August 10, 1936.

No renewals were found on any of these copyrights.

Coach", a tow truck, an
"Ambulance" which was otherwise
very close in design to the paddy
wagon, a dump truck, the "Oil"
tanker, a farm tractor, and
perhaps a few others, including a
silver zeppelin marked "USN". Again,
none of these were marked "Tommy Toy",
but Weldon is sure that all were done
by Tommy Toy, and Greene and Marjorie
Ross' husband Bob also mentioned that
the companies had manufactured vehicles

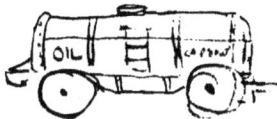

SONS of BARCLAY
Tommy Toy

Detective Story

by Richard O'Brien

Editor's Note: This article explains in depth the fantastic tale of how Richard
O'Brien located information on Tommy Toy, as reported in OTSN,
Volume 3, #3, and it could be a model for future research. So
imagine that you've closed the glass door stenciled "Spade and
Archer", told Effie to hold your calls, and settle back to listen
to Sidney Greenstreet as Guttman, the fat man, whisper to you a
history, "not Mr. Wells' history, but history just the same."

As mentioned previously, it was the copyright report on Tommy Toy that opened up what
had formerly seemed to be a permanently closed door. The report, an exceedingly
thorough one by Fred Steiner, Bibliographer of the Reference Search Section, immediately
provided three major points of information: dates, an address, and the names of two
Tommy Toy artisans.

The dates were June 10, 1936 and August 10, 1936, the address was 131 Palisade Avenue,
Union City, New Jersey, and the two artisans were sculptresses Margaret R. Cloninger
and--Olive Kooken, the woman who took over the toy soldier sculpting at Barclay after
Frank Krupp left to set up All-Nu. A bonus was learning the precise spelling of her
name, which I'd previously spelled phonetically (though, as it happens, correctly).
In my letter to the Copyright Office I had listed all the Tommy Toys I then owned--
soldiers as well as nursery rhyme figures. But disappointingly, although Tommy Toy
declared copyrights on all its figures, it appears to have actually filed for
copyrights only on its 10 nursery rhyme toys. According to Steiner, "Search in the
indexes and catalogs of the Copyright Office covering the period 1898 through 1970
under the names Tommy Toy (Mfg. Corp. Inc.) and the titles (where available) WOUNDED:
HAND GRENADE: GROUND ARMS: and OFFICER GAS MASK failed to disclose any separate regis-
tration for works of art identified under this name and these specific titles. Search
in the indexes and catalogs of the Copyright Office covering the period 1898 through
1970 under the name Tommy Toy...disclosed the following separate registrations for
works of art identified under this name in addition to the ones reported above
(LITTLE MISS MUFFET and OLD KING COLE)." Then he listed the remaining 8 nursery rhyme
figures, and nothing more, which would seem to be conclusive proof that Tommy Toy
filed copyrights for nothing but these ten figures.

It was disappointing to be shut out of finding the year or years that Tommy Toy's soldiers
were first produced, but on the positive side, Tommy Toy did give credit to the artist
on each of its nursery rhyme pieces. Since Margaret Cloninger, I'd recently been told
by an ex-Barclay employee, often accompanied Olive Kooken to Barclay in the early years
(the two may have done sculpting for Barclay pre-Krupp), sharper eyes than mine may be
able to decide, having observed their work on the ten Tommy Toys, which soldiers produced
by Barclay and Tommy Toy were the work of Cloninger and which that of Kooken.

Each of the ten is described in detail as "separate registrations for works of art
identified under this name and these specific titles." Thus, Little Miss Muffet, for
instance, reads: "LITTLE MISS MUFFET; by Olive Kooken. Clothed figure of small girl,
seated on hillock, holding bowl in extended right hand. Left hand held to face.
Spider at base of figure. Registered in the name of The Tommy-Toy Mfg. Corp. Inc.,

under G 23441, following the deposit of one photograph August 10, 1936. No renewal found."

Although all of this was fascinating to me, it was obviously not the whole Tommy Toy story. A fourth major point of information then made its impact felt. The report described Tommy Toy as a corporation. Therefore, it was likely I could find out the former owners of Tommy Toy by getting in touch with whatever New Jersey state office dealt with corporations. This turned out to be, after several phone calls, the Corporations Department, Secretary of State. I sent off a letter and check and soon received a photocopy of the incorporation papers. A quick read-through and I knew I had a new date, a new address, and at least three names. The date of incorporation was October 16, 1935, the address was 210 Palisade Avenue, Union City, and the names were Charles N. Caldwell, Jr., David H. Jackman and George V. Reilly, all, curiously, with a New York address. Two other names appeared: Charles E. Weldon was agent (I assumed this meant lawyer for the incorporation) and Edward S. Williams was the notary.

Since the three "owners" (which is what I assumed they were) had New York addresses, I picked up my Manhattan phone book, though not with much hope. After all, this was 44 years later, and the odds seemed long against finding anyone this way. Incredibly, one of the names--Jackman--was listed, though not at the same address, and when I called, it turned out he was the David H. Jackman. He and his secretary were out, but I knew--or thought I knew--in a matter of just a few minutes I would have the whole Tommy Toy story.

I called again. Jackman was on vacation for at least two months and would be unreachable during that time. Worse, according to his secretary, he would have no memory of Tommy Toy. He was associated with a firm which acted as agents for the incorporation of thousands of firms. The secretary also knew the name of Charles N. Caldwell, and said he had also been an agent of this type, and was dead.

I seemed to have run up a blind alley. A visit to the Hudson County, New Jersey, records office provided no new information. Another try with a different arm of the State of New Jersey told me only that Tommy Toy's corporation had been voided January 19, 1943, for nonpayment of taxes, and that corporations were voided only after two or more years' delinquency, which meant that Tommy Toy had to be out of business by at least 1940.

I was beginning to despair. It looked as if Tommy Toy was destined to remain shrouded in the mists of time. I took a drive to Union City to check out the company's two addresses, and the final Barclay building, all of which were located within a few short blocks of one another.

I found 210 Palisade Avenue first, and--it was a private home. Was it possible Tommy Toy had begun in this house's basement or garage? The other address offered even less information. Where the building should have been there was, instead, a park. I stopped a few elderly people in the street. Two had heard of Barclay (one's grandmother had sewn tents at home for Barclay, also farming them out to other women in the neighborhood), but none knew anything about Tommy Toy, or had even heard of it. However, the name of Dr. Greene (see "Sons of Barclay", Volume 3, #1) came up again, linked both to Barclay, and to another, unnamed company, which my informant told me had been co-owned by the head of a fleet of taxis. Although I'd previously been told Greene had been an owner of Barclay, every Barclay veteran contradicted this, and I began to suspect Greene instead was associated in some way with Tommy Toy. Two of my informants assured me Greene was still in business with his son, just a couple of blocks up. But when I walked to the indicated spot, there was no evidence of a doctor's office or offices, and the residents of the block said they'd never heard of any doctor named Greene. A call later to the Union City information operator also came up blank. And I seemed to be stymied.

At this point, as I say, I felt it unlikely I would learn much more, if anything, about Tommy Toy. I had gleaned a bit in the meantime from a couple of Barclay's old employees: that Tommy Toy was probably very short-lived and that Barclay had almost certainly bought it out, but that was about all. Finally, with no real hope, I decided to try

Jackman again. At least two months had passed, and he might be back at work. I
expected to speak to a feeble old man. However, he was surprisingly vibrant, interested,
and anxious to be of help. His files yielded nothing, but he asked me who the agent was
on the incorporation papers. I looked, gave him Weldon's name, and found out that
Weldon was not necessarily a lawyer for incorporation, but someone connected with
Tommy Toy, and that the address given might have been his home. I thanked Jackman and
hung up, hoping I had something. My first move was to check all the Weldons listed
in Union City. The operator gave me the two names and numbers she found, and I tried
both. The first had no connection with Tommy Toy, and the second didn't answer when
I called.

Before I got into this business of researching toy soldier companies, I'd have derided
anyone who suggested I could ever be a detective. It's not my bag, or at least that's
the way I've always felt. But more and more as I've researched these companies I've
come to understand what it might feel like to be Sam Spade. You try a lead, and if
you're lucky, it takes you somewhere for a while, and then you come up short and have
to backtrack and start all over again. And so I once more did just that.

A year before, while researching Barclay, I'd received a letter from a man named Joseph
A. Tighe. The information hadn't been much; he hadn't worked at Barclay, and simply
told me where the factory had been located, and that it was operated "by a son of
Dr. Albert D. Greene." I'd written him back in the hope that he might be able to tell
me more about Greene, but nothing substantial emerged. I'd nearly thrown away his
letter after completing my book on collectible toys, but luckily had decided not to.
What I remembered about Tighe was that he had lived in the same neighborhood Tommy
Toy was located in, and had known about Greene, whom I now felt strongly had been
involved somehow with Tommy Toy. I wrote him on March 30th, asked the first name of
the son of Dr. Greene, on the chance I could look it up in the phone book, mentioned
Tommy Toy, and the name Charles E. Weldon. In less than a week I had a reply, and it
was the "Open Sesame" to Tommy Toy.

Tighe wrote, in part, "Charles E. Weldon was a very close friend of Dr. Albert Greene...
Unfortunately, Mr. Weldon died about 18 months ago." He then, however, gave me the
address where Weldon had lived, and the name of his widow. After a couple of frustrating calls, when no one was home, I finally contacted her, and all the information
began to unravel.

Helen Weldon gave me some information and led me to her son, Charles Jr., who furnished
more. He led me to Dr. Robert Greene, who also was helpful and in turn referred me to
his sister, Marjorie Ross and her husband, Bob, who filled in yet a few more areas.
The results of my search appeared in "Sons of Barclay: Tommy Toy," OTSN, Volume 3, #3.

Photo by Bill Kaufman

Rare BARCLAY Box

These box photos were located for OTSN by Richard O'Brien and come courtesy of Al Rizzolo of the Red Pony. The box is probably circa 1937-39. To write that this box is rare is certainly an understatement. Most dimestore figures were sold singly, loose in the chainstore tray. There were boxed Happy Farm sets, Auburn Rubber's prize-winning boxes, and rare Grey Iron boxed sets. But a Barclay box is singularly rare. The faded end label is stamped 50/941 TRAIN FIGURE SET. The cover and side flaps suggest that soldiers, wild west, and boy scout figures would have fit into this box type.

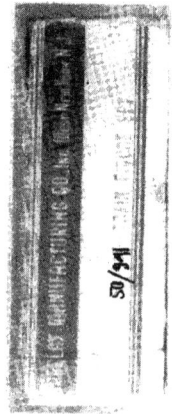

OTSN V3#6 12/79

37

UPDATE

DATING BARCLAY: SOME THOUGHTS

by Richard O'Brien

Since none of the many illustrated order sheets used by Barclay in the pre-WWII period have yet surfaced, dating just when certain soldiers began is difficult, perhaps impossible. However, here are three examples of clues I have found. Perhaps there are readers who can furnish prewar catalog sheets or other clues.

Historical chronology indicated that the Ethiopian officer was probably produced before the Japanese officer (which, of course, except for paint is the same as the Ethiopian). However, the issue was cloudy. Then one day, I noticed Steve White's note on a color photo of an Ethiopian officer which pointed out that the officer was supposed to have brown painted bare feet. It then occurred to me if he had been produced before the Japanese officer, and if he were supposed to have been barefooted, he might have toes. I went to my Japanese officer, and sure enough, although he obviously wasn't meant to be barefooted, his feet had toes. Thus, no question anymore about which came first.

The American Legionnaires were produced for the big New York convention of the era, and research of newspaper files proved that to be the fall of 1937.

Finally, Barclay employee George Fall would set up Barclay's figures around his Christmas tree and then photograph the result every year after his marriage. Although the following groups don't absolutely establish dates, they at least allow us to reach some reasonable conclusions. In Christmas, 1939, the following can be seen in the photo: Skiing Santa, Bride and Groom, Motorcyclist, Train, Preacher, Prairie Schooner, Santa in Chimney, Police Cars, Old Man, Old Lady, Black Porters, Man with Coat, Oil Truck, two different-sized Sedans. In Christmas, 1940, new figures were Little Girl in Rocking Chair, Conductor, Traffic Cop, Mailman, Woman with Dog, Male Skater, Oiler (train employee). In Christmas, 1941, the new pieces were Male Skier, Female Skier, Male Sledder, Female Sledder, and various animals. If only George Fall had married earlier!

OTSN V4N1 2/80

UPDATE   American Dimestore

by RICHARD O'BRIEN

Continuing research on the old toy soldier makers has resulted in a patchwork of new information; here is what I've come up with recently:

BARCLAY: Early Barclay employee Louis Picco is certain that Barclay was named after the West Hoboken Street on which the firm was located and that he went to work there for Barclay in 1924. (See OTSN, Volume 2, #7,6-8) We are now certain that the company began as Barclay in 1924 or at the earliest in late 1923, because Barclay co-founder Leon Donze was previously listed, with his son John, in a 1922-23 business directory as a toymaker at 23 Bline Street, in West Hoboken. Thus the move to Barclay Street must have taken place in 1923 or 24. Late phone books reveal Barclay to have been located at 934 Hoboken Street in North Bergen in 1931-32. In 1936 they moved to 567 9th Street in West New York, where it appears to have remained until the War, though the nominal address changed to 567 52nd Street, apparently as a result of a renumbering of streets...In 1938 according to a business directory, Barclay employed 150 men and 150 women, and in 1940-41 it employed 156 men and 126 women...In 1938 a "B. Bogaty - Lead Toys" company at 34 Montgomery Street in Jersey City was listed with a workforce of three men. This was a subsidiary of Barclay, owned by Barclay's Michael Levy (Bogaty was the original family name) and may have been set up in case of a strike at the main plant.

MANOIL: According to the records of Manoil relatives Arlene and Murry Bakel, Manoil began production of toy soldiers in 1935...It was in business earlier than previously thought, with "Manoil, Jack and Co. mtl. lamps and novlts" being listed at 34 West Houston Street in the Summer 1927 Manhattan phone directory...Both Jack Manoil and Man-O-Lamp were listed at the same address in the Winter, 1928 directory...The address changed to 114 Bleecker Street in the Winter 1929-30 directory...The next Manhattan directory I was able to check, Winter 1936-37, showed a move to 54 Bleecker Street... However Jack appears in the Summer 1935 Brooklyn phone book with a residential address... The move of the factory to 346 Carroll Street in Brooklyn is recorded in the Winter 1937-38 phone book.

AMERICAN ALLOY: Louis Picco now says this company made its molds directly from existing Tommy Toy soldiers...The company's address was 1016 Paterson Plank Road in North Bergen, New Jersey, and seems to have been in business for a very short time, not appearing in the 1940-41 phone directory or the May 1942 issue, but only in the August, 1941 listings...There was a fourth employee, a J. Bracco, who worked with Picco and the company's two women...The soldiers, still with World War I helmets, were also sold briefly after the War.

TOMMY TOY: Tommy Toy appears to have gone out of business between August 1938 and May 1939, according to the phone books. Tommy Toy does appear in the May, 1939 yellow pages, but not the white, and presumably the business page's listing was an oversight...In a 1938 business directory, Tommy Toy's officers are listed as "Pres. Albert D. Greene; V. Pres. Joseph Maulbeck; Sec. Treas. Chas Weldon; Pur. Agt. Pt. Mgr. George Ganzkow"...Employees listed for that period are seven men and three women... Maulbeck is dead, with no survivors, and the status of Ganzkow is unknown.

ALL-NU: According to Frank Krupp's widow, who recently remembered it, Krupp did have a partner from the start in All-Nu. The partner was David Reader, who may also have acted as the company's salesman, and who was a brother of Irving Reader, Barclay's chief salesman and the company's Secretary.

OTSN V4#2 4/80

AMERICAN LEAD TOY & NOVELTY CO. was entered in a new businesses directory
August 19, 1939. The officers were Charles Kremm, J. Bracco, Robert Bostwick, Louis
Picco, and George L. Miller. This would appear to be American Alloy, but Picco
doesn't remember Bostwick being with American Alloy. He does remember having a
company which made "six or seven" soldiers which were sold through Toy Creations,
another North Bergen company. These seem not to have been the Tommy Toy copies.

American Dimestore

COMPOSITION

by RICHARD O'BRIEN

Until recently, tracking down the composition
soldiers made in the United States during
World War II had been next to impossible.
Except for a P within a triangle on some of them,
they bore no markings, no company name, no place
of manufacture, and none of the many toy soldier
employees I've spoken to knew anything significant about
them. It finally reached the point where it seemed that
a lucky break was all that one could hope for.

Then, at last fall's Kennedy Toy Show, I got that break.
While idly inspecting a few composition soldiers at a dealer's
table, I was told by the dealer that if I were interested, he
had a whole box. Something clicked, and I told him I'd be glad to see them. Sure
enough, he had a box of them, all the same type--the stocky pot-helmeted AA gunner,
and on the side of the box were the words *Playwood Plastics Co. Inc.*, *200 Fifth
Avenue, Factory in Brooklyn*. At first I didn't think the box was original (the
dealer was not sure), as *Plastics* was the word I fixed on, but then when I realized
the second word was *Playwood*, I began to think I was onto something.

Within a few days I'd checked with the State of New York and found the company had
been incorporated March 17, 1942, which seemed right as I recalled buying the
composition sailor and Marine shortly after the start of World War II. I ordered
the incorporation papers, found no owner names, but instead the title of the law firm
handling the incorporation, and the names of four attorneys. As luck would have it,
one of the latter was still in the Manhattan phone book, 37 years later. He didn't
know much, but just enough to lead me onto the usual chain of informants, a chain that
terminated with Michael Weiss, the most informed source I've encountered in my research
of the last few years.

Weiss vividly recalled being approached in the spring or summer of 1943 by Reuben
Roth, a former classmate in law school, and by Roth's client, a Mr. Smith. Smith's
father had come up with a composition that could be molded into toy soldiers. They
had a mold of an English soldier, but nothing else. Weiss was with Transogram, a
company that had been in business since 1915, and they were looking for a new toy
product. A subsidiary of theirs, Anchor Toy of Coudersport, Pennsylvania, had been
making papier mache and wood accessories to go with nativity scenes (barns, wells,
campfires, nativity cribs, etc.), but the nativity figures themselves had been
imported. With the war on, they were no longer available and the accessories
had no value.

The year before, Transogram had incorporated a subsidiary company, Playwood Plastics,
planning to use it for something else; now they decided this would be the name of the
company making its soldiers. Weiss remembers frantically scrambling around, looking
for scrap metal. This was wartime, with all metal being diverted to war purposes,
but he finally found enough junk bronze to make the molds. Mold-making and figure
sculpting were entrusted to Max Peinlich (pronounced PINE-lick), an Austrian living
in White Plains, New York, who was in his 60s or 70s at the time. Weiss does not
know where Peinlich got his ideas, but from the look of the soldiers, it could have
been from his grandchildren's Manoils.

The composition of Playwood's soldiers consisted of triple zero wood flour from Wisconsin (very fine-ground, almost like talc), 20 Mule Team Borax, unbleached white flour (condemned by food inspectors who had marked the inedible flour with chicken blood), and water. The flour and water, of course, provided the glue binder. The blend was mixed in a high-speed dough mixer, and then extruded into bars 3" wide and about 1½" thick. These were cut into strips and fed through a hydraulic press which stamped out the soldiers, rather like cookies. The soldiers were then placed in wire trays and put into 8 foot high hot air bins, where they were cured. After their edges were buffed, they went into a centrifugal machine which coated them with khaki paint, and then onto a production line, where the details were hand-painted.

Although the selling office was located at 200 Fifth Avenue, the factory was at 133 Floyd Street, Brooklyn, formerly the home of Sklar surgical instruments. Originally Roth, Smith and Transogram went in on a 50-50 basis, but Roth and Smith had virtually no financing and Transogram eventually took over completely, entering into an employment contract with Roth and Smith (Smith was later fired), and with Weiss in full charge of production.

The company was successful for a time, employing 125 people, but never went beyond its original complement of (as Weiss recalls) 12 to 15 soldiers--partly because they were too busy, and partly because finding metal for the molds was too difficult. However, as the war ended and metal soldiers began to return, Playwood's days were numbered. It hung on for a while after the war, making such things as composition fingers with nails to be used with nail polish displays in cosmetics stores, but was eventually closed down by Transogram. No catalogs have yet surfaced, but the figures illustrated were issued by the company. Each soldier was numbered, and known numbers and poses are listed below.

401 marching slope in helmet

402 marching slope in softcap

403 2 man machine gun team

404 stretcher bearer

405 probably wounded man

406 gasmasked with flaregun
     overhead

407*

408 lying with machine gun

409*

410 kneeling with anti-tank gun

    *407 and 409 are motorcycle &
    advancing with machinegun, but
    numbers are not distinct enough
    to say which is which.

Book Review by DON PIELIN

COLLECTING TOYS NEW 1980 EDITION!

The second edition of Collecting Toys by Richard O'Brien is a price guide for thousands of old toys from iron and tin to premiums and comic character toys. A special feature of this guide is brief company histories for almost two dozen manufactuers written by experts in each field. As a prolific writer for OTSN, Mr. O'Brien's special interest in American toy soldier manufacturing is clearly reflected in the short company histories on All-Nu, American Alloy, Auburn, Barclay, Built-Rite, Grey Iron, Ideal, Jones, Manoil, McLoughlin, Metal Cast, Tommy Toy, Tootsietoy, and Warren. The book is particulary rich in toy soldier photos which help a collector to know what he has in his collection, or better yet, what he is missing.

In some cases O'Brien includes photographs of rare items in the collections of company relatives which may or may not have ever been commercially available. It is, however, a real treat to be able to see rare items so well illustrated. Since OTSN has already commented on the problem of price and rarity, I'll leave the subject out of this review.

All in all, Collecting Toys contains outstanding photographs and very interesting copy on company history and is, along with American Dimestore Soldiers Volumes I and II, the only photographically illustrated listing of American soldiers available.

OTSN V4#4 8/80

American Dimestore

BARCLAY AND TOMMY TOY FACTORIES, AND THE BROTHERS MANOIL

by RICHARD O'BRIEN

Living in New Jersey has been an advantage in researching the old American dimestore soldier companies. It's easy to visit ex-employees and relatives of owners, easy for them to visit me, phone calls are relatively inexpensive, and finally, it has enabled me to take photographs of the old factories while they still exist.

Photo 1 is the Barclay plant in West New York at 567 52nd Street, where the company was located from 1936 until World War II. (A company called Arrow, which has something to do with automobiles, now inhabits it.) Photos 2 and 3 show the front and back of the last Barclay plant, on Palisades Avenue in Union City, and photos 4 and 5 are of the Tommy Toy factory, front and side views. Tommy Toy was located on the second floor of the building, the bottom floor being used as a parking garage. "Helen Coat Co." is the current occupant, and the building is just a couple of blocks up Palisades from the final Barclay plant.

Before I'd visited the area, I'd expected Palisades Avenue to be mainly factories, but most of it consists of small one and two-family houses, with the Barclay factory and nearby Yardley plant (across from Tommy Toy) looking rather out-of-place. The Barclay building has been abandoned since the company folded in 1971. Many toys and materials were left behind, with children eventually breaking in and throwing the soldiers around in the street. Later, adults came in and literally shoveled out toys, with the police finally arriving and clearing out the plant. More frustrating than all those shattered toys is that there is a possibility that the company's old catalogs were left behind and then lost, as author Louis Hertz remembers sometime in the 1950s or 1960s borrowing, from Barclay, a 1931 catalog and another that illustrated the Italian and Ethiopian soldiers.

The final Barclay plant was located at the edge of a cliff, so that from the back, an observer gets a completely unimpeded view of the New York skyline. The building still contains some equipment in the cellar. The rest of the plant was located on the main floor, except for a few small rooms upstairs, and an outside shed that held lacquers. Although it may not look it in the photographs, it is much smaller than the West New York plant (which was located in a non-residential area).

Another advantage of living where I do is that, somewhat amazingly, Manoil relatives Marjorie and Peter Ruben live just a few blocks away. We met at a garage sale I had (I'd advertised Manoil soldiers for sale), and in addition to their eventually showing me some previously unknown Manoil soldiers (to be featured in a future article), they thoughtfully gave me these photos of Jack and Maurice Manoil, the two brothers who owned and ran Manoil. The photo of Jack, who was the creative head, was taken around 1945, and of Maurice, who took care of the business end, around 1969.

OTSN V4#5 10/80

44

1

2

3

4

5

Maurice Manoil, above;
Jack Manoil, left.

RARE MANOIL

by RICHARD O'BRIEN

Recently, a number of previously unknown Manoils were found in the collection of Manoil relatives Marjorie and Peter Ruben. Some of these are hollow, and may have actually reached toy stores, although none are known to have surfaced so far in any collections. The rest are solid cast, and presumably are prototypes which for one reason or another were never produced. In the following list, those marked with an "H" after the code number are hollow, and those with an "S", solid.

Those labeled with 500 numbers in the list below are not the same size as the ones they resemble in Manoil's 500 series; some of these prototypes also differ somewhat in position. Don Pielin points out that these prototypes for the 500 series are the ones actually photographed for the company's original catalogs; until now these discrepancies have proved a puzzle for collectors. Presumably economics suddenly dictated the substitution of smaller figures. A sample from the previously confusing Manoil 500 series catalog page is reproduced on page 8. (Figures have been rearranged to fit OTSN format.)

The third edition of Collecting Toys, due out this spring, will show all of these soldiers in color as well as in black and white. (Photos, page 7)

1.	MXS1	Military School Cadet	16.	MXS521	Flagbearer
2.	MXS2	Cadet	17.	MXS522	Parade
3.	MXS3	Sailor	18.	MXS523	Soldier in Poncho
4.	MXS4	Cowboy, gun raised	19.	MXS526	Observer
5.	MXH50	Bicycle Dispatch Rider, WWII helmet	20.	MXS527	Aircraft Spotter
			21.	MXS530	Machine Gunner (lying)
6.	MXH57	Camouflage Sharpshooter lying down, WWII helmet	22.	MXS531	Machine Gunner (sitting)
			23.	MXS532	Sniper (kneeling)
7.	MXS62	Soldier with Gas Mask & Gun, WWII helmet	24.	MXS533	Soldier with gas mask and flare pistol
8.	MXS82	Anti-aircraft with Range Finder, WWII helmet	25.	MXS534	Sniper
			26.	MXS536	Anti-aircraft Gunner
9.	MXS83	Soldier Trench Mortar, WWII helmet	27.	MXS535	Soldier Throwing Hand Grenade
10.	MXH88	Radio Operator Standing, one-piece puttees	28.	MXH45/18	Soldier w/Bazooka Cannon
11.	MXH89	Radio Operator Lying Down, one-piece puttees	29.	MXS/No#	Soldier w/gas mask, gun, camouflaged helmet
12.	MXS/No#	Standing w/Periscope, WWII helmet	30.	MXS/No#	Tommy Gunner, leaning back
13.	MXH94	Soldier Running with Cannon, WWII helmet	31.	MXS/No#	Tall cowboy, two guns
14.	MXS16	Sailor	32.	M23a	Sailor, hollow base, painted black, possibly for export to Cuba
15.	MXS24	Cannon Loader, WWII helmet			

Above, left to right from top:
    #1, 2, 3, 4, 32, 5
    #10, 11, 6, 13
    #16, 17, 18, 19, 20, 21
    #22, 23, 24, 25, 26, 27

Above, left to right from top:
    #28, 29, 30, 31
    #14, 15, 5, 6, 7, 8
    #9, 10, 11, 12, 13
Photos above by Norbert Schachter

47

521

522

524

523

525

527

536

538

533

534

526

532

529

BETON

PRE-WAR PLASTIC

by RICHARD O'BRIEN

Back in 1932, Metal Cast Products Company (also known as H. Sachs) offered the public a way to go into business for themselves, successfully, by buying Metal Cast's slush lead molds. In at least one case, there turned out to be some truth to this claim.

By tracking down names in the 1936 incorporation papers for Bergen Toy & Novelty Co., Inc., I was finally able to talk to William Nussbaum, the son of the company's accountant. Nussbaum got his first job in the summer of 1935 with Bergen Toy, working in a corner of a shop in East Rutherford, New Jersey. As one of their two casters, he turned out slush lead soldiers, cowboys and Indians, using Sachs' molds. The soldiers were then transferred to 417 Third Street in Carlstadt, where approximately ten workers trimmed, painted and packed the figures.

The company first appears in the Bergen County phone book in 1935, at the Third Street address. In 1938 it was listed for the first time as Beton (pronounced BEE-ton) as well as Bergen Toy. Nussbaum says Beton was simply a contraction of sorts of the original name, but doesn't know why it was done. 1938 also seems to have been the first year Beton turned out its toys in plastic, judging by a surviving catalog. Toys and Novelties magazine still listed it under "lead soldiers" during that year, however.

The type of plastic used was tenite, according to an April, 1940 article in Toys and Novelties (page 140), and it was supplied by a southern manufacturer. When Beton turned to plastic it farmed out the actual manufacture to a Carlstadt firm, Columbia Protektosite, which spent most of its time manufacturing sunglasses. Once cast, the soldiers were transported to 9 Rose Street in Wood Ridge, where about twenty workers finished, painted and packed them.

Nussbaum left the firm in 1940 to enter the service, and his father severed connections about 1948. However, it is his understanding, backed by the opinion of Louis A. Schiffman, who incorporated the firm on September 12, 1936, that Beton was never a particularly successful company. The firm's owners, Charles Marcak (pronounced MAR-sak) and his wife Elsie were at best middle-class. To me, this was surprising news since Beton appeared to be quite successful, particularly in 1942-45 when its products were ubiquitous in 5 and 10s across the country, with virtually no competition.

CATALOGUE OF

Beton Toys

BERGEN TOY & NOVELTY CO.
CARLSTADT • NEW JERSEY

Return Postage Guaranteed

(The owners of Barclay and Manoil are known to have become wealthy selling the same type of product.) However, it is possible that not doing its own manufacturing or distribution cut down its profit potential considerably.

On the incorporation papers, a third owner is listed, Mae Scheiblin, Nussbaum's stepmother. According to Nussbaum, she was simply a "dummy" for incorporation reasons, no more authentic than the "total authorized capital stock...of One Hundred Thousand Dollars" mentioned in the certificate of incorporation. The actual capitalization was considerably less.

Nussbaum believes the Marcaks, now deceased with no children, were born around 1896. On March 11, 1944, they bought a home in Hackettstown, New Jersey, eventually moving the business there (though perhaps not immediately, as a 1945 toy trade magazine ad places the firm in Rutherford, New Jersey). There, according to Schiffman, Marcak himself did the packing of the soldiers in his own ground-level basement. Nussbaum agrees this could be true, as he knew Marcak to be "frugal." One of the reasons for the move to Hackettstown, according to Schiffman, was that Marcak hoped to do "a little farming" on the five or six acres of land on which his stone house was located.

Possibly because Marcak was near retirement age, the company was sold, probably in the 1950's, to Rel Plastics of East Paterson, a company which produced plastic toys. This company is either out of business or has since moved, as I have not been able to track it down. Presumably this is where Beton's molds, which produced 25-50 pieces at a time, went. I do remember seeing bags of plastic cowboys and Indians in the 1960's which contained a few of Beton's large-size Indians, while featuring other non-Beton figures as well. Possibly these were all produced by Rel.

According to Nussbaum, one of the reasons some of the figures were painted was because every scrap of plastic, both from the trimming and the mold gates, was reground and recast, with some of the figures thus emerging in a varicolored state that necessitated a cover-up. (At least as early as 1940 they were sold both painted and unpainted, as I bought both kinds in the summer of that year.) Finding a paint that would adhere gave them many problems, Nussbaum remembers, with DuPont probably the company that provided the solution. It is not known who the sculptor of the figures was, but Marx Toys may have employed the same designer for some of their soldiers in the 1950's and 60's. Nussbaum does remember the moldmaker was an R. A. Koegel of Newark, New Jersey, who could perhaps have been the sculptor as well. Koegel, if alive, would be about 85 today. His name does not appear in the Newark phone book.

Nussbaum was in the Navy during the war and has no information on Beton during that period. It is my memory, however, that before the war ended--probably in the spring of 1945--metal must have become more available because Beton obviously was finally able to produce new molds. For the first time their figures emerged in World War II pot helmets.

Although discarding Metal Cast's molds for its own, Beton retained a tie of sorts to the company that gave it its start. At least two of its figures were close copies of Metal Cast's (the mounted officer in World War I helmet and the bucking broncho), and it even used two of Metal Cast's designations: "Big Chief" and "Broncho Bill." Finally, there is a possibility that Beton was in business even before 1935. The 1932 Metal Cast catalog contains a testimonial by a company calling itself "Toy and Novelty Mfg. Co.", although this company appears to have been only turning out Metal Cast's "Speedster," presumably a race car, and unlisted in the 1932 catalog.

Beton figures were previously pictured and discussed in OTSN, Volume 2, #8. In addition to 2-3/4" military figures pictured on page 10 (photo by Ed Poole), the company also produced farm, circus, railroad, and American West figures in the same scale. Civilian figures and circus box lid pictured on page 11. In a slightly larger scale, Beton produced several mounted figures, including hunt, polo, Indian, police, and others; a cadet is pictured on page 9. Beton's common mounted cowboys and Indians (not pictured) were approximately 54mm.

Dimestore Sculptresses

Kooken & Cloninger

by RICHARD O'BRIEN

Virtually everything about toy soldiers is cloaked in masculinity. Soldiering is almost wholly masculine; relatively few figures have been produced of girls and women. The toys were produced with boys in mind, and most of the buyers and collectors have been boys, and men. However, at the production end, women figured heavily. Nearly half the labor force of such companies as Barclay and Manoil consisted of women or teenage girls, who almost exclusively did the painting, and also packaged, did clerical work, and performed other duties. In the latter category was the key job of design. Here at least two women have figured, one of them quite prominently.

Olive Kooken (pronounced COO-ken) was one of the major sculptors of Barclay and Tommy Toy's toy soldiers. Her friend, Margaret Cloninger (pronounced KLAH-nin-jer) apparently did some work for Barclay, and definitely produced figures for Tommy Toy and Warren.

Olive Kooken was born December 12, 1904 in Kansas. Margaret Ruth Cloninger (known as "Margo" to her friends) was born July 17, 1905 in Jackson, Tennessee, with the two becoming friends as early as high school in Wichita, Kansas. According to a long feature story in the March 31, 1929 Wichita Eagle Sunday Magazine, Miss Kooken became interested in sculpture when she was a young child. Her high school yearbook described her in part, "Brushes and pallettes and flats, sharps and naturals..." so she was obviously interested in painting and music as well. In 1927, when she was 22, she moved to New York City and attended the Art Students League from 1927-1928. According to my informant at the League, "In looking over the records it is obvious that Edward McCartan was her most popular teacher as she attended his class most often. He taught sculpture."

The young artist's return to Wichita in March, 1929 (where she had earlier studied art) and her old job at the Mid-Continental Map Company, was an effort to save money to finance a trip to Europe, where she hoped to work as an artist. Presumably, the 1929 Crash put a temporary end to those hopes, and instead she returned to New York.

It is not known when Ms. Kooken began working for Barclay. Most of the company's workers didn't recall seeing her much before 1939, and two of her friends seem sure she did no work for Barclay during her first stay in New York. However, Sally Newman, longtime bookkeeper for Barclay, contradicts the others, saying that Olive Kooken did work for the company before 1929, when she lived in Greenwich Village.

Newman's memory does not square up with this account by Mildred Orr Hirth, a longtime friend of Olive Kooken and Margaret Cloninger: "You asked how she got started on the soldiers. She had some animals, lamps, bookends, etc., and they were expensive to cast. The steel foundries were close (she lived in Union City) and she started to do some of the casting herself. She met some of the toy manufacturers there, and Barclay's and another company asked her to do the soldiers." If this is true, then she couldn't have started with Barclay until 1936 or 1937, as she apparently moved to Union City around this time.

Presumably the other company mentioned by Mildred Hirth was Tommy Toy. It was at this point that Margaret Cloninger entered the scene. Miss Cloninger was an actress, and in 1935 had appeared on Broadway in "L'Aiglon", and then remained with the company through their winter tour. However, according to Anna (Mrs. Hugh F.) Cloninger, "Because of hard times in the theatre, she took up sculpting and became outstanding in the art...The girls roomed together. Most of their work was done by Epplesheimer and Company--the company made molds for Hershey bars among other things--but much of their casting was with this company, and Margaret Ruth married the vice-president and general manager, John D. Warren, whose father was owner and president." John Warren subsequently founded the Warren Lines soldier company. (See OTSN series continued in this issue.)

According to Mildred Orr Hirth, "I believe Margaret selected a subject to do, Olive helped her get started, corrected the figure when it was about half finished, and went over it at the end. She was trying to help her financially, but I think most of the work was Olive's." (Anna Cloninger remembers her relative also sculpted "zoo animals" in addition to her "figures of nursery rhyme characters, soldiers and horses.")

The fact that it may have been a collaboration of sorts makes separating just who did which work for Barclay and Tommy Toy difficult, if not impossible. Each artist did receive separate credits on the copyright for Tommy Toy's nursery rhyme figures, but to my eye at least, the figures are in the same style, with, if anything, Miss Cloninger's work slightly superior. However, Miss Cloninger is said to have given up all toy soldier sculpting when she married on March 26, 1941, so it can safely be said that all postwar sculpting of Barclay's soldiers was done by Olive Kooken. (Before that time, however, Barclay's Harry Bogaty remembers seeing the two women arrive together at the plant when new figures were needed.)

At least two of the Tommy Toy soldiers would seem definitely to have been done by Miss Kooken, since they turned up again as Barclay podfoot figures--the wounded soldier holding his helmet, and the nurse with the towel over her arm. Olive Kooken's work was generally distinguished by a smooth, nearly wrinkle-free look, quite different from the more realistic figures produced by Frank Krupp, who preceded her at Barclay. Unless Sally Newman is correct and Olive Kooken did begin work for Barclay in the late 1920s, the sculptress's first work for Barclay appears to have been its civilian train figures, and then, around 1940, its cast helmet soldiers.

Margaret Cloninger, according to Warren expert Steve Balkin, was brought in to improve the look of Warren's horses in its toy soldier line, and she may have sculpted some of the soldiers as well. It is known that horses were her prime interest. Collector Al Lane points out that she may have designed a lead toy train (possibly for Tommy Toy) as on the coal car and caboose are the initials "MCRR", presumably standing for "Margaret Cloninger Railroad."

Top, Margo Cloninger,193?
Below,Olive Kooken, 1943

According to Jeannette Vrancken, who was a ward of Miss Kooken's, toys were the artist's "bread and butter", but the pay was low. She was never an employee of Barclay, just a free-lancer, and she "sometimes hated" working on the soldiers, since she was given so little time to do them.

Perhaps this was truer after the war than before, when detailing certainly deteri-
orated on the figures. Olive Kooken thus had to earn her living through more than
soldier design. She sculpted jewelry, trophies, eight-foot tall angels and the
rest of the altar for a modern Catholic Church in Newark, New Jersey, Beaut
Manufacturing's toys from designs by its owner, modeled approximately half of the
black model ID planes produced by Design Center of New York in 1942-43 for the
armed services and the general public, did a sculpture in miniature for New York's
Museum of Modern Art of its Sculpture Garden, and undoubtedly a number of other
things. In addition, she had known the great American actress Minnie Maddern Fiske,
and in 1955, her book, Mrs. Fiske and the American Theatre, cowritten with Archie
Binns, was published by Crown.

Miss Kooken seems to have been liked by everyone I've been in touch with. She
appears to have been a very kind and generous person. Like many artists, she was
something of a nonconformist, wearing trousers most of the time, dungarees to the
Metropolitan Opera in an era when virtually everyone dressed up for it, even
getting up on the roof of her small stone home in Union City to make extensive
repairs herself.

For a while, Margaret Cloninger Warren's life ran more smoothly. Her husband had
money, and for a time they lived in a handsome home in the upper-class town of
Bernardsville, New Jersey, but eventually the money ran out, and her later years
seem to have been somewhat impoverished.

Unfortunately, both women died young. Miss Kooken died quite suddenly at the age
of 59 on June 24, 1964, of arteriosclerotic heart disease. Neither of her obituaries
mentioned her association with any toy company. Mrs. Warren died at age 61 on
November 15, 1966, while visiting in Wichita from her home in Merritt Island,
Florida. Her obituary, in the local Wichita paper, also made no mention of her
connection with the toy industry.

Unfortunately, friends and relations who survived the two women have not been able
to provide much specific data. Mrs. Hirth has a pre-1949 Barclay catalog or price
sheet but has not been able to locate it. She was, however, able to provide me
with photos of some of Olive Kooken's Barclay figures. These, using Barclay's
numbers, were 616 Little Boy in Jacket, winter figures 635, 636, 628, 495, 496,
500, 530, 498, podfoot cowboys and Indians 953, 951, 955, 956, 957, and HO train
figures 361, 351, 355, 359, and 354.

As for Margaret Ruth Cloninger, at the moment the only
works that can definitely be attributed to her are the
five nursery rhyme figures she produced for Tommy Toy.
One can only hope that eventually more evidence will
turn up, as both women deserve full credit for their
important contributions to increasingly prized
Americana.

****

*Richard O'Brien, a frequent contributor to OTSN, is
the creator and writer of the syndicated comic strip
'Koky' and author of several books. The 3rd Edition
of his price guide Collecting Toys has just been
published by Books Americana.*

The Second Composition Company

by RICHARD O'BRIEN

Perhaps the most frustrating of all my research into the old dimestore toy soldier companies involved the firm which manufactured the unmarked composition soldiers distinguished by a hole in the base and between the legs. Over and over again, I tried to find information on this company and each time came away empty. Adding to the frustration was the fact that twice I felt I had come close to the answer.

Barclay shipping department head George Fall told me that he had been hired once or twice during the war by Irving Reader, formerly Barclay's salesman, to help ship composition soldiers. Fall remembered working in a loft in Manhattan. Since Playwood Plastics, the only other known maker of composition soldiers, had its factory in Brooklyn, this sounded like it must be the company. However, Fall could not remember the name of the firm or its address, and a search of the period Manhattan phone books under Reader's name revealed nothing.

Then, collector Edward Szpond informed me he had once met a man in the Elizabeth, New Jersey area who had worked for the company and still had some of its soldiers. However, since this was before dimestore soldier companies were being researched, Szpond had neglected to ask the company's name or where it had been located. Furthermore, since several years had passed, he no longer remembered where the man lived. By this point I was sure, having tried everything I could think of, that I'd go to my grave still frustrated over the mystery.

But I had left a stone unturned. Recently, trying again, I visited the New York Public Library, requested-- among other things--the 1945-46 Playthings Magazine annual directory, and found a listing for "Soldiers (Wooden)".

There were four companies listed. Two I knew and the third seemed wrong geographically. However, the fourth sounded as if it were almost certainly right. The name implied figures made out of sawdust, rather than solid wood. When I got home, I called the State of New York, was given the incorporation date, and as a result, was more convinced than ever that this was the company. I ordered the incorporation papers. As soon as they arrived, I called one of the names on the papers--the only one listed in the Manhattan phone book. As it happened, he was the son of one of the owners (sharing the same first and last name of both), but said enough to make me almost certain this was the right company. Then he gave me the number of his father who, when I called, proceeded to furnish me with the full history of Molded Products, Inc.

The company was incorporated on November 29, 1941 under the ownership of Leslie S. Steinau and his son, Leslie

Steinau, Jr. The two had purchased the extruding equipment that Lionel employed when making the figures for its Mickey Mouse handcar during the Depression. The Steinaus were in the advertising display business, but felt that with World War II approaching, they had better get into another field since wartime shortages would limit marketing. Leslie Jr.'s brother-in-law at the time was the lacquer supplier for Barclay and knew Barclay's salesman Irving Reader. When Reader heard about the equipment, he got in touch with the Steinaus. He was sure the lead toy soldier market was doomed, again because of approaching wartime shortages, and convinced the Steinaus to go into the toy soldier business. While in advertising, the Steinaus had employed a sculptor named Bill Zegel to produce display figures like Old Grand-Dad (a brand of whiskey). They now hired him to design their soldiers, while Reader got in touch with his contacts at the dimestore chains.

The company was successful from the first ("They grabbed everything we could send them!" Steinau recalls), selling to all the five and dimes except Penney's, which Steinau remembers objected to war toys of any sort. The factory was located at 203 East 12th Street in Manhattan, and employed about thirty people. The soldiers themselves were made of wood flour, starch, whiting and water. This material was kneaded in a dough mixture and then poured into the extruders, from which it emerged "like strips of baloney", which then went into molds under hydraulic pressure. The resulting soldiers were placed on nails (which were attached to strips of wood) to hold them upright--creating the holes in stand and crotch. Then they were put in trays and dried by the warm air near the ceiling.

When the war ended, Irving Reader left, feeling there was no future in composition toys. The Steinaus were convinced otherwise, however, by a toy distributor who persuaded them to open a larger factory in Mamroneck, New York where they produced pull-toys of Mother Goose, a duck family and Easter rabbits. As Leslie Steinau Jr. said to me, "We didn't know when to get out." Just as Reader had feared, competitive materials gave them problems, and then a strike "broke our back." The company went into bankruptcy in 1945 or 1946. With wartime shortages a thing of the past, the Steinaus then returned to the advertising display business, until recently never knowing they had helped to create a bit of history in the field of dimestore toy soldiers.

Inside the *Beton* Factory

by RICHARD O'BRIEN

*This article continues information provided
in Mr. O'Brien's "Beton--Pre-War Plastic"
article published in OTSN, Volume 5, #3.*

Shortly after I moved to the Hackettstown, New Jersey area where Beton toys had been
manufactured, local collector Bill Adams told me the town hall had a temporary exhi-
bition of Beton soldiers. It was a small display--a few boxed sets and some individual figures--arranged by the Hackettstown Historical Society under the direction
of Raymond Lemaster. I sought out Lemaster, and he in turn put me in touch with
Harold Frutchey, who was the general manager for Beton, more formally known as Bergen
Toy & Novelty Company Inc., from January 1951 to September 1957.

Frutchey, who had also served as chief engineer for Ideal Plastics from 1942-45, had,
happily, saved a Beton catalog c. 1955. In addition, he had kept a few newspaper
and trade articles on Beton, plus two photos of Beton displays and five of six
photos illustrating the manufacture of Betons that appeared in a J.J. Newberry 5x10
display pictured in the November 12, 1953 Hackettstown Gazette. The accompanying
article further confirmed that Bergen Toy had begun as a manufacturer of slush lead
toys (using Metal Cast molds), and that 1938 was the year Beton became "the first to
begin acetate plastic figurine toy manufacture." Another article establishes the
move to Hackettstown from Bergen County as July 23, 1946.

Beton was located on Stiger Street in Hackettstown, where the city hall now stands.
(There is a Bergen Machine & Tool Co. on Hackettstown's Main Street, but there is no
connection.) According to Frutchey, the factory was a one-story building "little
bigger than a diner."

According to an article Frutchey showed me, "...the material from which the toys are
made is an acetate substance in the form of chips resembling the colored stones used
in goldfish bowls. As much as 50 pounds of the material may be dumped into the
hoppers of the moulding machines. The acetate material enters a heating chamber
where it is converted into liquid form by four 400-degree heating units and is then
forced into the channels of the solid steel molds which weigh from 400-1000 pounds
....For most of the toys, the actual moulding process takes about 25 to 30 seconds,

DECORATING TOYS
by TRAINED GIRLS

TOYS ARE SHIPPED
by RAIL·TRUCK·AIR·BOAT

after which the mould opens automatically, the jointed figures are removed and immediately immersed in water to retain their shape and then separated from the stem." (Frutchey showed me some figures which had not been cooled and had bloated; some were pretty hilarious looking.) These toys which were painted went under automatic paint sprayers, with any final touches of color being applied by hand-operated air brushes.

Frutchey did not remember the name of Beton's sculptor, but he did remember he was a man from New York who'd been born around 1900. Whether he was also Beton's first or only sculptor, Frutchey did not know. This sculptor would be paid from $200 to $1000 per sculpture, depending on its size, and seems to have done a lot of his work from life, studying animals in the field, according to Frutchey.

The company issued catalogs every year, and in 1952 had ten national sales representatives, the same year that it added circus animals to its line. That year, it shipped out 500,000 figures a week. Another article relates why Beton never produced cars, trucks, air planes, etc.: "Mr. Frutchey explains that the firm follows the example of English manufacturers in concentrating its production on figures rather than expanding to other varieties of plastic toys. All designs of the firm are copyright." I checked out the copyrights, all of which run in the 4th version of

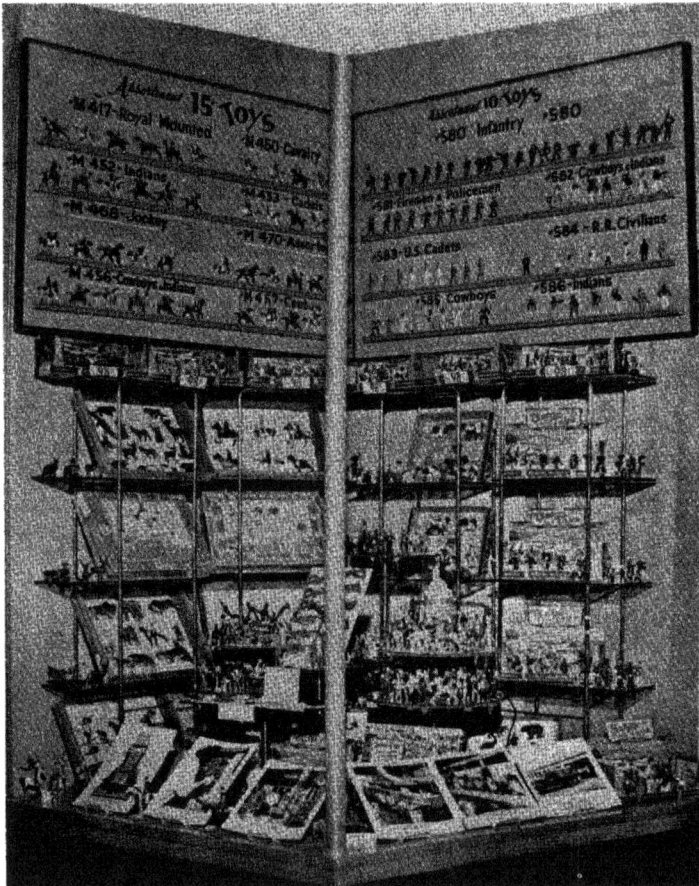

Collecting Toys. Unfortunately, unlike the copyrights for Tommy Toy, no sculptor's name appears, and the earliest copyright date is 1959, so there is no indication of when the individual earlier Betons were produced. (In 1938, without being more specific, Beton's catalog offered "Infantry, Cadet, Indians, Cowboys," mounted "U.S. Cavalry, U.S. Cadet, Big Chief, Broncho Bill.")

According to Frutchey, the company employed no more than 20-25 workers, running two eight-hour shifts a day. No workers were added during the busy season; overtime sufficed. Frutchey recalls that owner Charles Marcak died in 1959 or 1960, and that Beton "almost certainly" closed in 1958 after Marcak attended the New York Toy Fair at the McAlpin Hotel in March to take orders for Christmas sales. The Japanese had

Photo left: Beton window display reproduced from their mid-1950s catalog.

Beton INFANTRY

580 ASSORTED INFANTRY   RETAIL 10¢

BERGEN TOY & NOVELTY CO., INC. FACTORY and MAIN OFFICE. HACKETTSTOWN, N. J.

SMALL MOUNTED FIGURES

M-457 COWBOYS MOUNTED — ASSORTED HORSES   RETAIL 15¢

M-671 ASSORTMENT OF CAVALRY, OFFICER, CADET, JOCKEY, CANADIAN ROYAL MOUNTED — ASSORTED HORSES   RETAIL 15¢

1010 ASSORTED HORSES   RETAIL 10¢

BERGEN TOY & NOVELTY CO., INC. HACKETTSTOWN, N. J.

begun "copying his toys" and selling them at a much lower price. When Marcak saw the Japanese product displayed at the show, he realized there was no way he could match their prices and decided to sell out.

Among the Frutchey photos (two of which appear on page 2) was another photo of a mold captioned "Plastic Molds are Made by Special Tool and Mold Shops." Twelve different pieces were turned out in this mold. Rather oddly, in the one pictured, the mold produced three Indian chiefs with spear, three Indians with tomahawk touching head, three with bow and arrow, and then just one each of a brave with a spear, a brave holding an arrow, and a brave with a club raised in the air. Perhaps Beton had established that Indian figures sold in about that ratio.

Plastic Toys, Inc.

by RICHARD O'BRIEN

Recently, while going through back issues of Toys and Novelties Magazine of 1944 and 1945, I was startled to find ads for a company that made toy soldiers that looked exactly like Betons. The company was named Plastic Toys, Inc. and was located in Cambridge, Ohio.

Finally, I came across an article in the March, 1944 issue that at least partially explained the connection between the two firms. O. J. Sharpe, the executive vice president of Plastic Toys, after having been a department store representative for Auburn Rubber, had become sales manager for Bergen Toy and Novelty Co. (Beton) in the beginning of 1941. While Sharpe was at Beton, the article explained, "their line of toys was revamped—a proper merchandising plan mapped out—and a definite policy established." Sales went up almost 400% the first year "and the company was launched into the 'leader' class." The article continued, "Early in 1942, greatly increased quarters were required...and a complete building was obtained in Rutherford, New Jersey. By the end of that year, Bergen Toy and Novelty Co., Inc. had become just about the acknowledged leader in its field, and by April, 1943, orders received exceeded manufacturing possibilities for the year."

This unmet demand apparently put a bee in Mr. Sharpe's bonnet, and on January 4, 1944, he submitted his resignation, effective February 1, to become connected with Plastic Toys, Inc. As I recall, in some areas (and this might include toys), manufacturers during the war were allowed only a specified amount of materials. This might have been Beton's problem, and may have convinced Sharpe that a new company, allotted a reasonable amount of materials, could fill up the holes that Beton couldn't, and possibly capture some of Beton's business, too.

Plastic Toys' soldiers look just like Beton's, although they can be identified by an integrally cast round base without any manufacturers' markings. The question that follows naturally is did Sharpe, without authorization, copy Beton's soldiers, making molds based on Beton's models, or was there an arrangement between Plastic Toys and Beton? Since the two people connected with Beton I've spoken to never heard of Plastic Toys, Inc. and Mr. Sharpe's widow knew nothing about the subject when I called her in Byesville, the inclination is to believe it was simple, if legal, piracy. At that time Beton copyrighted none of its toys, so presumably it had no legal recourse. On the other hand, Sharpe hardly seemed to be trying to maintain a low profile, with both the article and an ad in Toys and Novelties establishing his previous tie to Beton. However, if piracy was involved, it must have been unsettling for Charles Marcak, owner of Beton, to thumb through an issue of a trade magazine that contained ad illustrations of Beton and Plastic Toys soldiers, all looking exactly alike (except for the bases).

MARCHING ONWARD TO VICTORY!

Soldiers That Are Successfully "Attacking" The Markets Of America!

ACTUAL SIZE

10c TOYS THAT SELL

★

PLASTIC TOYS, Inc.

CAMBRIDGE, OHIO

Advertisers wish to know where you saw this ad

Originally located in Cambridge, Ohio, where it had a brick building that contained over 15,000 square feet of floor space on two floors, Plastic Toys had moved to Byesville, Ohio by the middle of 1945. The Toys and Novelties article explains that the line had been planned carefully, "not simply allowed to 'grow up' as many toys do--and although the company is prepared to ship a tremendous volume in 1944, its schedule calls for shipments on farm animals and barnyard fowl from May 1, and on military toys from July 1." Just a few months later, in March, 1945, the company claimed that "several million" of its toys had been delivered.

As the accompanying illustrations demonstrate, Plastic Toys, Inc. also made plastic ships by 1945, including a submarine that must have been very popular, as I've seen it again and again. (The boxed set of ships that I've seen did not name the manufacturer; the boxed set of soldiers did.) Later, Plastic Toys produced cowboys and Indians of its own design; this box also named the manufacturer.

O. J. Sharpe died in 1977, and his wife seemed to know little about her husband's business when I called her. She did know he'd worked for Auburn about a year, and that Plastic Toys eventually turned from toymaking to custom molding for other companies, such as car parts, "because there was more money in that"; however, she did not know when the change was made. According to Mrs. Sharpe, her husband was the owner of the company.

In any event, we now know why Beton did not mark some of its soldiers. They weren't theirs.

Well known dimestore soldier authority Richard O'Brien is the author of Collecting Toys and writer of the syndicated comic strip, 'Koky'.

PLASTIC TOYS, Inc.

Each set in individual, 3-color carton having the appearance of a landing barge—a great selling feature in itself!

SOLDIERS... IN WONDERFUL GIFT BOX $1 LIST

Inner box lifts out as illustrated; contains 8 khaki-clad soldiers

A PATRIOTIC PLAY SET OF INSTANT APPEAL EVERYWHERE

Box lid is then stood up beside boat, cover illustration adding to effect

We are happy to present to the trade this amazing toy value, consisting of 8 plastic soldiers and a "landing barge" which is also a carton. Cover is finished in 8 process colors, beautifully done. The "boat" itself is in battleship gray and black.

This is without doubt one of the finest toy offerings of the present year, and dealers of all types will be able to do a real volume of business. It is too good to justify any delay in placing your orders. It is something in a quality product that you have been waiting for—yet the price at which it may be sold is low enough to assure many sales.

WRITE—WIRE—PHONE!!!

---

112   TOYS and NOVELTIES   March, 1948

"SHIPS THAT PASS IN THE NIGHT"

PLASTIC TOYS, Inc.

10c TOYS

Yes, They'll "Pass" Anywhere—Any Time!

Never a better, more popular, appealing 10-cent toy! Made of durable plastic, beautifully colored to catch the eye of any boat-loving child. They are marvelous little ships that really float. For outdoor or indoor play, you should be able to sell large quantities for Easter and Spring

Ready for Delivery

PLASTIC TOYS, Inc., CAMBRIDGE, OHIO

Advertisers wish to know where you saw this ad

PLASTIC TOYS

The Barclay Story

by RICHARD O'BRIEN

GRANDPA BARCLAY

The trouble with Barclay Mfg. Co. is that no one there seems to have had a sense of history. No "Founded in 1924" (or 1923); no "25th Year in Business"; no preservers of catalogs or other papers; no photographers; no diarists. For this reason, much of the information contained in this and subsequent articles is based on the memories of Barclay ex-employees. As some of these memories go back more than five decades, it follows that not all may be accurate; in fact, some do conflict. Since this article will frequently refer to the opinions of one Barclay veteran or another, readers may wish to refer to the biographical list of Barclay employees I spoke to which is provided at the end of this article.

Barclay probably began in 1924, and almost certainly not earlier than late 1923, as Leon Donze is listed as a toymaker, along with his son, John (who later worked at Barclay and died early) in a 1922-23 directory, with their address given as 23 Bline Street, in West Hoboken, New Jersey. Barclay was also located in West Hoboken, but on Barclay Street, which is how the company got its name. When West Hoboken became Union City, the street address of the original Barclay building became and remains 316 10th Street.

According to Louis Picco, Barclay's founders were Leon Donze, an elderly one-eyed Frenchman, probably in his 60s in 1924, and Michael Levy, who bought his way into partnership with $800 "he borrowed from Household Finance", which was the capital Barclay was founded on. At the time, again according to Picco, Levy had been working as a bookkeeper in the Brooklyn Navy Yard. Donze had the molds and the set-up, Levy the cash. Not until several years later, on April 18, 1929, did Barclay

December 21, 1949: A party given by Barclay owner Michael Levy for employees with over twenty years with the company. The site is the Claridge, at 11th Street and Central Avenue in Union City, New Jersey. Seated, from right, are: Mr. and Mrs. Frank Terminini, Harry Bogaty, Sally Newman, Michael Levy, Mr. and Mrs. Angelo Addeo, Mr. and Mrs. George Fall. Each of the veteran employees was presented with a gold Waltham watch. Photo courtesy of George Fall.

incorporate, with Levy, Donze and Peter Musto listed as owners, in that order. Levy owned 25 shares, Donze 25, and Musto one. Musto's connection with the business seems only to have been as a longtime boxmaker for Barclay, and he presumably served simply as the third name needed legally for incorporation purposes.

There was yet another interested party, one who comes up over and over again when talking to Barclay veterans--a Mr. Thompson, the toy buyer for Woolworth's. He was very important to Barclay, and according to Picco, "carried the company" in its early days. Thompson, now deceased, was probably from Montclair, New Jersey, and frequently traveled to Europe in search of new toys for the Woolworth's chain. When he returned, he would bring some of them to Barclay, with instructions to "make them cheaper." Although Barclay also sold to Kresge's from the beginning, according to Picco, Thompson bought "practically everything they made."

Barclay probably made toy soldiers from its start. My notes on Picco have him insisting more than once that no soldiers were produced in the early stages. He had joined the firm in 1924 when there were only "about five other employees." In our initial discussions, the one toy Picco did recall being made when he arrived was military in nature--a cannon whose lead muzzle was cast and then bent into circular shape. (Picco most recently says it was cast round, but George Fall disagrees.) It was modeled after "a French 75, with a brass spring." However, on my last and recent call, Picco insisted the company was making soldiers from the beginning. Harry Bogaty also believes that soldiers were produced in 1924, remembering that his brother brought them home to paint in that year. Certainly George Fall insists that soldiers were being produced when he joined the company in 1925.

According to Picco, Barclay's earliest soldiers were "knock-offs of European soldiers" which had been brought to the company by Woolworth's Thompson. Picco remembers "a man on a horse with an officer's cap, one of them having a moving arm, which used to break; a cowboy on a bucking broncho, hat in hand, a cowboy and an Indian, 'pretty crude', a soldier charging, another marching, a third prone with a machinegun."

Two of these last three sound like the so-called "small Barclays", but Picco, being shown photos of them, said they were not Barclay, the same reaction I got from all other Barclay workers queried. Also, no other Barclay workers remember small-sized foot soldiers. It may be helpful to point out here that Picco, although the president of American Alloy almost 20 years later,

George Fall confirms that this moving-arm cowboy is an early Barclay. The Indian had previously been confirmed. In addition, Fall stated the moving arms with bugle, pistol, rifle and sword were cast "at one time in a flat mold that they did not empty out, so the pieces were solid. They used a soft lead so they could be hand-bent. The mold was shaped like a triangle and cast about three of each piece. . When they were pulled out of the mold they were distorted; then they were flattened out with a piece of rubber on a wood handle. They used the same method on the first #1 cannon: the carriage was of soft lead, then bent over a form." Falls says the cowboy and Indian were numbered 90 and 89, respectively.

gave me two different answers at two different times about the soldiers American Alloy produced, some of which have yet to match up with known American Alloys. One simply doesn't remember everything after all these years, although, of course, the possibility remains that Picco is correct about the early Barclay soldiers he described.

Frank Cota remembers in 1928 coming across old molds at Barclay, which he described as "paperback" molds, apparently rather primitive. However, these were no longer in use in 1928; perhaps they predated Barclay and were used by Donze before he formed the company with Levy.

Cota remembers that the moving-arm figures were in production when he was hired in 1928, and also recalls that Barclay's first diecast toy was a cannon, produced in 1934 or 1935. The diecast machines were designed by George Buhler, a Barclay employee. By 1928, according to Cota, the firm had already grown to "probably 100 employees."

THE SOURCES

LOUIS PICCO was at Barclay before anyone else I've been able to find. He joined the company at the age of 17 in July, 1924, working as a caster, a mold repairman and a foreman until the end of 1937, when he left to work for Frank Krupp at All-Nu. He returned to Barclay from 1948 to 1951.

GEORGE FALL joined Barclay in 1925, at the age of 14, working in receiving and shipping, eventually becoming head of the shipping department. He left the company when it turned to war production in 1942, had his own business for a short period after the War and then returned to Barclay, remaining with the company until it closed.

FRANK TERMININI was in charge of the machine shop. He joined Barclay in 1927, and left in 1967.

FRANK COTA began his employment at Barclay in 1928, left for less than a year, and then came back in early 1930, working as an apprentice to sculptor Frank Krupp.

SALLY NEWMAN was the bookkeeper for Barclay, beginning there in November, 1929, and leaving when the war ended toy production, then returning until the company shuttered in 1971.

HARRY BOGATY was the brother of Barclay owner Michael Levy. The family's name was Bogaty in Poland, but was arbitrarily changed to Levy by a U.S. immigration official; Harry Bogaty legally changed his back. Bogaty officially joined the company in 1934 after graduating from college but finding no teaching openings in that Depression year. However, he had worked there from time to time from 1930. He later became plant manager.

ANGELO ADDEO was the shop manager and joined about 1929 or 1930. He remained with the company until sometime after the war.

BILL RUCCI worked at Barclay part-time 1937-1940, and full-time from 1946-1966. He sculpted virtually all the wheeled toys after the war.

GLORIA MARY ZULUMIAN worked for Barclay for approximately eight years after WWII, in time functioning as Michael Levy's secretary.

FRED KLUMPP was employed by Heyman Mfg. Co., which made Barclay's helmets, skis and aluminum trailer bodies.

AL JANITSCHEK is the current owner of the New Jersey Art Foundry, which under his father's regime made Barclay's molds, as well as Manoil's, Playwood Plastics', and possibly Warren's and American Alloy's.

REVIEW

First Annual East Coast
TOY SOLDIER SHOW
& Related Items

Sunday, November 13, 1983

by RICHARD O'BRIEN

"Beautiful! Beautiful!" was the reaction of a collector I spoke to yesterday about Bill Lango's First Annual East Coast Toy Soldier Show at Schuetzen Park Hall in North Bergen, New Jersey, and that seems to sum up the feeling about the show.

As anyone who reads collector periodicals knows, Bill advertised heavily for the show, and in addition outdid himself in his advance publicity efforts. WOR-TV did an interview with Bill about the show, and ran it three times. The Jersey Journal did more than a full page, and other notices of the show, often with illustrations, ran in such newspapers as the New York Post, the Bergen Record, and the Hudson Dispatch, with the New York Times reporting on the event a week later.

All this ballyhoo paid off: 106 tables bought by 78 dealers, and over 900 paid admissions, plus about 200 kids admitted free. The sum total of these figures ensures that this will indeed be an annual event.

I checked with many people, and no one had anything but praise for the show. Naturally, since this was dimestore territory, plenty of Barclays, Manoils, etc. were in evidence, but Britains and other foreign soldiers sold extremely well also. One dealer in imported figures reported, "I can't take the money from the customers fast enough." Another, who sold all types of soldiers, was from the area and went home three times during the show to replenish his stock.

Some rare soldiers turned up. Three very large hollow lead doughboys (the standing firing figure was 4-3/8" high),which all veteran collectors agree were Jones, were sold at $125 each, despite all having broken rifle tips. Manoil collector-relative Peter Ruben revealed he'd bought two Manoil composition motorcyclists and that each was a mirror image of the other. Seven Tommy Toy military figures were scooped up by one collector for $450! A few figures were there just to be shown: a Metal Cast World War I flagbearer, a Metal Cast soldier with searchlight, and some intriguing 3¼" solid lead replicas of Stalin, Chiang Kai-shek, and MacArthur which seemed to be produced by the same company which made a majorette that was discovered by a New Jersey collector a year ago.

The Best Toy Soldier Display award was won by Tom Fallon of Westminster Miniatures for his 800-piece "Trooping of the Colors." Joe Shimek copped the prize for the Most Attractive Dealer's Table.

Photo right: Bill Lango (left center, in shirt and tie) talking to Bill Rucci, postwar sculptor of Barclay's vehicles. Scene is the First East Coast Toy Soldier Show.

-18-

66

OTSN V7#6 12/83

The Barclay Story Part 2

by RICHARD O'BRIEN

GRANDPA BARCLAY

I suspect for those of us who have wondered about Barclay figures, the most frequently asked question would be: "When did the production of the 3¼" tin-helmeted soldiers begin?" Having had to wait years to trade a mint moving-arm early Barclay, I know that Barclay's pre-short stride figures attract only limited attention, whereas the soldiers of the tin helmet era are among the most highly coveted dimestore figures.

For years I've been talking to Barclay veterans, trying to determine just when production of the 3¼" figures began. Frank Terminini is emphatic in stating that the Ethiopian soldiers were Barclay's first in that size. However, that belief is almost certainly wrong because by the time the Ethiopians and their accompanying Italians emerged, the distinctive Barclay eye had shifted from the early sideways glance to the straight-ahead gaze. (To give an idea of what it is like to work from memories, neither George Fall nor Louis Picco remembers the Ethiopians, although Terminini remembers them as "good sellers.")

Harry Bogaty believes that the Barclay eye was designed and later modified by the late Dorothy Grisar (pronounced Grih-ZAR) and that she did not join Barclay until late 1934 at the earliest, and much more likely not until 1935. Grisar, an artist, was in charge of painting at Barclay. Since Bogaty later married her, it seems likely he would be fairly clear on when she had come to the company. Since all 3¼" Barclay soldiers have the Grisar eye except for a very rare aberration, 1935 or late 1934 would be the earliest date of production if Bogaty is correct. Furthermore, he states that it took "about two years" for the company to find that the glued-on helmets did not work, after which it turned to the clip.

Although I have seen blueprints dated February 1938 for the design of the clip, it seems certain that the clip helmets were in production in 1937, since long stride soldiers are known to have been made then, and all seem to have the clip helmets. Thus, if the glued-on helmets only lasted two years, 1935 again seems the likely start-up date.

George Fall and Louis Picco remember that tin helmet production did not begin until Barclay was in its West New York plant, between 1934 and 1936. Fred Klumpp, who worked for Heyman Mfg. Co. (still in business in Kenilworth, New Jersey), told me that he joined Heyman in May of 1934 and that he remembers someone making the die for the helmet, so it would have to be after that date. According to Klumpp, it "could even be 1936." (No one at Heyman remembered the flat tin tops for the caps of the short stride ensign and marine. Klumpp speculated that they were probably just purchased by Barclay on the commercial market, which seems likely.)

On left: Early Barclay eyes.
On right: Distinctive, characteristic Barclay eyes.

OTSN V8#1 2/84

Frank Cota, asked when the tin helmets began, says "about 1935 on Hoboken Street"--
which, to confuse matters, was in North Bergan and not West New York. So 1935 or
late 1934 would seem to be the date. One question remains. If the early Grisar
eye only lasted for about one year (remember, the Ethiopians and Italians had
straight-ahead eyes and were manufactured no later than 1936), why do so many
examples exist? Was production that enormous from the beginning?

Dated catalogs, of course, would provide the answer. Until then, all is at best
informed speculation, with the earliest definite record yet found of Barclay tin
helmet soldiers not appearing until 1936, in the May issue of Consumer's Union.
The soldiers pictured there were both short-stride; the kneeling machinegunner and
the standing firing rifle. Since they were facing away from the camera, there was
no way of telling whether they had the early or later eye.

According to Harry Bogaty, production of integrally cast helmets would have begun
about 1939 or 1940. I do remember receiving the #785 skier no later than the
summer of 1940, so they were available at least as early as that.

Barclay's production of toy soldiers would have stopped by April 1, 1942; an
article in Toys & Novelties, page 135 in the March 1942 issue stated the government
had decreed that "No lead toys can be fabricated after April 1st and the quantity
of lead used during the first quarter of 1942 must be restricted to 50% of the
amount used in either the 3rd or 4th quarter of 1941."

POSTSCRIPT

In February, 1984, I visited Charles Porretta, former head of maintenance at Barclay.
In our phone conversations he had sounded very assured, and knowledgable, claiming
Barclay began in 1922, and that the tin helmet soldiers were first manufactured
in early 1934, with Frank Krupp designing them in late 1933. During our visit,
however, his memory seemed far from accurate. However, what is shown in the photo
on the following page more than made up for it. Porretta had been in charge of
the final cleaning when Barclay shut down in 1972. He threw out most of the things,

including all the paper (which would have included catalogs!), but saved several hundred toys, most of them postwar, and 45 plaster castings: soldiers, Disney figures, vehicles, and an autogiro. Many of these were never produced. Using the code in the 3rd edition of Collecting Toys for the soldiers that were produced, here is a description of the figures shown in the photo above.

Top, left to right: Farmer with pitchfork; farmer broken, perhaps chopping wood or pumping water; B223 (in background);farmer harvesting corn; B189; tall WWII soldier, marching; supine wounded; soldier with horse; broken figure, probably farmer harvesting corn; B190; three soldiers firing from a window (I think the most fascinating of all of these); B127; B118.

Bottom, left to right: B73; B222 (in background); B170; B191; B172; B93; B20-21; B90; walking in cap; B195; Paratrooper with tommy gun, parachute trailing from his shoulder to the ground (if produced,this could have been Barclay's greatest piece; it's beautifully done and doesn't appear to have been by either Kooken or Krupp); woman with bucket; B159.

One note of interest: Bill Lango of Vintage Castings is planning to make molds of many of these. The first three may be available as early as April.

And a final note: the speculations about dimestore copies (Volume 7, #4, 1983 of OTSN) were correct. Porretta also took a number of Elastolins, Auburns, Warren, and other figures out of the factory, and told me owner Michael Levy often picked them up on his road trips and brought them back to the company on the chance they might prove worth copying. I hope to eventually have them photographed.

****

CORRECTION: OTSN apologizes for two errors in Part 1 of this Barclay company history, published in V7, #4, pp. 13-15. The negative for the photo on page 13 was reversed, so the caption reads improperly. In the section entitled "The Sources" on page 15, a typographical error has Frank Cota returning to Barclay in 1939 rather than 1930.

Well known collector and frequent OTSN contributor Richard O'Brien is the author of Collecting Toys. To shed further light on Barclay's company history, Mr. O'Brien continues to search for Irving Reader, "who seems to have been Barclay's only salesman up through 1941 or 1942 when he left to join Molded Products Inc. His last known address was Brooklyn." Mr. O'Brien notes, "Florida collectors might check their local phonebooks, since many Brooklyn natives retire to Florida."

The Barclay Story: The Factory

PART 3 OF A SERIES

by RICHARD O'BRIEN

In the January, 1938 issue of <u>Toys and Bicycles</u> (page 20), Robert H. Greenwell, a toy buyer, discussed a visit to Britains Ltd. He said, in part, "an inspection of the factory discloses the fact that most of the work is done by emaciated looking children fourteen years of age and over." The same description could probably have been applied to Barclay in its early years.

Many of Barclay's workers began at the age of fourteen, getting around the educational process by applying for their working papers and going to something called "continuation school", which meant turning up for classes just one day a week.

Probably one of the reasons so many children were employed is because in the 1920s and early 1930s the wages were too low for an adult to make a living. It was, as Harry Bogaty points out, "an unskilled industry." In 1928, when Frank Cota began, he remembers the rate of pay was 21¢ an hour. According to Bogaty, wages in 1933, just before the NRA took effect, were 25¢ an hour, or $10 a week.

Barclay was a patriarchy, with all that implies, both good and bad. For some it was wholly good: Gloria Mary Zulumian, who joined the company after World War II, has said, "There was a very pleasant atmosphere in which to work at that company and I look back upon those days with a great deal of happiness. I believe all the workers there shared the same sense of being one family--from the office to the factory and even to the maintenance men." About owner Michael Levy, Zulumian says, "That man was Barclay...he always wanted to do more," and that until the union was formed (around 1952), Levy "never laid people off...kept people employed 12 months of the year." She adds that "pay was good for the time." There had been a strike of a few weeks' duration about 1938, and this may have had an effect on wages at Barclay.

There was only one shift at the company, which began at 8 a.m. However, the lead pots were lit up about two hours earlier, by means of gas heat, so that when the workers arrived, the lead was ready.

There was a large remelt pot. No parts of excess lead were wasted. Excess lead from the dies went down a chute onto a belt and into the remelt pot. Soldiers with no future use, such as the Legionnaires made for the 1937 convention, were also melted down. The large pots were ladled from at first when casting was done, but later a faucet was used, with a flame kept on the pipe to keep it running. As the years went on the soldiers were reduced in size because of the higher cost of lead, etc. If a representative soldier from a batch weighed too much, the entire batch would go into the remelt pot, since anything above a certain weight would cause the company to lose money.

Barclay's soldiers were originally cast from slush molds, and later from diecast molds. With the slush molds, generally only one mold was made for a figure, and one man could cast up to five gross a day. Every three or four castings the mold would have to be dipped in water, or the mold would become so hot the lead would pour right out again, making the soldier too thinly fragile, if not completely nonexistent. The flashings were cleaned off with a knife, on a piece-work basis.

When the dies came into use (probably in the late 1930s), the soldiers were trimmed automatically in the die, with the trimmings dropping out on the other side of the mold. Once cleaned, the soldiers were painted.

Painting originally was done with a two-foot square screen on which the soldiers were laid face up, brought into the spray booth, and then hand sprayed; the sprayer was held about a foot above the screen, and the screen revolved three or four times so that all the sides and the top were done. Usually this was the basic khaki color. The figures were then placed in a rack and taken out, with girls then turning them over and returning the tray to the painters, who would spray the unfinished side.

For a time in the late 1930s, dipping the soldiers in a base coat was tried. The soldiers had a clamp attached to their base and then were moved via a chain through the tub of paint, where they were fully immersed. However, the process wasted paint, as the lacquer in the tub dried too quickly, so the company returned to spraying. Even spraying had to be done quickly, with a rack of figures being completed in five or ten minutes, because the lacquer dried so rapidly.

Finishing touches were added by women, and oddly, for most of its years, the factory used a table that revolved by hand, rather than a conveyor belt. When the belt came into use, three or four women would be on one side of the slow-moving belt, one painting the face and other flesh parts, another the green stand, another the rifle, etc. For many of the years, two sisters, Josephine and Mary Como, did the intricate work, such as the eyes.

CRIB WITH DOLL
"Barclay"—3½ in. pewter crib, asst. blue and pink, dressed china doll, mattress.
62-6599—1 doz in box..........Doz .86

▲5-379-2 **193**

Barclay's toys rarely turn up in catalogs. Hank Anton found these in one published by Butler Brothers, the May-June 1936 issue. The doll was almost certainly produced by another maker. George Fall remembers the wheeled crib.

"BARCLAY" PEWTER TOYS—Enamel Finishes—White Rubber Wheels

Tractor	Tow Truck	Stake Truck	Anti-Aircraft Gun	Coupe
4 in., asst. colors, hook connection on car, driver. 62-6512—2 doz in box.....Doz .39	3¼ in., asst. colors, dummy headlights and bumper, movable steel hook. 62-6514—2 doz in box.....Doz .42	3½ in., asst. colors, underslung body, dummy headlights and bumper. 62-6515—2 doz in box.....Doz .42	3¼ in., khaki color, on army truck chassis. 62-6516—2 doz in box.....Doz .42	3¾ in., asst. colors, dummy lights and bumper. 62-6517—2 doz in carton....Doz .42

Blue Bird Racer	Dump Truck	Streamlined Coupe
4½ in., asst. colors, replica of the "World's fastest car." 62-6519—2 doz in box...Doz .42	4¼ in., asst. colors, spring action dump, ratchet holds box at any angle. 62-6561—2 doz in box......Doz .80	5 in., asst. colors, silver trim, 2 cut rhinestones set in black receptacles—look like real headlights. 62-6562—2 doz in box.......Doz .80

71

After the toys dried, they were packed. The drying, which was simply done by air, with no machines used, would take about an hour. Taken to the shipping department, each soldier was individually wrapped in tissue, twelve to twenty-four to a box, then put in a flat truck, numbered for the stock bin. Mounted figures were placed in special cardboard crates and slid into the openings. Stores the toys were shipped to included Woolworth's, Kresge's, Lamston, Kress, E.C. Murphy, Ben Franklin Stores, Sears-Roebuck, W.T. Grant. Woolworth's appears to have been an outlet from the beginning.

Recently, when I interviewed Charles Porretta, former head of maintenance at Barclay, he stated unequivocally that production of the 3¼" tin-helmeted soldiers began in early 1934 at the West New York plant, with Frank Krupp having designed the soldiers in late 1933 (one of them, according to Porretta, copied from a photograph of an Italian soldier in Porretta's Italian-language newspaper--but designed as an American, not an Italian). However, since he was equally as firm that Barclay began in 1922, and then changed his mind to 1923 when his wife insisted it was 1923, confirmation of that date will probably have to await discovery of a catalog or two.

Porretta also gave a clue as to where some of the so-called "small Barclays" may have originated. According to him, Barclay's former owner, Leon Donze, after leaving Barclay, had set up a small company which produced toys. Barclay later bought out the company in the early 1930s, and Porretta cleaned out the factory, bringing everything salvageable back to Barclay. It's possible, then, if Donze produced small military figures (Porretta can't remember what Donze made), Barclay owner Michael Levy may have looked them over, and decided to turn them out in a larger size.

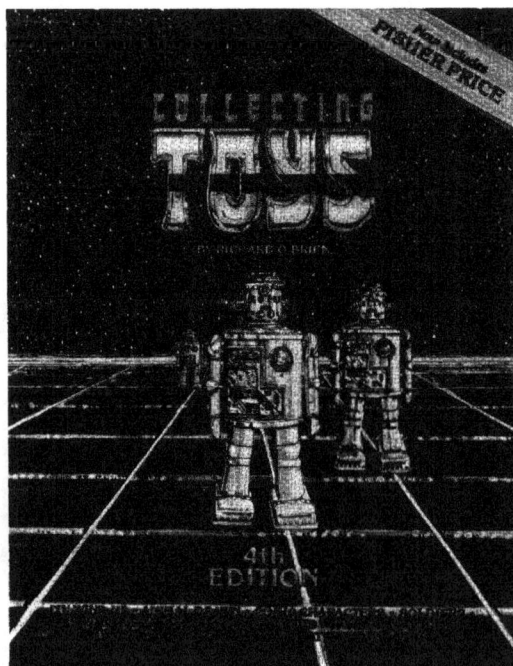

THE ALL NEW 4TH EDITION COLLECTING TOYS

by RICHARD O'BRIEN

The 4th edition of Richard O'Brien's "Collecting Toys" has been a long time coming, but an advance look by Toy Soldier Review indicates it will have been well worth the wait when it is officially published on September 1 of this year.

As with each of the previous editions, the 4th is an improvement and expansion on what has gone before. Newly discovered soldiers and variations are pictured and listed, histories of the major companies are revised where new information has come in, and a number of "new" American soldier companies, some previously unknown, have been added.

One highlight is O'Brien's listing of 3" high hollow lead figures produced by Jones in 1929-31, including a doughboy officer in overcoat with pistol which is a forerunner of the Jones J13. Included among the "new" companies are the pre-War American manufacturers of hollow lead soldiers, Cosmo Novelty and Soljertoy. All the known Ideal figures are now pictured for the first time. Miller Plaster has been added, as well as the plastic soldier manufacturers, Plastic Toys Inc. and Ausley. For those interested in plastic soldiers, some of the Marx Playsets have been listed for the first time, and the copyright dates and official descriptions of Beton's figures are now described in full.

Joe Wallis has done the Britains history for this edition and pruned the listing to those sets which are common enough to have an established average price. Another change is that the often misleading "Value Rare" designation has been eliminated from the book (which of course lists thousands of non-soldier toys as well), and replaced by the more accurate "No Price Found". As for the prices, the tremendous upward surge in soldiers prices, particularly among the less common pieces, is realistically reflected.

O'Brien has kept the military vehicles in the Vehicles section, but this time virtually all known military cars and trucks are pictured, as are many of the civilian items. Also, for the first time, all the Barclay, Manoil and Auburn vehicles are coded in the same manner as the soldiers, which should make things easier when buying, selling, and swapping through the mail. All in all, the forthcoming 4th edition of O'Brien's "Collecting Toys" is a must for the serious collector.

TSR Summer 1984

GREY IRON TODAY!

by RICHARD O'BRIEN

Want to have a whole army of Grey Iron Italian officers and infantrymen for the price of a single mint Jones? Read on.

Recently, having learned from OTSN that Grey Iron soldiers were
being produced again, having heard from Uncle Hank Anton that a great
variety were being made, and having a friend who was picking up some
very odd pieces (try a surrendering Chinese and a marching Anzac for starters, both
looking like Grey Irons) which I suspected might be being made currently from old
Grey Iron molds, I, with my friend, decided to take a trip to Wrightsville,
Pennsylvania to check it out.

The John Wright division of Donsco (which bought Grey Iron) has a factory outlet
shop on the banks of the Susquehanna River. We went in, and a few minutes later my
friend called to me. He pointed to wooden bins of Grey Iron soldiers, unpainted,
for $1.00 each. On a shelf there was a score or so of painted (badly) doughboys at
$4.50 each. I approached a saleswoman and asked a few questions. She wasn't able
to help me, but summoned Julie McNamara, the daughter of the owner. She's in charge
of the gift shop, is bright, amiable, pretty and informed, and within minutes had
spirited the two of us up to their warehouse, where she introduced us to Larry
Gilbert, who's the general manager of his particular division, which includes (quick
intake of breath) all the molds.

First Gilbert, who was also gracious and quietly friendly, showed us a book of photos
of all the soldier molds. Fascinating, mouthwatering stuff. Then, he took us to a
part of the building on which three rows of molds, scores of them, reaching from a
foot or so above the floor to several feet above my head, were hanging from iron
rods. Christmas in September!

There were at least three soldiers I was pretty sure Grey Iron would no longer have
the molds for: the original Continental flagbearer and the two "Italian" soldiers.
Well, they didn't seem to have the flagbearer, but the "Italians" were both there,
as well as the Evzone, ski troop, both Ethiopians, and virtually every piece Grey
Iron ever made, including what appears to be all the Greyklips, and all of the
American Family series, including the beach figures and accessories. The molds
hold multiple figures, sometimes all of the same type, and sometimes, as in many
of the American Family series, various kinds. I didn't count, but I'd say there are
about twenty figures to a mold, all looking exactly like the figures they reproduce.

Some of the molds have the mold numbers cut into them, some have the mold numbers
and the description of the figure, and some have the mold numbers, the description
and the catalog number of the figure. I forgot to check the ski troop, but the
Evzone had neither catalog number nor description. But the surrendering bandit did,
with the description noted as "Mexican." And the "Italian" officer had what appears
to be a catalog number, "C-1", but no description. But the "Italian" infantryman
not only had a possible catalog number, "C-2", but also a description. And guess
what it is? "British Soldier."

What about the famous palm tree, which OTSN reported is being made again? Neither
McNamara nor Gilbert knew anything about it, knew for sure they weren't manufacturing
it, and my admittedly incomplete study of the molds didn't reveal it. So if it
is being reproduced, it would seem likely it's coming from another place, and quite

possibly was never a part of the Ethiopians and "Italians" set. Does anyone have any definite knowledge here?

Anyway, I suggested to Julie McNamara that she get into mail order and she picked up on it immediately. (Previously, they'd been selling only through the store.) She requested we (my friend and I) take down a few of the molds which would interest collectors. As I recall we picked out the two "Italians", the Evzone, the wounded doughboy with nurse, the "Mexican" and I think one of the Ethiopians. I then furnished her with the address of OTSN, so if all goes well, in the next issue or two there should be an ad by John Wright which should make a lot of collectors happy.

Oh yes. Though they don't appear to have the palm tree, they do have the "treasure chest" for the pirates. Also, those aluminum Grey Irons that turn up from time to time were produced by Grey Iron, or at any rate, John Wright. They also produced the all-black G54 12/1 Hold-Up Man in the 1950s, produced a few soldiers along the way, and also sold off (for, I think, fifty cents each), all of their old prewar products in the 1960s or so to their employees. As for my friend's possible counterfeits? He was delighted to find that no molds for surrendering Chinese, Anzacs, etc. exist at John Wright. More "unknowns" for us to ponder.

   (Editor's Note: See palm tree Update on page 19.)

SOME DIMESTORE NOSTALGIA

By Richard O'Brien

What collector of dimestore figures doesn't remember, with nostalgia, the glass compartments in 5 & 10's that held our beloved treasures? Recently, I was lucky enough to acquire a mass of material on the Bergen Toy & Novelty Co. (Beton). Included was this photo, dated May 1951, featuring the old familiar glass separators.

Although the placards identify the display as being from the dimestore chain McClellan's, this doesn't appear to have been taken in an actual five and dime, but perhaps was set up at a toy fair, or as a display to be shown to the managers in each of McClellan's stores. But if not completely authentic, it's close enough.

Not just Bentons are represented. A close look with a magnifying glass reveals a number of Miller plaster figures, as well as plastic vehicles and planes by yet another manufacturer (Renewal?). The Betons are priced at 10 cents and 15 cents, the Millers at 19 cents, and the other toys range from 10 cents to 59 cents.

TSR Winter 1984

76

The Second Annual East Coast Toy Soldier Show

By Richard O'Brien

As I spent most of my time at the show selling books and soldiers, this will be a short report. From that limited point of view, a couple of quick tours I made, plus comments from all I spoke with, I feel this was the best toy soldier show yet held on the East Coast.

There were about 140 tables filled with toy soldiers, etc. Figures indicate over 1000 customers paid their way in. Prices were all over the lot. Personally, I picked up two soldiers I had been searching for for years--the Barclay officer without a strap, both in khaki and blue, for $2 and $4 respectively. At the other end, I bought for a friend who couldn't be there, the second All-Nu bugler known, and the first complete one in about 95% paint. It sold for $600.

There were a number of other rare pieces: an All-Nu firing rifleman with broken rifle tip, selling for $95 (and sold, though I don't know if it went for that price), *three* Metal Cast motorcyle officers (only one had been known previously) which went for a total of only $60. Word has it that another *fifty* will emerge!

Though apparently only for show, not sale, three other pieces turned up belonging to the group of historical figures recently found by Steve Balkin (shown on page 217 of the 4th edition of "Collecting Toys"). One appeared to be MacArthur, another was FDR, and a third was previously unknown: Winston Churchill in his naval coat and cap with cane. Nice stuff, and I think I'm in the middle of tracking down the manufacturer.

Although some dealers felt they had done better last year, most seemed to feel this was the best show yet in terms of sales (and buys). Certainly the beginning collector had a chance to buy a lot of soldiers at low, low prices ($5 and under), and most of the advanced collectors went away satisfied. The only low point was dealers in the back room tended to be unnoticed. Vintage Castings, who sponsors the show, has decided the cost of the back room isn't worth it, so there'll be fewer tables available next year (120 or so). Dealers who tend to put things off, take notice!

TSR Winter 1984

Major Barclay Find

by RICHARD O'BRIEN

Part I of this two-part article discusses the circumstances leading to Mr. O'Brien's recent important discovery of some Barclay records. Part II, which will be published in June, will detail other specific items Mr. O'Brien found and comments relating to figures shown on the lists published here.

Three cheers for Terry Culpepper! And while I'm at it, renewed respect for the keen eye and informed intuition of Don Pielin.

First to Terry. About eight years ago, during a vacation in which he visited the old Manoil and Barclay factories, Terry stopped at my house. He told me he'd recently met Stanley Goldsmith, the son-in-law of Barclay owner Michael Levy. Goldsmith had taken over the company when Levy died in 1964. According to Terry, Goldsmith didn't know much, and apart from a few Barclay postwar order sheets and a large painting chart to which postwar Barclay pieces were affixed, didn't have much. I wrote Goldsmith, but when he didn't respond, I let it go. It seemed unlikely he had anything to offer on prewar Barclay research.

The years went by, and although I got much information from ex-Barclay employees, many questions remained unanswered. Most of these, I felt, could be answered by dated Barclay catalogs, but although I did everything I could think of to locate them, none emerged. None. And then last fall, Terry called. He was very excited.

When he'd seen Goldsmith, Terry had left his phone number with him, should Goldsmith ever decide to dispose of anything. And finally, after all those years, Goldsmith had called. Immediately Terry, who lives in Georgia, had driven to Goldsmith's home in Florida. Stanley Goldsmith, it turned out, had thousands of pieces for sale, all mint. "Mostly postwar?" I asked Terry. "Yes," he answered. "Any prewar catalogs?" I asked. "No."

Since he'd told Goldsmith I might be able to help him in finding a market for his figures, Terry gave me his number. I called, though not with much interest because I don't collect postwar soldiers. But within the first minute of our conversation, I became very, very interested. Terry had been wrong. Goldsmith did have early Barclay order sheets, and over the phone he quite willingly furnished me with information I'd been wondering about for years.

But still, that wasn't the same thing as seeing the sheets themselves. A few days later a fellow collector and I drove 23 hours straight to Goldsmith's home. I was groggy from lack of sleep, but from the minute I walked into the house, my eyes couldn't have been wider open. There were two rooms, filled with soldiers and vehicles, and, in a folder, pages of order sheets. While my friend dickered over various

At right: Partial Barclay catalog from a book by Louis Hertz.

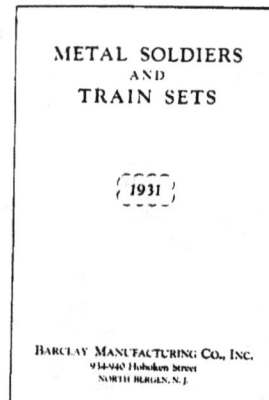

METAL SOLDIERS
AND
TRAIN SETS

1931

BARCLAY MANUFACTURING CO., INC.
934-940 Hoboken Street
NORTH BERGEN, N.J.

pieces (lots of stuff in bubble packs as well as countless loose pieces, all mint), I took a quick look at everything, and then rapidly began recording every bit of information I found.

Some years back I'd been tipped about Louis Hertz's book The Complete Book of Collecting and Building Model Automobiles, which reprinted two pages from a 1931 Barclay catalog (neither of which, unfortunately, showed soldiers, though the catalog advertised them). I got in touch with Hertz and found that when he'd borrowed the catalog from Barclay he'd also seen other catalogs, including one showing the Ethiopians, and he mentioned there hadn't been many--just a few sheets, as well as some printing blocks. Looking over the sheets Goldsmith had, they seemed to be what Hertz had seen, but there were two disappointments: the order sheets weren't dated, and the 1931 catalog Hertz had partially reprinted wasn't there. (Hertz thinks there were only four pages to the catalog.) On the other hand, the printing blocks were: a whole cardboard box full of them. In addition, there were sketches, rough sketches by two different artists of soldiers in various poses. They seemed to be ideas noodled out, and then presented to Michael Levy. I thought I recognized Frank Krupp's style, and decided the others must be Olive Kooken.

By the time I left, just a few short hours later, I had the descriptions and numbers of virtually every soldier Barclay had made from 701 to 773, plus descriptions and numberings for all the 800 pieces and most of the 600s, as well as numbers from some of the other series. And there was a great deal of other information.

Although I was unable to buy the order sheets from Goldsmith, I later asked if he'd photocopy a sheet and cut out a few pieces to illustrate this article, and that he did. They appear here. Let me state also that all the sheets were black and white, and except for the most recent one, which was probably postwar, they were scrupulously detailed, looking almost like photographs. And Goldsmith thinks he has the 1931 catalog, but so far hasn't looked for it.

The lists on page 9 show all the numbers and descriptions I found on the order sheets and printing blocks. Oddly, while a couple of numbers are blank, a couple of others are repeated, even though at least two of the pieces sharing the same number seem to be contemporaries. After the numbers and descriptions are the codings found in the 2nd, 3rd, and 4th editions of Collecting Toys. Some long stride versions of the short strides may have been produced later than others, i.e. the short stride marine appears on the order

No. 719—Sailor White Uniform

No. 708—Officer

No. 714—Pirate

No. 701—Flag Bearer

No. 706—Soldier Charging

No. 715—Cowboy

79

sheet that shows the long stride ensign. However, there is a mark by the marine that could indicate that it should be made as a long stride next, or that somehow the wrong illustration was used.

Words shown in all caps are
Barclay's own description.
1-5 are shown on p. 351, 4th
edition of Collecting Toys.

1 CANNON (top photo)
2 LONG RANGE CANNON (bottom
   photo, top row right)
3 REVOLVING CANNON (bottom
   photo, bottom middle)
4 COAST GUARD CANNON (bottom
   photo, bottom row left)
5 SEARCHLIGHT (bottom photo,
   bottom middle)
41 Fire Truck BV40
44 Steamroller BV64
47 ARMY TANK BV 56
48 ANTI-AIRCRAFT GUN
    TRUCK BV19
53 Racer BV53
55 Motorcycle with Flat Rider BV46
87 OFFICER ON HORSE B3A
89 INDIAN ON HORSE B1,B1a, &
    Pielin's B412
90 COWBOY ON HORSE B2,
    Pielin's B411
100 MASKED RIDER ON HORSE
     with lasso (facing front)
100/4 BUILD & PAINT AUTO SET,
       six vehicles, parts,
       paints, 1930s
151 ARMY TRUCK WITH GUN BV4
193 CANNON TRAILER BV78 with
     Howitzer
195 Aeroplane--"U.S. Army"
     single engine transport,
     p. 319, 4th edition
196 Cannon (apparently I did
     not record which one)
197 ARMY TANK TRUCK BV7
198 ANTIAIRCRAFT GUN TRUCK
     BV16
200 JOCKEY
204 U.S. ARMY TRUCK BV76
209 Fire Engine (shown in 4th
     edition as Tommy Toy,
     middle photo, right, top
     row left--Pumper)
303 Race Car, smaller version
     of BV65
307 Lindy-type plane, p. 318,
     4th edition
309 Delivery Truck BV33
310 COP B93a
363 LARGE STREAMLINE RACER
     BV65
365 STREAMLINE TRAIN
368 Pumper, large (see Tommy
     Toy, p. 54)
372 AEROPLANE CARRIER (air-
     draft carrier)
373 BATTLESHIP
374 ARMY MOTORCYCLE B152
486 CAVALRYMAN Bh
610 ROCKET SHIP
611 ROCKET SHIP
2004 BUILD & PAINT AUTO SET,
      early truck, coupe, sedan,
      parts, paints
701 FLAGBEARER B5
701 FLAGBEARER B6

702 MACHINE GUNNER B9
702 MACHINE GUNNER B10
703 SNIPER B12
703 SNIPER B13
704 SOLDIER ON PARADE B14
704 SOLDIER ON PARADE B15
705 SOLDIER AT ATTENTION B16
     (actually port arms)
706 SOLDIER CHARGING B18
707 SHARPSHOOTER B86, short
     stride, standing firing
708 OFFICER B23
708 OFFICER B25
709 BUGLER B29
709 BUGLER B30
710 DRUMMER B31
710 DRUMMER B32
711 DRUM MAJOR B33˙
712 KNIGHT B156
713 KNIGHT B155
714 PIRATE B154
715 COWBOY B94
716 INDIAN CHIEF B48
717 INDIAN BRAVE B47
718 WEST POINT CADET B36
718 WEST POINT CADET B38
719 SAILOR WHITE UNIFORM B49
720 SAILOR BLUE UNIFORM B50
721 NAVAL OFFICER, hard to
     tell from ill. if it's
     B54 or B55
722 MARINE, hard to tell
     from ill. if it's B57 or B58
723 MARINE OFFICER B24
723 MARINE OFFICER B26
724 ETHIOPIAN SOLDIER B39
725 ETHIOPIAN OFFICER B4
726 ITALIAN SOLDIER B42
727 ITALIAN OFFICER B41
728 MACHINE GUNNER LYING
     FLAT B61
729 SOLDIER WITH BINOCULARS
     B114
730 SOLDIER SIGNAL MAN B65
731 SOLDIER PIGEON DISPATCHER
     B66
732 SOLDIER TELEPHONE
     OPERATOR B67
733 SOLDIER BULLET FEEDER B68
734 SOLDIER AMMUNITION
     CARRIER B69
735 SOLDIER RANGEFINDER B70
736 SOLDIER SENTRY B71
737 SOLDIER CHARGING MACHINE
     GUNNER B72
738 SOLDIER BOMB THROWER B74
739 SOLDIER FIFER B78
740 SOLDIER FRENCH HORN B79
741 AVIATOR B80
742 No figure shown with this
     number
743 No figure shown with this
     number, but it's the
     West Point Cadet officer
744 NURSE B83
745 NAVY DOCTOR B81
746 ARMY DOCTOR B81
747 SHARPSHOOTER B87
748 SOLDIER, RUNNING B89
749 SOLDIER, GAS MASK B91
750 SOLDIER, CRAWLING B64

751 SOLDIER, SHARPSHOOTER,
     PRONE POSITION B84
752 COWBOY WITH LASSO B95
753 COWBOY TWO GUNS B96
754 INDIAN CHIEF B97
755 INDIAN, BOW AND ARROW B98
756 SAILOR, FLAGBEARER B53
756 INDIAN CHIEF B99
757 SAILOR WITH SIGNAL FLAGS
     B60
757 INDIAN BRAVE B100
758 CAMERA MAN B101
759 SOLDIER, STRETCHER
     BEARER B102
760 SOLDIER SITTING POSITION
     B115
760 SURGEON B104
761 Doesn't show in the order
     sheets; it's the supine
     wounded
762 WOUNDED B85
763 RAIDING B105
764 ADVANCE B106
765 BAYONETING B107 (although
     no bayonet)
766 CLUBBING WITH RIFLE B108
767 NURSE B82
768 Doesn't show in order sheets
769 COOK B110
770 AT MESS B151A (the typist
     without table or typewriter)
771 PEELING POTATOES B111
772 Doesn't show in order
     sheets
773 OFFICER READING ORDERS
     B116
951 SOLDIER WIRELESS RADIO
     OPERATOR B147
952 SOLDIER, DISPATCHER
     WITH DOG B148
960 SURGEON AND SOLDIER B146
961 AT TYPEWRITER B151
801 BOY SCOUT HIKING B182
802 BOY SCOUT SALUTING B183
803 BOY SCOUT SIGNALING B184
804 BOY SCOUT COOKING B185
850 POLICEMAN B189
851 FIREMAN B187
852 FIREMAN B188
610 WOMAN PASSENGER B157
611 MAN PASSENGER B158
612 CONDUCTOR B161
613 PORTER B160
614 RED CAP B159
615 ENGINEER B162
616 BOY B163
617 GIRL B164
618 ELDERLY WOMAN B165
619 OLD MAN B166
621 NEWSBOY B169
625 BRIDE B173
626 GROOM B174
627 GIRL IN ROCKER B175
Note: Numbers in the 600 series
don't come from the order sheets,
but from Barclay's tags that were
attached to the actual figures.

Major Barclay Find Part 2

by RICHARD O'BRIEN

Part 1 of this article revealed the circumstances behind Mr. O'Brien's recent discovery of Barclay production records and included a list of the Barclay pieces now identified by original number. In Part 2 Mr. O'Brien discusses secondary information he was able to discover as a result of Terry Culpepper's efforts in leading him to Stanley Goldsmith.

Here is some of the additional information I found at Stanley Goldsmith's, in no particular order. First, Barclay obviously did keep Tommy Toy's molds when it bought the company. All the nursery rhyme figures were there, but they were unpainted, and without the "Tommy Toy" underbase markings. Each figure had a tag attached to it, with a comment to the effect that the base wasn't good. Since none were painted, probably Michael Levy decided it just wasn't worth the effort to spend any more time on the molds. And for all those out there who might be drooling about the Jack and Jill, even if unpainted and with a rough cast base, I may as well mention it was (naturally) the only one of the figures that was broken--badly broken.

There were a few prewar Barclay soldiers, but the closest things to rarities were the Japanese officer and infantryman. (Figures pictured below) On the other hand, there were some plaster pieces, although not nearly as many as in the Poretta find and most were not in terribly good shape. Among those that had reached production were the Japanese charging infantryman (broken in two parts), the ski trooper, the diver, and the girl figure skater. Of those that hadn't been produced, two were outstanding: a long stride marching German (minus the bottom parts of his legs) in wax that I'm sure was sculpted by Frank Krupp, which would date it as 1936 or 1937, and a ski troop done by Olive Kooken. This is a real beauty; the soldier is in a deep crouching position, with a rifle slung across his back. At first I thought it was an Arab or foreign legionnaire because of the headgear, which seems to have a trailing neckcovering. Either it was meant to be that way, or in the process of moldmaking a helmet would have been affixed to it. (None of the Barclay cast helmet figures had helmets in the plaster stage.) Other unproduced pieces included a sitting civilian in top hat (an attractive piece); a soldier, rifle high, apparently being shot (in very rough shape); and what looked like a small copy of the Sun Rubber Scout Car (p. 53, 4th ed. Collecting Toys). The latter was also in pretty bad shape so I couldn't tell just how close a copy it was.

As in the Poretta find, there were a number of non-Barclay pieces: Britains, Manoil, Eire, Corgi, Tootsietoy, Beton, and a number of "small Barclays." This brings me to Don Pielin. In his The American Dimestore Soldier Book he lumped all the so-called "small Barclays" in the Barclay section, although none of the Barclay employees I've queried remembered them.

I argued with him about it, but it looks as if Don may be right--at least with
some of them. For one thing, the mounted cowboy and Indian he identifies as
B411-412 are Barclays. They're on the same order sheet with the Ethiopians and
Italians. Furthermore, the "small Barclays" in Goldsmith's possession were all
the same type--the 60-65mm with oval bases (top photo, page 219, Collecting Toys
4th edition). When I got home, I wrote Evelyn Besser, the daughter of Frank
Krupp. I'd remembered she had a few crude soldiers which she was sure her father
hadn't sculpted, but which were among his possessions. I asked her to ship them
to me and she did. There were five pieces: three of the 60-65mm type, and the
B411 and B412 of Pielin's. That makes it seem very probably that Barclay did
indeed make the 60-65mm figures. This is the conclusion K. Warren Mitchell had
reached some months before after careful scrutiny of them--while deciding none
of the other small Barclays were Barclays.

There were about 150 printing blocks, many of them of individual soldiers or
vehicles, some with identifications on the wooden parts of the blocks. One of
Barclay's veterans had once told me they'd made rocket ships. While going through
the printing blocks, there they were--two different types, numbers 610 and 611,
each labeled "Rocket Ship." I made hasty sketches of them, but they're so rough
I won't reproduce them here. If anyone has a lead rocketship, however, I could
probably confirm whether or not it's Barclay on the basis of those sketches. The
baby crib shown in a recent OTSN article was also among the printing blocks, as
well as a milk truck shaped like a milk bottle, and illustrations of five or so
Barclay boxed sets--soldiers and vehicles.

There are some collectors who believe there was no such thing as an "open-handed"
stretcher bearer, that it simply was a casting flaw. The order sheets are scrupulously accurate, and pictured on one of them is an open-handed stretcher bearer.

There were photos of painted Barclay plaster models. In one photo, along with
the smooth searchlight soldier and the two tall infantrymen (B19 and B75) was a
mounted Royal Canadian Mounted Policeman, leaning forward, which seems never to
have been produced. In another photo, either B62 or B63 is shown, only it has
wheels under the machinegun barrel. Also some of the painted soldiers in the photos
had light uniforms and dark puttees. I once saw a batch of these in a shop and
assumed they were repaints. Maybe not.

Goldsmith has a number of hollow animal heads, like the ones Metal Cast produced and sold as "Barking Dogs". (When a rubber ball is attached to the head and squeezed, it makes the dog bark.)

On the order sheets number 100 is called Masked Rider, on horseback with lasso, except instead of facing sideways as in B2B and B2C, he faces forward. Since it's on the order sheet, it would seem to have been produced, but if so, none as yet appear to have turned up.

And the sketches? Much there to make collectors think of what might have been. I believe I recorded all of the drawings (which were done in pencil); they were Soldier Digging, Soldier with Pickaxe (shades of the Jones order sheet!), Sniper Firing Upward, KP Sweeping, Barber giving soldier a haircut, Soldier Planing Table, Soldier Water-Carrier, Soldier Dancing a Jig, Officer Inspecting Soldiers at Exaggerated Attention, a Mailman (drawn, apparently, by Kooken, and like the one Barclay produced), Soldier with Pack Horse (like the plaster one by Kooken that was part of the Poretta find), Soldier at Attention in front of a sentry box, Soldier with some kind of longish gun, Two soldiers standing by an antiaircraft gun, and a Band.

All of the order sheets had the 567 West 9th Street West New York address, which Barclay occupied from 1934 until 1947. The only poorly drawn one appears to be postwar, as it contains B222 and B223 (the two soldier crews at mobile cannon and a.a. gun). Also on that sheet are three of the Boy Scouts and the B99 and B100 Indians. The first of the order sheets contains only short stride figures 701-723. The second earliest has 14 pieces on the order sheet, which is glued to the back of the printing plate. Eight are soldiers: the four Italians and Ethiopians, B3A, Bh, and Pielin's B411 and B412. Since it would help to date them, these are the numbers found on the order sheet with the Italians and Ethiopians: 724-727, 87, 89, 486, 90, 1, 196, 197, 204, 48, 198.

One final note. Soldiers from the prewar period that are not identified on the sheets, and the list compiled from them published in Part 1 of this article, include B79A (seated machine gunner), B112 (sitting eating), B145 kneeling with antitank gun, and the four Japanese and Chinese troops. In the later numbers, only 786 is blank. This could be B137, the skier in brown.

Photos for this article courtesy of Don Pielin.

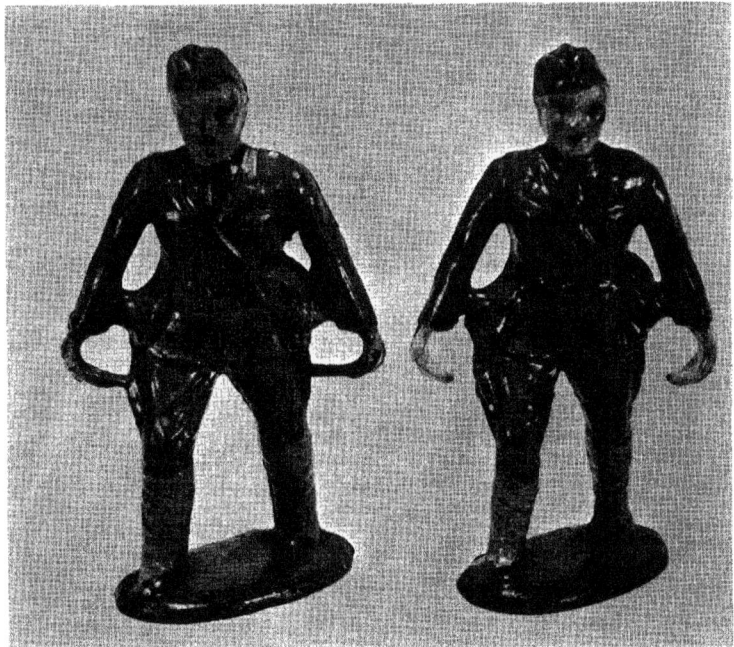

The 10 Rarest Dimestore Soldiers

by Richard O'Brien

Tommy Toy Soldiers

Recently, when the editor-publisher of Toy Soldier Review and I were talking over the phone, Bill informally asked me to send him a list of what I thought were the ten rarest dimestore soldiers, and I informally agreed that I would.

But, once off the phone, I thought it over and realized he was really asking two questions: what are the ten rarest dimestore pieces and what are the ten most sought-after? And then the more I mulled, the more I realized this might be a good time to list what appears to be the rarest and scarcest of each of the individual companies, which is a question I'm asked from time to time.

A few definitions and guidelines here: "Rare" to me means a piece which causes excitement *whenever* it turns up, even when found by someone else. "Scarce" is a piece

that's tough to find, but that almost certainly will wind up in a collector's hands within a three-to-five year period if he's diligent enough, is willing to dig deeply into his wallet, or is willing and able to trade high enough. And what is rare and scarce today is not necessarily so tomorrow. It wasn't long ago that Manoil's boxer, banjo player and paymaster evoked much more response in the salivary glands than they do today.

I'll skip the color and most other minor variations this time out, since I feel this falls more into the realm of esoterica. Suffice it to say that such pieces as the Barclay detective in tan (I know of one), the Barclay short stride cadet painted as a wooden soldier (I know of two), and the Manoil hostess in tan (I've heard of three or four, but have never seen one) are rare, and are certainly hungered

TSR Spring '85

for by at least a few. Likewise, the Barclay Cuban flagbearer (none known), and the possible Manoil Cuban flagbearer.

I'm also going to avoid the smaller early pieces by Barclay and Metal Cast which attract only a small number of collectors at this point.

Finally, "only four known" means four known to *me*. I've seen thousands of soldiers at shows and elsewhere, have seen even more thousands listed in catalogs, auction sheets, etc., and am in touch with a fair number of collectors. So although this isn't a strictly scientific survey (and I don't see how it could ever be), it should at least veer perilously close to the truth.

Let's start with the biggest of them all, Barclay. Oddly, Barclay has more truly rare soldiers than Manoil or Grey Iron. Odd, because one would assume their production runs would have been large enough to guarantee a fair number of survivors. On this, and all the following listings by company, are all arranged in their order of rarity:

1. 706 Rifle Across Waist, shorter rifle, sling around hand (B18a), rare, only one known.
2. 708 Officer with sword, long stride, no chest strap (B25a), rare, only two known in brown, one in blue.
3. 738 Grenade-Thrower, tall (B75), rare, only three known.
4. 954? American Legion Flag-Bearer (B150), rare, four, perhaps five known (the fifth could be a fake).
5. 706 Tall, rifle across waist (B19), rare, only five known.
6. 801 Knight with Red and Blue Shield and Sword (B229), scarce.
7. 776 Standing at Searchlight, smooth lens, elevation wheel (B120), scarce.
8. 776 Standing at Searchlight, smooth lens, no elevation wheel (B120), scarce.
9. Chinese Officer (B45), scarce.
10. Prone with short binoculars (B114), scarce.
11. 787 Diver with Axe (B139). This turns up more than all the above, but is still considered both scarce and more valuable than some of the above, since they're only variations.

Ed Poole's Out 'n Out Repro's of Scarce All-Nu Soldiers.

And now for Manoil. Manoil has no real rarities, except in its variations, but more of its pieces are scarce. Some, like the cameraman with thick or thin arm, are too newly-discovered to know which is the rarer, if either. The (M70)

Crawling Scout, incidentally, is an odd piece. When compared to the more common Crawling Scout, it appears to be exactly identical. That is, taken part by part, *every* part seems to be identical, and yet somehow the left leg is high.

1. 22 Indian with knives, sarong-like garment (M38b), rare, only one known, but possibly was never sold, as it's in the hands of Manoil relatives Marjorie and Peter Ruben.
2. 44 Crawling Scout with Gun, left leg high (M70), rare, only two known.
3. 32 Stretcher-Carrier, number on back, buttons on uniform (M58a), scarce.
4. 21 Nurse, no hemline (M36a), scarce or rare - I haven't kept tabs.
5. 47 Anti-Aircraft Searchlight with tin lens (M75a), only three known (possibly homemade variations, but not likely).
6. (M37) Indian with hatchet, scarce.
7. 10 Bugler, howllow base version (M11) scarce.
8. 12 Machine-Gunner, prone, no aperture between hands and gun (M19), scarce.
9. 8 Parade, number on back (M7), scarce.
10. (M173) Machine-Gunner sitting (thin), scarce.
11. (M174) Machine-Gunner lying (thin), scarce.
12. 540 Wounded Soldier, lying (M206), scarce.
13. 539 Stretcher-Bearer (M205), scarce.
14. 86 Aviator Mechanic with Propellor, away from head (M113), scarce.
15. 101 Soldier Jumping with Chute (M127), scarce.
16. 25 Sniper (kneeling), folding rifle (M44), scarce.
17. 26 Sniper (standing), folding rifle (M47), scarce.
18. All Manoil Composition Figures are rare to scarce.

Grey Iron has one of the toughest figures, the Colonial Flag-Bearer (really tough, and with the original flag possibly impossible; I know of none), and its Mounted Masked Cowboy is about as hard to find, but since it's non-military, is not quite as sought-after. Otherwise, it's not to hard to complete a set of Grey Iron, particulary since the two next-toughest, the mounted variations with horse's head and left leg up, may not have been made by Grey Iron, but by an affiliate. Replacement antennas make the other rare Grey Iron, the radio set operator, not so mouth-watering, since the figure itself is relatively easy to come by.

1. 1B Colonial Flag-Bearer (G3), rare, four known.
2. 12/1M Masked Cowboy Mounted (G59), rare, about five known.
3. 75 Radio Set, Operator and Aerial (G103), rare.
4. (G106) U.S. Cavalryman, possibly Grey Iron, like G34, but horse's head and left leg up, scarce.
5. (G107) U.S. Cavalry Officer, like G37 and above, possibly Grey Iron, scarce.
6. 4/4 U.S. Doughboy Ammunition Carrier (G21), scarce.
7. 11/1M Indian Scout Mounted, firing pistol rearward (G51), scarce.
8. 12/3 Bandit, surrendering (G56), scarce.
9. (G91) Italian Infantryman in Ethiopia, scarce.

Scare Tommy Toy Soldier Charging.

Auburn Rubber isn't widely collected, though now more collectible than it was just two or three years ago. Despite the relative lack of competition, none of its pieces come close to being common and some are real doozies for rarity. I'm still looking, after seven years of avid search and advertising, for the running "Pilot", looking up. Furthermore, since the standard early bugler, painted as an Ethiopian, exists, there are undoubtedly more regular Auburn infantrymen daubed with black skins, but none have yet surfaced. And how many original Ethiopian figures were made? Possibly only two, the two known, but quite possibly more. However, aside from those, and a couple more which qualify as scarce, don't get discouraged. Auburns are out there for the taking. It just requires more time.

1. (A35) Tank Soldier(?) running, looking skyward, looks like a pilot, but probably a Tank Commander, none known.
2. (A7b) Ethiopian with shield and rifle, in robe, only one known.
3. (A7a) Ethiopian Bugler, only one known.
4. (A7) Ethiopian with shield and rifle, bare-chested, only two known.
5. (A12a) Cavalry Officer, mounted, smaller version, only one known.
6. (A10) Charging Soldier with Tommy Gun, early version, scarce, or possibly rare.
7. (A33) Tank Defender (?), with tommy gun, scarce.

Just about all of Jones' soldiers are scarce. Perhaps only the Firing Machine Gun on Tree Stump (J10) comes close to being common, and it doesn't exactly jump out at you. So in this case, let's just list the truly difficult pieces, remembering that the Officer in Greatcoat (J13), while easier to come up with than many Jones figures, is still a great find for any collector, being both scarce and one of the most dramatice dimestore soldiers. And let it be noted that *any* Jones figure with an identifying number on it is a great find, even if it doesn't vary in any other way from its unnumbered brother.

1. (J39) Cowboy on Horse, firing backward, only one known.
2. (J17) Cook with chef's hat, scarce and maybe even rare.
3. (J25) Bugler, very scarce.
4. (J18) Ammunition Carrier, very scarce.
5. (J5) Wire-cutter, prone, scarce.
6. (J6) Soldier with rifle, gassed or shot in neck, scarce.
7. (J9) Charging, port arms, scarce.

And now we come to the toughest of them all. *Every* military piece made by All-Nu is rare. Many of the most advanced collectors don't own a single All-Nu soldier, and have never even seen one. All-Nu's other pieces, aside from its horsemen and horsewomen, are all scarce, and two of its majorettes are rare.

1. Prone, firing rifle (the owner's daughter is sure he made one), none known, even in photo form.
2. Advancing with Tommy Gun, one known, gun tip replaced.
3. Bugler, two known, one of them broken.
4. Signalman, two known, flag missing in each case.
5. Running in Gas Mask, one known.
6. Officer kneeling with binoculars, one known.
7. Majorette, baton held backward, capelike cloth trailing behind her, only one known.
8. Majorette in ensigns cap, only two known.
9. AA Gunner in campaign cap, only two known.
10. Standing, firing rifle, only three known, one with missing rifle tip.
11. Seated machine-gunner, only two known.
12. Advancing, fixed bayonet, only two known.
13. Grenadier, three known.
14. "Newsreel" Cameraman in helmet, four known.
15. Officer with Sword, four known.
16. Marching, slope arms, four known.

My guess is, along with all those rare birds, there could be a couple or more All-Nu's that none of us have yet heard of, a flagbearer, for one. It was one of Barclay's big sellers, and All-Nu owner Frank Krupp designed the Barclay flagman and didn't forget to include a colorbearer when the War forced him to turn to producing cardboard soldiers. So keep an eye peeled!

Since the son of one of the Tommy Toy owners has a welter of figures, none can be truly considered rare. However, all of them are scarce and two are especially hard to find. What I consider to be Tommy Toy's most interesting figure, "Wounded", is the easiest to come by (relatively speaking, of course). Herewith, the two toughest Tommy Toys (aside from the detail variation in the areas between the nurses' legs, but no one seems to care much about them):

1. "Port Arms"
2. "Stretcher-Bearer"

Finally, we come to Metal Cast, a company which either stole outright, with only minor changes, or turned out grossly ugly originals. Since Metal Cast sold its molds to the public, one can never be sure whether a piece has been produced recently or in the long ago. To the best of my knowledge, these are the hardest to find "original" Metal Casts.

1. 28A Wounded, lying down, head on hand, arm in sling, none known.
2. 33A Trumpeter, in campaign cap, none known.
3. 25A Signal Corps, with semaphore flags, none known (except for the ones now being produced by Vintage Castings, which located a mold).
4. 29A Machine-Gunner, WWI helmet, same situation as number 3.
5. 32A Flag Bearer, in campaign cap, one known.
6. 30A Motorcycle Officer, one known (cast solid).
7. 26A Anti-Aircraft Soldier, with searchlight, one known.
8. 21A Flag Bearer, two known.

Jones J34 Indian on Rearing Horse.

And now a list of not the rarest, not the most expensive, but what are probably the ten most sought-after pieces. Why do they make it over much more difficult pieces? Because they're hard to find, because they would complete a collection of one company's output, and/or because, as in the case of the "Newsreel" cameraman, of their unique quality. Listed in order of what I think are the most sought after to the somewhat less yearned for:

1. Grey Iron Colonial Flagbearer.
2. Barclay American Legion Flagbearer.
3. All-Nu Cameraman.
4. Tall Barclay Grenade-Thrower.
5. Tall Barclay, rifle across waist.
6. Manoil Aviator Mechanic, Propellor away from head.
7. Grey Iron Masked Cowboy Mounted.
8. Manoil Folding Rifle, kneeling.
9. Manoil Folding Rifle, standing.
10. Barclay Diver.

Since I wrote this article, a piece has turned up that would be right up there with the ALL-NU cameraman--a nurse pushing a wounded man in a wheelchair that I'm sure is Manoil, though neither of the Manoil relatives every heard of it.

Richard O'Brien has just completed a book on toy soldiers that should run at least 500 pages. It will be the same size and format as the fourth edition of his "Collecting Toys". American companies are represented in depth, as is Britains. Jack Matthews has contributed a large section on German Composition, Rusty Haller on G.I. Joe, Ed Poole on Home-Castings and Hank Anton on the new manufacturers. Japanese-made soldiers, Timpos, Mignots, Heyde, etc., will also be included. As with "Collecting Toys", this book will be a price guide as well as reference book. It will include all accessories as well, such as vehicles, etc. Publication is tentatively scheduled for March 1986. The title (also tentative) will probably be "O'Brien's Toy Soldiers". Publisher will be Books Americana, which also publishes "Collecting Toys".

Another Unknown Bites The Dust

by RICHARD O'BRIEN

This one was fun! It all began at the 1985 OTSN Show, when Gene Parker
picked up a boxed set of what appeared to be American Alloy soldiers,
though with a trademark on the box that showed the name Schranz and
Bieber, which was both a manufacturer and distributor of toys, games and paint sets.

What did seem out of joint was that the illustration on the box showed World War II
soldiers. But these figures all sported WWI helmets. Furthermore, two of them were
copies of Barclays: the B63 prone machine gunner and the B132 soldier with field
phone. I'd previously seen the antenna-shouldered doughboy with what appeared to
be American Alloy paint, but the machine gunner was a surprise. In addition, Picco
had stated that when he'd joined Schranz and Bieber's subsidiary company, Toy
Creations, after the war, sculptress Olive Kooken was involved.

Since Barclay was the main source of her income, it seemed unlikely that even though
they were no longer being produced, Kooken would have jeopardized her career by
pirating two of Barclay's figures. But it was mainly the World War I helmet turning
up postwar that bothered me. True, Metal Cast had offered World War I molds in
1946, but it seemed unlikely a company could stay in business selling prewar soldiers
during the immediate postwar period. And Picco had told me he'd been with the
company until 1949, involved only in the production of soldiers. The more I thought
about it, the more likely it seemed that Toy Creations would have been forced to
start producing World War II G.I.'s.

So there I was, with these thoughts nagging me, and the odd prone machine gunner
also occupying my thoughts from time to time. Then it struck me. Don Pielin has
two of the sharpest eyes in the hobby, and I had a feeling that in his The American
Dimestore Soldier book he'd lumped the machine gunner with a set of World War II
soldiers. I grabbed his book and looked. He had. Then I turned to my own book,
the 4th edition of Collecting Toys. There in the color pages was Hank Anton's
photo of the machine gunner, his paint seeming to match that of several other soldiers
in the picture. And they were the same as Don's!

I don't collect World War II soldiers, but a few days later at a friend's house,
I examined his "American Alloy" figures, the two Barclay copies, and the World War II
infantrymen I'd begun to suspect had been produced by Toy Creations. As it turned
out, there was a definite link between them: a copper-colored underbase that
matched none of the other paint on the soldiers. It was erratic, because not all
the World War II soldiers had it; but many did, as did a few American Alloys, and so
did the soldier with field phone and machine gunner.

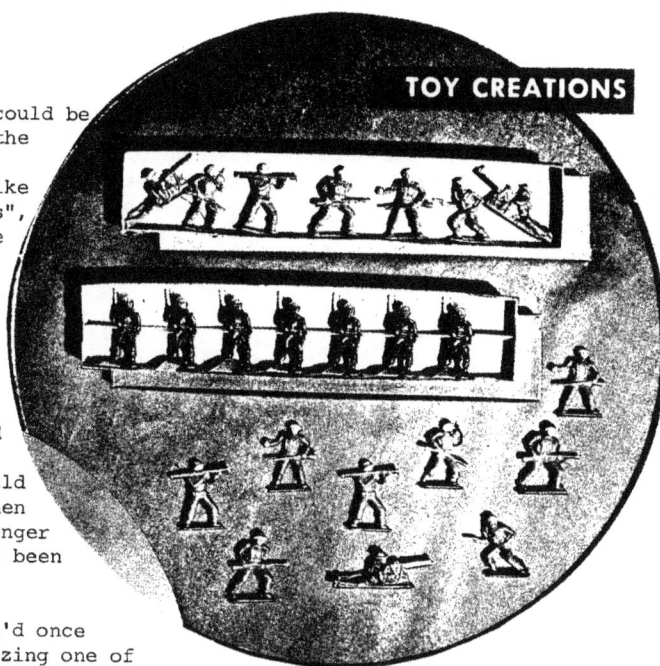

TOY CREATIONS

At this point I was as sure as I could be without actual confirmation that the World War II soldiers had been produced by Toy Creations, just like that boxed set of "American Alloys", and furthermore, sculpted by Olive Kooken--something more likely for her to have done than to have produced new molds of Barclay's soldiers. Although they don't greatly resemble the pieces she did for Barclay, they do sport her typical smooth, wrinkle-free look. Also, a friend of hers said at one time she had done her own casting. It seems possible it could have occurred at Toy Creations, when her services at Barclay were no longer required as frequently as they had been prewar.

Finally, I had another thought. I'd once chided Don Pielin about characterizing one of the soldiers in his book as a Tommy Toy, as it wears a World War II helmet, and Tommy Toy was out of business before the war. He'd replied he simply meant to point out that it resembled a Tommy Toy. I looked at his photo again. It was definitely a copy of the Tommy Toy charging soldier, only with pot helmet. Everything about it suggested a transitional figure between the World War I "American Alloys" and the World War II "Toy Creations" soldiers.

Then, a few months later, all but the last question was resolved. I was going through postwar Playthings magazines as part of the research for my forthcoming book on toy soldiers. My fingers were crossed, hoping to find ads for Toy Creations and Ajax, a company which produced plastic copies of Barclay's soldiers. Toy soldier ads are rare, and I hadn't much hope. In the case of Ajax what little hope I had was not rewarded.

But suddenly, in the March, 1947 Playthings, there it was! A two-page ad by Toy Creations. And there, on the top half of the first page, was the confirmation of my speculations! The soldiers that Don had coded MC21-27 (and which I had coded UD21-25a & U26) were all there, every one of them, including among all those pot-helmeted G.I.'s the WWI machine gunner. And so the list of "unknowns" continues to diminish, this time by seven. And if anyone has that "transitional" charging soldier with a copper-colored underbase, I think we can safely mark off an eighth.

On the homefront, no one in the USA is a more
tenacious toy soldier archaeologist than Richard
O'Brien. It should surprise no one that with the help of a couple of fellow enthusiasts
Richard has pulled together for publication the remains of the Barclay archive, an
American dimestore coup which cannot be overestimated. The Barclay Catalog Book,
with the exception of one photo and four previously seen postwar catalog pages,
is sixty oversized pages packed with never-before-seen material. Illustrated are
catalog print block proofs, photos of plaster master figures, sketches for
projected toys, catalog pages, and order sheets. Most of the material was saved by
the last Barclay owner, Stanley Goldsmith, when the factory closed in 1971. Collector
Lee Schaffer acquired the material in 1985, and Lee
graciously transferred it to Richard.

O'Brien's Catalog Book provides an impossible to
duplicate glimpse at paper prewar retailers would have
perused, used, and discarded. This includes ten pages
of catalog sheets from 1934 to the late 1940s and a
dozen pages of print block illustrations of soldiers
and vehicle boxed sets and individual items; most are
photo quality, not line drawings. Even more spectacular
is the chance to imagine your way into the Barclay
design studio through project sketches or the photos
of models like a plaster Mounted RCMP never in
production.

THE BARCLAY
CATALOG BOOK
by Richard O'Brien

MATERIAL FROM
THE BARCLAY ARCHIVES

Richard has kept his commentary to a minimum; contents
are identified, and in a few cases Richard has posed a
question or offered an interpretation, but basically
this is a collection of raw material. It is an archive
for dreaming about what was, what might have been, and
even what might be out there somewhere. No dimestore
collector should resist this one. See Richard's ad for
the book on page 14.

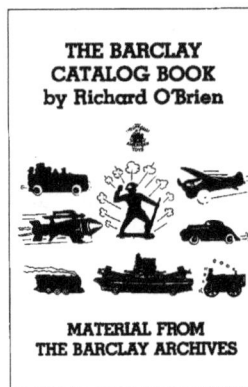

OTSN V10 #1 2/86

Book Review

THE SECOND CATALOG BOOK

Richard O'Brien's The Second Catalog Book
is just out. It is the same size, style
and format as his Barclay Catalog Book,
but covers a larger number of makers. Richard has gathered
catalog sheets, some of which have been previously available,
on All-Nu, Authenticast, Beton, Grey Iron, Manoil, even
Warren, and, of course, more Barclay. Again, the 50 plus
pages clearly reproduce original photos and illustrations
ranging from Beton cardboard trenches and teepees to Manoil
airplanes to boxed Barclay winter figures. At $15, this
book is another Dimestore must. See Richard's ad on the
inside back cover.

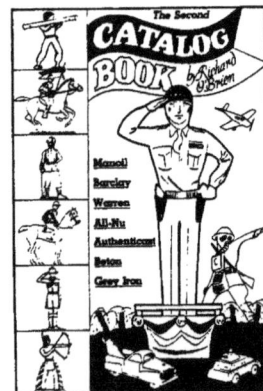

The Second
CATALOG
BOOK by Richard O'Brien

Manoil
Barclay
Warren
All-Nu
Authenticast
Beton
Grey Iron

JUST OUT!

THE BARCLAY CATALOG BOOK
by Richard O'Brien
(author of "Collecting Toys", etc.)
MATERIAL FROM THE BARCLAY ARCHIVES

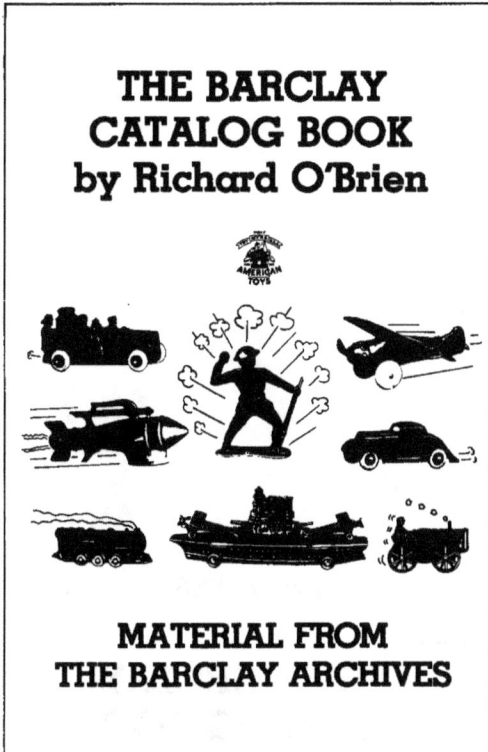

THE BARCLAY
CATALOG BOOK
by Richard O'Brien

MATERIAL FROM
THE BARCLAY ARCHIVES

Barclay Mfg. Co. was one of the largest toy manufacturers (and the largest maker of toy soldiers) in the United States in the period before the Second World War, and remained a significant force until it went out of business in 1971. The company issued catalogs from its beginning in the 1920s, yet despite years of search by collectors almost no company material surfaced.

Until now.

Here, from the personal files of Barclay's former owner are catalog pages, illustrated order sheets, photographs, sketches and illustrations pulled from Barclay's original printing blocks!

Almost three hundred separate toys and boxed sets (most of the latter previously unknown to collectors) are illustrated, some for the first time. In addition to soldiers, you'll find cars, fire trucks, airplanes, cannons, a dirigible, ships, military vehicles, trains, tractors, racing cars, trucks, even rocket ships and a baby crib. Dealers and collectors alike will now be able to identify many items for the first time as Barclay products.

A number of the photographs illustrate the original plaster castings of Barclay's toy soldiers, as well as prototypes that seem never to have made it to the market.

5½ pages of sketches of projected toy soldiers offer dreams of what might have been, and perhaps will even inspire current-day makers to follow through.

Most of the items pictured have company numberings and descriptions.

Every care has been taken to insure the best and most accurate reproduction possible. For this reason, the size of The Barclay Catalog Book is 8½"x13", allowing everything but one extra-large page of sketches to be printed full-size. The 56 interior pages are on 70 pound coated stock, and the wraparound cover 80 pound coated stock.

Price per copy is $15 plus $1 postage. For quantities of six or more, the cost is $8 each, postage paid. Order from:

Richard O'Brien —OTSN
135 Stephensburg Rd. RD2
Port Murray, New Jersey 07865

To The Editor,

I've realized recently that I may be incorrectly running the Barclay production number 785 next to the B135 and B136 skier in white. The piece I got in 1940 has no markings at all. The other skier I have (obtained considerably more recently) is only marked "MADE IN U.S.A." Does anyone out there have a Barclay skier in white with a number (Don Pielin reports only the brown version is marked 785). If not, it could be that the one in white was given a production number in the 724-727 sequence, like the Italians and Ethiopians and possibly Japanese and Chinese-Mongols. A small point, maybe, but it could indicate production earlier than B130, say (the size of the piece indicates this). It might also help in dating when production of Barclay's cast helmet pieces began. I received the B135 in the summer of 1940. Anyway, would appreciate hearing from anyone who has a number, or perhaps one painted in red as a Russian, which may or may not have happened.

Richard O'Brien

THE BARCLAY CATALOG BOOK
Richard O'Brien

While collectors await O'Brien's upcoming massive book on toy soldiers (now at the typesetter's, with a tentative Spring, 1987 publication date), he's given the dimestore buffs among us something to chew on.

If you've ever tried to find reference materials on American dimestore companies you know how little exists. However, Richard tracked down the sizeable archives kept by Barclay's last owner, and he reproduces it all here, with everything but one extra-large page of sketches printed in its original size. It's a treasure trove — catalog pages, order sheets, photos, printing blocks, sketches of projected toy soldiers — and it's all beautifully produced on heavy, glossy paper. The illustrations are sharp and crisp, and almost all of the toys bear Barclay's own descriptions and numberings. Some of the soldiers have yet to be found by collectors. The same is true for almost all the boxed sets shown here, and a number of the other toys, including two odd-looking rocketships.

The price is $15 for 56 oversized pages plus wraparound covers. For any true dimestore collector, this book is a must.

Another recent book by O'Brien is the second edition of his American Premium Guide To Electric Trains (Books Americana). At 463 pages, it's 172 pages longer than the first edition, and is a great source for those of you interested in military train sets. All the major manufacturers are represented, and most of the smaller ones. It's a price guide, and the prices I checked were right on the money. At $10.95 this is a real bargain.

THE BARCLAY CATALOG BOOK by Richard O'Brien

MATERIAL FROM THE BARCLAY ARCHIVES

HOLT'S HOBBIES
IN THE BARCLAY AND MANOIL TRADITION
Please note: these items contain lead and are not intended for use by children.

These hollow-cast metal figures continue where the old dimestore manufacturers left off.
They are the same scale as the Barclay and Manoil soldiers of the 1930's and 40's, are carefully
painted, and faithfully match the original toy soldier colors.

We are happy to announce the first in a series of dimestore soldiers sculpted from sketches attributed to the late Barclay sculptress Olive Kooken.

These soldiers are illustrated on pages 26 and 52 in Richard O'Briens newly published Barclay Catalog Book, as ideas that were never produced. We intend to release a continuing series of soldiers from the illustrations in the book.

Our thanks to Richard for graciously allowing us to reprint these sketches.

Soldier with Lewis Gun (This figure is heavier due to a 6 piece mold requiring solid arms and weapon) $14.00. Soldier standing firing up $12.00. Guard in campaign hat U.S. Infantry blue braid $10.00. Please allow 3 to 4 weeks delivery.

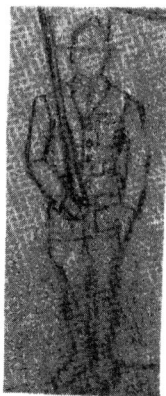

NAME _____

ADDRESS _____

CITY _____ State_____ ZIP_____

FLA Res. Add 5% STATE TAX.
OVERSEAS AND CANADIAN RES.
Add 10% of order.

PPD. UPS in USA.
MAKE ALL CHECKS OR MONEY ORDERS
PAYABLE IN U.S. DOLLARS TO:
HOLT'S HOBBIES, 19800 SW 180th AVE.
Box 40, MIA, FLA, 33187 (305) 253-4251

Charge to: ☐ MASTERCARD   ☐ VISA

_____
ACCOUNT NUMBER
Exp. Date _____

Signature _____

TSR Spring 1986

93

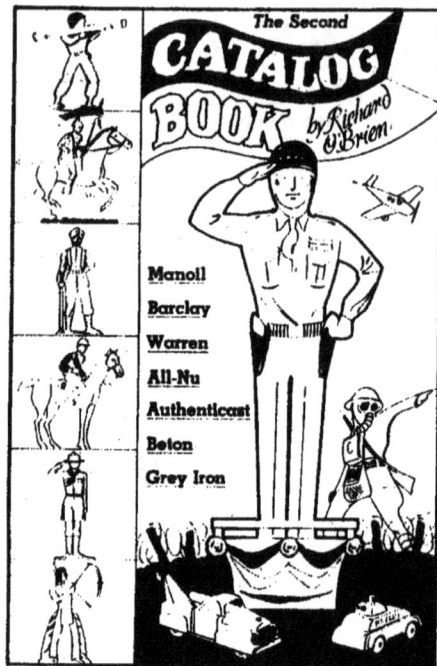

THE SECOND CATALOG BOOK (56 pages, $15.00) 8½ x 13″ soft bound by RICHARD O'BRIEN. As Richard explains in his introduction, this is a companion to the "The Barclay Catalog Book". Apparently because of the high quality job Richard did on those company archives, it brought a lot of other catalog material out of hiding. The same care has gone into this book, which covers a much wider range of material. Some of the highlights: the only known Manoil pre-WWII catalog (circa 1939 soldiers and related military toys), two very early Beton catalogs (one of which shows sets and accessories nobody seems to have seen before), and the first reproduction of a Warren catalog. A single page of post-war Grey Iron (John Wright) figures will be worth the price of the book alone to some collectors, as it solves a lot of mysteries. In addition, there's a bunch of post-War Barclay and Manoil illustrated order sheets, an All-Nu (Faben) catalog, and an Authenticast flyer that tantalizingly lists soldiers that never got produced. The book is the same size, page count and quality print job as the Barclay book. Still another highlight is the cover illustration itself, by artist-collector John Schmidt. Outstanding work, John! The price for The Second Catalog Book is $15 plus $1 postage. It's advertised elsewhere in this issue.

TSR Summer 1986

Sixth OTSN Show

The Hyatt was fully booked, the show itself sold out of tables, and the gate on Sunday morning was up by several hundred visitors as well. Some new toy soldier dealers said they had their biggest single sales day ever.

Photos on the next three pages tell much of the story of the weekend. Richard O'Brien took home this year's Bermuda-Texas Toy Soldier Society's Tommy Award for his research and numerous articles and books on dimestore soldiers. In fact, dimestore enthusiasts had quite a show. At least 30 excellent condition Jones figures changed hands, and three separate Manoil parachutist #58's in a light cream-colored paint variation turned up. Other rare figures seen included a mint painted version of the Metal Cast Products mounted colonial officer (MCP22 in Pielin's book) and a Playwood Plastics advancing rifleman in mint condition.

OTSN V10#5 10/86

"Gogo" Unmasked: Sheila Toys

by RICHARD O'BRIEN

When I was a boy, I spent all the holidays I could in Massachusetts
where I had three very good friends. We had remarkably similar
interests, the major one being toy soldiers. The three of them
had the only Joneses I'd seen, and one of them (naturally, the
rest of us thought he was rich, which was hardly the case) owned
six hundred soldiers, among them a number of Joneses, some
All-Nu majorettes, that running Auburn "pilot" I've been seeking
all these years, and an oversized, klunky-looking football player.

The latter, because of his unintelligent, hulking look, caught
my fancy. I named him "Gogo", and used him whenever I wanted
an amusingly dim-witted enforcer. Like the Joneses, he also
drove me to distraction from time to time, since there was no
indication of who had made him. And I wanted to *know*.

Decades later I got into this hobby, found out about Joneses,
and suggested to Jones expert Don Pielin several times that "Gogo"
might be a Jones too since he had that same bulky, clumsy look.
But no positive assurances issued from Don.

Then came the day when I heard from my favorite uncle, Hank
Anton. Hank wrote and said he'd found a couple of klunky football
players. And underneath their bases were labels reading *Copyright 1937 by Sheila Inc.,
Cleveland, Ohio*. (See author's note on page 7.)

About that time I had a day in New York planned with my wife. We were going to visit
the Metropolitan Museum of Art, dine at the Russian Tea Room and see the big comedy
hit of the day, Noises Off. I suggested to Mary Ann that a whirlwind visit to the
copyright records at the Fifth Avenue Library might prove an exciting addition to
the day. "Sensational!" she sighed.

Well, the art was great, the blinis terrific, and the show funny. But still, compared
to the copyright records...Because it was *all* there, all the information, and plenty
more. Unlike Tommy Toy, which had marked its soldiers with a copyright and never
followed through with the Copyright Office (or perhaps had been rejected), the
pieces marked *Sheila Inc*. had been copyrighted. Not only that, so had a number of
others, most of which--at least to my knowledge--have yet to surface.

All the pieces attributed to Sheila Inc. were sports figures. Two names were listed
in the records, and I presume they were the sculptors. The letters and descriptions
underlined in the list that follows are the company's description. The U30 shown
in the 4th edition of Collecting Toys (p. 218) is a Sheila (the kicker next to him
is a Hubley, according to dealer Bud Born). The new edition of Don Pielin's The
American Dimestore Soldier Book pictures "Gogo" and 4 other Sheila figures as
MC46 through MC50. That photo is reproduced on page 7.

*By now all but the most recent subscribers must be familiar with Richard
O'Brien's frequent articles based on his extensive dimestore soldier research.
Richard was recognized for these efforts by his fellow collectors when he
received the BTSS's Tommy Award at this year's OTSN Chicago Show.*

OTSN V10 #5 10/86

So here they are, "unknowns" no longer in the sense that we now know who manufactured them, but--many of them--still "unknowns" because we have absolutely no idea what they look like. Anybody got any hollow lead basketball players?

FOOTBALL PLAYERS (Jack Worthington), Copyright July 8, 1937

Back, copyright 7/8/37   Lineman, copyright 7/17/37
Ball Carrier, copyright 7/8/37   Kicker, copyright 7/17/37
Center, copyright 7/8/37   Football Referee, copyright 7/17/37

BASEBALL PLAYERS (Stephen A. Rebeck), all copyright 7/7/37

A. Baseball Umpire   D. Baseball Pitcher
B. Baseball Catcher   E. Baseball Fielder
C. Baseball Batter   F. Baseball Fielder

BASKETBALL PLAYERS (Jack Worthington), all copyright 7/17/37

A. Guarding   F. Pass Receiver
B. Shooting   G. Pass Receiver
(No C or D listed)   (No H listed)
E. Passer   I. Punter (listed with basketball players)

Author's Note: What would we do without the dealers in our hobby? And does any other hobby have the same caliber of dealers? What I'm talking about is the contributions our dealers keep making to the continuing research into American toy soldiers. It's not a thing they make a dime on; in fact it's a money-losing proposition for them, in terms of time and postage and film developing spent. But they do it. To give a single instance, the recent research into plastic Barclays spurred by three dealers: Gene Parker, who spread the word about his Ajax Plastics discovery, K. Warren Mitchell, who passed on the news about Thomas Toys, and Hank Anton's unearthing (and disseminating) the Royal Puddings toy soldiers offer.

From left: Sheila's baseball fielder, football back, football lineman, football center, and football runner.

American Dimestore

EMPIRE FORCES
by Richard O'Brien

It all began when first K. Warren Mitchell and then Hank Anton happened upon boxed sets of soldiers marked *Empire Forces*. Each found the same large set, and Mitch also came up with a smaller variant. The large sets were intriguing; they contained wood composition versions of Manoil's prone and seated World War I machine gunners. (The smaller set featured four inch-high composition paratroopers, all the same rather uninteresting type, and not at all Manoil-like.) The boxtops were just as compelling; there was no manufacturer or country of origin listed, and the seven soldiers illustrated looked more British than American. One was a trooper in a bearskin hat, another a highlander, a third a British Indian, and the remaining four could as easily have been Tommys as Yanks. Furthermore, the term "Empire" suggested these soldiers could have come from Canada, Australia, or England.

Still, New York is the Empire State, so I took a shot with the corporations bureau. They listed two Empires in business during World War II (obviously the period of Empire Forces' manufacture). I sent for the incorporation papers, and each company seemed a possibility, but I couldn't locate any of the listed principals. Frustration set in.

Months later, my wife suggested we take a drive to Bucks County, Pennsylvania. Furthermore, in some mad caprice (she hates flea markets), she asked if I'd like to visit the Lahaska flea market, where in earlier years I'd found a lot of soldiers. I gave her a quick yes, and not long after, we were there.

Not surprisingly, the elderly woman who'd dealt in dimestore soldiers years before virtually everyone else was gone. The other dealers didn't have much, and I was about to leave. But then I spotted a building that had gone up since I'd last been there, and I decided to take a fast look around. At the far end of the building, I found a dealer who specialized in paper collectibles. I asked if he had any toy catalogs. He handed me a couple.

In the second one I flipped through, a Christmas 1944 <u>Billy and Ruth</u> catalog, there it was: *Empire Forces*--the large set Mitch and Hank had found, priced at $1.29. And diagonally above it was a similar set. It had the prone Manoil machine gunners, what appeared to be the paratrooper, and several other figures. However, they were made of plaster and were dubbed not *Empire Forces* but *United Nations Forces*. As I looked at the name, a faint bell went off.

As soon as I got home, I grabbed the envelope that contains notes I've made over the years while searching through toy trade magazines. Eventually I found it: a cryptically penciled "Paint set: 'United Nations Forces'". And several spaces down, the notation "Gardel Ind. 106 E. 19th St. NY". It seemed to be the company's name, but I couldn't be sure since I had made the note years before. As soon as I could, I went to a New York research library where good old <u>Playthings Magazine</u> came through again, or nearly so.

From at least April, 1943 through March, 1944, New York's Gardel Industries of 106 East 19th Street (and after 179 Wooster Street) advertised its *United Nations Forces* sets. The owner was F. Gardelle. The plaster soldiers shown in the ads were the prone Manoil machine gunners, a sailor, and some other less immediately identifiable figures, but presumably "infantry, paratrooper, airman, RAF" as described in the ad. As in the Empire Forces large set, there was also a tank. Aside from the machine gunner, all the figures appear to be originals. (A notation that some of the soldiers were also available painted at ten cents each retail doesn't say whether these individual pieces were plaster or composition.)

Photos, page 18: Empire Forces boxed set, including tanks; page 19: Machine gunners--Manoil's at left, Empire Forces at right. All courtesy of K. Warren Mitchell.

Here I have to mention that though United Nations Forces and Empire Forces were coupled in the Billy and Ruth catalog, they shared the same prone machine gunners (and probably the paratrooper) and the same types of figures in their boxtop illustrations, but the style of art on the labels is not the same. United Nations were plaster, Empire composition, and Gardel seems never to have advertised Empire Forces even though in 1944 it did advertise a second set of plaster figures: The Kiddie's Circus.

So although a direct connection between Gardel and Empire Forces is virtually certain, it hasn't yet been proven. My guess, based on the date of the Billy and Ruth catalog and the more modern look of the art on its boxtop, is that Empire Forces was a late entry by Gardel. Possibly by that point the manufacturer had found, as had Playwood Plastics and Molded Products before him, that in those wartime years there was no need to advertise toy soldiers; hungry retailers grabbed them up as soon as they were available.

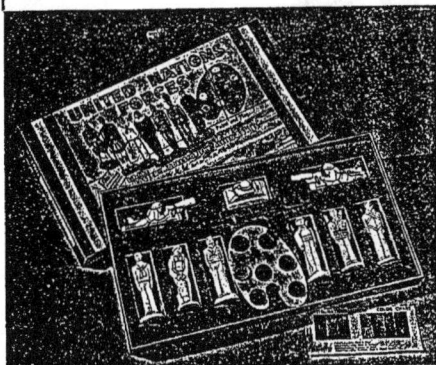

THANKS For The Way You Came, Saw and *BOUGHT!*

PAINTED SOLDIERS—10¢ each Retail
Infantry, paratrooper, airman, machine gunner, RAF and tank.

UNITED NATIONS FORCES SOLDIER PAINT SETS

Fun galore for young American patriots and quick profits for you.

No. 100 Paint Set, illustrated, contains 9 pieces, 6 assorted standing soldiers, 2 machine gunners, 1 tank, 1 palette with 6 assorted water colors, 1 camel hair brush, 1 color chart, and complete directions for coloring. Box 8¾x16¼x1½"; printed in 4 eye-catching colors; individually boxed; 2 dozen to corrugated carton.

Suggested Retail Price **$1.19**

Our No. 200 De Luxe Set Retails at **$2.00**

WRITE FOR FULL PARTICULARS

GARDEL INDUSTRIES
106 East 19th Street   New York

Represented by
TOM McGINTY — 200 Fifth Avenue, New York City

The ad above for United Nations Forces ran in the April, 1943 Playthings. Note that a larger set was available.

While going through Playthings of 1943-45, I found some other related toy advertised, so I thought I'd pass on the information at the tag end of this article through captioned illustrations. Carvatoy doesn't appear to have thought of its figures in toy soldier terms, but they seem quite toy soldier-like to me. I have no idea of how one carved a toy.

When I first found the ad for the Well-Made Doll and Toy Company's "Victory Toys" I was delighted because it seemed on first look to prove answers to Ed Poole's past OTSN article on wartime composition toys. Then I noticed many of the pieces were variations of the ones in Ed's report. I sent Ed the ad, and he says only the carrier, the destroyer and the sub are identical to the pieces shown in his article. Were there two companies making these pieces or did Well-Made, like Playwood Plastics, have variant molds made? I'd vote for the latter; Ed's not so sure. Perhaps more important to toy soldier collectors: what were the "military statuettes" described by Well-Made in its ad?

The KIDDIE'S CIRCUS

Brings the Thrill of the
Big Top into the Playroom

Every youngster loves a circus and every youngster will want this great new circus on sight.

Play value plus! It's fun painting the circus animals and performers and hours of fun afterwards playing with them.

Each Set contains 16 plaster figures to be colored, 1 Animal Trainer, 2 Clowns, 2 Elephants, 3 Tigers, 3 Lions, 3 Seals and 2 Animal Stools—also a circus ring, animal cage and a palette with 11 colors. Packed in colorful, illustrated display box. Approximate retail price $2.00.

UNITED NATIONS FORCES P....SET

The Famous Sales Tested Milit....

....utfit

For steady all-year sales make sure you also have this business-built $1.19 retailer in stock. A pro... from coast to coast. Y...

Each...

PAINT-PALS

HAVE LANDED AND HAVE THE MARKET WELL IN HAND!

We are at last in high-speed production on this amazingly popular new item! So, if you have been fretting over the non-delivery of your last order, rest assured that "it won't be long now!"

The coloring of PAINT-PALS—statuettes of authentically dressed and equipped Soldier, Sailor, Nurse, Marine and Aviator—is such an interesting and educational pastime that it is fast developing into a hobby! The ceramics used are non-critical, and the water colors furnished are non-poisonous.

NEW 3-PACK DISPLAY CARTON

This new package (not illustrated) is 15 x 5¾ x 1⅜ inches, printed in full colors, and contains one Soldier, one Nurse, one Sailor, one Brush, one palette of colors, and complete directions for coloring all three of the statuettes. Its size, vivid coloring and general attractiveness compel attention and make it a sure-fire self-seller! PAINT-PALS are also packaged singly, and two to a carton.

REPRESENTATIVES

Hugh D. Kenney, 1623 Merchandise Mart, Chicago, Illinois
A. Dartmoore, 242 Kasota, 2900 Woodward Avenue, Cincinnati, Ohio
R. J. Mattburn, 742 Kasota, 28th Street, Erie, Pennsylvania
Carl A. Sulzberg, Security Bldg., Seattle, Portland, Oregon
Arthur Niece, 2711 Ave. Star Dr., Dallas, Texas
W. Mossysmith, Room 313—200 Fifth Ave., Atlanta, Ga.
Chas E. Jacobus, Room 313—200 Fifth Ave., New York, N.Y.

DETROIT TOY COMPANY
17102 Mack Avenue   Detroit, Michigan

PAINT-PALS
will soon be joined by
PULL-PALS

An animated Uncle Sam, 14½ inches high, which, when assembled and operated, delivers a kick to the enemy and Hitler. It's a natural if ever there was one!

WAIT! WATCH!! OR WRITE FOR INFORMATION NOW!

DIVISION PRESENTS
Victory Toys
Popularly Priced

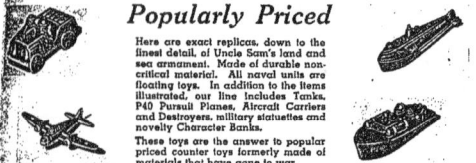

Here are exact replicas, down to the finest detail, of Uncle Sam's land and sea armament. Made of durable non-critical material. All naval units are floating toys. In addition to the items illustrated, our line includes Tanks, P40 Pursuit Planes, Aircraft Carriers and Destroyers, military statuettes and novelty Character Banks.

These toys are the answer to popular priced counter toys formerly made of materials that have gone to war.

TOY FAIR DISPLAY

HOTEL McALPIN
Rooms
800-801
803

SAM KALNER
RALPH KALNER
MURRAY HABERMAN
Representing

& TOY COMPANY
Permanent Showroom:
37-43 GREENE STREET   NEW YORK CITY

UARY, 1943—PLAYTHINGS   When writing to Well-Made Doll & Toy Co., will you please mention PLAYTHINGS?   93

AMERICAN
CARVATOY
TRADE MARK REGISTERED U.S. PATENT OFFICE

We take this opportunity of thanking the many buyers of Toys and Hobby Merchandise who visited our exhibit at the Toy Fair for their voluminous orders, and particularly for their instantaneous response to the initial showing of Carvatoy. We are now running to capacity to produce the merchandise for orders placed at the Fair so as to ship at promised date.
We want to remind you, however, that Carvatoy is a twelve months item in your stocks. It is pleasant, profitable entertainment for the recreation hours of the entire family, inviting friendly competition.
In addition to its other advantages, it is so well covered by patents, that there is no danger of uninspired imitations.

Sincerely,
Josef E. Princiotta
DIRECTOR

WAAC
WAVE
TANK
SOLDIER
SAILOR
PILOT

CARVIT
COLORIT

With these models the user can create
BOOK-ENDS
ASH-TRAYS
PLAQUES
and many other things.

CARVIT
COLORIT

Figures Portray "America On Guard"
10" to 12" High. No limit to combinations possible

Truly an educational toy, because it sponsors and develops the creative spirit in the individual. Designed by an artist to bring out latent talent and foster artistic ability.

Each Kit contains one Carvatoy figure. Six different powdered Colors in cardboard tubes. Two Brushes, sandpaper. Illustrated Manual of Instructions.

Designed and Created by

RONI STUDIOS
WHITESTONE, NEW YORK   Phone Flushing 3-9070

All the ad pages reduced and reproduced here are from the trade magazine Playthings, c1943-44. From top left they illustrate the plaster Kiddie Circus also produced by Gardel Industries. Top right is Sam and Ralph Kalner's Well-Made Doll Company's wartime offerings; below that the strange Carvatoy product, and finally Paint Pals, 5 inch "white ceramic figures" ready for coloring, by Detroit Toy.

"The Duke" Before He Got The Lead Out

By Richard O'Brien

John Wayne (front)
Photo by Ed Poole

John Wayne (back).
Photo by Ed Poole

I fell in love with the movies instantly, enduringly and obsessively before I was two-and-a-half. So when I ventured into a New Jersey antiques shop recently, there was little question in my mind as to what I had found.

I discovered it in a dim corner at the rear of the shop. It was a game by Parker Bros. called the "The Big Trail". At the bottom of the impressively drawn boxtop were words that instantly confirmed my suspicion: "A Fox Movietone Production - Under the Direction of Raoul Walsh". There was no mention of the star, but I knew who it had been.

"The Big Trail" was released on Columbus Day (October 12th), 1930. About a group of pioneers struggling along the Oregon Trail, the film seemed certain to make a star of its then-unknown young hero, John Wayne. But it was wide-screen, one novelty too many, at a time when audiences were still adjusting to the innovation of sound. "The Big Trail" flopped. Fox soon released the former Marion Morrison, and he had to stuggle another nine years before finally vaulting to stardom in "Stagecoach".

Although I don't know much about games, I did remember that, when I put together a possible section on them for the first edition of my book "Collecting Toys", I hadn't come across any mention of "The Big Trail". And in the weeks after I bought the game, all my subsequent efforts to research it failed. One expert did tell me that games based on movies are rare (four or five known, I think he said), and that there is absolutely nothing in the literature on "The Big Trail".

Which may be why the figure shown here, in front and back views, seems to have escaped toy soldier collectors. A toy soldier it is, of solid lead, almost one and three-quarter inches high. Four duplicates, each painted a different color, are used in the game (there are no other figures). Since Wayne was the star of the film, I think it's safe to say, that at least on some level, this is the first (and possibly only) "John Wayne" lead soldier.

TSR Summer 1987

MORE FORT-MAKERS

by Richard O'Brien

PLAYTHINGS

March, 1932

Terre Town Toy Houses

The child's desire to "play house" is intensi-
fied with the Terre Town line because they are
so realistic. So easily set up, so easily taken
down and constructed so correctly that the
strong, wood-fibre corrugated material with-
stands hard wear and abuse.

SPACIOUS PLAY HOUSES

There are no nails, brads or metal to injure little hands
in our life-size Play House which is 39" long, 34" wide,
42" high. The awnings and flower boxes are detachable.
French windows and doors open outward. Plenty of
room for several children and toy furniture. Can be
retailed profitably as low as $1.95.

TERRE TOWN FORTRESS

A real rugged fortress that combines maximum boy
appeal with popular price. It is one of our best
selling items, and has many excellent selling features such
as large entrance door, double floors, and watch
towers. 13½" high and 18" square. Retails at 75c.

ATTRACTIVE DOLL HOUSES

Children are delighted with our Doll House. 24" long,
15" wide, 19" high with four large rooms for toy furniture. Also Doll House, Item No. 200, one large room
with spacious opening on side for furniture. These
items retail at $1.00.

TERRE TOWN TOY TRADESMAN

200 FIFTH AVENUE   NEW YORK CITY

ROOM 538 — A. H. DELFAUSSE, Representing

Southern Representative: FREDERICK A. JONES, Hotel Henry Grady, Atlanta, Ga.

As a follow-up to Ron Fink's Spring, 1986 article on the forts made by Rich Toys, here are some other companies that made forts - and fortifications.

The Terre Town Fortress was advertised in the March, 1932 Playthings magazine. Originally I suspected the foot soldiers in the illustration were Cosmos (a circa 1931 New York company), but at the 1986 Chicago toy soldier show I discovered that a German composition company had produced the same officer and troop as Cosmo (which no doubt copied them), so the pieces here are probably German.

The Melso fort was advertised in the May, 1943 Playthings.

Till now no American trench-makers seem to have been known. Here are two: The toy soldiers in the trench made by Ideal Airplane and Supply Company are mainly (per-

TSR Autumn 1987

1936

TRENCHES IN MINIATURE

The Buterfield Toy Co., 1232 Montana St., Chicago, Ill., are making a line of miniature battle fields in two sizes; the small field with a single line of trenches and the large field with first and second line trenches together with communicating lines between the two. The fields are so constructed that as many as desired may be placed side by side making a continuous line of trenches. When placed end to end there are opposing sides. These toys are moulded in one piece from a paper pulp composition which is very durable and realistic. They are finished in attractive colors and are designed to add new equipment to toy soldier sets.

The Miniature Trench Made by the Ideal Airplane & Sup

DY TRENCH MADE ROVED PROCESS

.deal Airplane & Supply Company wing a new development consisting iniature Trench which can be used iy of the toy soldiers now on the , and will make mimic warfare more c for the youngsters. This Trench e by a newly developed process on patents are expected to be issued r. This new process is extremely nsive both as regards material and

labor and produces a muc artistically decorated, and item at a much lower cost. Trench 24 inches long, 9 in 2¾ inches high, complete wire entanglements, can now tail for about half the pr smaller ones have brought p Ideal people are exhibiti Trench at the Hotel McAlp during the Toy Fair, along line of Model Airplanes and

MELCO TOYS

Melco Forts Are Volume Sellers

A HIT!
MELCO
GARAGES
and
Wheelbarrows
Made of Wood

Big, realistic, durable! Made of hard pressed wood with solid wood towers, finished in brilliant colors. Each fort has wooden cannons with action. Most models have drawbridges that raise and lower. Fort F-300 illustrated—list price $3.00. Others from $1.00 to $5.00.

MELRATH SUPPLY & GASKET CO., Inc.
Tioga St. & Aramingo Ave., Philadelphia, Pa.
New York Sales Office: Herman F. Mack,
200 Fifth Ave.

haps wholly) Lincoln Logs. This illustration ran in the April, 1937 Playthings.

The Buterfields Toy Co.'s ad ran in the September, 1986 Playthings. Ideal and Buterfield weren't the only U.S. companies to make trenches; the Pulp Reproductions Co. of Milwaukee in 1944-45 advertised "trenches and

dugouts", among other toy soldier items (there was no illustration, unfortunately).

Finally, Rich Toys' greatest competitor in the pre-World War II period was probably Keystone, which made at least three fibreboard forts, one of them an Exploding Fort.

PHOTOS OF OLD TOYS WANTED BY RICHARD O'BRIEN FOR forthcoming book. Richard O'Brien is doing a coffee table-type book (not a price guide) to be called "A History of American Toys" and is looking for good black and white photos and color slides or transparencies of all American-made toys of all eras, he's pretty well stocked on soldiers photographs, but is open for just about everything else. Write Richard at 135 Stephensburg Rd., Port Murray, NJ 07865, (201) 850-08958 anytime before 10 p.m. EST. He's also interested in any company histories that haven't yet come to light.

Pearlytoys
—Soljertoys

by Richard O'Brien

Trade magazines have been only minimally helpful in researching American toy soldiers. Of the dimestore companies, only Grey Iron and Auburn Rubber did much advertising, and several did none at all. In addition, trade stories on the companies were both few and skimpy in content.

Luckily, Pearlytoys and Soljertoys escape this category. Although what appeared in the pages of Playthings magazine was minimal, it was enough to piece together the story of the two companies. What makes this particularly fortunate is that all my other tries at researching them had turned up zero results, aside from a mention in John Garratt's not always reliable World Encyclopaedia of Model Soldiers.

Soljertoys' cowboys, both foot and mounted. From Playthings, September, 1932.

Of the two firms, Pearlytoys shows up first, in the December, 1928 Playthings. Owner S. Rosenberg of S. Rosenberg Co. is pictured with a large display of his boxed sets of Pearlytoys soldiers. According to the short piece that accompanied the photo, Rosenberg was "well pleased with the way in which the trade has accepted their line of 'Pearlytoys' Soldiers during the past season." It went on to say that Rosenberg had said his 1929 line would offer many new features, including "several newcomers" in the Rosenberg line of musical toys and noisemakers. Unfortunately, the photo showing Rosenberg's soldiers was taken from too great a distance to provide much in the way of clues. However, it is obvious that there were both foot and mounted figures.

Unless I've missed something, Rosenberg next pops up in Playthings as the owner of Soljertoys. My guess would be that Rosenberg (possibly as a result of the 1929 crash) evaded creditors by reorganizing as Soljertoys.

It's possible that someone got the original Pearlytoys molds, because the Soljertoys mounted officer, who bears traces of the original Pearlytoys marking, is less defined in his details, suggesting a new mold was made that used the lead soldier as the model.

In any case, between Playthings ads and illustrations and a boxtop unearthed by Jack Matthews, it's possible we now know of the full line of Soljertoys (which included soldiers, sailors, Indians, cowboys, cadets and marines), all but the

OTSN V11 #6 2/88

Soljertoys boxed set, oddly combining an advancing doughboy with an Indian chief doing a war dance. From *Playthings*, April, 1930.

Soljertoys Paint-A-Toy ad. August, 1930, courtesy of *Playthings*.

marine. This box lid pictures their Indian chief, mounted cowboy, marching sailor and cadet. The box's wording proclaims: *An American product: Soljertoys. A lasting toy--that brings joy to both girl and boy--mounted and unmounted-- soldiers, sailors, Indians, cowboys, cadets, marines.*

Aside from the marine, the major question in my mind is whether the dimestore-sized doughboy (coded SO11) I've shown in the 4th edition of Collecting Toys and in Collecting Toy Soldiers is actually a Soljertoy. Unfortunately, the Indian chief doing a war dance who appears in the same set depicted in Playthings hasn't yet turned up to confirm the doughboy's size. The cadet on the boxtop appears to be the cadet I've shown in both books (page 219 of Collecting Toys, bottom left).

Rosenberg incorporated his second company as S. Rosenberg Toy Manufacturers on January 14, 1930. His sets in 1930 sold for 25 cents to $3.00, with single pieces going for a dime.

The company seems to have gone out of business about 1936 or 1936 after a reorganization about 1934, becoming the Illfelder Corporation. According to Garratt, Soljertoys used the molds of Metal Cast in 1936, but to date nothing has turned up to corroborate this.

S. Rosenberg

A frequent contributor to OTSN, New Jersey collector and writer Richard O'Brien sends word that his latest book, a 520-page guide to toy soldier collecting with eight pages of color, will be released this spring.

EUREKA!
THE AMERICAN SOLDIER CO.

By Richard O'Brien

The first important American makers of metal toy soldiers appear to have popped up around the turn of the century. All evidence suggests there were just three of them: McLoughlin Brothers, William Feix and American Soldier Co. As a firm, McLoughlin is pretty well-documented, but about all that's known of its soldiers comes from the boxed sets that have emerged. Feix is known only through a few early ads and directories. For a long time American Soldier was essentially a mystery too. Recently, however, a great deal of information has come to light.

Almost all of it stems from Playthings Magazine. Playthings, a monthly trade magazine for the toy industry, began publishing in January, 1903. In the past year I've been able to examine the issues from that date through 1909.

American Soldier Co. was mentioned in that first issue, and began advertising in the second. For some years it advertised heavily, and consequently was given a considerable amount of editorial space.

In January, 1903 it was mentioned that the company's soldiers were available in both gilt and regular paint. In March, there was a line about "a very neat catalogue" having been issued. In May, 1903, there was the announcement "The American Soldier Co. have moved their factory to Glenside, Brooklyn, N.Y." from a previous Brooklyn address. "Glenside" was probably a mistake, as American Soldier is quickly noted as being located in Glendale, Brooklyn.

The next month, Playthings reported "C.W. Beiser of the American Soldier Co. says that his new factory is running along smoothly."

For a long time there has been uncertainty and confusion about Eureka soldiers and American Soldier Co. The early ads give evidence that Eureka was simply the trademarked name American Soldier gave to its products, running both names in its ads until July, 1903, when the Eureka designation seems to have been permanently dropped.

In that same month, an article was written about Beiser, accompanied by his photo. It begins "Five years ago C.W. Beiser became interested in the manufacture of lead soldiers, having had no experience in the toy business before that time." Since an ad in the December issue states "the past five years our line of 'American Soldiers' was exhibited in the competition with the best of foreign makes", 1898 would seem to be confirmed as the year of the company's founding. Judging by this piece, all the company's ads and another article on the firm itself, Beiser was far more interested in his patented tray than in the soldiers themselves.

The tray was designed so that soldiers could be kept in a lying position or stood up without removing them from the tray. This enabled the figures to be displayed as easily as they were shipped. Furthermore, any single soldier could be slipped out of the tray without disturbing the rest.

Today, Beiser's brainstorm doesn't seem like one whale of an idea, but back then, according to that July story, Mr. J.T. Doll of Wanamaker's (then a leading department store), when shown the tray rhapsodized that Beiser had discovered "the art of display", and "that in all his experience as a toy buyer he had never seen any toys put up in a similar manner." Futhermore, "his opinion was backed by a substantial order given on the spot."

The 1903 article states that Beiser patented his tray in Germany, England and the U.S. In England, he seems to have worked out a deal with Britains, as they used his tray in some of their sets, and he used their soldiers in some of his. Beiser apparently patented his trays twice, probably when he changed from cardboard to metal, since the presently known patent dates are given as 1904 and 1905.

In February, 1904 a fairly long article ran on the company itself, though never naming it. However, there's no question it was about American Soldier, as it mentions the tray (and the only other soldiers advertiser in Playthings was Feix, whose ads were small, and few).

Unfortunately, the account doesn't give any indication of the size of the factory, the number of workers, or where the designs and molds came from. What does get considerable attention is the process by which the soldiers were made. There was a melting pot, an alloy of antimony and lead (originally made by Beiser, later ordered in bulk from an outside source) and two-part molds, with wooden handles.

Occasionally one or more cores were required in the molds (for more complex pieces evidently). They had to be removed after each soldier was cast, then replaced. The soldiers were slush molded, with the metal poured into the mold, which was then dipped to "flush" it, after which the excess metal was poured out. Even in those days it was considered important, according to the article, that the soldiers be the proper weight; too much lead in one and some of the profit was lost.

The story goes on to say that the German-made metal horse of the day was modeled "more along the lines of a racer, with slim legs and body, and these goods are cast solid. The American horse, on the other hand, follows the lines of a charger or campaign horse, and even with the added bulk is lighter in weight".

After the soldier had been cast and the metal cooled, the "gate" (where the alloy had poured in and out, leaving

A February, 1904 ad.

A drawing which makes the figures in the ad
of the month before a little clearer.

An impressive full page ad from July, 1903.

I goofed on dating this one, Circa 1905-08,
but almost certainly March, 1905.

An Inventive Toy Maker

Five years ago C.W. Beiser became interested in the manufacture of lead soldiers, having had no experience in the toy business before that time. He was impressed by the fact that German manufacturers of lead soldiers display their wares in a laid-down position sewed on cardboard and known in the trade as flat goods. Also that their standup soldiers are sewed or clamped on by wire, so that it would be impossible to disconnect

C.W. BEISER

one of the soldiers without disturbing the entire lot. He at once went to work on the problem of making lead soldiers assume a standing position without the support being visible or without the use of thread or wire.

With this end in view he set to work, but soon discovered that he had undertaken a difficult problem. Perseverance and close study won out, however, and the display toy tray was invented. A simple device consisting of a double cardboard onto which each toy fits, locking with a half turn and each individual toy being easily removed and replaced independent of the others.

Each tray has the appearance of a miniature camp scene with collapsable tents, revolving cannon, horses and soldiers in marching and battle array on a field of green. After perfecting the tray it became necessary to ascertain how the trade would take to it. The first tray was shown to Mr. J. T. Doll, of Wanamaker's, with a request that he should criticize it. At the first glance he expressed entire approbation, saying that Mr. Beiser had discovered "the art of display," and that in all his experience as a toy buyer he had never seen any toys put up in a similar manner. His opinion was backed by a substantial order given on the spot.

Messrs. Feder, Hess, Kesler and Walsh expressed similar opinions as well as gave orders, which was most encouraging to the inventor of the new device and augured well for ultimate success. Patents were issued in Germany, England and the United States, every claim asked for being allowed. It is the aim of the inventor to place this line before every buyer on its merits, feeling confident that if those who have not already handled the goods would order a sample line they would soon discover that the American soldiers are quick every-day sellers. Customers who bought them five years ago are ordering every year, showing conclusively that the line has been firmly established.

An illustration of these goods, together with a detailed description, will be found on another page of this issue. Handsomely illustrated catalogues will be sent by the American Soldier Company on request.

This is an actual article, with type reset for clarity, from July, 1903 Playthings *magazine.*

a residue) was sawed off to make the bottom of the base smooth. A boy then pared away the "fins" as they called it (and a good description too, of the flashing) with a knife. The guns, swords, flags, etc. were made of "half and half" -equal proportions of lead and "block tin" - and attached to the figure with solder. The "half and half" was deemed necessary because it allowed flexibility, helpful with the accessories but "not wanted in the soldier itself".

May, 1908. This was the year pop guns were added to the sets. Whether the "Little Daisy" was made by the famous Daisy company isn't known. Daisy was around by then, however.

Paint was put on "by a boy or girl with a multitude of brushes and paint pots." Enamel paints were used, and after each color was applied, the soldier was set aside to dry. Each figure went through "about fifteen handlings before it stands complete, a soldier, a sailor, a Rough Rider or whatever he may be." The remainder of the article devoted itself to the tray.

American Soldier Co.'s early distributors were Geo. Borgfeldt & Co. (probably the most famous of all American toy distributors, in business from about 1881 to 1962) and A.S. Ferguson. There's been some speculation that the Beiser-Britains agreement meant no Britains were sold here till sometime after 1907. However, an early, extensive Playthings article in the August 1903 issue on Britains makes it clear that the company's soldiers were sold here before that date.

Between the article and ads in Playthings magazine, some inferences can be made as to when particular sets were produced.

A 1903 Brooklyn directory shows American Soldier Co. at 127 Wyckoff Ave. The later 1903 move to Glendale was probably to Myrtle Avenue and De Boo Place (apparently also, or later, known as Debevoise Place or Avenue) since that Glendale address is given in a later ad, circa 1905-08.

Further dating can be done by the following: Rough Rider types first appear in 1904 ads. A running soldier with movable arms was added in 1907. In 1908, cork-shooting rifles debuted in the sets, and Indians and Phillipine warriors were sold. That also seems to be the first year the sets were sold as a game. By 1909 American Soldier was advertising "sold as a game—not as lead soldiers", suggesting the bloom was off the lead soldier rose.

July, 1907: The first ad for the company's new running soldier with movable arms.

By 1922 Wm. M. Ferguson (A.S. Ferguson's son?) was listed as the president of the company and Beiser its treasurer, with both men the firm's directors. This indicates that Beiser may have run into trouble and taken in a cash-infusion senior partner. It's not known when American Soldier Co. went out of business, but it's likely that the 1929 Crash finished it off. By September, 1930 Selchow & Righter was advertising that it had acquired certain of the firm's "rights, patents, trade-marks, machinery and stocks".

The first Rough Riders ad, from March, 1904. These don't appear to have emerged in any lists, auctions or collections.

Just where does Beiser's baby figure in the history of American toy soldiers? At this stage it's hard to assess. Certainly, it was one of the important early manufacturers of metal, domestically-produced soldiers (there are strong indications that very little happened with metal soldiers in America before the turn of the century). But perhaps it was more than that.

Ads are ads, and have to be taken with a certain degree of skepticsm. Still, in February, 1903 Beiser claimed that his tray "created an American industry". All evidence suggests Beiser got there before Feix. It could be he nosed out McLoughlin too. In which case, Beiser could easily have been just what he claimed, the father of American metal toy soldiers.

109

Which would mean he was also something more: the spiritual progenitor of every besotted collector of Manoil, Grey Iron, Barclay, Comet, Beton, Auburn Rubber, etc. who's come down the pike.

PLAYTHINGS.

To the American Toy Buyer

The best line of lead soldiers are now made in your own country; if in doubt, ask the leading buyers what they think of the

Eureka American Soldiers

TRADE MARK

The first Playthings ad: February, 1903 Volume I, Number 2.

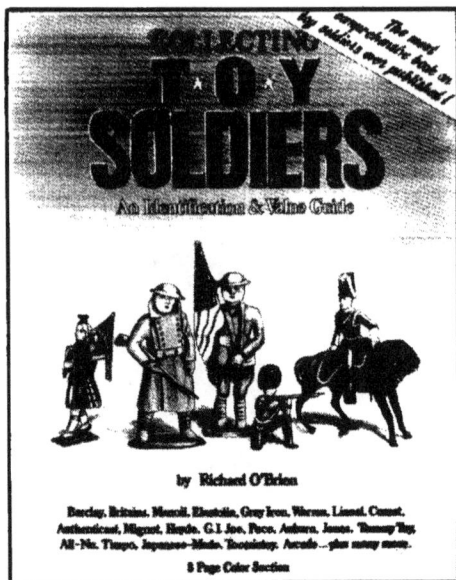

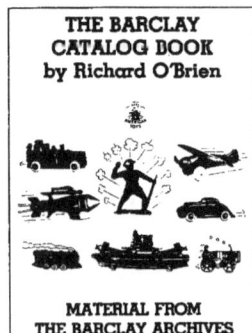

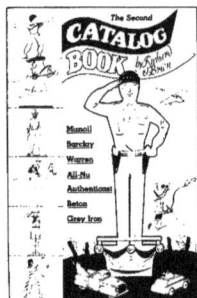

TSR Spring 1988

William Feix—
American Manufacturer

by Richard O'Brien

Until recently, when early American metal soldiers were the subject, only two manufacturers' names came up: McLoughlin Brothers and the American Soldier Company, which until mid-1988 also used the trademark *Eureka*. However, in recent months another company has emerged, and it's possible it was at least as important and prolific as the other two.

About a year ago, I went through the earliest issues of Playthings Magazine. In the sixth issue (June 1903) I found an arresting ad. I had never heard of William Feix, and when I checked with other collectors, including those who had made considerable study of turn-of-the-century American soldiers, found they hadn't either.

Recently, I've had the time to go through more issues of Playthings (1903-1909). I found two more Feix ads. In June, 1908 one appeared without an illustration. The only new information was an address: 58 Troutman Street in Brooklyn (near American Soldier Company), and the statement: *Our line has been greatly improved, and many new features added. We can fill orders from stock. Shown by all leading commission houses.*

In the July 1909 issue, there was no new information, but the drawing used in the first Feix ad reappeared. I checked a New York directory I have for 1923-24. Feix was still in it at the same address, listed in the toys section with the description: *Mfrs. Metal.*

Bill Nutting has been doing much investigation of early American soldier companies, both paper and metal, and when I told him about the Feix ads, he hied himself to the Brooklyn Historical Society. There he came up with a single find in a 1900-01 directory. It read: *Fiex, Wilhelm, pinmfr. 58 Troutman.* Bill and I take "pinmfr" to mean pin manufacturer, but we're willing to be enlightened.

Presumably Fiex instead of Feix is a typographical error. Wilhelm may be too, but perhaps not, if William was his son and found toy soldier making more fun (or profitable) than spewing out pins. (Feix is not listed as a pin manufacturer in 1923-24.) Many toy companies originally started out as something else. If Wilhelm Feix was in business as a pin manufacturer circa 1859, it would be quite significant, as Uncle Hank Anton has discovered a mounted Indian that at least one Barclay veteran has labeled as Barclay (B1 on page 176 of the 4th edition of Collecting Toys) that is marked on the bottom---EST'S 1859 BROOKLYN, N.Y. This would strongly suggest that Feix was turning out soldiers in the 1920s, which is the approximate era of that mounted Indian (and that Barclay may have gotten some of its early molds from Feix; co-owner Michael Levy was from Brooklyn).

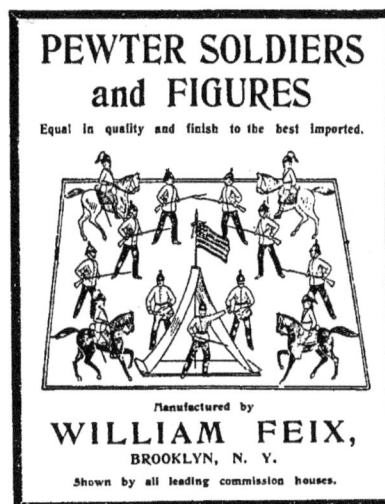

The soldiers in the Feix illustration look like copies of Britains, with the exception of the officer with the sword. John Garratt in his *Model Soldiers for the Connoisseur* (1972, p.4) identifies this group as McLoughlin, but at this point it would seem more likely Feix was the manufacturer, unless he pirated McLoughlins. Or...

Donald Wollheim, who knows more about McLoughlin than anyone I've come across, suspects that McLoughlin never made any of its soldiers. So Feix could have supplied McLoughlin with these, and perhaps sold some on its own. Or....

The soldiers in the illustration may <u>never</u> have been made by Feix. Beginning in the October 1907 <u>Playthings</u>, Henry C. Nathan of New York offered advertising cuts for sale. One of the cuts it sold was the Feix illustration. So Feix may have used a generic drawing in its ads. On the other hand, Butler Bros. in later years offered its customers cuts of any illustration in their catalog, with most of the photos and drawings obviously originating with the manufacturers, so it's possible that the cut originated with Feix, and that he allowed Nathan to sell it as a service to Feix customers.

For this reason, an ad that ran in a 1908 Steinfeld Bros. catalog can only suggest the possibility that Feix had a large line of soldiers (note the listing of Japanese troops). The same can be said of a similar illustration from 1914 reprinted in the book *The Wonderful World of Toys, Games and Dolls* (1971).

My guess is that Feix was a major toy soldier maker, possibly operating circa 1903 into the 1920s (perhaps with lapses during periods when soldiers were in relative disfavor), and that all the early hollowcast American soldiers with the large blowhole in the head were produced by Feix (even if he only sold toy soldiers from 1903-1909, think of how many soldiers Barclay manufactured from 1934-41). But this is only a guess. Obviously, there is a need for more research here. I had no help with the one Feix in the Brooklyn phonebook, who incidentally pronounced her name "fakes". The discovery of a box or two of soldiers marked "William Feix" would certainly help. Anyone out there have one?

Richard O'Brien's long anticipated toy soldier book is now available. See the review on page 4 and Richard's ad on page 26 of this issue.

Soldier Sets

Description of Soldier Sets

		Doz. List
No. 11.	Five American Soldiers	$ 3.00
No. 1.	Three American Soldiers and one Officer on Horseback	3.00
No. 3.	Four American Soldiers and one Officer on Horseback	3.50
No. 2.	Six American Soldiers and one Officer on Horseback	3.50
No. 6.	Four American Soldiers, one Officer on Horse and one Tent	4.20
No. 29.	Six American Soldiers, one Officer on Horse and one Tent, one Cannon	6.50
No. 20.	Six Volunteers, one General on Horse and one Cannon	6.50
No. 46.	Nine American Soldiers, two Officers on Horse	7.50
No. 17.	Twelve American Soldiers on Horseback	13.00
No. 48.	Fourteen American Soldiers, two on Horse, one Cannon and one Tent	13.00
No. 73.	Seventeen Japanese Soldiers, two Tents and two Cannons	15.50
No. 67.	Twenty-two Sailors and two Cannons	15.50
No. 66.	Sixteen American Soldiers, two on Horses, two Cannons and two Tents	16.00
No. 38.	Twenty American Soldiers, two on Horses, two Tents and two Cannons	18.00
No. 33.	Twenty-four Indians, two on Horses and one Tent	19.00

Book Review

Collecting Toy Soldiers:
An Identification and Value Guide

It's hard to imagine any collector who wouldn't want *Collecting Toy Soldiers: An Identification and Value Guide* on his reference shelf. Richard O'Brien gave a good taste of what this book would be like in the soldier sections of his *Collecting Toys* guides, but this book is special: 500 big pages, packed with photos, devoted exclusively to soldiers and related items from every manufacturer under the sun.

Old and even current manufacturers, over 50 strong, are covered through figure photos, box art, catalog pages, and even some factory photos, accompanied by Richard's famous thumbnail and not-so-short company histories. This book also uses the photo identification style and "good, v.g. and mint" grading scale Richard has employed in each of his books.

It has been Richard's attempt to put together an extensive, if possible comprehensive, list of each maker's range. The book includes over a thousand photos, most very high quality courtesy of New York auction houses or soldier enthusiasts like K. W. Mitchell and Ed Poole.

As you would expect, the book ranges from Beton to Britains, Johillco to GI Joe, Manoil to Marx; included are many unusual makers like Peco soft plastic 88mm figures with separate equipment. Section length has been determined both by information available and collector interest. For instance, no attempt has been made to create a comprehensive list of Heyde or German composition figures, although in the latter case Jack Matthews has written a very sophisticated overview. The Britains section is a 150-page long set list which even includes items like the garden gnomes. Like every section it is packed with hundreds of clear, sharp photos; but unlike the Dimestore section, the photos show only a sample, making figure identifications for the novice unlikely.

Richard has not in all cases created a figure by figure price guide. If this is your desire, he is most consistent in Dimestore; some maker's sections, like Warren or composition, include only general price comments and in some cases, frequently in Britains, Richard has used good restraint and simply noted "no price found." As with any price guide, particularly one developed over several years, collectors will debate and disagree. But this book is least important as a price guide. It is a festival of toy soldiers, from color photos of the Dimestore wounded in wheelchair duplex figure to pages of strange Japanese soldiers to Barclay prototypes and World War II paper toys. Quite simply, this book has a tremendous amount of useful information and it is great fun.

To order directly from Richard O'Brien, see his ad on page 26.

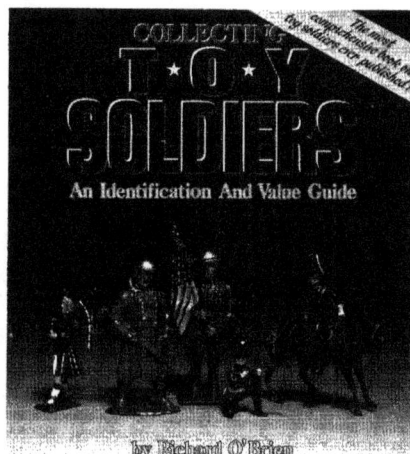

OTSN V12 #2 6/88

COLLECTORS ARE TALKING ABOUT

bOOKS

By Bill Lango

COLLECTING TOY SOLDIERS, *by Richard O'Brien. Books Americana, 1988; P.O. Box 2326, Florence, AL 35360. 505pp. $19.95. (Softcover 8½ x 11).*

When Richard O'Brien entered the battlefield of antique toy books with his *Collecting Toys* Vol. 1, (1978), he devoted a portion of that book to toy soldiers. Through subsequent printings and updated editions, he fine-tuned the toy soldier portion with cautious approach. A decade has passed since *Collecting Toys* sparked a growing interest in toy soldiers in the U.S. and truthfully, most of what is known today about American toy soldier makers is a result of his efforts. However, with his latest release *Collecting Toy Soldiers*, O'Brien has unknowingly laid claim to the toy soldier hobby and has decisively seized it as his own.

48

For openers, O'Brien's comprehensive coverage of American dimestores is the best of anyone's to date. Being a dimestore collector himself, it comes as no surprise to learn that American makers comprise almost half the book. Figures are arranged in rows and are listed by their manufacturers catalog or reference numbers, when known. Photos are large and easy to view. Variations are shown in detail, standing alongside their corresponding non-variation brethren. New, as well as long time collectors, will see first-hand the missing pieces in their collections. All the major makers are listed, as well as lesser makers and many formerely unknowns. Many previously unpublished photos are also included. Eye-poping color photos of extremely scarce dimestores are sure to reawaken the appetite of any complacent collector.

O'Brien lists many newly discovered facts on some of the little known and formerly puzzling toy soldiers, such as a group of plastic Barclay look-a-likes which turn up on dealers lists as plastic Barclays.

A chapter on miscellaneous equipment adds a refreshing change to military toys and shows some highly collectible accessories many toy soldier collectors use as adjuncts in their collections.

Jack Matthews did an excellent job of editing the German Composition chapter. Just eighteen pages are devoted to German composition, but Jack's lucid commentary runs six pages and reads as a primer for both new and older collectors of composition figures.

One hundred and twenty-five pages are devoted to Britains. Compared with volumes of information published elsewhere on Britains, we like the way O'Brien handled this chapter. No fluff here, instead, after a brief introduction, O'Brien gets to the point with a concise, yet exhaustive listing. Many other British makers are represented such as Johillco, Timpo, Cherilea, and Courtenay.

Mignot of France is given a brief listing, but the highly collectible Lucotte figures are absent.

Collecting Toy Soldiers is a workhorse of a book. Before diving into its pages, all readers should first read page 1, Condition of A Toy Soldier and its Relation to Price. O'Brien's comments here are right on the mark. Despite some minor pricing inconsistencies, (no price guide is going to meet with all collectors' approval), *Collecting Toy Soldiers* is a must buy book.

TSR Summer 1988

Dimestore Scale *Historical Miniatures*

by Steve Balkin, Bertel Bruun and Richard O'Brien

At the First Annual East Coast Toy Soldier Show in 1983, Richard O'Brien noted three unusual 3-1/4" solid lead figures (OTSN V7,6:18). Almost simultaneously, among the various toy soldiers of a collection bought by Steve Balkin, a number of solid lead figures were noted to be different from previous figures known to him. In 1984 he wrote about these unknowns in OTSN V8,2:14 and speculated that other figures might have been made as well as mentioning several others owned by other collectors. Basically that article was a cry for help.

Later, in early 1988 when even more of these mysterious figures had been discovered, O'Brien tentatively ascribed them to James Miniatures (Collecting Toy Soldiers, Books Americana, Alabama, 1988). He notes, however, that R.E. James' widow claimed that these figures were not made by her late husband.

Since that time, documentary evidence which had already been hinted at in 1984 by Balkin has surfaced. Among the well-known collector and dealer Gus Hansen's papers obtained from J.E. Jones, creator of the famous dimestore figures (193?-1941) and a partner in Metal Miniature Co. (1940-42) and Moulded Miniatures (1946-1955), were several referring to these figures.

These papers not only solve the mystery of the figures, but also document the existence of a formerly unknown manufacturer and cast considerable light on this company's production and early history, as well as indicating some of Jones' modus operandi.

The documents consist of a cardboard flyer by Historical Miniatures introducing the series (apparently produced specifically for the Hobbies Fair in Chicago in November 1941); a one-page article about the figures and their creator, Michael Gera, from the Sunday Mirror Magazine Section (N.Y.) dated January 11, 1942; a letter by J.E. Jones, partner of Metal Miniatures Co. of Chicago to Montgomery Evans of Historical Miniatures Inc. of N.Y., dated February 28, 1942, seemingly a response to a previous letter; Mr. Evans' response, dated March 21, 1942; and an undated handwritten note in Jones' handwriting summarizing his knowledge of Historical Miniatures (H.M.).

From this evidence the following can be pieced together about H.M. The company began about June 1941 and was located at 416 Fourth Avenue; New York City. The sculptor was a Michael Gera, or in his native land Russia, Mikhail Z. Gerashshenevsky. He is said to have been a former captain of body guards for Russia's last czar and wounded seven times in World War I. The newspaper photograph of Mr. Gera taken in late 1941 or early 1942 depicts a relatively young man who appears to be in his mid- to late thirties, making at least his military rank of captain somewhat suspect. He is also said to be a "distinguished Russian-American veteran," and to have produced "animated circuses for Beech-Nut Company, work for the New York World's Fair, and in (sic) many other commissions."

OTSN 2-3/89 V13#1

The aim of H.M. was "to do American history in figures of solid metal (3 inches high), designed from famous statues, as well as from the best material obtainable from the best collections and libraries" and "to present for collectors, amateurs, educators, and buyers of toy soldiers, figures which will be superior in quality of material and in design to any obtainable in any country."

The figures were 3" to 3-1/4" tall and weighed 1/4 pound. They were handpainted and the flyer states that "for those who are not as yet collectors, (they) are suitable as desk and table ornaments,or as paperweights." The figures are marked with a rubber stamp "Made in U.S.A." (white), or "Made USA" (black), or in one known case, with a dark blue paper label marked only "USA".

H.M. divided their figures into three categories: United States (historical figures, mainly from the Revolution); foreign figures (historical personalities from abroad and a charging Highlander), and contemporary figures (both soldiers and personality figures).

All the figures appear to have been created by Mr. Gera who "sculptures with surgical implements, mainly tiny instruments employed in delicate brain operations." In the correspondence between J.E. Jones and Mr. Evans (probably the business manager of H.M.), the former offered his only remaining metal casting from his 3" figures made in 1932 for sale to H.M. It does not appear that this deal was consummated.

It seems that Historical Miniatures switched to producing at least some of their figures in composition during the Second World War, and after the war sold at least a few GI's in pot helmets (first produced in composition). F.A.O. Schwarz is known to have sold the metal GI's, which suggests this could have been a continuing outlet for Historical Miniatures.

In Jones' correspondence he offers to help distribute the figures, either by buying them outright or on a commission basis, but it is not clear if this offer was acted upon. He also indicates an interest in the use of plastics but rejects it because of expense. He is more enthusiastic about his idea of pasting on faces so the likeness would be the same each time.

Mr. Evans mentions in his letter that he is contemplating "A 'V' display, a wooden V, 24x18, with 16 American figures attached by screws. Some advertising friends see in it possibilities for sale to stores, banks, etc. and suggest a retail price of $25." It is not known if such a display was ever made.

Prices for H.M. figures were high: regular figures went for 50¢, more complicated figures (drummers, flagbearers, etc.) for 75¢ and the Forty-niner with a genuine gold nugget in the pan, a unique feature among toy soldiers, for $2.50. Considering most dimestore figures at that time retailed for a nickel, it is understandable that H.M. figures are rare indeed. The very high quality of both casting and painting makes these figures both aesthetically very pleasing and well worth collecting.

Photo, page 22, George Washington.
At right, "Forty-Niner" with real gold nugget
   in his pan.

Photo above: World War II Allied leaders.
From left, Churchill, FDR, Stalin, and de Gaulle.

It is not known exactly when H.M. ceased production, but it was probably in the late forties.

Known Historical Miniature figures listed, as far as possible, in the order used by the company.

UNITED STATES

George Washington
Benjamin Franklin
John Paul Jones
Lafayette
Steuben
Pulaski
"Spirit of '76" (four figures in a box--son,
  father, grandfather and Massachusetts
  regimental flagbearer, with American flag
  with stars in a circle)
Officers and soldiers, marching and charging,
  of Continental, Massachusetts and
  Pennsylvania regiments*
Flagbearers of these regiments**
Nathan Hale
Forty-Niner, with genuine gold nugget in pan
Lincoln
Lee
Martha Washington
George Washington, mounted

  *Continental: dark blue jacket with orange
    piping, red vest, beige pants
   Massachusetts: dark blue jacket with white
    piping, white vest and pants
   Pennsylvania: brown jacket with white piping,
    white vest, beige pants
  **Massachusetts Regiment flagbearer carries
    flag with pine tree, the others the American
    flag with stars in a circle.

FOREIGN FIGURES

Charging Highlander
Simon Bolivar (liberator of South America)
Florence Nightingale (founder of Red Cross)***
Baden Powell
Martin Luther
Napoleon

CONTEMPORARY FIGURES

U.S. soldier with flag
U.S. Legionnaire with flag
Winston Churchill
Black Watch with flag
Greek Evzone with flag
Greek Evzone charging
Cossack in red or green uniform
Franklin D. Roosevelt
General MacArthur
Stalin
Churchill (in naval dress)
General de Gaulle
Chiang Kai-shek
G.I. charging with bayonet (composition)?
G.I. charging with bayonet (metal)?
Stalin, composition ?

***The Red Cross was founded by Henri
   Dumont, but Historical Miniatures
   catalogued her this way.

Photos opposite page, clockwise from top left: Washington's foreign lieutenants--Lafayette, von Steuben, Pulaski, John Paul Jones, four patriots, wartime composition Montgomery, and center--Nathan Hale with Ben Franklin.

Early American Soldier Makers
Part 1
by Richard O'Brien

Originally, my toy soldier research was confined to American dimestore companies. It's still my primary interest. But, having stumbled on the earliest (January 1903) issue of Playthings, it was hard not to become intrigued by the wealth of information its pages contained.

Consequently, I've found myself thumbing Playthings and Toys and Novelties (which began a few years later) straight through the World War One period. A number of American soldier companies appear in those pages. Some, as far as I know, have never been documented: companies like North American Toy, R. Gricks-Liberty Toy Soldiers, Western New York Toy, and Standard Map Company. Others have been limited to a few lines in Garratt's Encyclopaedia. In this series, I hope to expose all of them to considerably more light.

Fellow collectors Bill Nutting and Ed Poole have been sent copies of all that's been uncovered, in the hope they could add their expertise on early soldiers and molds. Since, as Bill has said, "Loebel, Widmann...is turning out to be a distinctive and important company," we'll start with it.

Those who insist on consistency from their toymakers won't be happy with Loebel, Widmann. The firm made at least three different styles of soldiers, as the accompanying illustrations from the 1916-1918 period demonstrate. According to Bill Nutting, these types are: 1) homecast types using German molds; 2) hollowcasts of the types usually attributed to William Feix, McLoughlin and, later, Ideal; and 3) solid cast soldiers in the Heyde style. According to Bill, it's these

Below: August 1917 advertisement depicting Heyde-like figures from the very eclectic Loebel, Widmann & Co.

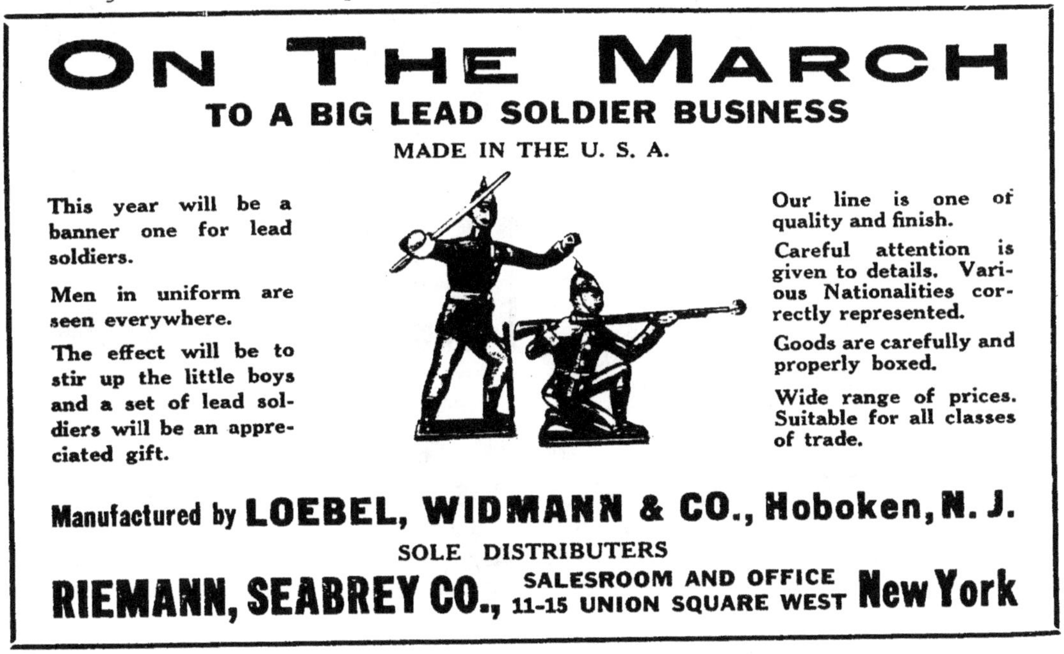

DO YOU BUY LEAD SOLDIERS?
See our line before you place order!
LARGEST AND MOST COMPLETE LINE MADE IN THE U. S. A.
HOLIDAY SEASON 1917

AMERICAN
MADE

BIGGEST VARIETY OF DESIGN
AND COMBINATIONS:
Good or elaborate according to price.
The line that is different—
Right goods, properly boxed.
WIDE RANGE OF PRICES.
Goods to retail at 10c to $25.00.
Good low, medium and high priced values.
Suitable for all classes of trade.

LEAD
SOLDIERS
Correctly representing various nationalities

Manufactured by LOEBEL, WIDMANN & CO., Hoboken, N. J.
RIEMANN, SEABREY CO., Sole Distributers
SALESROOM AND OFFICE
11-15 Union Square, West   Broadway and 15th Street,   NEW YORK

An impressive display in December 1916. Everyone agrees these soldiers appear Germanic. Produced from German-made molds?

Germanic figures, which if they were really manufactured in the U.S. as advertised, are the most extraordinary.

In December, 1917 Playthings ran a five-paragraph story on Loebel, Widmann. The occasion was its consolidation with the Maiden Toy Company. Loebel, Widmann was located in Hoboken, New Jersey. According to the story, "upon leaving the ferry one soon reaches the building where the cornerstone has been laid for this growing concern. Long since, however, this place had to be abandoned for larger quarters, as, in addition to the original manufacture of Lead Soldiers, they engaged in the manufacture of Doll Heads. One year of successful business has put them among the leading doll manufacturers in the East."

"And now we hear," the story continued, "that Loebel, Widmann, in order to expand their business still further, have consolidated with the Maiden Toy Company, Inc. of New York, the manufacturers of the country-wide known 'Maiden America.' This charming doll has unfortunately been out of the market for the last six months through the serious illness of the former manager of the Maiden Toy Company." Bill Nutting's research shows that in 1917 the Maiden Toy Co., Inc. (also known as the Maiden Toy Shop, Inc.) was run by Joseph M. Kalvin, as secretary, and

14   PLAYTHINGS   March, 1917

IT IS QUALITY THAT COUNTS
IN LEAD SOLDIERS THESE DAYS

We have perfected a line, the QUALITY of which is UNSUR-
PASSED—A FINISH that is DIFFERENT—and with EVERY
DETAIL COMPLETE.

Among our Feature Numbers are:

UNCLE SAM'S REGULARS, ROUGH RIDERS, and BLUE
JACKET Sets

FOR PATRIOTIC AMERICAN BOYS

Other Nationalities, too, correctly represented
SEE OUR LINE BEFORE YOU PLACE YOUR ORDER

Manufactured by

LOEBEL, WIDMANN & CO., Hoboken, N. J.

SOLE DISTRIBUTORS RIEMANN, SEABREY CO. 11-15 Union Sq. W. NEW YORK

JUST THE THING
FOR THIS YEAR'S

FOURTH OF JULY

LEAD SOLDIERS

UNCLE SAM'S REGULARS
UNCLE SAM'S ROUGH RIDERS
UNCLE SAM'S BLUE JACKETS

Largest and Most Complete Line.

MANUFACTURED BY

Loebel, Widmann & Co.

HOBOKEN, N. J.

SOLE DISTRIBUTORS

RIEMANN, SEABREY CO.
11-15 Union Sq. West, New York

Above, left: A March, 1917 ad. The mounted figures, top left, resemble Barclay's Bg, which was copied from a French soldier (the latter in turn, according to Bill Nutting, probably copied from an English-made figure). In the same box the infantrymen resemble Ideal's I-1, which also was probably copied from a French soldier. The sailors greatly resemble Ideal's I-8. Note the combination of flats and what appear to be fully dimensioned hollowcasts. Right: An April, 1917 ad. Ed Poole says the two bottom sets come from the molds made by Germany's Gebr. Schneider or their successors.

1

2

3

Louis Kalvin, as manager, both of whom lived on West 112th Street. Possibly it was Louis' illness which pushed the sale forward.

The Playthings article showed photos of two buildings, captioned "Doll Factory, New York" and "Soldier Factory, Hoboken". (Is it possible Barclay's Leon Donze got his start there?) The piece went on to say that in the future the two combined concerns would do business as "The Maiden America Toy Manufacturing Company, Inc. with headquarters at 101-103 Varick Street, New York City." (In February 1918 an ad shows both New York and Hoboken addresses.) Representation was to be by the well-known jobber Riemann-Seabrey and the more obscure (to me, anyway) Tip Top Toy Company. Both firms were located in New York. The final line of the piece gives the salient information that Arthur Loebel was the firm's president and general manager, and "through his long experience, is known as an expert in the toy line."

Picking up a clue in Ed Poole's files, Bill Nutting recognized an "unknown" set in Steve Balkin's personal collection as a likely candidate for a Loebel, Widmann/ Maiden America set. Bill and Steve spent a large chunk of an afternoon at Burlington Antique Toys literally digging out the huge, dusty box which Steve had squirreled away. Steve acquired the set in 1979. The set probably dates between 1916 and 1920 when the Playthings ads were appearing. The disruption of normal Atlantic commerce and growing American patriotism were obviously twin stimulants of the American toy soldier industry at this time.

The box is 24-3/4" x 33" and covered in black paper. The small label in the center of the lid incorporates a drawing pictured here and reads: "Made in U.S.A. Lot No. 195. Nation - American." The "Made in U.S.A." also suggests a circa 1916 date, as buying American-made toys was of considerably more significance then than earlier. (Photo 1)
Wired into the insert's slots, the soldiers are olive khaki-clad doughboys, standing approximately 48 mm. (Photo 2) There are several paint variations such as red, blue and green saddles, but, since this is such a large set, it's quite possible that it took the handiwork of several different painters to put together the set. A similar but smaller 11 piece boxed set of Scottish Highlanders is number 850 "Scotch". It contains a flagbearer, bugler, men on guard and firing. These figures have red tunics and green kilts. (Photo 3)

Special thanks to Bill Nutting and Steve Balkin for contributions of information and photographs.

——— Update ———

William Feix

Updating the article on William Feix which appeared in Volume 12, #2, page 22, Richard O'Brien writes that Feix is also listed in 1920 as "William Feix Lead Soldiers" and in 1921 as "William Feix Pewter Soldiers and Sailors." He last appears, with "Metal Toys" after his name, in the Winter 1926-27 phonebook, and is out of the Summer 1927 (and subsequent) phonebooks.

American Soldier Co. last appears in the Winter 1928-29 phonebook and not in the Summer, 1929 phonebook, which suggests it folded before the 1929 Crash.

-21-

OTSN V13 #4 8-9/89

A Nu All-Nu

by Richard O'Brien

Fellow collector Monty Mitzelfeld sent these photos to editor-publisher Bill Lango. Bill in turn passed them on to me for comment.

Previously known version of All Nu's scarce NewsReel cameraman.

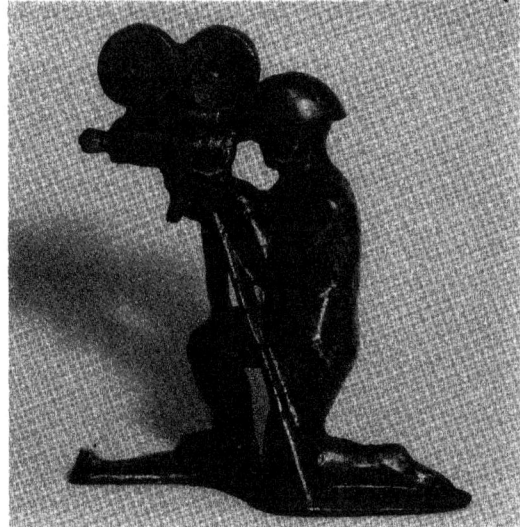

Monty Mitzelfeld's bronze painted, helmet variation All Nu NewsReel cameraman.

The soldier shown, of course, is All-Nu's highly sought-after newsreel cameraman, but with a double difference. The entire piece is painted bronze and the helmet is different from the previously known version. (The front leg of its tripod stand is also broken off, a not uncommon condition.)

Monty picked it up at an antique show from a dealer who specialized in various "bronze" souvenirs and novelties, which gives us all a new area to explore. All-Nu advertised to the novelty market (it seems likely its various jockeys and hunters were geared to those shops), and All-Nu owner-sculptor Frank Krupp's daughter has in her possession several All-Nu military figures painted the same way. I thought at the time I saw them that they might have been experiments that never left the factory, but Monty's find implies that at least a few were distributed. The shape of the helmet suggests that this is a post-World War try; a not-great attempt at updating (similar, of course to what Manoil seems to have tried with a few of its figures, and what Barclay did only somewhat more successfully). In no other respect, by the way, does the soldier seem to have been changed.

Thinking about all this has recalled a cloudy memory of mine; I'm in a tacky New York City souvenir shop during the World War II period, buying some airplane cards. And seeing for the first time All-Nu's bare-breasted cowgirl on bucking broncho. Quite possibly that's the kind of place virtually all of All-Nu's products (but its majorettes) were relegated to.

Not so incidentally, Ron Eccles has turned up a Breslin catalog showing non-military figures. The illustrations demonstrate that Breslin copied not only Barclay and Manoil, but All-Nu as well. So there could be a few Canadian military All-Nus out there as well.

TSR Autumn 1989

127

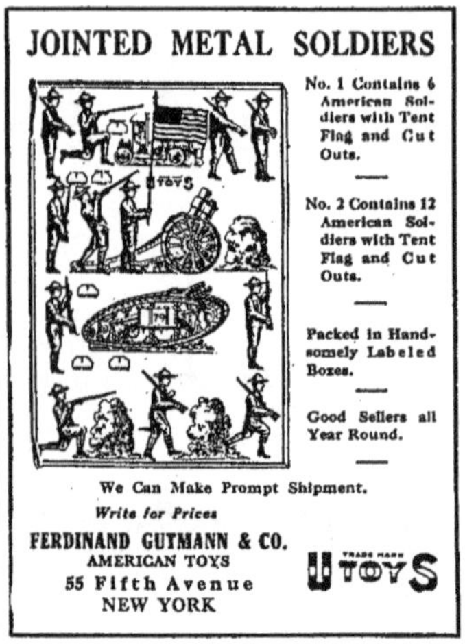

Early American Soldier Makers
Part 2
by Richard O'Brien

A Novel Toy With Action and Pep. That's how Ferdinand Gutmann advertised his impressive line of soldiers in the December, 1918 Playthings. Collectors who've been to a few shows or pored over a score or so of illustrated sale and auction lists have probably seen an example or two of the toys in which Mr. Gutmann took such pride. In person at least, it's hard to avoid noticing them. Their art is attractive and their color lithography eyecatching.

That December ad is the first I've seen for these soldiers, and its clarion call of *The Line Is Now Ready For Your Inspection* suggests that these were new in 1918.

Emphasized in the ad was that U.S. Army and Navy and British, French and Italian armies were represented. Since the ad shows five pieces and Gutmann ads which feature just Americans illustrate only the soldier in soft hat, my guess is that the infantryman in steel helmet represented the British and (with a different uniform color) the French. But possibly the bloke in the kepi represented, via color changes, both French and Italian.

The ads shown here give a good indication of how much variety could be packed into a single jointed tin Gutmann. A few adjustments and he'd march, run, present arms, stand and fire, kneel and fire, etc. In other words, a flat version, much earlier, of G.I. Joe.

Bill Nutting has checked into Gutmann and has found the following: In 1917 and 1918 Gutmann was at the same address shown in the ads, 134-40 West 29th Street. Ferdinand was president and seemed to be involved in several companies, including the Jam Perfecto Bottle Cap Co. (same address) with Jesse Gutmann as its vice-president. Bill suggests that probably tin bottle caps are what led to the soldiers. He adds that the soldiers stand 5" high, and "Pat. Pend." appears on the upper side of the tab on the figures' right foot. The tanks, bushes, etc. are thin cardboard, printed in color. The bush is 3¼" high, the tank 3-3/4" high. More importantly, Edward Ryan passed on patent information to Bill that suggests strongly that Gutmann

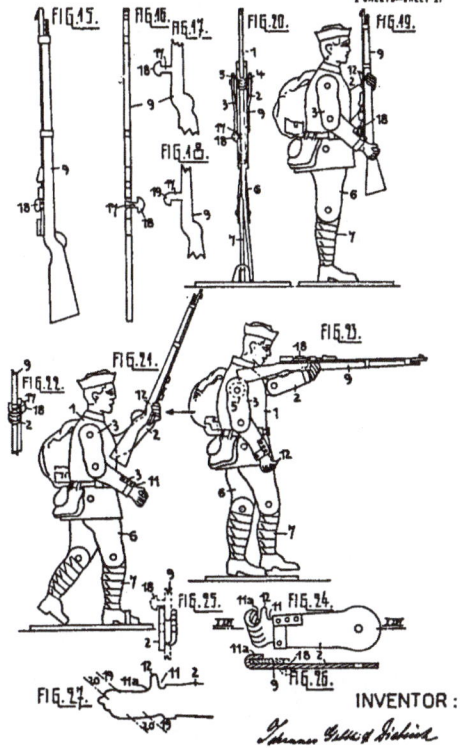

INVENTOR:

was not the originator of these pieces. Johannes Gotthilf Dietrich, "a citizen of the German Empire residing at Berlin-Tempelhof, Germany" filed a similar toy soldier design in the U.S. on January 17, 1921, with the patent approved November 28, 1922. But he had already filed for a patent in Germany on August 17, 1915. Bill has a set of the German-made figures which he says are indistinguishable from the American. The box for these "Gloria-Lino Soldiers - Marke Erhala" bears a logo that suggests the initials EHL. No one Bill has checked with can shed light on this company.

The Gutmann line seems to have consisted of the U.S. soldier, U.S. sailor, U.S. bugler, U.S. flagbearer, U.S. officer with sword and the three foreign soldiers, possibly with the same variations. The last ad I've been able to find is October, 1919. This doesn't necessarily mean anything, as soldier company ads were erratic, but it does at least suggest that the toy soldier fad was over, and possibly Gutmann's contribution to it.

Illustrations, Page 6: left, reduction of ½ page Playthings ad, December 1918; note U.S. Toys trademark; right, Toys & Novelties, October 1919; note flagbearer, officer with sword, plus tank and bush. Page 7: above left, Gutmann boxed set jointed figures and paper tank and bush identical to Gutmann's illustrations; right, U.S. Patent Office drawings of Dietrich figure.

Illustrations: At top, what seems to be the first ad for the Metal Toy Soldier Company. From the April, 1916 Toys & Novelties magazine. At left, cadets, etc. by the Metal Toy Soldier Co. from the December, 1916 Playthings. Photo left: two solidcasts which look similar to the cadets illustrated in Metal Toy Soldier ad. Photo and comment from Bill Nutting. Below, this cannon might be a clue to the firm's toy soldiers--from the February, 1917 Playthings.

An important company of the period seems to have been the Metal Toy Soldier Co., which appears to have been in business from at least 1915 through 1925, a considerable span of time. In its first ad (April, 1916) all its soldiers appear to be flats (demi-rounds; homecast types). Then in December, 1916 a new ad appears. This time the drawn figures, all cadets, look fully-dimensioned. And in fact they are, as Ed Poole via Al McGuire, has found a soldier in peaked cap that looks exactly, in every respect, like the cadets. A cannon and what seems to be a trench with both the American and British flags are also shown. These are the only two ads that illustrate the firm's soldiers.

In April, 1916 a toy trade magazine stated, "Because of the large demand for their products in 1915, the Metal Toy Soldier Co. was forced to enlarge their quarters this Spring and have recently moved into a two-story building in Jersey City, N.J. Sixty-five sets of lead soldiers representing every nationality are manufactured, besides a totally new line including mountain scenes, etc." The article went on to say that the firm employed a special artist to make window displays for dealers, and that a new catalog would soon be sent out, showing the complete lines.

In August, 1916 an article stated: "Metal Toy Soldier Company is about to market a new toy cannon that shoots." It would be ready by September and sell for 15 cents. The text isn't clear, but it also sounds as if the firm put out unpainted soldiers that were sold with watercolors. It was during this time that the firm advertised: "We Do Any White Metal Casting Works."

Judging by ads and text, cannons seem to have been an obsession with the firm. In February, 1917 it was announced "The Metal Toy Soldier Co...are now making the toy cannon formerly manufactured by the Art Metal Toy & Novelty Works. This cannon is made of solid cast metal, attractively decorated." They also advertised, at various times, a "Big-Bang Cannon," "Topsy-Target Cannon" and "A New 10¢ Toy Cannon That Shoots."

The final announcement I've found ran in February 1921 and stated: "The Metal Soldier Company are showing many sets of lead soldiers from ten to fifty in a box, 32 different sizes. Soldiers, marines, sailors, Indians, regular infantry, West Point cadets and aviators. Highly colored and complete in all details."

A 1918 City Directory lists the company and suggests the owner was a Carl Dickmann.

Editor's Note: Special thanks to Ed Ryan and Bill Nutting. Bill's research has added significantly to our knowledge of these early companies. Look forward to an article by Bill on the early British firms of Abel, Beaumont, and C.F.E. slated to appear soon in OTSN.

Book Review

OTSN V14 N3 6-7/90

The Story of American Toys by Richard O'Brien

Richard O'Brien's personal, conversational yet always analytical voice has been enjoyed again and again in the past decade of OTSN. More than in any of his previous books, The Story of American Toys shows off the quality of Richard's intricate and deceptively relaxed prose. Decade by decade from pre-Civil War America to the 80's, Richard points out the toy fads and the manufacturing trends; he provides biographies of key people in toy making and highlights great and typical toys of each era. Particularly in the outstanding color and black and white photographs, boys' toys predominate. This is not a soldier book, but there is interesting soldier commentary and great color photos of military related toys like Arlan Coffman's wonderful Captain Kidd's castle or Perry Eichor's photos of Hubley's diecast P-40, or Marx Mac army trucks from the Bizarre Bazaar's collection in New York City.

Abbeville Press is a standard setter in publishing toy books for the collector which become collectibles themselves. Their latest, O'Brien's The Story of American Toys, continues this tradition. This indexed book with over 200 color photos is available at $49.95 from book retailers or directly from Richard O'Brien; 135 Stephensburg Road, RD2; Port Murray, New Jersey 07865.

OTSN V14 #3 6-7/90

Part 3: *Ideal Wasn't*

Early American Soldier Makers

by Richard O'Brien

"Ideal" wasn't Ideal.

In September, 1977, Gordon F. Christie sold a group of toy soldiers to the Little Old Clockmaker's Shop in Bridgeport, Connecticut. He also wrote an accompanying letter addressed to the shop's owner as a way of establishing the provenance of the soldiers. It read: "Dear Mr. Josephson, The lead soldiers that you have purchased came from my father's estate, who owned the Ideal Toy Co. in Bridgeport. He ceased operations in the late 1920s. These are hollowcast and hand painted, and were sold in sets in N.Y. to the top department store. Glad you like them. Cordially, Gordon F. Christie."

When Hank Anton later interviewed Christie, Christie again said the name of the company was Ideal. Hank reported what he'd been told, but did feel there was some question of Christie's reliability when it came to facts. Later, when I discovered a "Metal Toy & Soldier Co." listed in a 1923-24 toys directory at the same address as "Ideal", Hank wrote me in 1985 that he felt Christie's credibility was questionable, and "as far as I am concerned," he went on, "I think the firm's name was really Metal Toy & Soldier Co."

I had my own questions. In 1981 I had written Christie, and he again said, "My father, Lewis D. Christie owned and operated the Ideal Toy Co. at 252 Middle St. Bridgeport CT. during the early 1920s...I have no knowledge of the Metal Toy and Soldier Co. but it may have been the name of the company before he bought it."

So it was no longer "late 1920s". Then in 1985, when I wrote and asked if a photo of a ballplayer "is Ideal", he responded with, "Do not know about 'Ideal' but the lead soldiers made by my father were identical to the pictures you enclosed."

Christie's waffling, combined with the company I'd found at "Ideal's" address, began to gnaw at me. Finally, in 1989 I sent off a letter to the Bridgeport Public Library. Their reply was, "In response to your letter...we find the Atlantic Metal Parts Company operated at 252 Middle Street, under the ownership of Albert A. and Lewis D. Christie from 1917 through 1921. In 1922 the Metal Toy Soldier Company is shown at the same address and owned by the Christies. The 1923 directory shows a different tenant at the address, and each of the Christies is shown as employed elsewhere."

"Ideal" seemed to be crumbling.

I knew Lewis D. Christie was Gordon Christie's father. But Albert A. was a new name. I wrote Christie about all this. Atlantic Metal, he reported, did metal stamping and had nothing to do with toys. It also did no lead casting.

Albert A., he disclosed, was Lewis' brother. He also told me Ideal was <u>never</u> the firm's name or even trademark!

OTSN V14 #4 8-9/90

I asked if it were possible the soldier company had lasted only one year, as the Bridgeport Library's report suggested.

"Yes," he replied, "They sold out the metal business to Warner Bros. Co. (corsets) and toy business could not support 2 people." (I assume the Warner Bros. made corset stays - O'B.)

I wrote again, asking if another of his statements in the previous letter, that "Lewis Christie took the Metal Casting Business home and ran it from there" meant that his father then cast soldiers at home. "No," was the answer. "He sold any finished inventory he had and that ended the matter." He also said, in reply to yet another question of mine, that the name "Ideal" wasn't used when he sold off inventory.

I had two more questions. One I'd obviously had from the first but had thought it wiser to put off till last. The other question was whether Christie was sure that the toy soldier molds his father and uncle had used originated in Germany. He answered, "That was what was told to me."

I then asked the question I'd decided to save until I had all his other answers: "You had originally said the name of the soldier company was Ideal Toy Co. but now you say it wasn't. Can you explain the discrepancy?"

Christie answered, "Tell me the original question asked, and the reply in each case." I then quoted his letter to the shopowner and his two letters to me. Christie never responded. My guess is that when he sold the soldiers and was asked to provide provenance, being anxious to sell and not remembering the firm's name (perhaps he never even knew it), Christie plucked the name from the air. There has <u>never</u> been any indication--in the form of boxed sets, catalogs, etc.--aside from Christie's first statements, that the firm was <u>ever</u> called Ideal.

Summing up, it appears that "Ideal" was a very minor company, lasting for just one year (the listing for 1923-24 is a little worrisome, but toy directories weren't always terribly accurate). On the other hand, Theodore Hahn of Jersey City (see page 318 of <u>Collecting Toys No. 5</u>) which made soldiers of the same design, and lasted for at least six years, is at least as important as "Ideal" was once thought to be. According to early American soldier specialist Bill Nutting, the way to tell Christie's product from others is by the paint, a "combination of very metallic paints, such as for the blue tunics, and very flat paints, such as for the bases."

Since it would be very easy to confuse this company with Jersey City's Metal Toy Soldier Company of the same general period, from now on, in future books and articles, I'll refer to it as Christies' Metal Toy & Soldier Co.
***
Photo right: The soldiers of Christies' Metal Toy & Soldier Co. These were part of the collection sold by Gordon Christie to Bridgeport's Little Old Clockmaker's Shop in September, 1977.

OTSN V15#2 4-5/9

Goodbye "Two Guys From Barclay"
Hello H.B.Toys!

by Richard O'Brien

In 1985, at Bill Lango's New Jersey show, I saw a toy train that I thought had the same look as a group of "unknown" soldiers that had been plaguing me. As I remember, it was attached to a colorful cardboard backing which contained the name and location of the company that had made it: M&L Toy Co., Inc. of Union City, New Jersey.

I went after the incorporation papers, received them, and hit a dead-end; the people named in them were either dead or knew nothing. I then wrote the local newspaper, the Hudson Dispatch, asking for help from their readers. The story ran February 27th, 1986 and the next day a fellow sent me a postcard. He'd worked for the company. I called him, and he filled me in as best as he could. But then he broke my heart. He told me the firm had made no soldiers. And that was that.

Somewhere along the way Barclay veteran George Fall told me he thought "two guys from Barclay" had left that company and started making the soldiers I was trying to research. So, having nothing else to go with, I pinned that name on the company.

I wasn't happy about it. I wanted the real name. As the years accumulated I assumed I'd never get it. But I couldn't quite get M&L out of my mind; somehow, that train looked so much like the soldiers.

Recently, I began work on the forthcoming 6th edition of "Collecting Toys". A contributor sent in a photo of a small toy car, and I forwarded it on to an expert for possible identification. "M&L", he wrote back, and went on to say they'd made a number of similar vehicles, usually unpainted with black plastic wheels. I decided to put the company into the book, and, for further information on

M&L, called the fellow who'd once worked for them.

I reached his wife, and in the course of our conversation, found there was a former M&L worker they were still friendly with. Eventually I called him. It was M&L I was calling about, but also with the very faint hope that my first informant had been wrong; that M&L had made soldiers.

Well, they hadn't. But when Walter Helm's wife answered the phone, within seconds I was almost positive I had the answer to the mystery. "Yes, he worked there for a while," she told me, "and then he and his brothers formed their own toy soldier company." Oh boy.

Her husband wasn't available at that time. I had to wait five hours before I got to speak to him. A long five hours. But the wait was worth it. "Two Guys From Barclay" is now officially H.B. Toys!

H.B. stood for Helm Brothers. Walter and Frank were the active half, with Joseph and Charles silent partners. H.B. Toys was formed in 1947 or 1948 and was located in the bottom half of a two-story house at 208 63rd Street in West New York, New Jersey. Both the first floor and a loft-like structure behind it were used.

There were twenty workers. Four cast during the day and four at night (there were no other night workers) on eight-hour shifts. Each caster produced 16-17 gross of soldiers a day (the firm, aside from their Number 1000 Horse, made no other toys). Usually, the company was on a five-day week, but in busy seasons it went to six, suggesting the firm produced about 75,000 soldiers a week.

The figures

TSR Spring 1991

were slush cast. They used the same alloy as that used by M&L - more than 99% zinc, with a smidgen of aluminum. The look this metal produced, and possibly the paint, must be what caught my eye when I saw the train. Molds were made in New York by the Facci Studio, in the 14th Street area. H.B. Toys paid up to $250 per mold, and it was the moldmaker who made whatever changes were done that distinguished the pieces from the Barclay and Tommy Toy soldiers they copied. No old Barclay molds were used. Frank Helm had worked at Barclay, and it was his stint there that had given the brothers the idea to form their own company.

I asked Walter Helm about the molds. He told me his brother had sold them to a junk dealer in Hoboken, so they may still be around. More tantalizingly, he said H.B. had bought about sixty to seventy molds from a man in Jersey City, which were also eventually scrapped. It seems likely these were Barclay molds, sold to Jersey City's New Jersey Art Foundry, but my research on the foundry suggests they could have been Manoil's.

H.B. Toys' soldiers turn up in more than one size. I had assumed the firm had some means of pantographing them. However, when I asked Walter Helm about this, I drew a blank. As far as he remembers, the soldiers were made in just one size. The answer would seem to be that the alloy "exploded" outward over time. This can happen when a zinc toy is made from a mold contaminated by lead, although this doesn't seem to be the case here.

The soldiers were priced at ten cents for the foot figures and fifteen cents for the mounted. Despite what the H.B. catalog indi-

cates, "Robe Man" and "Robe Boy", which were given more detailing and seem to have been larger, sold for about 25¢ and 50¢ each. The high price seems to account for their scarcity; few were sold. I have a feeling I've seen one at one of Bill's shows, quite possibly at the same show where I found the M&L train, but on a different dealer's table.

Robe Man and Robe Boy were the firm's only original figures, and seem to have been the idea of H.B.'s jobber, Al Farber. The company tried to secure rights to existing comic book heros (Walter Helm doesn't remember which), but failed. As a result they created their own, though obviousy closely based on Captain Marvel and Captain Marvel Jr. To my knowledge, these were the only superheroes produced by a dimestore company; an idea a few decades ahead of its time.

H.B. Toys' soldiers never sold at Woolworth's, but did reach the counters at such dimestore chains as Newberry's and W.T. Grant. They were also available (presumably only the boxed sets, which sold for a dollar) at Macy's department store in New York.

H.B. had been started on something of a shoestring. Though relatively prosperous, it remained economically vulnerable. Thus when the Korean War came along, there was no alternative. The company had to close. It was using five tons of metal a week; the Government allowed them a quarter of a ton. H.B. Toys folded in 1951 or 1952.

Some of the company's figures were also sold plated; H.B. bought a plating apparatus as a way of trying to stay in business by additionally selling their soldiers as souvenirs to novelty shops, etc.

Happily, Walter Helm's wife prevented him from throwing out the firm's brochure, which is reproduced here. The gaps in the numbering are for soldiers the Helm brothers hoped to produce in the future from their extra molds.

H.B. Toys

A Follow-Up

By Richard O'Brien

A few weeks after I'd obtained, via phone, the history of H.B. Toys from former co-owner Walter Helm, I paid him a visit. There were some soldiers of unknown origin I hoped he might identify as H.B. products, and two vehicles I thought might have been made by his former employer, M & L.

Unfortunately, no IDs were obtained. But the visit did result in more information on H.B. This time Walter Helm was sure H.B. set up shop in 1947. He also disclosed for the first time that he'd also worked briefly at Barclay before the Second World War (his brother Frank was emloyed there pre-War for a much longer time) so in fact "Two Guys From Barclay" had, with their two other brothers, founded the company (the Frank Keller who some at Barclay thought might have co-owned the firm was in fact an employee).

Barclay is known to have farmed out some of its work, not infrequently to its own workers. For instance, Helm worked nights in his short time there (on the diecasting machines) but he also did work at home for the firm, putting wheels on their vehicles.

He is sure that H.B. Toys, which never advertised, made more soldiers than are shown in their brochure (which was the only one they had printed). The ones he could remember were a cowboy on a rearing horse which rested on its tail, and seems to have been a larger-than-normal size; a mounted Indian with a headdress; and a mounted Indian with a rifle (presumably just like the Barclay one; that shown in the H.B. brochure has had the rifle changed to a tomahawk). To my knowledge none of these pieces has surfaced.

H.B. also briefly tried to cut down on the weight of its soldiers (thus lowering shipping costs) by sawing off parts of the bases after the figures were cast. So if you own an H.B. minus part of its base, it's likely it was sold that way. The experiment was brief because of complaints by parents that the resulting edges made the toys "too rough".

There was no particular order to the company's releases. Helm told me the first three or four pieces cast were the No. 1002 Cowboy, perhaps the No. 1016 Cowboy Shooting, and 1500 and 1501, the Mounted Cowboy and Indian. I'd wondered if the soldiers had come much later, sparked by the Korean War in 1950, but Helm and his wife said no, the soldiers were issued soon after the first Western figures.

Since H.B. produced Tommy Toy-type soldiers I asked if there were any connection between it and another Tommy Toy swiper, Toy Creations, but Helm said no.

Previously, he'd told me that in addition to the molds made

TSR Summer 1991

for H.B. by the Facci studios based on the Barclay figures, the company had bought two large batches of soldier molds. This time I pressed Helm on them. He couldn't remember what any of them looked like, but finally remembered they'd bought one batch from a Paul Paragine of Union City, who had worked with M & L. However, they didn't come from M & L, which never made soldiers (I tried to track down Paragine, but he's not listed in the Union City area).

I later called Frank Helm, the other active partner at H.B. Two important bits of information emerged. He had worked off and on at Barclay from 1928. I'd already sent him a copy of "Collecting Toy Soldiers." When I asked him to check the "Early Barclays" on page 34 (the approximately 60-65mm size) he became the first Barclay veteran to positively identify them as being from that company. The only piece he was uncertain about was the drummer, although it seems clear it belongs in that group.

I quizzed him about the molds that came from Paragine. All he could remember was that he had tried casting from some of the molds H.B. had acquired, but wasn't happy with the results, and said the firm didn't try selling the castings. I asked him to describe the bases. He said they tended to curve at the top, and underneath were (his word) "hollow". Soldiers like this have turned up. One is the kneeling firing soldier I mistakenly thought was Manoil's and coded M43. Another is shown at the top of page 72 of the soldiers book, and another on page 261. Some of these, like H.B. Toy's soldiers, are oversized, but possibly as a result of something happening to the alloy. In any case, they obviously are from Manoil's old molds. or copies of those soldiers. Further, the metal they employ appears to be the same as H.B.'s, which was the same as M&L's. I began to wonder if Paragine had done any toy soldier-making.

I called Walter Helm. He said Paragine (company name unknown, if there was one) had rented a small loft above a bakery in the vicinity of 27th Street and Center Avenue in Union City, where he cast "heraldics" and perhaps some toys. He seems to have used the same HB-M&L alloy. If in fact Paragine was the man producing the above-mentioned soldiers, as I now strongly suspect, they would have been on sale in the late 1940's or early 1950's, as H.B. bought the molds "for almost nothing" just before they went out of business. These soldiers, of course, were among the small group I had brought Walter Helm to see if they'd been made by H.B.

Then, while trying to persuade Helm to supply photos of himself and his brother, I turned to pages 125 and 126 of "Collecting Toy Soldiers" to illustrate what I meant by showing him the shots of Frank Krupp, Olive Kooken and Margaret Cloninger. Helm started staring at one of the pages, and asked to have the book so he could see it better. Then he pointed to the photo I'd taken of the former Tommy Toy building. "That's where we bought the other molds," he said.

What this means, of course, is that Tommy Toy didn't turn everything over to Barclay when it folded. Helm also believes H.B. used the *original* molds when they cast the wounded and doctor soldiers (presumably changing the base so that it wouldn't read "Tommy Toy"). What it could also mean is that the molds are still out there someplace. (Bill Lango knows of someone in the Jersey City area who's sitting on toy soldier molds that sound as if they could be H.B.'s.)

48

I was told by Mrs. Helm that the wives of the brothers often did the painting, and in fact an entrance, via window, from Mrs. Helm's kitchen to the work area out back was created so it'd be easier for her to come and go.

Previously, collectors had known of one type of boxed set for H.B.'s figures. When I showed Helm a photo of it, he said there was a second type, which was about half the size.

Although Al Farber is noted on the brochure as the company's sales representative, Walter Helm did a lot of the selling himself, the Newberry's five and ten account being one of the many he landed. Farber became H.B.'s sales rep. as a result of seeing their soldiers in a local candy store that Walter had sold to, and then presenting himself to the Helm brothers as someone who could considerably expand their sales.

Helm has retained only one of the firm's soldiers. Luckily, it was the extremely rare Robe Boy. It was unpainted, and on examination there was no question it was a copy of Captain Marvel Jr.; it even had the lightning bolt carved onto the chest.

Two soldiers I had thought were H.B. Toys and showed as such in *"Collecting Toy Soldiers"* turn out not to have been. One was the TG15 Flagbearer, which is now generally agreed to have come from American Alloy-Toy Creations. The other is TG25, a copy of the Grey Iron officer. Ed Poole has since written me that this figure is solid lead, rather than hollow cast. This one remains an "unknown" (possibly even made by Grey Iron or John Wright, as they occasionally cast in lead).

Part 4

Early American Soldier Makers

by Richard O'Brien

For years, collectors have thought that McLoughlin Brothers was the first important manufacturer of American-made metal toy soldiers. That may be, but the research of the past few years argues against it. The soldiers' uniforms and the lithography on their boxes suggest the late 1800s, but the earliest that they appear in any known McLoughlin catalog is 1911 (with the same page, even to the printing defects, repeated in the 1914 catalog). Bill Nutting, who found these pages, has looked at about 15 McLoughlin catalogs from 1879 to 1920, and these are the only references he found to lead soldiers. For identification, readers should remember that the underside of the base of McLoughlin's 48 mm German-style solidcasts has two circular depressions. Pictured here is an officer in red (one of four color variations).

McLoughlin seems to have taken no pride in its metal figures; none appears in the firm's many ads in toy trade magazines of the era. So for the moment at least, we can consider American Soldier Co. the first significant maker, and William Feix the second, which more and more Feix gives evidence of having manufactured many or even all of the approximately 54mm hollow lead soldiers previously attributed to McLoughlin.

76   McLOUGHLIN BROS' CATALOGUE

LEAD OR "TIN" SOLDIERS

60 CENT SETS

SET A
Contains 11 pieces, viz.: 1 horseman, 1 captain, 2 drummers, 1 flagman, and 7 privates.

SET B
Contains 6 horsemen.

$1.00 SETS

SET C
Contains 17 pieces, viz.: 3 horsemen, 1 Captain, 1 flagman, 2 drummers, and 14 privates.

SET D
Contains 9 horsemen.

$1.25 SET E
Contains 23 pieces, viz.: 1 horseman, 2 captains, 2 drummers, 1 flagman. and 16 privates.

$1.25 SET

SET F
Contains 12 horsemen.

$1.75 SETS

SET G
Contains 17 pieces, viz.: 11 horsemen, 1 captain, 2 drummers, 1 flagman, and 12 privates.

SET H
Contains 18 horsemen.

SET I
Contains 37 pieces, viz.: 1 horseman, 1 captain, 2 drummers, 1 flagman, and 32 privates.

$2.50 SET

SET K
Contains 37 pieces, viz.: 11 horsemen, 1 captain, 2 drummers, 1 flagman, and 22 privates.

Some odd, intriguing, and at present very obscure soldiers first appear in the December, 1917 Playthings. They were featured in a full-page ad for "Camouflage Toys" and Liberty Toy Soldiers, all manufactured by R. Gricks at 524-526 W. 166th St. in New York. This may have been the same firm mentioned in the September issue; Liberty Toy Co. of N.Y. was featuring a "Modern Trench Warfare" set in white pine. The January 1918 issue had an ad with the same art but different, and far more extensive, text. The firm was now known as Liberty Toy & Novelty Co. In the same issue, the lead soldiers were noted as being under the "personal supervision" of Gricks, suggesting he may have stepped down from ownership.

Photos: This page, McLoughlin 10x10 inch Set D cavalry box; opposite, McLoughlin 48mm figure from Set A; boxlid is 6x11-1/2 Inches. Photos courtesy of Bill Nutting.

OTS V15 #3 6-7/81

The Liberty Toy Soldiers are dwarfed in the ads by the "Castle", "U.S. Signal Station", "Windmill", and "Fort & Battlefield" they're arranged on. The first ad states that they're of lead and hand-painted. The second goes considerably further, headlining that they come with "Interchangeable heads and arms." Furthermore, in addition to being "the acme of perfection in workmanship and finish", they were "as different from the old fashioned lead soldiers as a live man is from a corpse." They could be transformed into "288 different models" and "into an American, English, French or Italian soldier as quickly as you can say it. At your command he will present arms, swing a sword, wave a flag..." Furthermore, Liberty seems to have designed its own molds, as the ad claims: "we are the only manufacturer of these new, unique and epoch-making lines of toys mentioned above."

There is no mention in the ad that the soldiers, the same as shown in the previous issue, are made of lead, and there's the curious statement that no "spirited American boy" would prefer the "old fashioned stiff pieces of lead" to the new Liberty brand. There's a small possibility they were not lead. A year later, in the February 1919 issue of Toys & Novelties, there was a mention of "Liberty Toy & Novelty Co. papier mache soldiers with moving arms and interchangeable heads." However, the last

appearances I've found for Liberty Toy & Novelty are in the February and March, 1920 Playthings, each once more citing the firm's (still at the same address): "Lead soldiers of all nations with moveable heads and arms." Its "Camouflage Toys" are also mentioned.

Fichtman & Alexander, of 325 Lafayette Street, New York, first shows up in the July 1915 Toys and Novelties with a story that proclaims the manufacturer of jewelry novelties had begun to make "very high grade lead soldiers...being in color, finish and design an exact duplicate of imported lines, which manufacturers have failed to initiate in the past." In August, the firm ran its only known illustrated ad.

The soldiers, as drawn, appear to be copies of German-made soldiers and are distinguished by a thin, flat and rectangular base. They are described as "Boys of the U.S.A." and "fully equal to the finest soldiers made in Germany." The last mention I've found is in February 1916, when it was announced Fichtman & Alexander had prepared fifteen new models, including sailors, soldiers, Indians, mounted officers and "similar characters." Incidentally, I have a photocopy of an article on this company (with the name misspelled "Fitchman") that runs an illustration purporting to show the firm's soldiers. For anyone who has this article (I don't know where it ran), be advised the soldiers shown are not by Fichtman and Alexander but are actually four-inch high composition soldiers produced by another firm called Indestructo, about which more will appear in a future article.

Little can be found on toy soldier companies in toy trades of the 1920s. So it was something of a jolt, and an exciting one, when I unexpectedly happened upon the March, 1921 ad for Theodore Hahn. No one seems to have heard of this company, and yet it appears to have been a significant one. It was in

business for at least five years (at 16-18 Hopkins Avenue; Jersey City, NJ) and appears to have been, with the Christies' Metal Toy & Soldiers Co., the first American firm to produce steel-helmeted doughboys. Several of its soldiers turn up with some frequency; doughboys in the charging, advancing and kneeling-firing category. Furthermore, it sold mounted soldiers with moving arms just like, or very similar to, Barclay's.

Although Hahn advertised several times, it showed no other toys than those found in this 1920 ad. Luckily, the ad is stuffed with information; photos of two trees; a circular tent; and eight different soldiers, mention of another (a sailor or sailors), drawings of a plane, a cannon, a canary whistle, the firm's "factory and office", mention of toy trains and automobiles as being part of its line, an address and the name of the owner.

10

Hahn was not listed in city directories in 1918 or 1927, so unless he moved, we have a pretty good idea of the firm's duration. The 1922-23 city directory shows Theodore Hahn as president of the firm, Jack Pflug vice-president, Louis M. Schmidt secretary, and John Slack treasurer. The 1925-26 directory finds Hahn now both president and treasurer, Conrad Koegel the vice-president, and John Slack the secretary. Theodore Hahn's home, incidentally, was in South Orange. A call I made to Information revealed a Theodore Hahn still in the area, but the number, alas, was unlisted.

Many of Hahn's soldiers seem to be copies of French-made soldiers, and perhaps even came from the same molds. Bill Nutting notes that these French figures have very thin, flat bases with France debossed on the top or bottom. Will Beierwaltes has found a set that is almost certainly from Hahn, even to the round tent, cannon, and what appears to be one of the same trees. However, in addition to the Barclay-type horsemen with moving arm, there's also a mounted figure that resembles Barclay's Bg. According to Barclay's Louis Picco, this was modeled after a French-made soldier. Other early companies also produced this piece (William Feix, I suspect, among them). There are also more types in the doughboy hat; one at right shoulder arms, one apparently emptyhanded, and a bugler in a cap. Paint and mold styles suggest a third U.S. company, in addition to Hahn and the Christies, sold the doughboys in steel helmets.

After finding the Hahn ad, I contacted two Barclay veterans, on the chance that Barclay had purchased Hahn's molds. However, there was no memory of this, and none of the pieces rang any bells with one of the former workers. George Fall, who began a few years earlier, thinks the doughboys look somewhat familiar, but he was far from sure of this.

Soldier Set No. 240
Soldier and Sailor Sets in 31 Styles

Finally, Jones Metal Art and Dimestore visually linked.

More
Jones Catalogs

by Richard O'Brien

Back when we were all little (August 1981), OTSN scored a coup, reproducing the first two catalog pages anyone had found which showed photographs of dimestore soldiers. One was a 1939 Butler Brothers illustrating Barclays, and the second a 1939-40 L. Gould which listed what seemed to be the figures attributed to J. Edward Jones.

There was one mildly worrisome element in the latter; the knight shown (though not listed) appeared to be Barclay's. Some time after the article ran, however, the ever-sharp-eyed Don Pielin found a couple of knights which looked a little different to him. He discovered they were a bit shorter, and when he turned them over, there was the tell-tale sign of a Jones piece: flat underbase with a tendency toward choked pourholes.

Since then, three more catalogs have surfaced, each of them significant. I've discovered a Spring and Summer 1938 catalog from N. Shure; Don has turned up a coverless item that appears to be Johnson-Smith from the fall of 1938; and most recently, I've found a 1940-41 L. Gould.

The Shure catalog is the only one to offer the knights for sale: Knight with Shield and Knight with Flag. This suggests why they are so rare: probably offered for a short time, perhaps because they reeked too much of Barclay. Only nine soldiers and a stretcher could be ordered, suggesting this was a new line, an assumption buttressed by the line of copy that reads: "The New Three-inch Metal Figures the boys are demanding...." My guess would be that Jones' dimestore line first emerged about February, 1938.

N. SHURE CO., CHICAGO

1003

Soldier, Cowboy Figures, Rubber and Metal

The New Three-Inch Metal Figures the boys are demanding with plenty of action. Full form and hollow cast. Brightly painted with chipproof enamel. May be had in the following numbers: Packed 1 dozen of number to box. Sold in original boxes only. When ordering, be sure to specify number wanted.

No. 50N520.	Cowboy shooting.	No. 50N520/5.	Indian kneeling—shooting.
No. 50N520/1.	U. S. Machine Gunner.	No. 50N520/6.	Knight with Shield.
No. 50N520/2.	U. S. soldier kneeling—shooting.	No. 50N520/7.	Knight with Flag.
No. 50N520/3.	U. S. soldier with gas mask—charging.	No. 50N520/8.	Stretcher Bearer.
No. 50N520/4.	U. S. soldier marching.	No. 50N520/9.	Stretcher.

Per dozen...42

Don's catalog, which oddly uses the same codings on some of its other items as N. Shure's, is a real find. Who ever figured Jones' dimestores came **boxed**? Most of all, it shows the gas-masked bayoneter, a Metal Art 1/24th scale figure, in the **same box** as dimestore figures. Since there was some uncertainty about Jones' connection to the dimestore soldiers, that figure really provides a reassuring link (as does the illustrated cowboy); the bayoneter is the same one which recently turned up in Jones' Metal-Art displays of his 1929-31 soldiers (OTSN V14, 2). Finally, this catalog shows how extensive Jones' line was by late 1938 and exactly what the stretcher looked like with its distinctive cross at the center.

Only two real pieces of information come out of the 1940-41 L. Gould catalog. The Pill Box is listed, finally tying it absolutely to this group of soldiers, although collectors with trained eyes have never had trouble placing it there. The other help is a little card at the beginning of the catalog. It says the prices shown are list, "subject to a universal discount of 50 per cent", so whatever price is shown should be halved. That 92 cents-per-dozen price in the 1939 Gould catalog had bothered me, as it suggested Jones soldiers went for a dime, which would have been very uncompetititive. This way, it's obvious they went for a nickel, just like Barclays and Manoils. One small note: the officer in greatcoat is dropped. Just an accident, or was Gould getting too many complaints about that vulnerable arm breaking off?

If only more of the pieces in the Goulds and Shure were illustrated, as in Don's catalog, because some of the listings are a bit worrisome. The "Indian Kneeling--Shooting" which appears from 1938-1940: who is he? My guess would be the one shown in Collecting Toy Soldiers on page 262. What about the "Indian Standing with Bow" which appears in 1939 and 1940? Is it the one shown on page 136 of Collecting Toy Soldiers or the one on page 263? Or neither? My guess would be the first, but in the past Don's disagreed with me on this, and as I've noted, he has highly trained eyes.

Metal and Rubber Soldier Sets, Children's Play Sets

3-inch Metal Soldier Set. An assortment of U. S. Soldiers in action. Machine gunner, officer, flag bearer, etc. Set of 7 packed in display box.
No. 50N523. Per Set $0.70

U. S. Army Medical Unit. All 3-inch figures. Consists of two wounded soldiers, two stretcher bearers, stretcher, nurse and doctor. Packed in display box.
No. 50N525. Per Set $0.70

Marching Soldier Set. All 3-inch figures. Cast metal. Consists of six U. S. Soldiers marching and one flag bearer. Packed in display box.
No. 50N524. Per Set $0.70

U. S. Army Medical Unit with Red Cross nurse, doctor, stretcher, stretcher bearers, wounded soldiers and an assortment of U. S. Soldiers in action. Packed in display box.
No. 50N526. Per Set $1.50

Shelter Tents and Doughboys. 3 tents, 1 mounted U. S. soldier, 1918; 4 on foot, 1 machine gunner.
No. 50N503. Per Set $1.50

U. S. Soldiers and Opposition Soldiers. Opposition soldiers have olive green uniforms. An appealing set from a play value standpoint. Set of 14 pieces packed in display box.
No. 50N527. Per Set $1.50

All Rubber Soldiers. Unbreakable, washable. 4-color box.
U. S. Infantry, 3-inch, 1 bugler, khaki, 7 privates, khaki.
No. 50N516. Per Set $0.70
U. S. Marines, 3-inch, 1 bugler, white, 7 privates, blue.
No. 50N517. Per Set $0.70

This is a partially reproduced page from Don Pielin's catalog find, probably Johnson-Smith c1938.

For that reason, nearly everyone's gone along with him on attributing that AA Gun (his The American Dimestore Soldier Book) to All-Nu. However, in 1939 and 1940 there's a listing for an "Anti-Aircraft Gun." Since the only AA gun I know that's turned up is the one Don attributes to All-Nu, isn't it more likely it's a Jones? Or...I've seen it come two ways: one quite sharp in its details, and one in a larger size and a crummier-looking metal. Could be Jones produced only the latter one, but my guess would be it has this look because the metal Jones used had an occasional tendency to "explode" outward, the way the H.B. Toys ("Two Guys from Barclay") pieces do.

And what were the "Cannons" listed in 1939 and 1940? Maybe two or more that we collectors have assumed came from Barclay?

The "U.S. Soldier with Pix axe" listed in both 1939 and 1940? I've never been too uncomfortable about this one. When I was a kid, my friends and I could never figure out what the wirecutter was holding in his hand. Could be Gould's lister couldn't either.

Finally, wholesalers rarely showed a manufacturer's entire line, but the pieces left out suggest they came later. I've always felt that Jones lasted into 1941 with his dimestore line because of the anti-tank gunner, which copies Barclay's. One can't be 100% sure Barclay didn't come out with that figure until 1941, but it seems likely as it's in Barclay's late pre-war style and its absence of a number suggests it was the last pre-war piece to be issued.

Anyone out there with a 1941 catalog that shows Jones figures?

Richard O'Brien is the foremost researcher of American toy soldiers; see page 11 for information on the second edition of his Collecting Toy Soldiers.

Finally, Jones Metal Art and Dimestore visually linked.

146

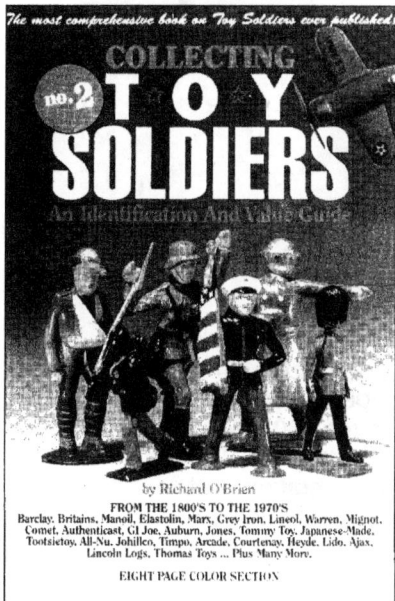

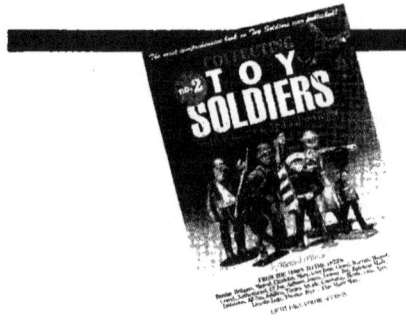

PUBLICATIONS

Just in time for this publication is Richard O'Brien's 2nd edition of **Collecting Toy Soldiers**--and even a quick look attests to its scope and quality. First the basics. It is 625 pages, over 100 pages longer, with little from the first edition dropped. The homecast section is not in the second edition, but the additions are significant. First, it is easier to use, with a table of contents arranged alphabetically by maker: Ajax to William Feix.

All areas of the book seem updated or expanded. For the American collector, there is much information on WWI era firms like American Soldier Company and George Grampp, plus great original advertising from trade magazines on companies from Hahn to Jones. Plastics from Marx to Premier are expanded. There is more on American paper toy production. Also among the U.S. niceties is a silhouette chart for Warren Lines horses, center color photos of an Auburn Rubber ad, and a box of Guttman jointed soldiers. New from across the sea is a French dimestore section, a section on Danish soldiers, and a much expanded Johillco photo section. Most of all, K. Warren Mitchell, one of the major toy soldier dealers in the U.S., took weeks to revamp the whole Britains Ltd. section. It begins with charts on uniforms and color, and includes photos often placed near the set information.

Like the first issue, this is a price reference, but clearly Richard O'Brien researches for the serious collector, not for the novice. The old lady with two dozen in a cigar box will find this a tough search. So as long as we all remember the inherent problem of price guides, this book will be a must for the reference shelf. It is available for $29.95 from Richard O'Brien; 135 Stephensburg Rd. RD2; Port Murray, NJ 07865.

Dear Editor:

In answer to Ken Chamberlain's question about those soldiers in candy tubes, I remember there was a Foreign Legionnaire (I think with a moustache and goatee) and an American soldier in campaign cap at a rakish tilt. I also think there were other American soldiers. My memory is that there was art on the <u>back</u> of the soldier. I remember buying them as early as 1940, and probably as late as 1942 or even 1943. I believe all of them had big grins on their faces. The colors were bright and sharp.

Although they were cartoony, they weren't as Elmer Fuddish as Ken stated, and therefore were good enough to play with. Ken's drawing is actually a good representation; a devilish grin would have brought it close to the real thing.

I've enjoyed Ken's full-pagers, but this one was special for me. For years I've asked collectors if they remembered those soldiers, but no one had. Could be it was a New York-area company. I bought mine in Sayville, Long Island and Brooklyn.

Now that the first step has been taken, can anyone out there provide photos? They could make up a very colorful cover.

Richard O'Brien
Port Murray, NJ

TSR Autumn 1992

Early War Toys

by Richard O'Brien

While researching early American toy soldiers I've come across a number of ads for war toys in the magazines Playthings and Toys and Novelties.

Since many toy soldier collectors collect war toys as accessories, the following may be of interest, and perhaps even unravel a few mysteries.

From the May, 1918 Playthings. The truck at the bottom left is the No. 476 Army Truck

From the June, 1918 Playthings. I think I've seen the tank around.

TSR #36

THE DRIVE OF THE BIG TOY EIGHT

GILBERT Mechanical Toys

The 1917 Automobile
Toys with these BIG
Improved Features:

1. EACH TOY LITHOGRAPHED IN BRIGHT, ATTRACTIVE COLORS.
2. EACH MACHINE WITH LITHOGRAPHED DRIVER.
3. IMPROVED AND MECHANICALLY CORRECT SPRING WOUND MOTOR.
4. MORE SUBSTANTIALLY MADE THAN EVER BEFORE.
5. HEAVIER MATERIAL.
6. SEPARATELY PACKED IN LITHOGRAPHED BOXES.
7. CORRECT DESIGN—REALISTIC APPEARANCE.

The Best there is in
Mechanical Toys—
Workmanship,
Material
and Finish

P74
GILMOTOR
AMBULANCE
PRICE 75c
(CANADA $1.15)

P76
GILMOTOR
RACER
PRICE 75c
(CANADA $1.15)

P77
GILMOTOR
TRUCK
PRICE 50c
(CANADA 75c)

P78
GILMOTOR
MAIL WAGON
PRICE 75c
(CANADA $1.15)

THE A. C. GILBERT CO., NEW HAVEN, CONN., U. S. A.

A 1917 ad. A.C. GIlbert of course is best known for its Erector sets. In October, 1989 the ambulance was offered for sale at $400.

TOYS AND NOVELTIES

Introducing
THE YANKEE TANK

An almost exact replica of the fighting monster; equipped with a powerful spring motor and the real caterpillar traction, perfectly imitating the tremendous driving action of the real tank. Reports of orders from the Toy Fair in New York forcibly indicate the great enthusiasm with which this wonderful toy is received. Made of steel; 14 inches long; enameled grey.

Orders for early delivery should be placed at once.

The Walbert Line of Quality Toys is on display at the IMPERIAL HOTEL, New York, Room 204.

In charge of B. C. McHENRY.

The Australian Boomerang

WALBERT MANUFACTURING CO.
225 West Illinois St. - - Chicago, Ill.

A circa 1931 photo of a display of Jones' soldiers shows a similar tank. It could have been made by Walbert, as both Jones and Walbert were located in Chicago. From the February, 1918 Toys & Novelties. Walbert also made a "Sinking Battleship with Torpedo"; the ship split apart and sank when hit by the torpedo.

PLAYTHINGS

ORKIN FLEET
OUR NAVY IN MINIATURE

U. S. S. CONSTITUTION—Superdreadnought
Length 35 in. Beam 4½ in. Draft 2½ in.
Triple Screws

U. S. S. PENNSYLVANIA—Dreadnought
Length 30 in. Beam 4½ in. Draft 2½ in.

U. S. S. MARCELLA—Cruiser
Length 19 in. Beam 2½ in. Draft 1½ in.

Nine Models, consisting of two types of Superdreadnoughts, four Dreadnoughts, Sub-Chaser, Destroyer, and Cruiser.

WRITE NOW FOR CATALOG AND PRICES
Sole Distributors

Geo. Borgfeldt & Co.
16th Street and Irving Place   New York, N. Y.

From the August, 1919 Playthings. These ships were big, the lengths running from 19 to 35 inches. This could have been Orkin's debut ad.

152

From the August, 1918 Toys and Novelties. This is the earliest ad I've found for Grey Iron's soldiers.

War toys quickly disappeared after the end of WWI, so it's not likely this sold well. It's even less likely, given its cardboard body, wings and rudder that any have survived. Too bad; how many other war toys had this much action going on? From the September, 1919 Playthings.

TOY SOLDIER REVIEW

AUTUMN 1992

No. 790 Soldier Shooting Anti-Tank Gun

No. 788 Soldier Marching with Gun Slung Behind Back

No. 789 Soldier Shooting Triple Barreled Gun

No. 791 Soldiers with Mortar

No. 701 Flag Bearer

No. 702 Soldier Machine Gunner

No. 703 Sniper

No. 705 Soldier, Port Arms

No. 792 Airplane Mechanic

No. 793 Soldiers in Boat

No. 706 Soldier Charging

No. 708 Officer

No. 707 Soldier, At Attention

No. 709 Bugler

No. 710 Drummer

No. 731 Soldier Pigeon Dispatcher

No. 711 Drum Major

No. 730 Soldier Signal Man with Flags

No. 728 Machine Gunner, Lying Flat

No. 733 Soldier Bullet Feeder

No. 734 Soldier Ammunition Carrier

No. 735 Soldier Range Finder

No. 736 Soldier Sentry

No. 740 Soldier, French Horn

No. 741 Aviator

No. 738 Soldier Bomb Thrower

No. 737 Soldier Charging, Machine Gunner

No. 760 Soldier Sitting Position

No. 749 Soldier,

MAJOR BARCLAY FIND

BY RICHARD O'BRIEN

At this September's Old Toy Soldier show in Chicago, I ran across collector Bill Dunfee, who told me the postwar Barclay order sheet on the bottom right of page 90 in "Collecting Toy Soldiers No. 2" was originally his. He then told me back in 1955 he'd written Barclay, asking what soldiers they had available. They sent him two postwar sheets, indicating that everything on them was available, and this 1941 sheet with the notation at top "1935-1946 – NOTHING AVAILABLE".

It's a major research find. It furnishes missing numbers and descriptions, and shows what are probably all the military

numbers introduced by Barclay in 1941 – 788-793. Since all the soldiers have ties and solid puttees, they represent, where it applies, the cast-helmet soldiers that replaced the tin-hat ones, in 1940 and 1941. That the anti-tank gunner is a late number indicates that Jones, which almost certainly copied it, was around as late as 1941.

Till we spoke, Bill Dunfee apparently didn't know what a gem he had. Anyone else out there with toy soldier catalogs and order sheets they'd never thought of as important to anyone?

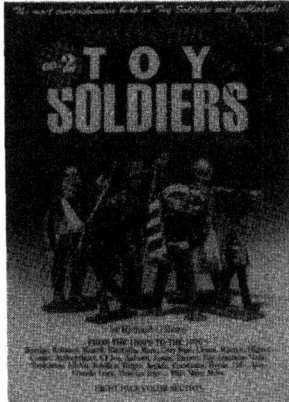

TSR Autumn 1992

157

Barclay
More Catalog Pages

by Richard O'Brien

It's been seven years since the discovery of the order sheets and printing blocks Barclay's last owner had retained. Since then only a single pre-WWII page has surfaced. However, along the way a sprinkling of information has turned up via general catalogs and trade magazines of the period.

Though Barclay is said to have issued catalogs since its beginning in 1924, nothing before 1931 has surfaced. In that year, however, information appears in four different places, suggesting an expansion caused by Michael Levy's taking full charge of the firm. A Playthings magazine photo, a Butler Bros. catalog illustration, a book reprint of the cover and an interior page of a Barclay catalog and a listing in a Shackman catalog make up the quartet. Unfortunately, all but the Shackman concern themselves with vehicles and trains.

I've been in touch with Daniel Jacoby, former president of Shackman, and the grandson of its founder (in 1898), Bertha Shackman. Jacoby claims to have all the Shackman catalogs, but has been reluctant to part with more than a few photocopied pages. It's Jacoby's memory that Barclay toys were always listed with a numerical prefix of 51 (51/125, 51/129, etc.). Gauged against known Shackman pages, this appears to be true. It is important to note, however, that illustrations for Barclay items, despite the use of a "51" in the caption, are **not** necessarily Barclay. As Jacoby explained to me, because illustrations were expensive and Shackman was a small house, generic cuts were often used. Thus, 51/126 and 51/129 on the 1931 page do **not** represent actual Barclays.

Twelve Barclays are listed in 1931. Most of the descriptions could apply to any company, but the "51/141, Canadian Northwest Police, 2-1/2" high" does seem to confirm this as a Barclay group. Also on the list is "51/33, Soldier with moveable arm and sword in hand. Sitting on black horse. 3 in.", and in this case the illustration may actually be of a Barclay soldier, though there's no way of being sure since several firms made a similar piece. (Note: Jacoby says any item **without** a slash in its numbering means the toy is imported.)

Illustrated below: 1931 Shackman catalog page.

B. SHACKMAN & CO. 906 BROADWAY
"THE NAME IS IMPORTANT" At 20th Street, NEW YORK

METAL NOVELTIES (Continued)

51/126 51/133 4850 19305 51/129

PAINTED METAL SOLDIERS

		DOZEN
51/125	Painted Metal Soldier. Khaki uniform. 2¼ inches.	$0.85
51/129	Soldier with gun and khaki uniform. Charging position. 2¼ inches.	.85
4889	Sailor (marine) with blue uniform, white hat and gun. 2¼ inches.	.70
51/126	Sailor (marine) with blue uniform, white hat and gun. 2½ inches.	.85
51/127	Indian with gun. 2¼ inches.	.85
51/131	Indian with gun, on black metal horse. 3 inches.	1.20
51/133	Soldier with movable arm and sword in hand. Sitting on black horse. 3 in.	1.20
4884	Red Cross Nurse. White uniform. 2 inches.	.75
43/779	Kneeling Soldier in Kahki uniform, with machine gun. 2¼ inches.	.65
43/783	Soldier in kahki uniform, with sword. Flat, painted on both sides. 2 inches	.40
43/782	Soldier in kahki uniform, with gun. Flat, painted on both sides. 2 inches	.40
43/781	Soldier in kahki uniform, with U. S. flag. Flat, painted on both sides. 3 in.	.50
51/138	West Point Cadet with gun. 2½ inches.	.85
43/776	Foreign Soldier with long lance. Mounted on horse. 3½ inches.	1.00
43/775	Foreign Soldier on horse. Assorted uniforms. 3½ inches.	1.10
43/777	American Cowboy with lasso. Mounted on prancing horse. 3½ inches	.85
4850	Soldier with gun. Soldier with sword, bugler, and drummer, assorted, with different style uniforms. 2¼ inches.	.78
4851	Soldier with sword, mounted on horse. 4 different styles assorted. Made of heavy metal, and beautifully painted. 3½ inches.	1.60
4854	Cowboy with gun, mounted on horse. 3½ inches.	1.20
19305	Indian with tomahawk doing a war dance. Very well made. 3⅓ inches	2.60
51/132	Marine with gun and dark blue hat and coat, and light blue trousers. 2½ in.	.85
51/139	Drum Corps. Fife, bugle and drum assorted. Khaki uniforms. 2½ inches	.85
51/140	Officer. Khaki uniform and hat, leggings and sword. 2½ inches.	.85
51/141	Canadian Northwest Police. Red coat and hat, black pants, and pistol. 2½ in.	.85
51/134	Cowboy with pistol, bright color blouse and pants. 2½ inches.	.85
4852	Soldier with khaki uniform and pistol, mounted on motorcycle. 3¼ inches	1.70
		PER SET
4855	U. S. Soldier Band of 8 pieces with overseas khaki uniform. Leader with baton, and 7 different instrument players. Each 2¼ inches.	$0.48

Illustrated above: 1934 Butler Bros. catalog; below: clipping from 1935 Shackman catalog.

The next known appearance of Barclay's soldiers occurs in the September, 1934 Butler Bros. catalog. Most of it concerns vehicles, but three "building and painting sets" with soldiers are shown. Of particular interest are the officer and bugler on horseback, both with moving arms. Also, the second series of "small Barclays" appears here, apparently for the first time (those that average 54mm in height). Among them is the distinctive left-handed Indian with tomahawk, which with a cowboy is part of the "Army Set."

Barclay troops next show up in a fall or winter 1935 Butler Bros. catalog. The Army Set is repeated, but this time the illustration is a photo, not a drawing. The contents of the set seem to be the same, but in the fuzzy photocopy I have, a mounted figure shown outside the box appears to be the mounted cowboy.

Though it's just a listing, the 1935 Shackman is significant. At the bottom of the page Jacoby notes "1935. Out of place. Must be brand new items." The list itself is headlined, "A new line made of metal, nicely painted. Each about 3 inches." This list almost certainly represents Barclay's first 3-1/4" soldiers, and over the years of my research into Barclay, more and more 1935 seemed to be the likely start date. Since Shackman seems to have sold Barclays on a regular basis, it's almost certain it would have carried a new line as soon as it emerged. Some, and perhaps all, Shackman catalogs were issued more than once annually, but unfortunately Jacoby furnished me with only the year. My guess would be that the 3-1/4" line debuted about February, 1935.

st.
...
ally.
wide, 2 yards long......
on
d in co
lots only.
e Fringe. Whi
an be had in colors i

SOLDIERS, Etc.

A NEW LINE MADE OF METAL, NICELY PAINTED. EACH ABOUT 3 INCHES. PER DOZEN. $0.48.

51/125 West Point Cadet
51/126 Sailor in White
51/127 Knight
51/128 Flag Bearer
51/129 Soldier with Gun
51/131 Doughboy

51/133 Indian
51/134 Cowboy
51/135 Soldier Musicians
51/137 Naval Officer
51/142 Pirate
51/143 Sailor in Blue

109

Illustrated at right: 1936-37 Shackman page.

B. SHACKMAN & CO.
"THE NAME IS IMPORTANT"

34th STREET and MADISON AVENUE NEW YORK

PAINTED TIN NOVELTIES (continued)

		DOZEN
10560	Circus Elephant. Press cricket lifts tail and head. 2¼ inches	$0.45
4726	Sewing Machine. When catch is released cabinet opens and sewing machine lifts to the top. 2½ inches	.85
4727	Modern gasoline station 2¾ inches and limousine, 2 inches	.90
839	Battleship. Press cricket and gun lifts and recoils. 3 inches	.45
895	Acrobat. Twirls over bar when two metal sides are pressed. 2¼ inches.	.45
10555	Traffic Cop. Lifts hand when cricket is pressed. 2¾ inches	.45
1112	Cockfight. Squeeze handle and two roosters peck. 5 inches	.85

51/145 51/136 51/148

SOLDIERS

WELL MADE OF NICELY PAINTED METAL AT $0.48 DOZEN.

51/148 Soldier with signal flags. 3"
51/146 Soldier with field phone. 2¼"
51/153 Soldier with carrier pigeons. 2¼"
51/145 Soldier and rapid fire gun. 2½"
51/147 Soldier with hand grenade. 2¾"
51/134 Cowboy. 3 1/8"
51/142 Pirate. 3"
51/135 Soldier with drum, bugle and baton, ass't. 3"

51/128 Soldiers with U. S. flag. 2 7/8"
51/130 Soldier and gun. 2 7/8"
51/129 Soldier with machine gun. 2"
51/131 Soldier with gun, ass't positions. 2¾"
51/151 Soldier with large shell. 2 1/8"
51/149 Aviator. 2 7/8"
51/144 Soldier with machine gun. 2 5/8"
51/152 Soldier with great coat and gun. 2¾".

51/154 Doughboy with field radio. 2¼ inches........ $0.80
51/136 Cannon Pea Shooter. 4½ inches........ .85

The winter 1936-37 Shackman catalog illustrates two Barclay 3-1/4" soldiers and a cannon, but oddly, though the descriptions are obviously of Barclay's 3-1/4" soldiers, the sizes mentioned are in the 2-1/2" range. No doubt just a Shackman mistake, but what to make of the different 1936 page, probably from earlier in the year, that Jacoby sent me? These sound as if they could be Barclay's 54mm range. Were they still being produced, or is this just another Shackman mistake?

The earliest appearance of long-stride Barclays (and the first appearance I've found of Manoil figures) is in the February, 1937 Toys & Bicycles magazine in the photo taken that month. A toy display is shown, and thus the soldiers are quite small. The Barclays I can make out are the long-stride ensign, the Indian with rifle across his waist, the cowboy with tin hat-brim and the mounted cowboy. The more visible Manoils are the nurse, a bugler, the cowboy shooting up, and the doctor. Some Grey Irons are also present. Manoils and long-stride Barclays also appear in the May, 1937 Playthings. The Barclays include the Soldier Range Finder, marching officer and kneeling with shell. The noticeable Manoil is an early drummer.

A circa November, 1937 Spiegel catalog shows all the Barclay cowboys and Indians of the period, including the long-stride cowboy firing a pistol. The 14-piece set sold for 98 cents.

The 1938 Playthings offers a Barclay boxed set of infantry. Included are several soldiers that probably debuted that year: 761, 763, 764, the first 765 and the first 766.

The 1939 Butler Bros. catalog page has already been shown in Old Toy Soldier, Volume 5, #4, August 1981. Playthings for November, 1940 offers a store window with several Barclay boxed sets, but nothing startling. However, the 1940 Butler Bros. catalog, circa that fall, shows several "new" figures. Using my codes in Collecting Toy Soldiers they are B20, B126, and B153. The Fall, 1941 Butler Bros. adds two "new" figures, probably first produced in 1940: B118 and B134.

The 1992 OTS Chicago Show's highlight, for me, was meeting fellow collector Bill Dunfee. Bill had received three catalog sheets in 1955 from Barclay and had held onto them all this time. One was pre-WWII and almost certainly from 1941 as it shows the last of Barclay's pre-war production: numbers 788-793. (The numbering of 790, which Jones almost certainly copied, suggests Jones was still producing dimestores in 1941.)

Since all the soldiers are shown with solid puttees and ties, they represent, where it applies, Barclay's cast-helmet versions of earlier numbers. This is a color page in the sense that the uniforms are khaki. Everything else is black and white.

Above: Shackman 1936
Left: 1939 Butler Bros.

That, for the moment, is all the known pre-WWII Barclay material, aside from what I've shown in the Barclay Catalog Book. Does anyone have anything else, whether of Barclay or other dimestore companies? And for that matter, does anyone have anything on Barclay's podfoots that show an earlier date than the Christmas 1951 Woolworth's page that's turned up (shown on page 90 of Collecting Toy Soldiers No. 2)? Oddly, far more dated material has been located on the earlier Barclays than on the pods.

Below: 1941 Barclay catalog sheet showing their 700 Series.

SHEET NO. 1

BARCLAY MANUFACTURING CO., Inc.   567 52nd Street, West New York, N. J.

No. 788 Soldier Marching with Gun Slung Behind Back

No. 789 Soldier Shooting Triple Barreled Gun

No. 790 Soldier Shooting Anti-Tank Gun

No. 791 Soldiers with Mortar

No. 792 Airplane Mechanic

No. 793 Soldiers in Boat

No. 701 Flag Bearer

No. 702 Soldier Machine Gunner

No. 703 Sniper

No. 705 Soldier, Port Arms

No. 731 Soldier Pigeon Dispatcher

No. 706 Soldier Charging

No. 707 Soldier, At Attention

No. 708 Officer

No. 709 Bugler

No. 710 Drummer

No. 711 Drum Major

No. 730 Soldier Signal Man with Flags

No. 728 Machine Gunner, Lying Flat

No. 733 Soldier Bullet Feeder

No. 734 Soldier Ammunition Carrier

No. 735 Soldier Range Finder

No. 736 Soldier Sentry

No. 740 Soldier, French Horn

No. 741 Aviator

No. 737 Soldier Charging, Machine Gunner

No. 738 Soldier Bomb Thrower

No. 760 Soldier Sitting Position

No. 747 Sharpshooter

No. 751 Soldier, Sharpshooter Prone Position

No. 749 Soldier, Gas Mask

No. 758 Camera Man

No. 748 Soldier Running

161

GEORGE GRAMPP

by Richard O'Brien

Revisited

George Grampp, in a photo taken about 1945.

When Bertel Bruun reported on his major George Grampp find in the Autumn, 1991 TSR, I was delighted. A year or two before I'd found a smidgen of information on the previously unknown Grampp in a 1920 Playthings magazine; a few lines of text, a very small and blurred photo... just enough to tantalize and frustrate me.

But as exciting as Bertel's discovery was, it still left some questions unanswered: how long Grampp was in business, when he began, how successful he was, etc. I also couldn't keep from wondering what he looked like.

Then in March of this year it all turned around. I got a call from fellow collector Hank Anton. He'd heard from a woman who said she was Grampp's granddaughter. She had some of his soldiers and wanted to know their value before she donated them to a museum. Hank gave me her number.

I called her immediately. Her name is Lois Dmytryk. She was not truly Grampp's granddaughter, but had always thought of him as her grandfather (her mother was the sister of Grampp's daughter-in-law, Corinne, making Lois Dmytryk, Ed Poole suggests, actually a "Gramppdaughter".) Until my call she hadn't been aware of collectors' interest in Grampp and his soldiers. She immediately promised to do some research and send it along with photos of soldiers not previously attributed to the firm.

According to Mrs. Dmytryk, George Grampp was born about 1874 in Dresden, Germany. This could account for the strong resemblance his soldiers have to Heydes. He may have owned Heydes as a child, worked in the factory, or both. Grampp migrated to America about 1908. He seems to have begun producing soldiers almost immediately as Mrs. Dmytryk remembers a Grampp box (which she no longer has) with the label reading "West Point Cadets - Class of 1910". Incidentally, she says the boxes she saw were plain - no art on them.

Grampp had a wife, son and daughter, but both the daughter and wife were deceased by 1919. The "Mrs. Grampp", mentioned in the Playthings article as representing the company at the New York Toy Fair, was actually Corinne, the wife of Grampp's son William. In addition to acting as a sales representative, she also sewed the soldiers into their boxes.

TSR #37 1993

162

GG35   GG46   GG39   GG47
Courtesy Lois Dmytryk   GR5

7   GG49   GG50   GG51

GG42   GG43   GG44   GG45
GR4   Courtesy Lois Dmytryk

R6   GG48
Courtesy Lois Dmytryk

163

Grampp was a skilled wood carver, so the likelihood is that he sculpted his own soldiers. (Oddly, his wood carvings show far more artistic skill than the soldiers, which can generally be distinguished by an outsize nose.) Aside from whatever money he may possibly have made from his carvings, Grampp's main, and perhaps sole income was from the soldiers and the reindeer and other animals he produced. The latter "were used in a trade that Mr. Grampp had in the Catskill resort area", to quote Mrs. Dmytryk. Some of his molds—presumably the animals—were sold after Grampp's death to a client of his in Freehold, New York.

George Grampp was still casting his reindeer in 1945, and had the business in Patchogue, Long Island ever since Mrs. Dmytryk can remember (she was born in 1919). Although there was a house (and a barn) on the property, in Mrs. Dmytryk's memory Grampp always lived in the two sheds that made up the rest of the buildings, in rather "primitive" conditions. Nevertheless, it is her impression that he was economically in the middle class. (When he died circa 1955, he left behind about six thousand dollars—an impressive amount at the time.)

Though Bertel Bruun was in touch with at least one of Grampp's ex-employees, the firm seems to have been close to a one-man operation. Mrs. Dmytryk remembers no workers, aside from her aunt.

There is no indication when Grampp stopped producing military figures. Mrs. Dmytryk does remember that he sold them to F.A.O. Schwarz, the one known outlet specified in Bertel Bruun's article. Mrs. Dmytryk knows of no connection between Grampp and the "Anthony Grumpp" mentioned in that report.

In sum, George Grampp appears to have been a small, basically one-man operation whose longevity and presumably substantial output make it an important, if not major, American soldier company.

(The photos of Grampp's figures from the Lois Dmytryk collection were taken by Irene Lawrie of the Lightner Museum, St. Augustine, Florida. Mrs. Dmytryk's daughter also has a collection. If any turn out to be different and significant, they may appear in a future issue of TSR.)

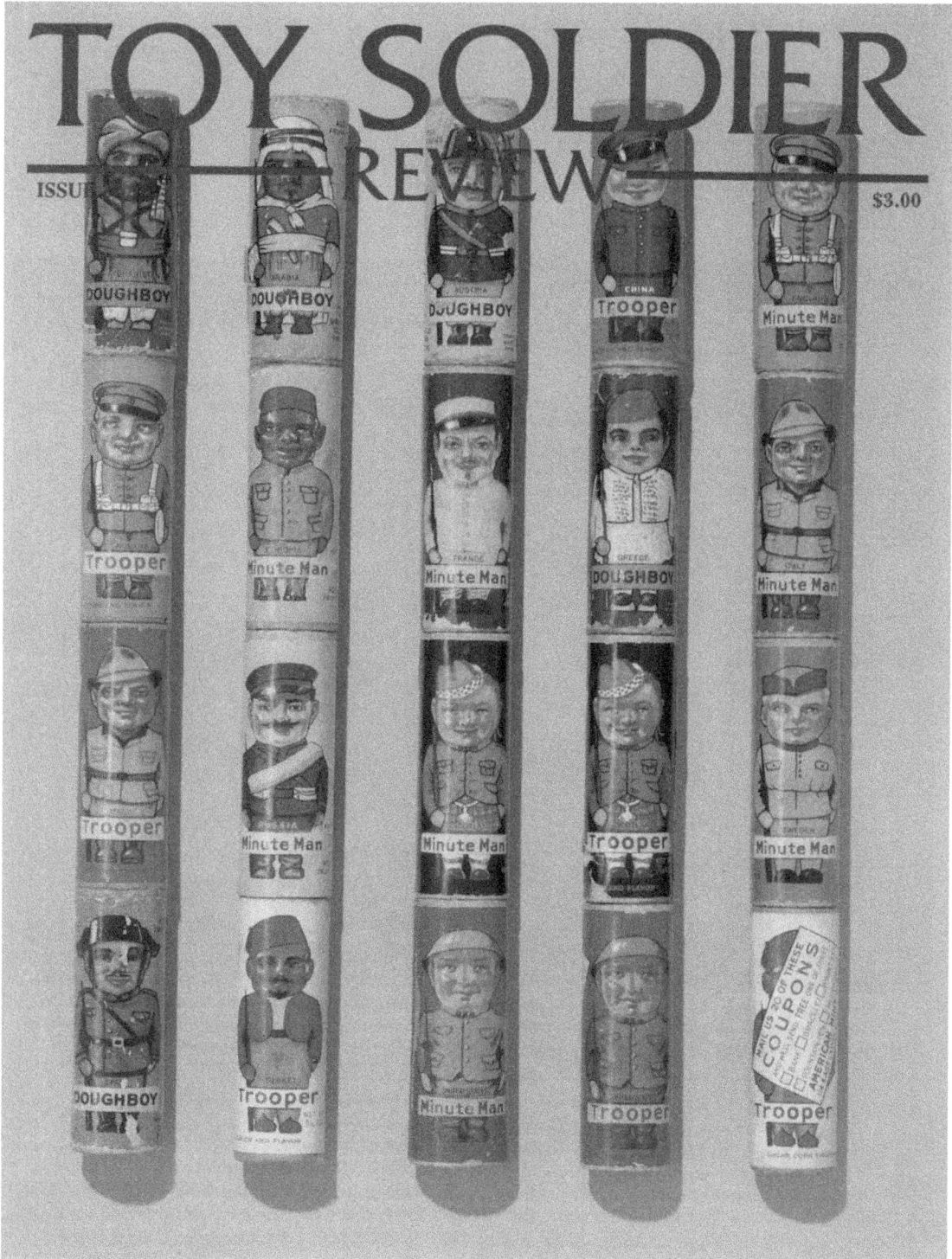

TOY SOLDIER REVIEW

ISSUE

$3.00

#37

Some "NEW" Soldiers

By Richard O'Brien

A magazine like *Toy Soldier Review* can serve its readers in a number of ways. One is as a forum; an information-swap that can even expand the hobby.

Close readers of TSR may remember that (a) in the Summer, 1992 issue Ken Chamberlain did a drawing from memory of a "cardboard tube" soldier he'd owned circa 1939-40, and (b) in the next issue I wrote that for years I'd been asking collectors if they remembered them (I'd received my first in the summer of 1940), with absolutely no luck. I then asked if anyone else out there knew about them and could provide photos.

Joseph Saine and Ted Bruce responded. Joseph wrote that these soldiers were produced by the American Mint Corporation of New York, N.Y. and were 2-9/16". (The tubes of cardboard, with a plain cardboard cap, contained small candies.) He mentioned there were twenty known titles in four categories: Doughboys, Minute Men, Troopers and Nurses (actually, Yanks).

He further mentioned that they are very collectible, and have been since at least the 1950s. Oddly, though, not by toy soldier collectors, but by gum card and candy wrapper aficionados. To my astonishment, he said they sold for $100 to $200 apiece, depending on rarity. He then listed the known soldiers for me, as noted in a non-sport price guide (he didn't specify the title) by Benjamin & Eckes, published by Sport Americana. He later sent a color Polaroid of his one American Mint soldier and Xeroxes of pages 55 and 56 from the book. (It's the book that got the "Yanks" listing wrong.)

Top, left to right: Afghanistan, Arabia, Austria, China, England.
Second Row: England, Ethiopia, France, Greece, Italy.
Third Row: Italy, Russia, Scotland, Scotland, Sweden.
Bottom Row: Spain, Turkey, United States, United States, Coupon Offer.
Courtesy Ted Bruce

Shortly after Joseph wrote, Ted Bruce got in touch with TSR. He said he owned 27 (some of them duplicates), all bought from his local candy store in Chicago circa WWII. I immediately got in touch with Ted and made arrangements to have his soldiers photographed. He in turn was astounded to find out how valuable they've become.

The photos eventually arrived, and though I was delighted to see so many of the soldiers, I still wasn't satisfied. By now I knew there were more out there, and suspected there were even more that the book hadn't listed. I then remembered that Tony Salamone, one of the major dimestore collectors, also was involved with gum cards. I queried Tony at the Rochester show this past spring, and to my delight found he not only had a number of them, but knew John Neuner, known as "The Wrapper King", who may have the largest collection of all. Tony sent me a Xerox of the pieces he has, and also of the ones John had. John had all of Tony's and more. So I called him, and found he recently had even added a couple more previous "unknowns". To my surprise and delight, even though he seemed to

TSR #37

166

know nothing about our hobby, he immediately agreed to send me Xeroxes of the pieces in his collection.

As far as I know, the figures shown and listed here are all (with the exception of Switzerland) the presently-known American Mint soldiers. The Yank Parachutist and Gob have only just turned up, and I think there is at least one more; I have a strong memory of a U.S. soldier in a tilted campaign cap that I suspect belongs in the Yank category. If anyone has that one, or any other still-unknowns, I'd love to hear from him.

Little is known about these soldiers. The suspicion is that the Doughboys came first, then the Minute Men, then the Troopers and finally the Yanks. I have a vague memory of thinking, shortly after Pearl Harbor, that the manufacturer had finally realized, what with the war, that kids would want a larger variety of American soldiers. If I'm correct, the Yanks would have emerged in early 1942. I first saw the soldiers in 1940. Tony Salamone thinks they may have been around at least as early as 1939, but isn't sure. He also thinks they sold for a penny apiece. I suspect it was two cents, but that's more a guess than a memory. The address for the company was given on a coupon that ran on the back of the Troopers (and apparently the Yanks, judging by a mention on the side of the Gob; the Doughboys and Minutemen showed the same illustration on both front and back). It was 114 East 13th Street. 20 of the coupons would get you a "free mouth-organ, pop-gun" or "globe-bank". Distribution seems to have been pretty wide; I know of Long Island, Brooklyn, Philadelphia and Chicago. It's not known when these were last produced, but I wouldn't be surprised if it was 1943 or even 1942, possibly as a result of wartime shortages.

As can be seen in the cover photo, these soldiers are very colorful, and designed by a skilled artist. Though the bodies on all but the Yanks are simple cartoons, each of the faces is very well done, probably in water color. To my eye at least, they're also excellent attempts at depicting each individual nationality. Almost all of the Doughboys, Minute Men and Troopers have a rifle at their side. The only exceptions I've noted (I've yet to see anything other than the photos) are the Pole (sword) and Zulu Warrior (spear). The three known Yanks seem to have nothing in their hands, and that's my memory of the fellow in the rakish cap.

If I've counted right, 24 different types are now known, though the Japanese and the Chinese look exactly alike (the Japanese functions as a Doughboy and the Chinese as a Trooper), and 21 countries, counting the Zulu, are represented. I'd been a little disturbed when Ted Bruce's photos came. I have a pretty good memory for such things (when Joseph Saine told me there was a nurse, though I hadn't remembered her in fifty years, she immediately sprang to mind, and as it turns out, exactly as she looks), and was surprised to find them looking so squat. But then the three Yanks arrived, and sure enough, they're thinner. There are two other differences; unlike their predecessors, their

faces all look very similar, as if they could be siblings. Additionally, their bodies, not just their faces, are in full detail.

Seeing all of these has been a joy for me. I owned a few when I was a kid, and played with them a lot. Now I know why. They're really neat. As for those of you out there who have about all the dimestores, Marx or Britains you want: here's a new collectible. Let me know how many years (and thousands of dollars) it takes you to find them all.

DOUGHBOYS: Afghanistan, Arabia, Austria, England, Ethiopia, France, French Foreign Legion, Greece, India, Italy, Japan, Poland, Russia, Scotland, Spain, Sweden, Switzer-land, Turkey, United States, Zulu Warrior.

MINUTE MEN: China, England, Ethiopia, France, Italy, Russia, Scotland, Sweden, Turkey, United States.

TROOPERS: China, England, Ethiopia, France, Italy, Russia, Scotland, Sweden, Turkey, United States (The exact replication of the Troopers and Minute Men—the same ten countries—suggests this may be all of them).

YANKS: Gob, Nurse, Parachutist.

Top, left to right: Zulu Warrior, Japan, Parachutist, Gob, Nurse.
Bottom, left to right: Poland, French Foreign Legion, Afghanistan, France, India.
The only known figure not shown in this article is Switzerland.
Courtesy John Neuner

Bill Hanlon has written a superb book called <u>Plastic Toys</u>. While reading it, I came across a passing mention that got my antennae quivering. I immediately wrote Bill and requested a photocopy of the article he'd briefly referred to. He sent it. Suddenly I found our hobby had a mystery it had never suspected it had.

Beton
Toys

"Betons" Before Beton!
A Mystery Discovered and Resolved

by Richard O'Brien

While doing research for his book, Bill had come across a magazine called <u>Modern Plastics.</u> The top photo of their August 1939 issue included Beton figures. (Shown page 22.) The magazine attributed them to Columbia Protektosite. That was okay; Columbia did Beton's casting. But on the bottom of the page were two photos of what I--perhaps all of us--would have assumed were Betons. However, the caption read: "Believing that metal toys are dangerous when broken or put in a child's mouth, that they were heavy and not easily handled, Universal Plastics Corp. is experimenting with a line of molded plastic soldiers, Indians and such."

That was enough of a jolt. But there were two more. The soldiers in one of the photos were wearing soft caps. I, and all the collectors I've spoken to since, had assumed they had been produced by Beton during the Korean War, not eleven years earlier! And the Indians in the second photo...they had rectangular bases! *In 1939.* Beton doesn't seem to have sold its figures with rectangular bases until late 1941 at the earliest. So my dim memory of receiving the same three Indians, with rectangular bases, in early 1940 (or perhaps Christmas, 1939) hadn't been wrong!

But had Universal actually marketed these pieces, or like Columbia Protektosite, simply cast for Beton? Or for perhaps yet another firm? Bill Hanlon's conjecturings were in the same ballpark. I wondered if we'd ever find out.

I spend of couple of days mulling. I'd often wondered why some of Beton's figures are so similar. But if some had been produced first by another firm...I have a circa 1940 Beton color catalog whose illustrations have been reproduced in a couple of my books. However, the detail is sharper in the original catalog. There I saw quite distinctly that Beton's soldiers BT1-BT11 (my codes) had bandage-type leggings, whereas the rest, with the exception of the drummer, had what Bill Holt tells me are spats. They also looked like (aside from the caps)

the Betons that run from BT12 on. It seemed likely that Universal had made soft-cap versions of the entire group: BT12-BT17. The catalog's drummer (BT16) displayed the bandage leggings, but the figure was drawn. Perhaps, I thought (and hoped) the artist had simply made a mistake. After all, the Universal Indians follow the Beton Indians numerically (Beton's numbers as well as mine).

The 1939 all-text Beton catalog stated its foot figures consisted of "Infantry, Cadet, Cowboys, Indians." Therefore, it seemed almost certain Beton had made multiples of cowboys and Indians. I'd always been puzzled by the two sizes of its Indians. Now it appeared likely that BT18-20 (the smaller ones) had come out in 1938, along with BT1-BT11, and probably just two cowboys, with Universal initially producing the other two, plus the later soldiers and larger Indians.

So already some mysteries appeared to be clearing up. I'd often wondered what Beton's first group of foot figures had been, and now it seemed likely it consisted of those eleven infantrymen, three smaller Indians and perhaps only two cowboys.

At this point, I called Bill Holt. He had written me sometime before, stating that Beton soldiers had come out in at least two or perhaps three sizes. A few years prior to his letter I'd noticed smaller Betons, the early ones, turning up at shows. I was intrigued, but finally decided it was probably shrinkage. Bill had written me a letter, with drawings, attempting to persuade me otherwise. So, knowing he was interested in Beton and assuming this startling new development would fascinate him, I picked up the phone.

While we talked, Bill rummaged around in his boxes of Betons. Finally, he found one soft-cap soldier: the saluter. For the first time since he'd owned it he turned it over and examined the underbase. It said: "U P Made in U.S.A" . *Horray!!*

We'd taken the first step. Now it was clear Universal had sold these figures under its own name. But so far we had only seven Universals. I was sure there were more and contacted Neil Wenberg, whom I knew was a dedicated Beton collector. He became excited too and sent me a photo of his three Universals. All had rectangular bases and "UP" markings. Two we already knew about, but he'd added a cowboy, BT26. That was kind of surprising. I'd expected it to be BT24, as the pose resembles BT15. But perhaps the Universal sculptor used BT24 as a guide to his design of the BT15. For somewhere along the way I'd noticed that with two exceptions, the saluter and the drummer, all the Universals echoed the poses or attributes of the early Betons. And even the drummer could be considered "inspired" by Beton's bugler.

Something else emerged. The helmets on Beton's BT12-BT17 are all odd-shaped, with the crown much too high. It now seemed obvious that Beton had obtained Universal's molds and then chased in helmets, the resultant crown being so high because the original caps rose high. So no longer any reason to wonder why some, but not all, of Beton's infantry sport incorrectly-designed helmets.

By this time, word had gotten around and suddenly I heard from Ron Steiner. He had much news. He had the "missing" soft-cap Universals: the drummer (in spats) and the kneeling machine gunner. He also had a second cowboy: Beton's BT25. He'd remembered buying the latter around 1941. However, it's possible he bought it a year or two earlier unless it was old stock. I checked through all my catalogs. A Christmas, 1940 Billy and Ruth catalog shows the Universals already incorporated into the Beton line (**all** of the figures on **oval** bases). An April, 1940 photograph of Beton soldiers in the Magazine Toys and Bicycles shows only original Betons, and just one foot cowboy, BT24, suggesting BT25, BT26 and BT27 all originated with Universal as, like all the other Universals incorporated into Beton's line, their Beton numbers are in a later sequence. (At this point, no Universal BT27 has been found, however.) It also suggests Beton didn't acquire the Universal molds until sometime in 1940.

It seems likely to me that when Beton finally turned to rectangular bases, it used Universal's base mold. To Ron Steiner too, who checked and found that Universal underbases read "Made in U.S.A" (no final period). When he investigated his rectangular-based Betons they too had the same missing period. Later, he really got busy,scrutinizing the underbases of all his Betons. Beton had added an X-shaped brace under the original base, which in its Universal guise, had serious warping problems. It occurred to Ron, as it had to me, that perhaps if the "Made in U.S.A" marking hadn't been changed, a bit of the U or P might also show below or above the brace. For some reason there's considerable variation on this, with some Beton underbases showing various lengths of the P's descender. But on one of Ron's, both some of the U and P are evident (see his diagram). So no question any longer that Universal produced its pieces and bases first.

Bill Holt, after photographing several of his Betons for me and then looking at them with a magnifying glass, noticed something he never had before. His Beton signalman, the one originally produced in soft cap by Universal, had on the front of the top flag the initials "PU", and on the front of the bottom flag, "FF". It seemed likely the PU stood for Universal Plastics, somehow reversed, and FF the initials of the sculptor. Bill later sent me a drawing showing how easy it would be for an absent-minded engraver to reverse the letters. It's possible that the second F stands for Ferriot, as the Ferriot brothers are known to have sculptured many soldiers for Marx. To my eye, some of Marx's designs seem to be from the hand of Beton-Universal's unknown sculptor. Unfortunately, no one seems to have the Universal signalman with intact flags, so for the moment we can only assume that once found, the initials will be there too.

It's possible Universal made a few more figures. I'd always wondered why Beton had two signalmen and two marching figures which had no real differences (no slung rifle or different headgear, for instance, to differentiate them). Now we know. But I've also wondered why Beton made two cops. And some very similar civilians. Could it be some originated with Universal? Perhaps OTS readers could check underbases and supply answers.

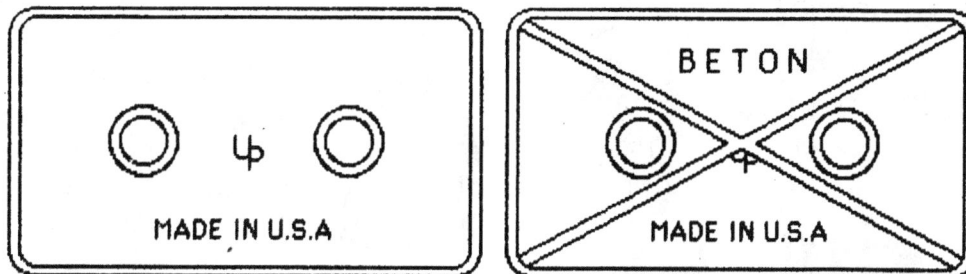

Ron Steiner's diagram of the Universal underbase and the Beton underbase. Note, in the Beton, the portion of the "UP" marking and the carryover of the lack of a period after "A" in "U.S.A".

As early as 1936 Universal was located at 235 Jersey Avenue in New Brunswick, New Jersey. Bill Hanlon has discovered its officers in 1946 were Charles A. Wyman, president; and H.N. Macdonald, vice-president; Paul LeB Whitney, another vice-president. Benjamin Kay was secretary and the treasurer was John F. Dunnigan. I couldn't track down any of them. The firm cast toys (no other soldiers known) and non-toys for several firms from at least 1939 through 1946. The state of New Jersey dissolved its corporate status in 1950, and usually the state waits about three years before it goes through this process.

As to whether Beton did originally make its soldiers in a smaller size, enlarging them only about the time it

Opposite: Ron Steiner's Universals. All Universals seem to have come unpainted, unlike Beton's pre-WWII pieces. The known Universal bases are invariably green or reddish. Below: These are the poses of UP figures, later seen here as Betons from their catalog illustrations. The original square base versions of these figures were pictured in August 1939, Vol. 16, #12 of Modern Plastics, but the photo is too dark to reproduce here. The discovery that Universal originated the plastic Indian brave with bow and arrow (shown in the August, 1939 Modern Plastics article), rules out the metal version as having been first produced by Beton (see page 202 of Collecting Toy Soldiers No. 2). The likelihood seems to be that American Metal Toys of Chicago copied Universal, since it's not listed among their pieces until 1939.

172

Beton Toys

somehow got Universal's molds, my guess is they did (Bill Holt is convinced of it) while other collectors seem uncertain and want to check further. And is it possible Universal was inspired by every one of Beton's foot figures? I have a very fuzzy Xerox from the early 1940s that suggests Beton may have made a saluter who stood at attention. Does anyone out there have one?

One final question. Why did Universal put soft caps on its soldiers? It seems like a death wish. If they'd gone to helmets instead, Universal and Beton might have been rivals. Or the tables could easily have been turned, with Beton giving up the ghost and selling its molds to a far more successful Universal. But then, we wouldn't have had all this fun.

RICHARD O'BRIEN LOOKING FOR HELP ON NEW BOOK

Richard O'Brien has begun work on a new toy soldier book. Like his preceding ones, this will also be a reference book and price guide, but this time it will confine itself to American makes (plus Canadian, Japanese and French "dimestores").

Richard is, as usual, open to all contributions, whether it be photos, catalogs, company histories, price information, etc. New makers who'd like to be in the book should send him a brief history of their company and a representative photo of their figures. Owners of U.S. toy soldier shops who'd like to be listed should let him know their address and the types of soldiers they carry.

As of November 18th, Richard's new address will be 705 Greene Street, Beaufort, South Carolina 29902. Phone number: 803-521-9983.

It's **NOT** "Jones" Dimestores:
It's American Metal Toys

by Richard O'Brien

For a long time I'd known Don Pielin didn't believe J. Edward Jones had produced the dimestore figures attributed to him. A couple of years ago, when I came across Jones' 1941 notes on Historical Miniatures, I fell into Don's camp. Jones had written the approximately 3-1/4" size they employed was the same as he himself had used "back in 1932." First of all, the 1932 soldiers Jones produced were more in the three-inch range. Secondly, why would he have reached back to 1932 if he had been selling 3-1/4" dimestores circa 1938-41?

Later, in the 1939 Playthings Directory, I came across a listing under "Soldiers (Metal)". My heart leapt. There, included with Barclay, Manoil, Grey Iron and John Wright, was "American Metal Toys, 215 N. Racine, Chicago". What got me excited and hopeful was that I knew Bill Long, who cast the postwar figures for Lincoln Log, had called his Bay City, Michigan firm American Metal Toy Company. And, of course, some or all of those Lincoln Log figures were said to have been sculpted by Henry Kasselowski, the same man who'd probably designed the "Jones" dimestores. It seemed very likely American Metal Toys was the company Don and I had been trying to track down, with Long somewhere along the way having moved from Chicago to Bay City.

Not long after, Don and I got in touch. I informed him of my find, and he in turn told me about once interviewing a relative of a man named "Riff", the relative claiming it was his relation's firm that had made the purported Jones soldiers. When Don mentioned his rather vague source had stated Bill Long was one of the three owners, I became sure we'd found the answer. All we needed was some verification. I called Springfield, Illinois, hoping American Metal Toys had incorporated. I was informed it had, and that there might be papers on file. Crossing my fingers, I ordered them. Shortly after, to my delight, they arrived. The day they came I called Don. Soon it was obvious the longtime mystery was solved.

But I wasn't satisfied. Where was that relative? Don hadn't been able to track him down again, and he might be able to answer all sorts of questions about the plant, the workers, the sculptor (was it Kasselowski?), the individual soldiers and accessories. Alas, he was no longer in the Chicago phonebook. Although the major part of the mystery had been solved, I still felt stymied.

Months passed. Then one day a friend, apropos of nothing, mentioned his brother had a computer program which could give you the phone number and address of anyone anywhere in the United States. A bell rang. One of the owners' last names was unusual. I asked my friend if his brother would feed it into the program. On Sunday, October 2, 1994, my friend called me. It had been an unusual name. Only a handful had surfaced. He gave me the two most likely. It was early in the morning. I waited an hour, then called. Bingo!

I'd got the co-owner's grandson. He gave me the son's number. Double Bingo! The son not only knew virtually the whole story, he had inspired some of the toys, and had even done some casting—just for fun—on Saturdays at the plant.

Stan Reyff was his name. His father was Royce Richard Reyff (pronounced "Reef", not "Riff"; it's Swiss), born 1898, died 1985. I asked him a number of questions; he gave me answers for almost all of them. I then sent him pages from Collecting Toy Soldiers to look over and comment on. A few days later I received the pages back, plus a two-page, single-spaced letter on the company. What follows has been altered slightly for style. I've parenthetically interjected a few of my own comments.

"My father, Royce R. Reyff, began his business career with the S.S. Kresge store in Bowling Green, Ohio as a stockboy in 1913 at age 15 years. Upon his completion of high school in 1915 he applied for management training with Kresge Co. In 1921 he was rewarded with his first managership at the store in Warren, Ohio (O'Brien: A significant location, as will be seen later.) It was the Kresge policy to transfer their managers from store to store every two to four years. As a result, Royce (the family moving with him) managed stores in Iowa, Michigan, Wisconsin, and finally a new location in Oak Park, Illinois (suburb of Chicago) in 1934.

"At the end of 1936, Royce resigned from Kresge Co. after 23 years of service. (O'Brien: The family then went to California, where Royce searched fruitlessly for business prospects. They finally returned to Oak Park.) In the spring of 1937, Royce and Raymond Pierson (O'Brien: Actually, according to the incorporation papers, C. Raymond Pierson), an "outside" sales rep, formed a partnership and created the American Metal Toy Co. in Chicago. (O'Brien: According to Stan Reyff, his father seems to have had no personal interest in toy soldiers.) The first shop was located at about 2900 West 39th Street, Chicago (a "storefront" shop), during the summer of 1937. The company started production with about twelve molds. The casting, trimming, and basic dip-painting was done in the shop. Detail painting was pieced out to local residents and paid on this basis. (O'Brien: According to Stan Reyff, this initial plant had only three or four inside workers, plus the co-owners, who pitched in when they weren't out selling.)

"One of the first substantial accounts was the N. (Nathan) Shure Co. in Chicago, as both Royce and Ray had worked with Nathan prior to the creation of American Metal Toys. Royce, having worked for Kresge, went to Detroit, Michigan (Kresge's headquarters) and was able to secure them as a main account. (O'Brien: N. Shure was a jobber.)

"The need for expansion room was obvious by the end of 1937. At the same time the boys were buying additional molds. The first week of 1938 the company was moved to a larger plant at 215 N. Racine. (O'Brien: Stan Reyff describes this as a one-story building, about 75-100 feet by 50-75 feet. Some of this space was rented by airplane model kit maker Joe Ott.) As it turned out, the new location was near the makers of Lincoln Log, which became important in 1941-42, when American Metal Toys was sold to them. (O'Brien: According to Stan Reyff, the sale was essentially a transfer of the molds, done by Pierson.)

"The company grew rapidly through 1938 and 1939. New molds were being acquired constantly. The casting material was a lead-zinc alloy."

One of my first questions when I spoke to Stan Reyff was whether Henry Kasselowski had been the sculptor. He immediately responded that he was, and that as far as he knew, he had sculpted all the figures and had furnished all the "dies" or molds. He didn't know what the molds were made of, but did a drawing of one. He also remembered that when Kasselowski and Royce Reyff had first hooked up, the sculptor-moldmaker was dying of lead poisoning. Doctors could do nothing for him. So in the summer he lay in the sun for long periods, which "cooked the poison out of him" until he was cured.

Reyff also stated that Kasselowski already had the molds, and Royce and Pierson bought about a dozen to begin with. He is very certain that three of the first soldiers were Germans: the charging German I've coded J2, the kneeling firing (J1) and the machine-gunner firing from a stump, but with a **German helmet**. I've twice asked Reyff if he simply remembered it that way because it was a doughboy painted German gray, but each time he insisted he clearly remembered the helmet. And he doesn't seem to be confusing it with the prone German, because he doesn't remember that one at all. (The prone machine-gunner seems to have been a late addition, and by about 1938 Stan Reyff had turned from collecting toy soldiers to making model airplanes, thus being far less aware of his father's later product. He has no idea of the size of the second plant's workforce.)

Also early were the two knights. It took a moment or two for Stan Reyff to remember them, and then he recalled they were planned to tie into the "Medieval Castle" (Reyff's description) that Built-Rite was beginning to market (presumably the no-ramp fort). Reyff remembers they didn't sell well, nor did the foot cowboy (MA17 in my book), and this seems to be true, as they appear only in an early listing in a general catalog. (N. Shure, spring and summer, 1938.)

The cowboy had originally been made by J. Edward Jones, as had the J26 gas-masked bayoneter and presumably the J1, J2 Germans (thus more in the 3" size than 3-1/4"). Did Kasselowski, after being approached by American Metal Toys, buy the molds from Jones? Or did he simply have them on hand after Jones abandoned the 3" line? Or...did he create new molds based on those figures? Examining photos of the 3" soldiers definitely produced by Jones that are in the collection of the Chicago Historical Society, it seems to me there are subtle differences between his piece and those of American Metal Toys. Perhaps a Chicago-based collector can make comparisons and let us know the results.

In any event, this seems to be Jones' sole connection to American Metal Toys. Stan Reyff had never heard of him (nor had he heard of Bill Long).

Stan Reyff remembered many of the soldiers in the J1-J41 listings, including J35a, the kneeling firing Indian. He also identified other pieces as American Metal Toys: The Beton (also Universal)-like Indian with drawn bow on page 202 of Collecting Toy Soldiers No. 2, the cannon on the bottom of pages 99 and 100, and the AA Gun on page 374. All this makes sense, as every one of these pieces is described in lists of American Metal Toys found in jobbers' catalogs.

Reyff says he actually inspired a number of the company's products, sometimes from his own ideas, sometimes from what he saw in Life and other magazines. Ed Poole says the AA Gun ran in the December 13, 1937 issue of Life. Reyff remembers seeing a photo in Life of a soldier being shot during the Spanish Civil war and saying "Dad, this'd be a great figure." This is almost undoubtedly the photograph that made Robert Capa famous, and Ed dates it as July 12, 1937. Thus, perhaps for the first time, we actually know the approximate date some dimestore toys were inspired (thought the Capa shot was the inspiration, Kasselowski then obviously used a different photograph as his basis for the wounded soldiers; that photograph shows a soldier—posed—ostensibly being gassed.) The 105 howitzer was also Stan Reyff's idea. "Looks like a pretty good piece," he remembers telling his father.

Another anecdote concerns the pillbox (JVA5), which collector Don Mueller says is copied from "Horrors of War" card number 172. Reyff's father wasn't happy with it because it didn't sell well. And it probably was included in an otherwise all-Barclay section in a Butler Bros. catalog because, seeing the war coming, Reyff opened a Ben Franklin store in 1939. Ben Franklin was a Butler Bros. franchise. (Stan Reyff remembers the pillbox being inspired by the Maginot line.)

Reyff remembers nothing about the sand bags shown on the lists of American Metal Toys, but does remember that the wheel assemblies (wheels and axles) for the cannon were subcontracted from Tootsietoy, suggesting that's where Barclay got them too. American Metal's stretchers also came from Tootsietoy, of which Nathan Shure was a major stockholder.

He also believes the initial pieces produced by American Metal were J1, J2, J10 (in German helmet), J23, J26, J29, J32, J35A. My guess would be he's right on some of them, but not all. (See the first known list, page 177 of Soldiers 2.)

Stan Reyff remembers the soldiers were dipped in one of two paint vats (enemy color in one, khaki in the other), about two dozen at a time as they hung suspended from a wooden rack. He remembers the doughboy kneeling firing with the long rifle, and that the rifle was modeled on a Springfield .03. He doesn't remember the short rifle, but speculates that it was "maybe done as a carbine" (presumably to reduce breakage). Reyff, incidentally, was eleven when the company began, and a collector of Manoils and Barclays. He remembers being disappointed with the look of his father's line. He agreed "klunky" is a pretty good description of Kasselowski's work.

A kneeling nurse has turned up, a copy of Barclay's, that appears to be from American Metal Toys. Alas, he does not remember it. However, he also doesn't remember the standing nurse, though he remembers telling his father the doctor in white, another Barclay copy, "wouldn't sell."

Although both Royce and Raymond acted as sales representatives, it was Pierson who did more of it, with Royce more or less the plant manager. The proportion of American figures to "Germans" (anything in gray paint), was two to one. Stan Reyff remembers the farmer and farm wife (though not the tramp) and a number of the animals distinctly, and that all of this was inspired by Built-Rite's "Farm Barn" set.

Though there was a big volume of soldiers cast, the Reyffs did not get wealthy from American Metal Toys. As for the boxed sets shown in catalogs, Stan Reyff remembers none, suggesting the boxing was done by the jobbers, although it should again be pointed out that as he grew older, Reyff paid less attention to American Metal. Despite that, he remembers suggesting the J16 anti-tank gunner, which almost certainly came late in the game as it seems to have originated in 1941 with Barclay. As with another of his ideas, the J8 soldier with AA gun, he was disappointed in the results.

Though American Metal began in 1937, it wasn't incorporated until October 24, 1939. It remained in business until late 1941 or early 1942 (probably the latter), and was officially declared out of business in December, 1944. Four names appear in the incorporation papers: Royce R. Reyff, Gertrude M. Reyff, C. Raymond Pierson and Gertrude Pierson. The women seem to have been listed only for legal purposes. Wives of the owners, they, according to Stan Reyff, had nothing at all to do with the

business. Reyff was listed in the initial papers as the firm's agent, and in February 1940, as its President (with Gertrude Reyff as Secretary and the Piersons not mentioned).

The incorporation papers list the firm's stock at 50 shares, and their total value $5000. Presumably this too is legalese. Perhaps also legalese was the firm's estimate in the same papers that its gross amount of business during the following year would be $150,000, but perhaps it was expectations back ed by past experience. Any Illinois lawyers out there know for sure?

Luckily, the firm occasionally slipped up on paying its state taxes. (Stan Reyff's memory of the firm's longevity was hazy.) For this reason we have the information on the Reyff's official titles, and the fact that on December 1, 1941, they paid up their back taxes of $11.40 (plus a ten-cent surcharge for delinquency), thus establishing they were still in business. Also, sometime after October 15, 1942, the sheriff's deputy sent out with a warrant to collect $11.50 in back taxes and fines found no evidence of the corporation's existence.

Some last notes. Another Indian with bow, the one with the long headdress on page 363 of Soldiers 2, has long vexed me. Its paint or lacquer is of a very high quality, suggesting it came from a successful company, yet it seems to go with none of the known firms. American Metal's lacquer was also of a high standard. Is it possible this was a late substitute for the Beton-Universal copy? Perhaps even by Lincoln Log after it bought American Metal's molds? A comparison of its paint to the Lincoln Log Indians might help provide an answer. I also sent pages to Reyff that showed still unidentified pieces, in the unlikely hope they were also from American Metal Toys. He said "no" to all of the following: the two

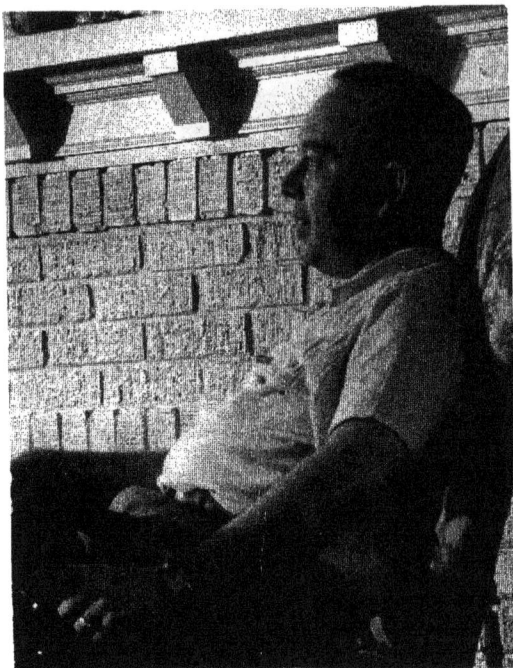

rocketships at right on page 87 of <u>Collecting Toy Soldiers No. 2,</u> the BC7 cannon on page 99, the early Jones Germans on page 170 and 172, the Indian with bow and diver on page 363, the nurse pushing wheelchair on page 366, the top left doughboy and divers on page 369 and the "U.S.S. New Mexico" and "Texas" ships on page 373. Although they almost certainly were made by American Metal Toys, Stan Reyff doesn't remember its tanks, suggesting they were late starters; they're not listed on any pre-1941 or 1942 lists and no lists from 1941 or 1942 have yet appeared.

Finally, since some collectors have become confused when I've told them about this: Yes, J. Edward Jones did make toy soldiers. He made a lot of them. He just didn't make the range of soldiers and toys mentioned here. And now we know who did.

Photos: On preceding pages, a selection of American Metal Toys, Reyff's, no longer Jones. At left, Royce Reyff, c1942.

Editor's Note: Oak Park has been homebase for OTS since we began 18 years ago. Roger Garfield, who grew up in Oak Park, remembers shopping at Reyff's toy store and dimestore on Oak Park Avenue. Small world is an understatement!

American Metal Toys
An Unexpected Part Two!

by Richard O'Brien

Recently while doing research for the third edition of Collecting Toy Soldiers, I came upon Glenn F. Ridenour's extensive article on Tim Mee in Plastic Figure and Playset Collector No. 20. In it he mentions that the firm was inspired by a salesman named Ray Pierson. Ray Pierson was the name of the co-owner of American Metal Toys, he had been a salesman before its formation, and both companies, American Metal Toys and Tim Mee, had Illinois locations. The odds were great it was the same Ray Pierson. I began to chafe, wanting to find out for sure. I hadn't tried Pierson's name in the computer system that had given me Stan Reyff's phone number. Ray Pierson had seemed too common a name, possibly requiring scores of calls in search of someone who quite likely was no longer around. But then it dawned on me. "Ray Pierson" may be common, but Pierson had appeared in American Metal's incorporation papers as C. Raymond Pierson. Not too common-sounding, that. I called my friend whose brother has the computer program. He came back to me with three names. The date was February 14, 1995. I tried the first. Then the second. Happy Valentine's Day! I had him!

Carl Raymond Pierson was born December 17th, 1904. Thus he was ninety years old when I called. He has also been stricken with Parkinson's disease. Nonetheless, his speech and memory are good. Between what he told me and what Stan Reyff had previously contributed (I sent Pierson the first American Metal article, which was based on Reyff's information, and he said it was correct), we now essentially have the whole story of American Metal Toys.

I asked Ray Pierson how he and co-owner Royce Reyff had gone into business together. He had to think for a moment, and finally said he believed it was simply a matter of his walking into Reyff's store as a salesman, as he had many times before. They talked, and the two off them finally made the decision. However, a third person also had input. He was a salesman named Sidney Worthen. It was his suggestion that Pierson and Reyff's business be soldier-making, and he was the one who led them to sculptor-moldmaker Henry Kasselowski. (Like Reyff, Pierson had had no previous interest in toy soldiers.)

When questioned about Kasselowski, Pierson said he was from Germany, had been in the German army, and "brought his know-how" with him when he immigrated. Kasselowski was married, childless, and did his sculpting in wax, Pierson added. About half of American Metal Toys' soldiers were copies. A collector had recently suggested this might have been at the direction of such buyers as Kresge's and N. Shure, if they had been unable to get stock from Barclay or Manoil. I asked Pierson if this were so. He said no. I then asked if he'd been aware Kasselowski had done so much copying. The answer again was "no".

The capitalization for American Metal Toys was about three to four thousand dollars, Pierson noting "that was a lot of money in those days." Some of it was his and Reyff's, some borrowed from friends.

Stan Reyff had remembered the address of the first factory as about 2900 West 39th Street in Chicago. Pierson says it was on California Avenue. (Editor's note: California is a north-south street which crosses 39th Street at 2800 west.) He did agree with Reyff that at the first location they had about four employees and several outside workers who did the detail painting at home.

Surprisingly, the number of workers didn't pick up much at the second location, 215 North Racine. Pierson informed me there were only about seven, but then allowed in the busiest times the number might go as high as twelve (plus, of course, the outside workers). I asked how many were in the shipping department. "Just one" was his answer.

In connection with that, I mentioned the boxed sets that appear in at least two 1938 general catalogs. Stan Reyff hadn't remembered them and thought perhaps the boxing had been done by jobbers. But Pierson says the soldiers were boxed at American Metal Toys, apparently mainly or entirely by the two owners. Furthermore, he says, the boxes, none of which has yet surfaced, had drawings on them (not by Pierson, Reyff or Kasselowski).

Photo opposite: C. Raymond Pierson in early 1994 at the age of 89, courtesy C.R. Pierson.

OTS 4-5/95 V19#2

Drawings, rather than photographs, also figured in the company's catalogs. Pierson stated there was about one a year. He thinks he may still have some, and when he feels better, might be able to provide them. Since I knew he had acted as salesman for the company, I asked if he remembered any of the firm's descriptions and numbers for their figures. He recalled two numbers: *One* for the machine gunner behind the stump and *Ten* for the officer in greatcoat pointing. Both sound as if they could be right. Some of the machine gunners have been found with the numerical "one" on them, and there are only nine figures in the first known listing of American Metal figures while later that same year (1938) the officer appears in the boxed sets. "U.S. Soldier" may have been the only written description for each of the American military, including the officer.

As for Reyff's memory of a German-helmeted soldier firing a machine gun on a stump, the first time I asked, Pierson said there was none. However, during the next call, he said he thought he did remember it and as he spoke became more sure as he thought about it. At this late date it seems highly unlikely such a piece could have eluded collectors, but I'm still searching for that running Auburn pilot I know existed, and what seems to be an American Metal Toys kneeling nurse (a copy of the Barclay) has just surfaced, so it's possible such a soldier was made. As for that nurse, like Reyff, Pierson doesn't remember it, though he recalled the standing nurse. However, he did remember both former "mystery Indians" on pages 202 and 363 of Collecting Toy Soldiers No. 2 as being from American Metal Toys. Since they're both standing with bow and arrow, I asked if the one in long headdress had supplanted the other, but he said no, they "just wanted to have different ones." As for the tanks, which Reyff hadn't remembered, Pierson did. When I suggested they might not have emerged until 1941, he said that sounded right.

Now, **J. Edward Jones**: When I first asked if he'd known Jones, Pierson said yes, and then immediately, without prompting, echoed seemingly everyone who knew the improvident soldier-maker: "He was a very poor businessman." Pierson wasn't quite sure how he met Jones. It was one of two occasions, about the same period of time. Pierson was a buyer of toys for Woolworth's and Jones had approached him, trying to sell his line of soldiers (both Pierson and Reyff were to some degree absentee owners, each working another job). Pierson did take on the line, and in addition, though he says he's sure American Metal's first molds came from Henry Kasselowski, he did buy some from Jones, whether before or after the Woolworth's encounter. When I suggested they might have been the molds for the three-inch American Metal soldiers, rather than their standard 3-1/4" height, he said, very forcefully, "Yes. That's what they were." This was--another firm statement by Pierson--Jones' only connection to American Metal Toys. However, both Pierson and Reyff did help finance--"not that

much"--Jones' own soldier-making enterprise. Incidentally, Pierson had no memory of Bill Long, who later had a soldier company of nearly the same name as American Metal Toys, nor had he ever heard of soldier makers William Feix, Theodore Hahn or Barclay salesman Irving Reader.

Pierson says he and Reyff stayed with the company until the end, the end being April 1, 1942, when wartime restrictions marked the close of metal toy soldier-making. He then sold the molds to Lincoln Logs. Asked how well he did with the sale, he said only "we came out pretty good." He doesn't think Lincoln Logs used the molds.

How successful was American Metal Toys? Not very. "We kept our heads above water," Pierson said, and then explained that they continued to pour money back into new molds, and molds cost a lot: $75 to $80 each.

Thus, American Metal Toys, though it did get its two owners through the Depression, was hardly a thriving enterprise. But Pierson got luckier with his second, and only other, try at soldier-making. He and John Baumgartner, the owner of Anchor Brush (which made brushes) had met each other at Chicago's Merchandise Mart. About 1948 Pierson persuaded Baumgartner to use the company's down time (and scraps) to make plastic toy soldiers. The new firm that emerged was called Tim Mee, after Timmy, the nephew of Baumgartner's secretary, Cora Kaiser. Pierson had a piece of the business, did the selling, and oversaw Tim Mee, staying with the firm until about 1964, when it was bought by Processed Plastic (Tim Mee is still in business under that name, Stan Reyff providing me with its current address--Aucutt Road, Mongomery, Illinois). At its peak, under Pierson's helm, Tim Mee grossed one million dollars a year.

And who was Tim Mee's moldmaker (though not sculptor)? That's right. Pierson brought in Henry Kasselowski, thus tying him to at least four toy soldier makers: American Metal Toys, Tim Mee, Lincoln Logs--Noveltoy and Jones.

Now to cross our fingers about those catalogs!

Earliest Sighting
of Manoils and Long-Stride Barclays

by Richard O'Brien

Bill O'Brien recently put me in touch with Steve Feile, whose huge collection of Warrens went on sale a year ago. Steve had much to tell me about Warren, and in his generous way then sent me a huge number of photos to look over. They were fascinating, but it was this one that got my old dimestore pulse racing. Luckily, it was taken by a professional photographer, and he dated it on the back: December 30, 1936.

This is the earliest documentation yet for Manoils and long-stride Barclays. The Manoils shown in the photo are the ensign, marching sailor, nurse and sailor signalman. The detail painting on the naval figures suggests they're all hollow base.

As for the long-stride Barclays, shown are the marching with rifle, officer with sword (and chest strap), flagbearer and bugler. Some time ago I'd concluded none of the long strides had reached the market until early in 1937, so this was an eye-opener for me.

Anyone out there who can provide an even earlier date for any of these?

Update on American Metal Toys

Fellow collector Chandler Gardiner, after reading my [American Metal Toys] article (V18,#6:8 and V19,#2:8), wrote and said that about ten years ago, in a small hardware store in Intercourse, Pennsylvania, he bought two toy soldiers that he was told had been salesman's samples. Each had a tag attached. The pieces were the ones I've coded J34 and J39. He Xeroxed the tags. Each was hand-written and dated 3/7/39. Each noted that they were from American Metal Toys, Chicago, Illinois, that they appeared on the 3/1/39 S.S. Kresge check list (one tag says "check sheet"), and that the price was 65 cents a dozen F.O.B. factory. This of course suggests they could have sold anywhere from seven to ten cents apiece. Interestingly, both pieces don't appear in any known catalog listings until 1939, which suggests they were introduced in March, 1939. This was about the time of year companies like Barclay introduced their new lines. Now how about someone tracking down one or more of those Kresge's check list-sheets?

OTS 8-9/95 V19 #4

Another Jones Diorama

by Richard O'Brien

OTS 10-11/95 V19 #5

Turn back the clock! Become a kid again! Stare into this shop window for hours. I have!

Terry Culpepper was one of the earliest researcher-collectors in the hobby. When Dick MacNary and Terry Sells, who have formed "S & M Toys", purchased much of his collection recently, they found this wonderful photograph. All the earthbound wheeled items and presumably the airplanes are Tootsietoys. All of the three-inch-size soldiers are Jones, and probably the few small ones are too.

According to my files, each of the wheeled Tootsies shown here began in 1931. And that's my guess for the date of this diorama, since the soldiers are of the same period.

Starting with the foreground: at left, the marching Jones soldiers that until now had been known only through a single, headless find. Since the latter has bandage-type puttees, one would assume its headgear would be the WWI doughboy's steel helmet. But the angle on each of these marchers makes it hard to be sure. The flagbearers are almost certainly the campaign-cap wearer coded MA42 in *Collecting Toy Soldiers No. 2.* The 1930 Jones Metal-Art catalogue mentions two flags: American and 308th Infantry, so presumably the latter is the dark one behind the Stars and Stripes. Finally, the huge formation in the right foreground is made up of MA23, doughboy in greatcoat standing at attention (also spotted throughout the trenches at rear). Until now some of us probably suspected Jones never cast nearly that many of them!

(continued, next page)

VANDERVOORT HARDWARE CO.

(**Jones**, continued)

In the background at left are the two three-inch Germans: officer with binoculars and standing firing rifle. The doughboys facing them include at least twenty gas-masked bayoneters (also later sold by American Metal Toys), a few of the pointing officer in greatcoat (MA22), and a scattering of grenade throwers (MA21), the most prominent of them facing forward directly over the "AN" in VANDERVOORT. At the extreme right is the mounted doughboy shown some issues back on the cover of OTS. Very near him, in front of the marchers at back, seems to be the smaller horseman shown on page 173 of *Collecting Toy Soldiers No. 2*. Presumably the small marchers at farthest right are the ones also shown on that page.

However, directly beneath the last plane at right (in front of the marchers) are what appear to be small prone machine gunners that don't seem to be the ones on page 173 (the shape of the gun looks different, and seems to have a curved underbrace not shared by Lincoln Logs' gunner). Some as-yet-undiscovered small Jones?

Finally, the three-inch marchers beneath that same plane and at far right: are they the same as the ones shown in the foreground? If so, there's nothing that suggests they're wearing a doughboy's helmet. Is it a cap? Or a German helmet? Or is this an entirely different piece? Perhaps Don Pielin, who's seen all of these close up, can clarify things. And maybe also let us know if VanDervoort Hardware Co. was a Chicago store which I suspect it was.

Everyone who knew him has agreed that J. Edward Jones was a terrible businessman. But as a promoter he gets higher grades. There was his publication *The Prospector*, his art-filled boxes, his various catalogues, and now this, the second all-Jones-soldiers diorama to emerge (the first has been shown in OTS and *Collecting Toy Soldiers No. 2*). Which makes him two up on the far bigger Barclay, Manoil, Grey Iron, and Auburn Rubber.

Editor's Note: Chicago and St. Louis phone directories from the 1930's list no VanDervoort's Hardware Store. We will check further in Chicago suburban directories, but if anyone remembers this store in your area, please let OTS know.

Previous Metal Art articles appeared in OTS, V14, #2:20-25 and V15, #6: 11-13.

The Jones' Kingsart—
American Soldier Company Connection

Richard O'Brien

The Terry Culpepper collection of toy soldiers, toys, pulp fiction magazines, and reference material is huge and S&M Toys, which bought it, is still sifting through everything. Recently they found this letter: a significant one for both American Soldier Co. and J. Edward Jones.

As I've mentioned in the American Soldier Co. article in *Collecting Toy Soldiers No. 2*, Jones' notes state that the firm's founder, Charles W. Beiser, died in 1924 and his successor, William Ferguson, offered to sell the assets of the company in a letter of December 24, 1925. The contents of this letter (reprinted here in reduction) put a new spin on things.

Kingsart, in business by 1925, seems to have been Jones' first toy soldier firm. A one-page order sheet from that year and a later ad suggest he began by selling flats and semi-rounds. However, this letter indicates he was already thinking of competing with Britains by obtaining American Soldier Co.'s molds and its patented display tray. Since Ferguson seems to have been willing to dispose of its entire line of figures, it's not clear why they wanted to retain the tray. Perhaps they used it in their games, which they may have hoped to continue; possibly there would have been problems with Britains, which had obtained rights to use their tray.

The discontinued "little booklet" referred to is most likely the firm's toy soldier catalog, which was mentioned in a 1903 *Playthings* article. Finally, this letter indicates that by December, 1925 American Soldier had moved its New York address from 48 East 21st Street to 215 Fourth Avenue.

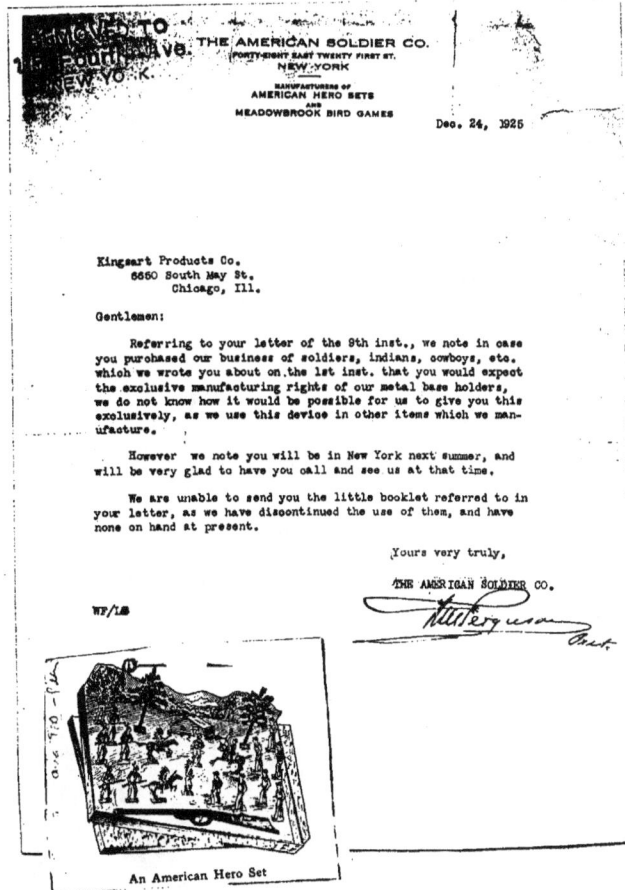

An American Hero Set

The illustration that looks like a part of this letter is actually pinned on, presumably by Jones. It's part of the August, 1930 announcement that Selchow and Righter had purchased rights to American Soldier Co.'s cowboy and Indian sets. Selchow and Righter's restricted pickup illumines why American Soldier may have been anxious to dispose of its line of figures; the military pieces probably drew minimal response from buyers of the postwar period.

OTS 2-3/96 V20 #1

New Dimestore Discoveries

by Richard O'Brien

The major dimestore research seems to be done, but there are still a lot of unanswered questions. Happily, things continue to pop up and here are two of the latest.

Dick MacNary sent me both. He found the "Dafar" ad in the August 1947 *Toys and Novelties* trade magazine, and asked me about it. It was immediately obvious to me this was H.B.'s Toys (and the only known ad for its product). The foot figures even had the same numbering as found in H.B.'s brochure. I called Walter Helm (for those who came in late, "H.B." stands for Helm Brothers), who was one of the firm's two active owners, and he was able to answer my questions. Dafar was simply the name H.B.'s jobber, Al Farber, used for his firm. Helm further said that by the time H.B.'s brochure came out the company had changed the numbering on the mounted figures to a 1500 series to indicate they sold for fifteen cents. The 1001 number on the mounted cowboy in the ad suggests this was the firm's first figure. A small print ad in the same issue by Dafar lists several of the jobber's offerings, including *Metal Cowboy and Indian Toys*, suggesting that H.B.'s military figures had yet to emerge.

The *Suggested Ranch Layout* by Manoil is large-sized, about 16-1/2" by 12", and unfortunately shows no date on either the front or the blank back. What's interesting is the prices, which suggest a late date, and the inclusion of the 3-1/4" Indian and Cowboys with these newer prices. As the copy I've made is a bit unclear, I'll point out the following: the compartment at front left, with a 10 cent price, holds horses. The one next to it, same price, seems to have the cow or bull or both. The mounted cowgirl and cowboy, which come next, show a 30 cent price. Finally comes the cowgirl and cowboy seated on the blanket over fence section, but the price is obscured.

The next row, from left, holds the Indian with knife, the surrendering cowboy and the cowboy shooting up, all 3-1/4" high, and each priced at 15 cents. Finally in that row is the cowboy on what seems to be the feeding cow for a "30 cent Complete" price. The rest is a little hard to figure out, but the M209 and M210 mounted cowboys seem to be in a "15 cent" compartment.

Part of the fun of this, of course, is simply being able to see these figures in the fondly remembered glass compartments from our old five and ten days.

SUGGESTED
RANCH LAYOUT

Illustration No. 1 is suggested window, island or pedestal display.

Illustration No. 2 is suggested merchandising display for Manoil Western Figures. Individual sections are 8 x 8 inches with mirror platform.

Above display occupies 24 x 32 inches comprising 12 – 8 x 8 inch sections.

Pedestal displays shown above and at rear of counter display add realism and greater visibility.

BETTER DISPLAYS MEAN MORE SALES

Made by **MANOIL MANUFACTURING CO. WAVERLY, N. Y.**

187

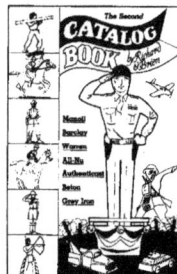

188

Collecting American Made Toy Soldiers, 3rd edition

Richard O'Brien's twenty years of research on toy soldiers is so extensive that it now demands two phonebook size volumes to contain it! OTS readers have shared years of Richard's discoveries which included last year's revelations on the real source of Jones Dimestore figures to be the Chicago firm American Metal Toys. This story and dozens of others are contained in O'Brien's 700 page American Made book. Like his previous editions, this covers U.S. toys from exotic early makers like George Grampp and Theodore Hahn to the giants Auburn, Barclay and Manoil to Marx plastics and on to current new toy soldier makers. There are special sections on vehicles and equipment, foreign Dimestore types, and "unknown companies". This book overflows with several thousand black and white photographs, always rare catalog illustrations and it is centered with ten pages of color. I don't know how any American collector can do without this book. The equal size European companion volume is just out. See Richard's ad on page 37 for ordering details on both books.

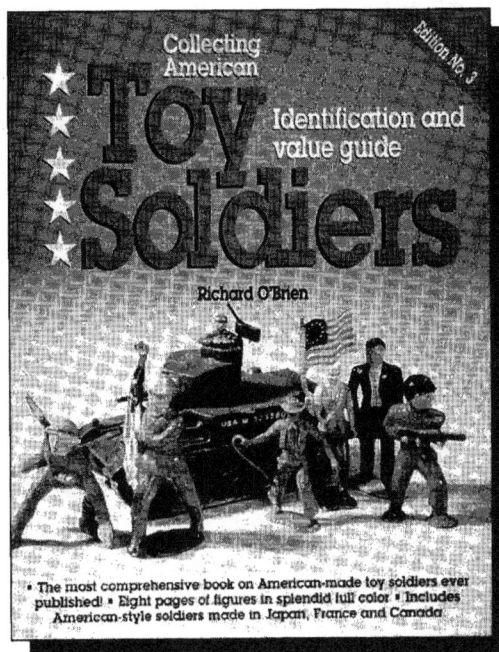

O'Brien, Richard; Collecting American Made Toy Soldiers,
Krause, (3rd Ed.) Iola Wisconsin, 1997, 717 pages, 36 colour and a great number (over 2000) black and white photographs. First two editions were entitled Collecting Toy Soldiers.
The encyclopedia of American manufacturers. This book must illustrate well over 10,000 figures. O'Brien is a prolific author of books on toys. Over eighty company histories are set out, and the text is organized by manufacturer. Catalogue excerpts and contemporary advertising enhance various articles. Current values are given. This is the key reference text for U.S. products, so much so that its figure numbering system used to key photographs and descriptions has become the standard method for referring to the products covered (original manufacturers' numbering is often provided). You simply can't collect American Dimestore without a copy.

O'Brien, Richard; Collecting Foreign-Made Toy Soldiers,
Krause, Iola Wisconsin, 1997, 493 pages, 2,500 photos, over 50 in colour.
This is an extensive listing and price guide for figures manufactured outside the United States that were generally obtainable as toys in the U.S. The book is organized first by country of origin and then by manufacturer. Not surprisingly, British companies take up over half of the book; Britains alone has over 150 pages. In many cases civilian figures are also covered. The listings deal with over 50 manufacturers. This is an essential book at a-not-to-be-beat price. The price guide is good but inevitably not 100% reliable.

OTS Fall '98 V22 N3 (Stewart D. Saxe article excerpted)

—Early Plastic—

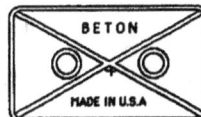

Beton's First Catalog

by Richard O'Brien

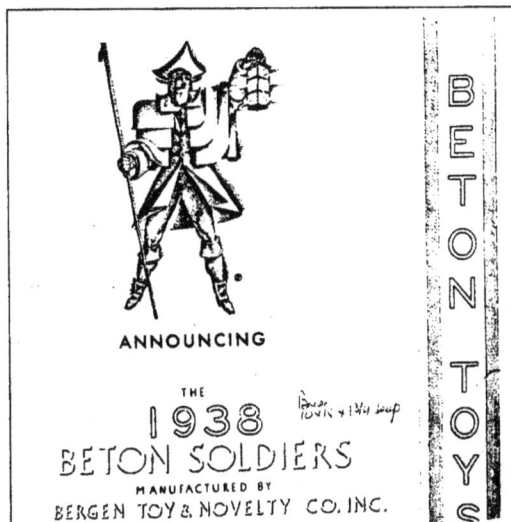

Another find by S&M Toys from the Terry Culpepper collection is this original 1938 Beton catalog, which announces its new line of plastic soldiers. A poor photocopy of this catalog has circulated in the hobby, but probably hasn't been seen by most collectors. The last one of its four pages is blank.

As I've noted in *Collecting Toy Soldiers No.2*, the listing reveals Beton's antecedents, employing the same names for its mounted cowboy and Indian as Metal Cast did: *Big Chief* and *Broncho Bill*.

What I find intriguing in this new look at the catalog is the small circle by the left foot of the figure on the cover. The circle seems to contain an "f". "FF" appears on the bottom flag of one of the Beton signalmen (and presumably on its Universal Plastics predecessor). Was the artist also Beton's (and Universal's) sculptor? The Ferriot brothers designed much of Marx's line and to my eye their work looks similar to Beton's and Universal's. But I've checked and there was no "FF" in their family. They also have no record of doing work for Universal and Beton.

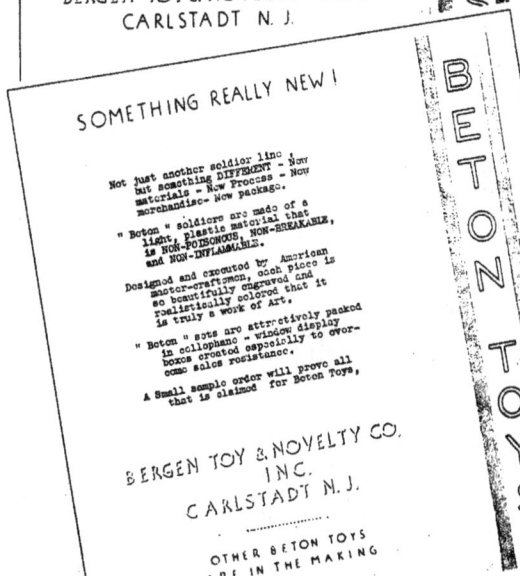

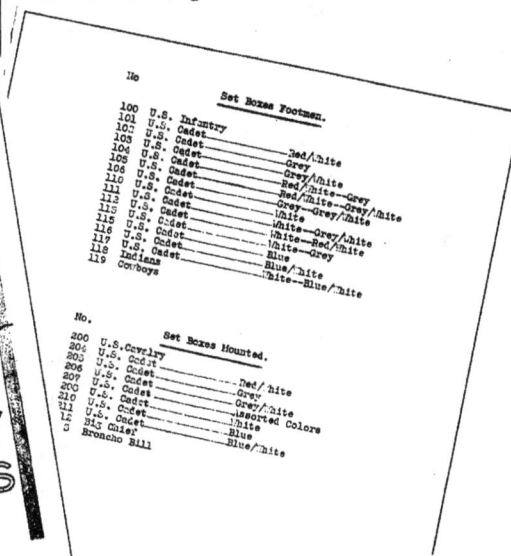

BETON
MADE IN U.S.A

BETON TOYS

ANNOUNCING

THE
1938
BETON SOLDIERS
MANUFACTURED BY
BERGEN TOY & NOVELTY CO. INC.
CARLSTADT N. J.

SOMETHING REALLY NEW !

Not just another soldier line
but something DIFFERENT - New
materials - New Process - New
merchandise- New package.

" Beton " soldiers are made of a
light, plastic material that
is NON-POISONOUS, NON-BREAKABLE,
and NON-INFLAMMABLE.

Designed and executed by American
master-craftsmen, each piece is
so beautifully engraved and
realistically colored that it
is truly a work of Art.

" Beton " sets are attractively packed
in cellophane - window display
boxes created especially to over-
come sales resistance.

A Small sample order will prove all
that is claimed for Beton Toys,

BERGEN TOY & NOVELTY CO.
INC.
CARLSTADT N. J.

OTHER BETON TOYS
ARE IN THE MAKING

No

No.		Set Boxes Footmen.	
100	U.S.	Infantry	
101	U.S.	Cadet	
102	U.S.	Cadet	
103	U.S.	Cadet	
104	U.S.	Cadet	Red/White
105	U.S.	Cadet	Grey
106	U.S.	Cadet	Grey/White
110	U.S.	Cadet	Red/White—Grey
111	U.S.	Cadet	Grey—Grey/White
112	U.S.	Cadet	White
115	U.S.	Cadet	White—Grey/White
116	U.S.	Cadet	White—Red/White
117	U.S.	Cadet	White—Grey
118	Indians		Blue
119	Cowboys		Blue/White
			White—Blue/White

No.		Set Boxes Mounted.	
200	U.S.	Cavalry	
204	U.S.	Cadet	
205	U.S.	Cadet	Red/White
206	U.S.	Cadet	Grey
207	U.S.	Cadet	Grey/White
200	U.S.	Cadet	Assorted Colors
210	U.S.	Cadet	White
211	U.S.	Cadet	Blue
1	Big Chief		Blue/White
3	Broncho Bill		

Book Reviews

Richard O'Brien's

Collecting Foreign-Made Toy Soldiers

Published by Books Americana, now a division of Krause Publications, c1997. Available for $32.95 at bookstores or shipped postpaid directly from Richard O'Brien; 705 Greene Street; Beaufort, SC 29902.

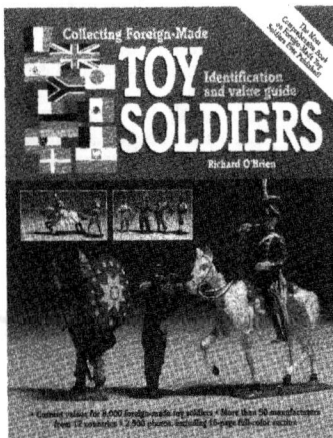

Collecting Foreign-Made Toy Soldiers is the companion volume to Richard O'Brien's recently published American-made book. Previous editions of *Collecting Toy Soldiers* had packed company histories and price guide lists into a single volume, but fortunately Richard was able to talk his publisher into splitting the coverage, thus literally doubling the size to a now two part reference series.

Collecting Foreign-Made Toy Soldiers is first an outstanding book because of its scope and the consistently high quality of its 2500 plus black and white photographs, but also because of the generous support of two dozen fellow collectors who contributed the research, writing and photographs which made this book possible. Richard O'Brien is, of course, the power behind the project, but in the Preface he graciously acknowledges that more than anyone, K. Warren Mitchell deserves the major credit for the book. Several other collectors familiar to OTS readers contributed sections of the book as well: Bob Hornung, Joe Saine, Jack Matthews, James Theobald, Steve Balkin, Lou Sandbote, Vadis Godbey, Lenoir Josey, and Will Beierwaltes. But the major project credit is Warren's.

Besides writing some sections himself, Warren enlisted fellow collectors to write others and also supplied the majority of photos. I talked with Warren about the finished product and quite frankly he said that it exceeded his expectations: both b/w and color photo quality is better than the American book and the final printing is more than a hundred pages longer (495) than his initial hope.

The book is arranged by country with each maker's section starting with a thumb-nail company history. Countries include England, France, Germany and Austria, Poland, Belgium, Italy, Denmark, South Africa, Japan, Mexico, Spain, and Argentina. For example, there are sixteen British makers listed; Denmark and South Africa have only one each, Krolyn and SAE respectively. Each entry has a head note after the brand name listing country, material, and size; this is a real boon to the novice and for most of us at least some of these companies will be new. The goal of the book was to be a useful guide to the average collector. As a result companies included were those with a broad U.S. distribution of factory painted figures. Figures listed are graded and priced with restraint.

So this is not a comprehensive survey of world makers and despite very extensive lists of Britains, Johillco, and Mignot, for example, it shows only a sample of the ranges of some major makers like French Starlux or German Elastolin. Realistically anything more would probably have been impossible. This is a monumental task well done and Richard O'Brien is already planning for an even more comprehensive edition in a couple of years. But don't wait! This is plenty good right now.

Mexican Asturias

by Richard O'Brien

About the time I began working on <u>Collecting Foreign-Made Toy Soldiers</u>, Jack Matthews sent me a couple of full-page ads from 1946 and 1947 toy trade magazines. One firm, Skinfill, had won first prize at a Mexico City fair, so it seemed likely its soldiers were made in Mexico. A weaker candidate for Mexican origin was a firm called Asturias since its address was San Francisco. But Garratt's <u>Encyclopedia</u> mentions a firm of that name, saying simply: "Mexico. In 1978 Wade had a model of a parachutist, the parachute itself of cloth with wire strings." Not much to go on, but I decided to put it, along with Skinfill, as tentative additions into the "Mexico" portion of my book.

About six months after the book came out, I heard from Jean Hathaway. Jean wrote, "In the Mexican section you have an advertisement for Asturias soldiers saying nothing else is known of this company. I bought a 12 piece boxed set of Asturias in Fullerton, California in 1950 while I was attending Fullerton Junior College for about $3.50." The end labels reads: IT'S ASTURIAS FOR SOLDIERS! AMERICAN Set No. '2' Model No. 200 ARMY. The box, Jean wrote, is 14-3/8" long by 8-1/4" wide by 1-1/8" deep. The box top label reproduced in reduction here clearly says MADE IN MEXICO in English and Spanish. The box has a red tie card which is riveted by four nickel-plated rivets. Some of the soldiers have a 5x10mm paper label glued to the bottoms of their bases which reads: MADE IN

MEXICO FOR ASTURIAS. The balance have MADE IN MEXICO FOR ASTURIAS cast into the base. Eleven of the 12 figures are in a running left knee raised pose (probably two slightly different castings); another casting, the officer(?), is walking with a drawn raised sword. Running figures are differentiated by their moveable arms: bugle, rifle slung, rifle trail, rifle bayonet, sword, and what may be a short sword.

Asturias is a province in Spain. Thus there may be some kind of Spanish connection as well. But though Asturias was based in the U.S. and may have had ties to Spain as well, there's no doubt now where these figures were actually made. Thanks, Jean! Now, anyone out there have a Skinfill or two?

THE MCCANDLISH DIARIES

By Richard O'Brien

I've long been curious about the people who designed and sculpted the dimestore toy soldiers I've loved all my life. Dimestore figures had long been ridiculed by collectors of other types of soldiers for their lack of artistry. Perhaps the carping was true, but there is no question that sculptors Frank Krupp (Barclay and All-Nu) and Olive Kooken (Barclay-Tommy Toy) had considerable training as artists, and there is a strong likelihood that Manoil's Walter Baetz had a similar artistic background, since he's known to have spent much time painting, drawing, and selling his work.

The fourth major designer of dimestore soldiers was Edward McCandlish. Till recently, all that was known of him was that in 1936 Auburn Rubber advertised him as its toy designer. I'd also come across a reference to an Edward McCandlish who'd had a syndicated comic strip. It seemed likely it was the same person, but that was as far as I could take it. McCandlish, wished I could take it. For years I wondered about McCandlish, wished I could find out more about him. But after all this time, it seemed unlikely I'd learn anything further.

Then this past spring (1996) I received a call from toy collector Dave Leopard. He was aware of my interest in Auburn, as many years before, in answer to an ad of his, I'd sent him all I knew about the company. In 1994, Dave self published a book, "Rubber Toy Vehicles." The reason for his call was that he'd recently heard from a woman

A really unlikely find: a photograph of the clay model of the Ethiopian Private! Sculpted by McCandlish from his design, this is the only known photo of any of his models.

who'd come across his book. Her name was Hope McCandlish Rider. She was one of the daughters of Edward McCandlish! Furthermore, she'd sent Dave a Xerox of the 1936 Auburn catalog showing her father's work!!

For me, it was like Christmas. For years I'd also wished, without any hope, that a 1936 Auburn catalog would turn up. It was the only one likely to

*Edward G. McCandlish 1887-1946
Artist, Cartoonist, Author, Illustrator and Sculptor. Toy Designer*

contain Auburn's Ethiopians, and I'd long been curious about how many the firm had produced. In the 1970s a former employee had mentioned to me that there'd been an Ethiopian with a spear, which has never turned up. But since two of the three known Ethiopians seem to be one of a kind, it didn't appear unlikely there were others out there. I begged Dave to send me a copy overnight, which he did. He also enclosed the names and addresses of three of McCandlish's daughters - Hope, Margaret McCandlish Edwards and Phoebe McCandlish Klaes.

The next day I found there are two Ethiopians in the catalog, and there's no indication any others were designed (the third known one is the doughboy bugler, with brown skin). Meanwhile, I quickly called all three women, and almost as quickly material began coming my way; color copies of the 1936 catalog, newspaper articles on McCandlish, letters from Auburn Rubber to McCandlish, photos, etc. And, miraculously, the highly-talented McCandlish had a feeling for posterity. He had kept diaries, and perhaps even more miraculously, noted much of his work for Auburn in them.

McCandlish was a man of many accomplishments; staff artist for such newspapers as the Washington Post, writer-artist of at least one syndicated comic strip, "Folk Tales," writer and illustrator of fourteen books, and designer of hundreds of toys manufactured in Germany, Japan and at least seven U.S. cities.

Margaret Edwards painstakingly went over the diaries and sent me notes of everything that pertained to Auburn. McCandlish, who studied art at Maryland University, the Penn Academy of Fine Arts (three years) and the Philadelphia Institute of Art (one year) told his children that most artists aren't recognized till fifty years after their death. Thus, it's significant that exactly fifty years after he died, McCandlish's book art has just been made a part of the Mazza Center For the Arts collection at the University of Findlay, Ohio, his drawings just been donated to the National Gallery of Caricature and Cartoon Art in Washington, D.C, that a number of pages were devoted to him in my book "Collecting Toy Soldiers No. 3," and that, for the first time, once this issue is published, notes from his diary will be accessible to collectors.

A quick background: As is indicated by the illustrated letter, Auburn had approached Kresge's toy buyer, a Mr. Jillson, with a line of toys designed by a high school girl. Her work was obviously not good enough. McCandlish had already designed a number of toys for Kresge's, and thus Jillson, who'd become a friend, recommended him to Auburn. As will be seen, A.L. Murray wasn't a easy man to deal with. He continually change his mind, (at that time an Auburn vice president, and later its owner) so that often toys had to be redesigned, often more than once, or even scrapped. Murray, presumably for monetary reasons, also seems to have played McCandlish against the diemakers, the Ferriot Brothers, so that at times, but not always, it was the Ferriots who took over the sculpting. (The Ferriots, incidentally, later did much of the sculpting as well as diemaking for Marx's toy soldier playsets.)

And now, with much thanks to Margaret McCandlish Edwards, notes from the diaries.

1934

11/1: McCandlish contacted by Lee Shimer, recommended by Jillson.
11/9: Off to Auburn: Three sets wanted; Farm, Soldiers, Train.
11/30: Modeled "soldier" after putting aside animals.
12/1: Finished it, nearly finished "officer figure."

1935

1/1: Molds for Toyland Soldiers to Auburn.
1/13: Worked all day on colt.
1/14: Letter changes size of soldiers to 5".
1/15: In Auburn, Murray, McCandlish decide to let Jillson establish size.
2/8: Colored 3 sample Toyland Soldiers and "sent back."
3/15: Modeled 4 1/4" modern soldier. M. offered $10 a day for "extra" work.
3/17: Finished second soldier.
3/18: Modeled farm horse, sketched soldiers.
3/19: Finished farm horse, modeled calf, blocked in cow.
3/20: Modeled English soldier 2-3/4" high, nearly finished cow.
3/21: Modeled & finished 3" English soldier (private) Finished cow. 3" English officer begun and nearly finished.
3/2?: Murray decides to make all figures 1/2" to foot. Animals OK "by chance."
3/22: Finished English officer and nearly finished khaki bugler started today.
3/23: Modeled Khaki Private at the "Ready," began & finished calf; made skeleton for a sheep. Finished khaki bugler.

3/24: Modeled second calf, began sheep.
3/26: Went to Akron Die Makers Ferriot Brothers, today, 9 figures. (O'BRIEN: must have been four soldiers, sheep, calf, horse, colt, cow.)
8/35: Murray says he wants an Ethiopians-Italians set. (O'BRIEN: No Italians were modeled, and no Ethiopians till months later, However, it's possible doughboys painted as Ethiopians and Italians ((yellow helmets)) were sold.)
11/25: Designed Circus Set.
11/27: Modeled "Ethiopian with shield and rifle at trail."
11/28: "Designed" Machine Gunner, officer on horseback (for 3rd time), Sambo, Tiger, collie and bulldog.
11/29: Finished Ethiopian in clay. Turned in 15 sketches drawn this week.
12/2: Started Circus Pony about noon, almost finished.
12/3: Finished pony, modeled circus clown, blocked in elephant.
12/5: Fly Swatter.
12/14: Took nine figures to Ferriots in Akron - circus clown, pony, elephant, circus poodle, Little Black Sambo, Tiger, Ethiopian leader, Ethiopian private, officer on horseback.

1936

1/8: Ethiopian remodeled, had been wrecked in transit (?) from Akron. Sent to Ferriot.
1/9: Finished collie for Auburn, and sent it to Auburn.
1/13: Modeled Easter rabbit, sent to Auburn.
1/16: Finished kitten, sent to Auburn.
1/17: Started machine gunner for Auburn, nearly finished.
1/23: Worked on correcting kitten model.
1/24: Sent drawings of dogs to Murray, designed a farm boy.
1/29: Rec'd $60 royalty advance for Ethiopian and 2 machine gunners.
2/7: Painted 2 tigers and sent to Auburn, also larger tigers cast in zinc.
2/11: Painted 3 collies for Auburn today.
2/17: Sent collie samples to Auburn.
3/2: Designed box for Circus set (2 sketches).
3/11: Rec'd 3 machine gunners to color.
3/25: Auburn requested drawings for a G-man, traffic cop and policeman. sent 3/26.
4/20: Painted 3 collies and sent to Auburn.
4/26-5/1: Worked at Auburn. $40.
4/28: Laid out a catalog in rough for Murray.
5/6: Finished catalog at Auburn.
5/7: Made final (3rd) Scotty sketch and began modeling large Scotty. Using new plan for modeling, wood cut-outs pinned with dowels.
5/9: Finished large & small Scottie pull toys in clay and gave them to Foley for casting. Murray ordered clay models of 2 frogs for artificial fish bait, will pay only $10 for two.
5/14: Carved a horse in wood for Auburn.
5/16: Wire to Murray re frogs: "Unable to sidetrack other work for less than fifty."
5/27 Sketches for Auburn: Jackies 3-3/4" & 4 1/4" high,

cadets 3-3/4" & 4 1/4" high.

6/25: Began modeling 10¢ size cadet.

6/26: Worked on cadet & Jackie (O'BRIEN: No one knows what a "Jackie" was.)

8/20: Designed hen & chicks for Auburn.

8/28: Murray "wants me to model (new toys) in 'Plasteline'."

9/13: Made wood models for six Auburn Easter toys: rabbit in egg, chick-in-egg, another chick in egg; gosling in egg; hen for pull-train, chick for pull-train.

9/23: Working at Auburn, finished equestrienne, started soldier charging with automatic rifle.

9/25: Worked on soldier with automatic rifle. Woolworth & Kresge originally turned down Clatter Ducks & Hop Bunnies but now find they do sell.

9/29: At Auburn finished (1) soldier throwing grenade (2) soldier signaling (3) soldier charging (4) equestrienne.

10/16: Remodeled Rabbit in egg, chick in egg, hen for train, chick for train. Auburn is working 24 hrs per day on toy orders, unable to fill orders. Sold $22,000 of my toys in Sept.

11/28: Considered remodeling toys in plastic wood.

11/29: Modeled a goat, buffalo & bear (no mention of medium used).

12/8: Made 2 plastic wood models but Murray insisted on clay. Almost finished one Infantry soldier.

12/10: Remodeled 3 soldiers in larger size (1) bomb thrower (2) rifleman (3) signal man.

12/14: At Auburn, made sketches of (1) pitcher (2) catcher (3) infielder (4) outfielder (5) base runner (6) batter. Drawings of (A) China girl (B) Eskimo Baby (C) Dutch girl. Worked on clay models of the new Bomber, charging soldier, bugler, signal man & infantry man.

1937

1/16: Began clay model of a reindeer.

1/18: Finished reindeer. Letters to and from Murray discussing terms for fish bait modeling work.

1/20: Began model of a small-sized draft horse with harness.

1/21: Finished draft horse.

1/22: Began to model an elephant.

2/12: Finished clay model of a charging infantryman.

3/29: At Auburn. Designed for Murray: 3 duck "bathing wings"; 3 scotties on a tricycle; frog bathing wings not ordered; fish bathing rings not ordered; 77mm gun designed for Ferriot to model.

3/30: At Auburn. Murray asked me to "put on my thinking cap for new items:. I immediately suggested a pig doll - calf doll - rabbit doll - puppy doll and kitten doll. Made drawings. Murray liked the five drawings, said he would make one up and try them out. I told him they should be dressed in regular doll dresses.

3/31: Began modeling 2 pig dolls, one 10¢ size 4 1/2" high, 20¢ size 6 1/2" high.

4/1: Finished two pig dolls in clay.

5/8: Letter from Murray asking me to model 3 baseball players in wax. I replied, promising the figures next week in clay.

5/19: Started modeling 3 ball players for Auburn, got them blocked in.

5/20: Continued work on ball players.

5/22: Finished 3rd Auburn ball player.

5/25: Made plaster mold of baseball catcher.

5/26: Worked on casting 3 baseball players.

6/1: Wired Murray "Work finished last week clay, plaster molds & wax awaiting instructions."

6/4: Delivered pitcher, catcher & batter to Auburn.

6/5: Gave Murray the idea for step-in galoshes for kids.

6/12: Worked all day on Pig doll for Auburn.

6/13: Cast the pig & spoiled because of interruption when pouring plaster.

6/19, 6/21: Worked on Quickie Boot models.

6/24: Finished plaster model of the Piggie doll & also the step-in Quickie.

6/25: Mailed doll & boot to Murray.

7/16: Letter from Murray saying "better let Ferriot do the modeling on the toys."

8/14: Made plaster molds of small farm horse w/harness, reindeer (3-piece) started & nearly finished a cow (NOT for Auburn) (Note: This work was done on spec, hoping to cast toys as samples to sell directly to retailers).

8/15: Trying to find a way to prevent Plastic Wood from sticking to molds (unsuccessful).

8/16: Finished modeling cow for farm set.

8/28: Designed 3 flyswatters for Auburn: Indian, Peacock and Charlie McCarthy.

9/4: Order from Murray for 3 fly swatters @ $10. "Expect soon to be America's Greatest Fly-Swatter Designer!" Auburn sales for three years from 30 designs I have made were $200,000.

9/5: Finished modeling fly swatters today & packed them in a special box.

9/20: At Auburn. Made designs, drawings, in color of: 1-soldier lying down; 2-soldier crawling; 3-officer in dress uniform; 4-officer in overseas cap; 5-charging soldier wearing gas mask; 6-Indian; 7-cowboy; 8-soldier telephoning; 9-soldier with carrier pigeon; 10-Red Cross Doctor.

9/21: Today made color drawings of: 1-Drummer (my idea in suggestion); 2-Flag bearer; 3-Soldier in a pup tent; 4-Soldier firing anti-aircraft gun; 5-Two soldiers lying behind machine gun-firing; 6-Soldier with police dog; 7-West Point cadet (better than previous drawing); 8-Jackie - also better than previous drawing.

9/22: Spent the day redrawing various soldier items that Murray wanted redrawn.

9/23: Further redrawings of soldiers. Murray wanted corrections in modeling of fly-swatters. Finished models of swatters in clay.

9/24: Murray wanted another fly swatter of his own design, a lily.

10/4: Wrote to Murray & advised trying Ferriot out with

one or two soldiers first before ordering all models.

10/6: Wrote asking Murray for permission to submit animal character dolls to firms making rubber dolls, since he has had them a long time now & failed to produce.

10/7: Murray asked me not to submit animal character dolls to other mfr. as he planned to add dolls to his line soon.

11/27: Began soap dish designs for Murray, Peacock & shell.

1938

1/3: Reference to Bunny Tot doll, made in Germany, had arms made in Japan: "I had designed both the Bunny Tot doll & the Japanese doll (made in Japan) & the arms were interchangeable. I didn't model the B.T. doll."

April - Worked on soldier sets but for Van Wert (Ohio) investor group, to be cast in a composition (we) are yet trying to develop.

5/22: Murray wants some sand toy rubber items.

June - Working on bandmen sets for Van Wert mfr. and finished a total of 40 soldier items.

7/28: Murray ordered some advertising drawing for Sanit Soles.

7/29: Made 4 pencil sketches for cartoon advertising for Sanit Soles.

8/16: Sent total of 8 cartoons to Murray.

8/27: Another cartoon for soles.

Oct. Designed & modeled a religious set to be cast in composition.

1939

3/1: Made pencil sketch of 3 monkeys for Murray.

3/3: Murray requires re-drawing of monkey ring-toss game. Re-drew in pencil & sent to Auburn.

3/7: Murray wants drawing of large monkey, made it & sent it.

3/20: In Auburn today. Made drawings of a Hula Girl, standing monkey, Galloping Cowboy, Cowboy on Rearing horse.

3/22: Nearly finished (modeling) a Hula Girl dancing.

3/23: Finished Hula Girl, almost finished the mounted cowboy.

3/24: Finished the monkey, cowboy & hula girl.

5/17: Auburn asked for sketches of 2 small dolls (to be solid rubber) 3 1/4" high. Made 6 groups of 2 dolls each.

5/20: Order from Auburn to model 2 dolls.

5/23: Started group #2 in clay for Auburn (boy & girl).

5/25: Boy & girl dolls for Auburn nearly finished.

6/1: Auburn returned the dolls, damaged.

6/2: Returned reconditioned dolls to Auburn.

6/15: Auburn asked for sketches of football players. Sent them about 15.

6/17: Letter from Auburn saying they were returning Mounted Cowboy (purpose is to make a mold & cast it in type metal).

7/1: Auburn asks me to decorate some pigs.

7/8: "Decorated 6 pigs for Auburn modeled (badly) by someone else."

7/18: Cast the galloping Cowboy.

NO FURTHER MENTION OF WORK FOR AUBURN IN 1939.

1940

2/7: Auburn wants models of 10 vegetables. Quoted $10 each for modeling them.

3/19: Received order from Auburn for 4 sketches.

3/21: Went to Auburn to work 2 days.

3/22: Saw Murray. Made about 6 sketches of the Elephant & donkeys. "Murray went with me to Foley's & I started carving the elephant out of poplar - got it about half done today & the pattern-makers (wood-workers all) were complimentary about the result."

3/23: Finished carving the Elephant in wood in Foley's shop, 1/2 day.

3/24: Carved the donkey today at home - Decorated the Elephant.

3/25: Sanded the donkey & decorated it. Touched up the elephant & decorated it & delivered both toys to Auburn by noon. Murray ordered 6 more drawings - These to be re-drawings of the kitten, puppy, pig & other animal character dolls which I designed for him 2 or 3 years ago.

3/28: Began & finished 7 drawings for Auburn, designs for hollow rubber items - "Andy," "Boys," etc.

5/8: Letter from Murray - Auburn admitting that they did have some chickens, ducks, etc. modeled by the Italian lad at Auburn.

11/22: Check today from Auburn. It was the biggest month since we started, over $25,000 (O'BRIEN: For which he probably got $250, minus his advances).

11/25: Arrived at Auburn early as requested, but no one in town to give orders. Was asked to return Wed. afternoon.

11/27: In Auburn early afternoon. Began an infantryman marching in the "carry arms" position.

11/28: Continued work on the marching soldier, blocked in the rifleman.

11/29: Finished the soldier firing automatic rifle. Started a new machine gunner.

11/30: Finished the machine-gunner.

1941: There were no more diary entries in 1940, and none at all in 1941. However, Auburn continued to send royalties, and $50 a month to keep McCandlish exclusive to them, either from all toy companies, or just rubber toy companies; it's not clear.

1942: In April, McCandlish received a letter from Auburn asking for a meeting. They wanted cardboard or wood items to substitute for rubber. McCandlish made drawings, and later worked on, "Smiling Sam," "Uncle Sam," "Toy Soldier," "Santa Claus," all six inches high, and a 10-inch "Uncle Sam." They were all walking toys. There was also a pony pull toy. Later the same month McCandlish worked on a wooden roller-skate and a Circus Parade. There is no indication of whether or not the toys were produced, but the likelihood is they weren't. The monthly $50 checks continued, and he was paid $80 for all the above work.

In 1943, there was mention only of a January check

and return of the toy designs made in 1942. There was no mention of Auburn at all in 1944. In June of 1945 McCandlish wrote Auburn Rubber. He received a quick reply, saying Auburn would visit him to look over his "lines." He replied a couple of days later, received one more letter in early July from Auburn, and that was it. In 1946 there were no references to Auburn. On December 6th of that year McCandlish died very suddenly on his way to an appointment with the toy and game company Milton Bradley.

AUBURN RUBBER CORPORATION

CEMENT APPLIED SOLES
CEMENT APPLIED HEELS
U-FIX-ET CEMENTS
NAIL ON TAPS
SPORT SOLES AND HEELS

QUALITY

RUBBER KNEELING PADS
RUBBER FLY SWATTERS
RUBBER JAR-OPENERS
RUBBER DOOR MATS
RUBBER TOYS

FACTORY AND GENERAL OFFICES

AUBURN, INDIANA

May 20, 1939.

Mr. Edw. McCandlish,
Van Wert, Ohio.

Dear Mr. McCandlish:

The following is an accounting on your royalty items for April, 1939:

Soldiers	890.84
#232 Soldier On Horse	86.85
#240 Motorcycle Soldiers	77.02
#242 Anti Aircraft Gun	116.94
Baseball Players	1,911.92
Small Animals	139.91
Large Animals	116.62
#4046 Animal Asst.	49.93
#1028 " "	16.38
#112 Chicken	4.60
Scotty Dog	1.59
Small Boxed Sets	4.00
Large " "	8.70
	3,425.30

$3,425.30 @ 1% royalty $34.25

40% check herewith ---- $13.70
60% credit to Adv. ---- 20.55
34.25

In regard to back royalties on which you should have had the above proportionate settlement -- this from actual records checks up as per the attached itemized accounting. The total is $18,344.45 and this would call for:

$18,344.45 ---- @ 1% ----- $183.45

40% check herewith ---- $73.38
60% to advances ------- 110.07
183.45

This, we believe, brings the entire royalty accounting to date and the above back items will be included in future accountings.

EAK/1

Yours very truly,
AUBURN RUBBER CORP. By: E. A. Kalbe Sec'y. to Mr. Murr

ALL ORDERS, CONTRACTS, OR AGREEMENTS ARE TAKEN SUBJECT TO DELAYS CAUSED BY STRIKES, FIRES, ACCIDENTS, OR OTHER CONDITIONS BEYOND OUR CONTROL. ALL QUOTATIONS ARE MADE BY US SUBJECT TO CHANGE WITHOUT NOTICE.
ORIGINATORS AND LARGEST MANUFACTURERS OF CEMENT APPLIED SOLES (AUBURN PATENTS 1,577,349 AND 1,624,300)

What at first seems an impressive royalty statement. But, like many others, McCandlish, who had done well in the 1920s, struggled during the Depression, even to working for the WPA. He had started off with a two percent royalty, but about 1937 or 1938, needing a large advance from Murray, he got it; but with his royalty rate cut in half as a result.

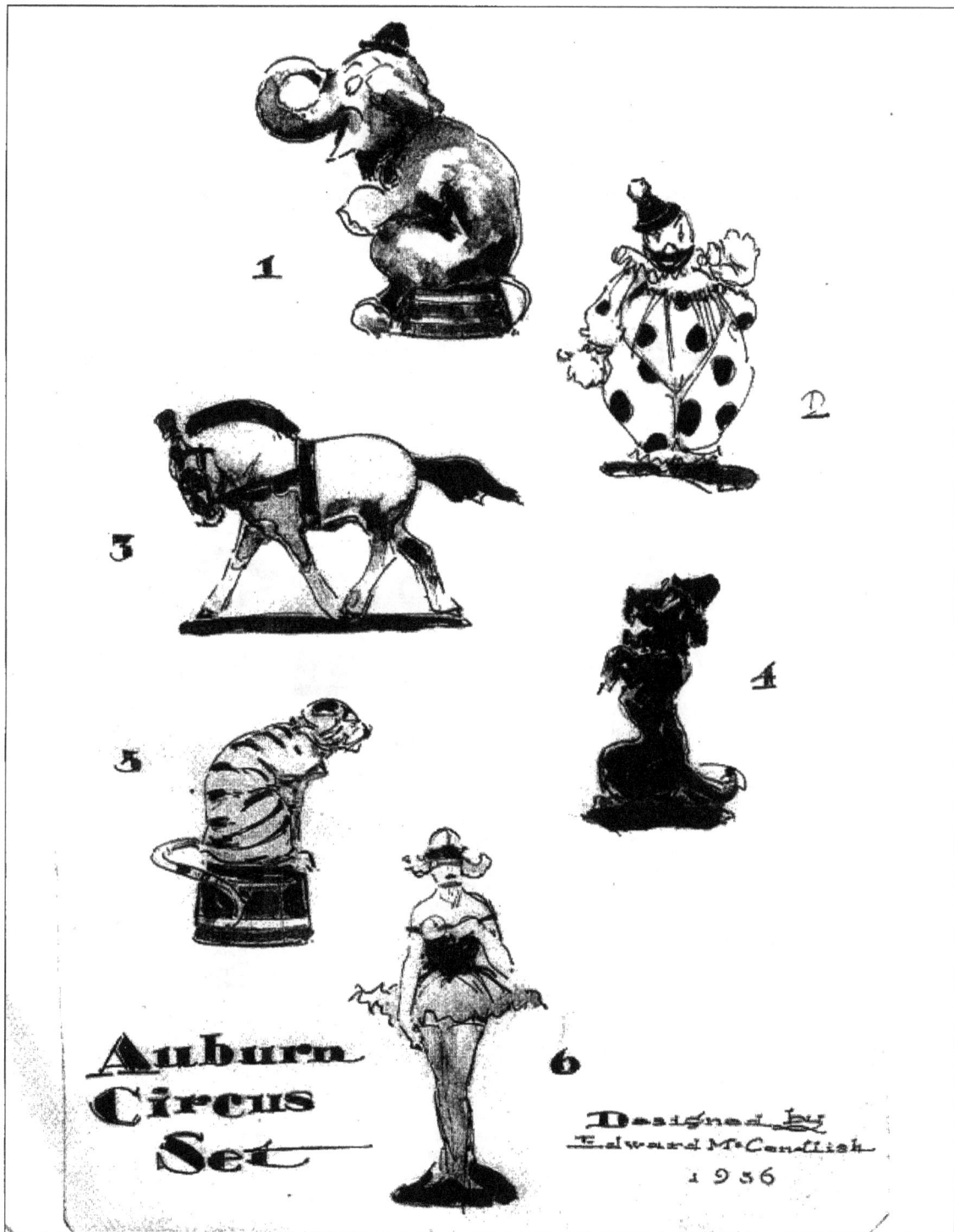

1

2

3

4

5

Auburn
Circus
Set

6

Designed by
Edward McCandlish
1936

Dated 1936, it's likely this page was drawn by McCandlish in November, 1935. Though he later sculpted the equestrienne, she seems to have gone unproduced.

Large Size SOLDIER SET — 4 color box 16 x 9".

No. 203 — U. S. Infantry: 12 Privates, 2 Buglers.
No. 213 — U. S. Marines: 12 Privates, 2 Buglers.
No. 233 — Assorted Foreign Soldiers: 7 Legion, 7 White Guard.
No. 231 — (illustrated above) U. S. Officer on Horse, Machine
Gunner, Bugler and 10 Privates.

Large Size FARM SET — 4 color box 16 x 9".

No. 105 (Illustrated above) 1 four-panel fence with gate, 1
horse, 1 colt, 1 cow, 2 calves, 1 collie, 4 sheep.

Medium Size SOLDIER SET — 4 color box 16 x 4½".

No. 201 U. S. Infantry: 6 Privates, 1 Bugler.
No. 205 U. S. Marines: 6 Privates, 1 Bugler.
No. 209 Foreign Legion: 6 Privates, 1 Officer.
No. 211 Ethiopians: 6 Privates, 1 Chief.

Medium Size FARM SET — 4 color box 16 x 4½".

No. 101 (as illustrated) 1 horse, 1 colt, 1 cow, 1 calf, 2 sheep.

No. 403 Boxed CIRCUS SET (Box not illustrated)

1 Circus Ring, 3 Circus Ponies, 2 Elephants, 1 Clown, 1 Poodle, as
shown on page 5, in large 17 x 12" attractive 4-color box.

No. 311—Three kittens in gray with
red, blue and yellow dresses
and contrasting bows, in cellophane faced 4 x 6" box.

No. 313—Black Sambo and yellow
Tiger, in cellophane faced
4 x 6" box.

No. 315—Baby's Pink circus elephant, and light Blue Scotty, in
cellophane faced 4 x 6" box.

1936 Catalog Page.
Note the Listing for boxed set No. 211, "Ethiopians". No. 207 is missing; this could have been the number for an Italians-Ethiopians set sold around
September-December 1935, with the Auburn doughboys painted with brown skin for Ethiopians, and the Italians with yellow helmets and white or yellow
uniforms, as some of these types have been found. However, this is just speculation on my part.

Designs
by
Edward McCandlish

(Soldiers Continued)

No. 224 Royal Guard Officer: Dark blue — red and yellow.

No. 222 Royal Guard Trooper: Dark blue — red and black.

No. 228 Ethiopian Chief: Black — red and white.

No. 226 Ethiopian Private: Black — red and white.

No. 232 Soldier on Horse: Brown — red and yellow.

No. 216 Foreign Legion Officer: White — red and yellow. (Same as 220)

No. 214 Foreign Legion Trooper: Red — black and blue.

No. 220 White Guard Officer: White — red and yellow. (Same as 232)

No. 218 White Guard Trooper: White — red and black.

No. 230 Machine Gunner: Khaki — yellow and black.

CUTS ARE ACTUAL SIZE

No. 202 U. S. Infantry Bugler: Khaki — red and yellow.

No. 200 U. S. Infantry Private: Khaki — red and black.

No. 212 U. S. Marine Bugler: Light blue — black and yellow.

No. 210 U. S. Marine Private: Light blue — black.

This 1936 page was drawn by Edward McCandlish, who also designed and sculpted these soldiers.

AUBURN RUBBER CORPORATION

AUBURN
DELUXE
RUBBER PRODUCTS

CEMENT APPLIED SOLES
CEMENT APPLIED HEELS
U FIX-ET CEMENTS
NAIL-ON TAPS
SPORT SOLES AND HEELS

RUBBER KNEELING PADS
RUBBER FLY SWATTERS
RUBBER SOAP DISHES
RUBBER JAR OPENERS
RUBBER DOOR MATS

FACTORY AND GENERAL OFFICES
AUBURN, INDIANA

October 31, 1934.

Mr. Edward McClandish,
Plymouth, Michigan.

Dear Mr. McClandish:

The writer recently called at the S. S. Kresge
Company General Offices at Detroit, with a line of rubber molded
toys. At their suggestion and high recommendation, I am writing
to you as having experience in modeling toy animals, etc. I am
wondering if you would be willing to work with us on a proposition
we have in mind of making up a farm set of rubber toys.

If you are interested, we will be glad to stand
the expense of a trip by you to Auburn to go over the matter. I
believe by making a personal call at the factory, we can better
discuss the matter and, of course, no doubt we can work out a satisfactory plan of having you model these items for us.

If you can arrange to come to Auburn, please write
us when you will be here so that our General Manager will be at the
office to go over the entire proposition with you.

Yours very truly,

AUBURN RUBBER CORP.
By:

Asst. Sales Mgr.

LAShimer/E

*Lost in the shuffle as TSR got back into action is this letter that Richard O'Brien referred to in his article (Issue 43)
on Auburn sculptor Edward McCandlish's diary entries. Remarkably, McCandlish saved this letter, which tells us the
story of how his association with Auburn actually began. As can be seen , at the time the folks at Auburn had yet to
learn how to spell his name.*

TSR #44 1999

DIMESTORE BREAKFAST AT OTS 1999 SHOW

From left to right, Mr. & Mrs. Donald Hovde and Mr. & Mrs. Richard O'Brien

O n Saturday, the day before last September's Old Toy Soldier show in Schaumburg, Illinois, approximately 50 of the top Dimestore enthusiasts assembled for a breakfast buffet hosted by American Dimestore Collector, Don Hovde, in honor of Richard O'Brien's many contributions to the hobby.

TSR 2000

Update

Dimestore Plastic
(and a bit of Toy Creations too)

by Richard O'Brien

Okay, disbelievers, I'm still searching for that running Auburn "pilot" looking up and to his left that only I and **Gene Parker** seem to have seen. But meanwhile, other previously unknown pieces do continue to turn up.

When I wrote about Universal Plastics, I suggested that it might also have made some civilians. The reason was that, like the Beton soldiers, which, because of Beton's obtaining the Universal molds, duplicate poses (two signalmen, for instance), some of Beton's civilians also fall into that category: two cops, two women and two men who are very much alike. **Ron Steiner**, an avid Beton (and now Universal) collector, has been keeping an eye out ever since. Recently, courtesy of the Internet, he's found what may be the first of several: a traffic officer. Like most of the Universals, it's unpainted and with very sharp details. Then, a few weeks later, Ron found yet another Universal that we'd had reason to believe preceded its appearance in the Beton lineup. This is the cowboy that Beton numbered 833. Thus, it seems even more likely that Universal could have originally produced at least a couple of the civilians later marketed by Beton. So come on, everyone; keep an eye out. Check for a rectangular base with a "UP" under it. Generally, Universals come unpainted, and have equally sharp details. But at the most recent Chicago show, I found a drummer with blurred features (Ron's drummer is cleanly detailed) and a kneeling machine gunner with paint on its face, weapon, and one hand which suggests either that Universal did paint some of its soldiers or that Beton put out a few of the soft-cap soldiers before chasing in helmets. (To my eye, the paint looks like what Beton used.) Please also keep a look-out for the cowboy, hand on holster that Beton numbered 833; because of the numbering, I suspect it, too, originated with Universal.

Ron Steiner has also had another eBay-Internet find: a Plastic Toys, Inc. catalog that includes the two pages shown. The most unusual figures here are the P-1 Space Office, P-2 Pre-Historic Man (who looks like the comic-strip character Alley Oop) and P-3 Space Fighter. These pieces seem to be extremely rare. I've asked a number of plastic collectors about them, and only one has seen any in this group: the Space Officer. Incidentally, though Plastic Toys showed a charging soldier in an ad (page 315 of <u>Collecting American-Made Toy Soldiers</u>), Ron thinks it may never have been produced. Anyone disagree? And Ron adds that the Plastic Toys prone machine gunner, neither seen nor listed in these two catalog pages (though seen in a photo in this catalog) is rare.

How rare are some soldiers? Well, as far as I know, only **Don Pielin** owns the presumable American Alloy-Toy Creations solider I've coded as TC?7. This is the piece that looks like the Tommy Toy-American Alloy charging, only with pot helmet, puttees and bloused trousers. It appears to mark a transition from the American Alloy pre-WWII uniform to what eventually became Toy Creations' postwar line. But it always seemed odd to me that only one in this niche had been produced. Thus it was both unsurprising and exciting to hear from New Jersey collector **Howard Gries**, who wrote and said "I came across this soldier and think it might be a new variation" on TC2. It sure is (I'm coding it TC?7A). Anyone else have another? Or yet another previous unknown in this category?

American Alloy-Toy Creations TC?7A. Photo by Howard Gries.

PLASTIC TOYS CORP.
BYESVILLE, OHIO

PRICE LIST
Subject to Change
Without Notice

NET 30
F. O. B. FAC

5 CENT SOLDIERS . . . Bulk

No.		Price Per Gr.	Packed	Weight Per Gr.	Ship's Chg.
S-1	Marching Soldier	$3.24	2 dz.	4½ lbs.	5 gr.
S-2	Machine Gunner, standing	$3.24	2 dz.	4½ lbs.	5 gr.
S-3	Machine Gunner, kneeling	$3.24	2 dz.	4½ lbs.	5 gr.
S-4	Bomber	$3.24	2 dz.	4½ lbs.	5 gr.
S-5	Charging Soldier	$3.24	2 dz.	4½ lbs.	5 gr.
S-6	Charging Soldier, gas mask	$3.24	2 dz.	4½ lbs.	5 gr.
S-8	Bugler	$3.24	2 dz.	4½ lbs.	5 gr.
S-9	Rifleman, firing	$3.24	2 dz.	4½ lbs.	5 gr.

ASSORTED SOLDIERS . . . Bulk

No.		Price Per Gr.	Packed	Weight Per Gr.	Ship's Chg.
S-102	10c Ass't Soldiers	$3.24	2 dz.	4½ lbs.	5 gr.

5 CENT FARM ANIMALS . . . Bulk

No.		Price Per Gr.	Packed	Weight Per Gr.	Ship's Chg.
A-2	Sheep	$3.24	2 dz.	4½ lbs.	5 gr.
A-3	Hog	$3.24	2 dz.	4½ lbs.	5 gr.
A-4	Colt	$3.24	2 dz.	4½ lbs.	5 gr.
A-5	Calf	$3.24	2 dz.	4½ lbs.	5 gr.

5 CENT FARM FOWL . . . Bulk

No.		Price Per Gr.	Packed	Weight Per Gr.	Ship's Chg.
A-6	Turkey	$3.24	4 dz.	3½ lbs.	10 gr.
A-7	Rooster	$3.24	4 dz.	3½ lbs.	10 gr.
A-8	Hen	$3.24	4 dz.	3½ lbs.	10 gr.
A-9	Duck	$3.24	4 dz.	3½ lbs.	10 gr.

ASSORTED FARM ANIMALS, FOWL . . . Bulk

No.		Price Per Gr.	Packed	Weight Per Gr.	Ship's Chg.
A-100	10c Farm Animals, Asst.	$3.24	2 dz.	4½ lbs.	5 gr.
A-102	5c Ass't Farm Fowl	$3.24	4 dz.	3½ lbs.	10 gr.

5 CENT COWBOYS, WESTERN FIGURES . . . Bulk

No.		Price Per Gr.	Packed	Weight Per Gr.	Ship's Chg.
W-1	Cowboy ("shorty")	$3.24	2 dz.	4½ lbs.	5 gr.
W-2	Cowgirl	$3.24	2 dz.	4½ lbs.	5 gr.
W-3	Bandit	$3.24	2 dz.	4½ lbs.	5 gr.
W-4	Rancher	$3.24	2 dz.	4½ lbs.	5 gr.
W-9	Indian Chief	$3.24	2 dz.	4½ lbs.	5 gr.

ASSORTED WESTERN FIGURES . . . Bulk

No.		Price Per Gr.	Packed	Weight Per Gr.	Ship's Chg.
W-102	Asstd. Western Figures	$3.24	2 dz.	4½ lbs.	5 gr.

5 CENT SPECIAL FIGURES . . . Bulk

No.		Price Per Gr.	Packed	Weigh Per Gr.
P-1	Space Officer	$3.24	2 dz.	4 lbs.
P-2	Pre-Historic Man	$3.24	2 dz.	4 lbs.
P-3	Space Fighter	$3.24	2 dz.	4 lbs.

5 CENT ASSORTED SPACE FIGURES . . . Bulk

No.		Price Per Gr.	Packed	Weight Per Gr.
P-100	Ass'd. Space Figures	$3.24	2 dz.	4 lbs.

3-SECTION ROCKET

No.		Price Per Gr.	Packed	Weight Per Gr.
B-1	4-inch Rocket		2 dz.	2 lbs.

25 CENT MARBLE DISPENSER

No.		Price Per Doz.	Packed	Weight Per Doz.
M-1	Marble Dispenser	$2.70	2 dz.	3 lbs.

ROCKET SET DELUXE . . . $1.80

No.		Price Per Doz.	Weight Per Doz.	Ship'g Chg.
B-100	Rocket Fleet w. Launcher	$5.40	13 lbs.	

BOX SETS . . . $1.50
30 Assorted Bulk Figures (entire line)

No.		Price Per Doz.	Weight Per Doz.
150	30 Ass't Figures	$8.10	9 lbs.

Courtesy Ron Steiner

HAND COLORED
ONE PIECE
PLASTIC
•
DURABLE   WASHABLE
SANITARY   SAFE

A-2—2½x1¾" High

A-3—2½x1½" High

Plastic Toys catalog, courtesy Ron Steiner

Hovde Hosts Dimestore Breakfast

Collector Don Hovde graciously hosted a Saturday morning breakfast at OTS for over 50 fellow Dimestore collectors. OTS had sent up trial balloons on collector dinners before, but Hovde, a man with political know-how, simply made one happen. From the "eye openers" to the breakfast buffet, it was a great occasion which may turn into an annual Dimestore event (without Don Hovde having to pick up the tab, of course!). Don Hovde made some remarks and thank you's on the joys and friendship of collecting which we all echoed. Richard O'Brien, premier Dimestore researcher, spoke. Don Pielin, OTS partner and show organizer, remarked on 19 years of OTS shows and 23 of our sponsoring magazine, and Bud Born thanked Don Hovde for his hosting the occasion and regaled us all with his now infamous Korean war toilet paper saga. No, we're not repeating it here; just ask Bud!

Photos, this page from top: Host Donald Hovde flanked by Richard O'Brien and Ron Eccles (right); center photo: O'Brien remarks; bottom right, OTS Show coordinators Don and Linda Pielin; lower left facing camera, from left: Bill and Sharon Holt; Bud Born and his wife.

Correction

Richard O'Brien's *Dimestore Plastic Update* in the last issue (V23,#4, p. 36) come to us in two stages, and we made a mistake in the editing we did combining the two parts. The last sentence in the second paragraph should have been deleted. The Universal cowboy that Beton later numbered 833 obviously was found by Rob Steiner and is the cowboy pictured in the article. While writing to alert us to this problem, Richard also pointed out "...re the *U.S. Ski Troopers* article [by Don Pielin and Ron Hillman, V23,#4, p. 23], it might be proper to point out that Manoil sold its ski troops not as Americans but, according to one of its order sheets, as 'Finns'."

OTS Spring 2000 V24#1

American Dimestore

McCandlish Speculation and Plastic Toys Update

by Richard O'Brien

Don Pielin has long owned a couple of toy soldiers that have intrigued me from the first moment I saw a photo of them. To my knowledge, he's the only one who owns any. Considering that one of them seems to be being shot and the other is kneeling, it seems likely other types were made, and may be out there somewhere. For years I've wondered who made them and why they're so scarce.

An inkling began to dawn when I found out, via Auburn sculptor Edward McCandlish's diaries, that he had also sculpted for something he called "the Van Wert group", investors from Van Wert, Ohio, who, in the 1938-39 period, were hoping to come up with a line of composition soldiers, presumably to take over for the metal ones when the impending war broke out. It eventually struck me that the two figures Don has look very much like the early pieces McCandlish designed for Auburn. At the 1999 OTS Show I suggested this to Don, and he agreed. Since I've always felt he has a couple of the sharpest eyes in the hobby, I felt encouraged. More recently, I wrote about this to one of McCandlish's daughters, Margaret Edwards, who has possession of the diaries. She agreed to look through them.

Recently, she wrote and had this to say: "the following entries jumped out at me: One: 'Mon., Jan.16' (1939) - 'Gun Bearer' was in a list of plaster toy samples which included 16 items, mostly animals from Africa. Two: Several entries of casting items in 'type-metal', including: June 5 'Bandsman' (O'Brien: in June, 1938, McCandlish mentioned "working on bandmen sets for Van Wert mfr."): July 18 'Cast the Galloping Cowboy'."

Obviously, this is far from conclusive, but does at least suggest McCandlish cast some of his own work in metal. Possibly enough were cast so that McCandlish or someone in Van Wert tried selling them that way when it became obvious they weren't going to come up with the composition they were seeking. Anyone in the Van Wert area feel like doing a little research?

Photo above right, this page: Were these soldiers designed by Auburn's Edward McCandlish for the Van Wert investor group?

Recently, Ron Steiner's find of a Plastic Toys catalog was reprinted in OTS. Since the figures drawn in the catalog don't look much like the actual figures, Ron has supplied photos of the pieces he's come up with. The missing-legged colt is Ron's from childhood. Ron, via eBay, has also come up with yet another unknown "company": two solid-cast copies of the Barclay B79a cast-helmet machine gunner. What suggests production, rather than simple copies for home use, is that each is stamped underneath the base, one reading "Army USA 13" and the other "USA 29". But if sold commercially, why two numbers for the same piece?

Ron also collects Universals, and recently found that that short-lived company produced its traffic cop in two variations: one has a ridged belt buckle and ridged lanyard ring, and the other has them without ridges. Beton, which obtained Universal's molds, also has those two variations.

Finally, back in the 1930s, the toy soldier field was obviously a volatile one. On October 28, 1935, the New York Times reported, under the headline "War Games Absent in Toys This Year", "Toy soldiers and war games are no longer being featured. Violence is represented in toyland this season only by G-men in the Federal war against crime and by miniature cowboys and Indians." Less than two months later, on December 5th, the Times said, under the headline "War Toys Are Leading in the American Market": "The demand for war toys came with the advance of Italian troops in Africa and found the great toy shops of the country unprepared. Since then, however, they've been turning out 'troops' by the thousands." Possibly these troops came from Britains, but it seems more likely they were from Grey Iron, Barclay and/or, their U.S. soldiers painted with

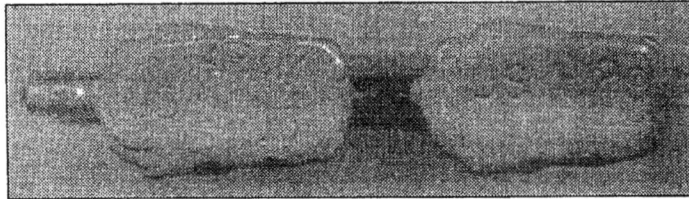

Images above: two solidcast Barclay copies with base inscriptions: left, "Army USA 13", and right, "USA 29".

brown faces and hands, Auburn Rubber. (We now know, via the McCandlish diaries, that the pieces designed specifically as Ethiopians wouldn't have been available until after the <u>Times</u> article was published.)

Images above: Plastic Toys' cowboys, cowgirl and Indian, and farm animals.

Dating Dimestores

by Richard O'Brien

Despite years of research, there are still plenty of questions about the soldiers sold in the five and tens before the Second World War and after. Just when did certain pieces appear, when did paint styles change, when did prices escalate? Luckily, at least one collector kept records, and he recently sent me that information.

Bill Dunfee has already done a lot for the hobby by sharing the catalog pages he got from Barclay in 1955. Now, with his notes, he gives us a pretty good sense of when some things may have happened, since he says he bought new soldiers as soon as they appeared. As a result, we can say with some certainty that the Barclay pot helmet soldiers emerged in 1947 (and certainly by that date) priced at a dime, that Manoil's price for a figure in 1948 had risen to fifteen cents (except perhaps for Happy Farms — see 10/17/50) and Barclay's apparently to thirteen cents. 1948 also could be the year that Manoil introduced its 45/7 through 45/16 line, despite the prefix that suggests initial 1945 manufacture.

1950 may have marked the first appearance of Barclay's white-helmeted bandsmen and Barclay's WWI-helmeted figures (though apparently in green helmets) were still on sale. Finally, as late as December 1950, Barclay's podfoots may still have been unborn since Dunfee is pretty sure he would have bought the smaller-sized pieces if he'd found them, as they'd have looked right as figures in the distance in his dioramas (1952 is the earliest date I've been able to find for them). At any rate, here is Dunfee's list. As a bit of confirmation, his buying Toy Creations pieces in 1947 echoes the information I've found that those soldiers did debut in that year. If anyone wonders why Dunfee didn't buy more pieces, it's possible these are all his local stores offered (many five and tens only carried some of a firm's line), or that they were all he could afford at the time; his notes also show plenty of buys from his friends during this period, at various prices.

Anyone else out there have similar records they can share with us?

Note: The figure designation numbers in Bill's list are those used in O'Brien's books, like his Collecting American-Made Toy Soldiers, not the Barclay or Manoil factory numbers. For example, O'Brien's B132 is Barclay number 782, or O'Brien's Manoil M181 is Manoil cataloged as 45/11.

Figures illustrating this article are reproduced from O'Brien's The Second Catalog Book, p. 10,12-13.

OTS Summer 2001 V25#2

Updating Dimestores

by Richard O'Brien

The years go on, and amazingly, things continue to turn up. Recently, the Barclay cook with timer sold on eBay for an astonishing $470. So here might be a good time to mention that **Gene Parker** has found out who offered this piece back in the pre-war period. The box it came in reads: "Paul A. Straub & Co., Inc. New York, N.Y." Presumably, Barclay just provided the cook and Straub did the rest.

Still with Barclay: **Fred Corcoran** recently sent me a photo of yet another variation of the soldier with searchlight (why did they make so many?). I've coded this B124a. It's the same as B124, but with a projection above the lens. It's probably pre-WWII, as the eyes have no whites, unlike at least some of the postwar pieces. If you've got all the variations, you've got nine of them.

A mounted Indian turned up recently on eBay that had some of us excited. The seller said it had no markings. Since the horse looked just like Barclay's Bn (the mounted officer with sword pointing forward), it seemed likely this was also a Barclay. Even the color of the Indian's jacket seemed to match the officer's tunic. Alas, the Indian turns out to have markings after all: Britains. But at least now some of us know where Barclay's sculptor got the idea for the Bn's horse.

Ron Steiner has also found yet another "civilian" by Universal Plastics that later found its way into Beton's line. This one is a fireman, meaning we now know that fourteen Betons were originally produced by Universal. And I'm still betting some of Beton's figures in mufti originated with Universal. Keep checking those underbases!

Finally, what I think is a terrific find: an L. Gould catalog from 1937. When I interviewed the late **Stan Reyff** (see O'Brien's two articles in OTS on Jones and American Metal Toys: V18,#6: 8 and V19,#2:28), he told me he remembered Germans were among American Metal Toys' earliest figures. Since mail-order catalogs from 1938 and 1939 showed none, and the firm's co-owner, **C. Raymond Pierson**, disagreed, I assumed Stan was wrong. But then I happened upon this. Since it's an all-toys catalog, it was probably issued in time for Christmas. Most likely it was printed about September. As American Metal Toys was formed only months before (in the spring), this is probably the earliest evidence we'll ever find for the company. And in that list of nine figures (surprisingly, only two of them doughboys), there they are: "Kneeling German Soldier, with Rifle" and "Charging German Soldier, with Rifle". These molds were among those bought from Jones when the company began.

Soldiers and Forts

THREE-INCH FULL FORM METAL FIGURES

Hollow cast type finished in bright chip-proof enamels. All items packed one dozen in an attractive box.

No. 3328—Machine Gunner and Gun.....................Per doz. **$0.90**
No. 3329—Kneeling U. S. Soldier, with Rifle............Per doz. **.90**
No. 3330—Kneeling German Soldier, with Rifle.........Per doz. **.90**
No. 3331—Charging German Soldier, with Rifle.........Per doz. **.90**
No. 3332—Knight with Shield.........................Per doz. **.90**
No. 3333—Knight with Flag............................Per doz. **.90**
No. 3334—Kneeling French Soldier, with Rifle..........Per doz. **.90**
No. 3335—Kneeling Indian, with Rifle..................Per doz. **.90**
No. 3336—Standing Cowboy, with Pistol................Per doz. **.90**

No. 3336

No. 3333

No. 3886—Assorted Rubber Toys. Five piece contains one each 6¼ inch Cord sedan, 4 inch coach, 4 inch coupe, 4x3 inch airplane and 5½x4¼ inch airliner. Packed one set in a built up display carton 5x16½ inches...Per doz. sets **$8.00**

No. 3088—Soldier Set. Consists of six only 3½ inch lead soldiers, including flag bearer, bugler, captain and infantry troops. Complete with silk American flag. Enameled in assorted colors. Packed one set in a carton 6x7¼ inches. Per doz. **$4.00**

Plus, there's a ringer on this list: "Kneeling French Soldier, with Rifle". I was startled by this, and then got the feeling I'd come across something like it. I searched through my files, and twice went through **Don Pielin**'s self-published books. On the second go-round, I found what I was looking for: in two of his books, Don shows two kneeling firing Germans, the second in blue. My guess is this is American Metal's French Soldier. And yet...there's something nagging me about it; as if somewhere along the way I saw the American doughboy with a slightly different helmet, one that could look at least vaguely like the Adrians the French wore. Anyone out there have a clue?

More from that 1937 L. Gould: An Auburn boxed set with airplanes and cars. I've never seen that boxtop, let alone the set. Finally, what may be a toy soldier company new to all of us! A "Soldier Set" with a generic drawing of an admiral, a doughboy, a pilot, a

sailor, a cadet, etc. and the following information: "3-1/2 inch lead soldiers including flagbearer, bugler, captain and infantry troops. Complete with silk American flag".

These could be homecasts, but I don't know of any this big. Cosmos were about that size, but the company seems to have been out of business before 1937. I've checked the "Miscellaneous Soldiers" section of my book, and all I can find that seems likely are the flag bearer on the bottom of page 627 and the officer and marcher on the top right of page 628. I got into toy soldier research decades ago to clear up all the mysteries, and yet here it is, over thirty years later, and we've got a brand new one!

EXTRA! EXTRA!
LATEST DIMESTORE NEWS!
By Richard O'Brien

Page from May 1940 Playthings Magazine

First off, my apologies to Jim Casey. It was Jim who discovered the original retailer of the Barclay cook with timer, not Gene Parker. Secondly, my apologies to everyone. Recently, I went over the notes I'd made decades ago when I was researching toy soldiers in the pre-WWII toy trade magazines. When I originally began, I was only interested in finding out the histories of the dimestore soldiers I'd grown up with. So this note never got into any of my books: "Lincoln Logs soldiers made of zinc alloy - also made 4" high U.S. Soldiers of 1918 - set for $1.00". Unfortunately, I didn't note source or date, but the next two notes are from 1941, with the second being from the March 1941 Playthings, so presumably the first item was also from that year. As I looked at the note, it occurred to me that the page I'd stumbled on some years later, from the May 1940 Playthings could be reproduced in OTS, since its photographic quality is so high. So, here's the photo that shows the large doughboys listed in my American made toy soldiers as LL53 - LL58, Page 536. It's the box on the right, just above the lowest row. There is something else I'd like to point out there that I've never mentioned before - we may have another doughboy to discover. The figure second from the right doesn't seem to have a rifle and the arm is crooked, unlike the pilot's (LL59) (not shown in this box), whose arms hang straight down, so it's quite possible it was an officer, possibly with a sword. Anyway, we now know Lincoln Logs' description of these soldiers (same as their small doughboys), and that seven of them in a box sold for a dollar, a pretty stiff price in those days of nickel-apiece soldiers, at least one reason why they seem not to have sold well.

Another Shackman catalog has turned up. Shackman, you

may recall, carried Barclay's soldiers from about the time the company began. This is dated 1938-39, and since the catalog leads off with Halloween items, then goes to Thanksgiving, Christmas and New Years, in that order, I think we can assume it was printed no later than early October, 1938. A 1936-37 Shackman's catalog was reproduced earlier in OTS and many of the same items appear here. New, though, and probably new in 1938, are the fireman, cop and Boy Scout signaler. Also new, and again probably first sold in 1938 are, as described by Shackman, "Cannon. Coast Guard"; "Cannon. Long Range"; Searchlight Mounted on Stand" and "Cannon Howitzer". This almost certainly is the revolving cannon. All four were found on a Broadway sheet I reproduced in "The Barclay Catalog Book".

Also in this catalog, and something I somehow never expected to find anywhere, especially after 1937, are the American Legionnaires. Interestingly, Shackman lists them this way: "American Legion Soldiers" and "American Legion Marine Soldiers". No way of knowing if this was also Barclay's description, as Shackman's designations weren't always the same as Barclay's.

Shackman seems to have sold all its Barclays at retail. Thus, the common soldiers are listed at a nickel each, the legionnaires and the "Soldier with Radio Signal Set" at ten cents each, and the cannons, etc., fifteen cents apiece.

Recently, John West, who does cartoons for Antique Toy World, drew "A Few Toys That I Can't Remember As A Child". Included were six Barclays: Bh, 2B11, 2B9, 2B3, 2B2 and 2B5, thus all from the second series of Barclays. I wrote John and asked if he knew, or could at least guess, when he'd gotten these. He didn't know for sure, but his guess was 1933, which seems likely. I asked if they came in a box, but he says he never saw a box. Barclay did seem to have boxed sets of soldiers at this time, but I've never come across one.

I recently heard from collector James Brady, who seems to have found a new Manoil paint variant - the fellow with a barrel of apples in white. The scan he sent me seems genuine and he says veteran collectors like Bud Born also feel it's the real thing.

Recently, eBay ran an auction of drawings by the fellow who seems to have designed and presumably sculpted many or all of Grey Iron's soldiers. Presumably the high bidders (I dropped out at $300) will eventually make all of the art available to collectors, but meanwhile here are two drawings: one of soldiers known to us and a mounted piece that I think would have been Grey Iron's most dramatic. I got in touch with the seller, Charles K. Kuhns, Jr. and he said the artist, whose last name

was Young (first name possibly Russell), worked at Grey Iron and Wilton from the 1920s into the 1960s. Back when I was researching Grey Iron, Young's name never came up, but then neither did anyone at Auburn have any memory of its designer-sculp-

tor. Anyway, we now know what the drawings of Frank Krupp, Olive Kooken, Edward McCandish and Young looked like. Now to find some art by Manoil's Walter Baetz!

Finally, Charles Kuhns sent me scans of a farm set that seems to have sold for a quarter during World War One. The copyright is 1914, with the box top reading "Made in U.S.A. Buy, Boom and Conserve". This set is new to me. The milkmaids are about an inch and a half high. The material is lead. I think Kuhns told me he owns three of these sets. The manufacturer's name doesn't appear anywhere.

DIMESTORE UPDATES *by Richard O'Brien*
BARCLAY, SOLJERTOYS AND AUBURN

B. SHACKMAN & CO. 906 BROADWAY
"THE NAME IS IMPORTANT" At 20th Street, NEW YORK

METAL NOVELTIES (Continued)

51/126   4850   43/403   51/129

PAINTED METAL SOLDIERS

		DOZEN
51/125	Painted Metal Soldier. Khaki uniform. 2¼ inches.	$0.85
51/129	Soldier with gun and khaki uniform. Charging position. 2¼ inches.	.85
51/126	Sailor (marine) with blue uniform, white hat and gun. 2½ inches.	.85
51/127	Indian with gun. 2¼ inches.	.85
51/131	Indian with gun, on black metal horse. 3 inches.	1.20
51/134	Cowboy with pistol, bright color blouse and pants. 2½ inches.	.85
51/132	Marine with gun and dark blue hat and coat, and light blue trousers. 2½ inches	.85
4850	Soldier with gun. Soldier with sword, bugler, and drummer, assorted, with different style uniforms. 2¼ inches.	.78
43/776	Foreign Soldier with long lance. Mounted on horse. 3¼ inches	1.00

METAL SOLDIER SETS

METAL SOLDIERS ABOUT 2¼ INCHES EACH. WELL MADE. PAINTED IN APPROPRIATE COLOR UNIFORMS. MOUNTED ON 6 COLOR SCENIC BACKGROUNDS WHICH ARE TO BE REMOVED AND USED AS A PLAYSETTING. EACH SET IN A NICELY LITHOGRAPHED BOX.

		PER DOZEN SETS
43/400	Cowboys. 4 assorted in set.	$2.00
43/401	U. S. Infantry. 4 assorted in set.	2.00
43/402	Indians. 4 assorted in set.	2.00
43/403	West Point Cadets. 4 assorted in set.	2.00
43/404	U. S. Sailors. 4 assorted in set.	2.00
43/405	6 Standing Indians. 1 mounted in set.	4.00
43/406	6 U. S. Infantrymen. 1 mounted officer in set	4.00
43/407	6 West Point Cadets. 1 mounted officer in set.	4.00
43/408	5 Mounted U. S. Officers in set.	4.00
43/409	6 U. S. Sailors. 1 Mounted U. S. Naval Officer in set	4.00
43/410	6 Standing Cowboys. 1 Mounted Cowboy in set	4.00
43/411	5 Foot Knights in Armor. 1 Mounted Knight, movable arms, in set.	4.00

Another Shackman's catalog has turned up, this one No. 70, from 1932-1933. I didn't have much hope before I bought it that it would have anything significant re Barclay, and it doesn't much, but it did furnish a surprise. I never expected to find anything regarding Soljertoys.

The cadets shown on this page look like Soljertoys, and the listings in the 43/400 series seemed like Soljertoys, too. But the cadets and the listings are so generic, they were frustratingly vague. Then I noticed the background in the box of cadets (43/403). It looked very familiar. I checked the top left photo on page 55 of "Collecting American-Made Toy Soldiers", and there the background was, in another box of Soljertoys. Anyone owning a copy of my "Collecting Toys", fourth edition, can see an even clearer picture in the color pages.

Essentially, what all this (43/411 in the listing) does is confirm that Soljertoys and Pearlytoys did make the knight I show on page 58 as SO18, which is marked (two words) "Pearly Toys". Further, that a mounted knight, with moving arm, was definitely produced by Soljertoys (which started about January, 1930) and probably by Pearlytoys as well. Now, how about someone finding that mounted knight?

As for Barclay, the only items from that company are soldiers, just seven of them, from the 51 series, and nothing I haven't seen listed before. But in this catalog, unlike the one I cited in my last report, the prices here are all wholesale, not retail. Thus, a dozen Barclays selling for eighty-five cents suggests they were probably retailed at a dime apiece. However, this being the Depression, it could be they sold for eight or nine cents each, at least in some stores. Just a few years later, the much larger Barclays were selling for just a nickel. Just one word of caution to any newcomers; those illustrations of 51/126 and 51/129 are not Barclays, they're generic drawings used by Shackman long before Barclay came on the scene.

Catalogs by American toy soldier companies are excruciatingly hard to find. A long-time want of mine was a 1941 Auburn Rubber catalog, but I had little hope it would turn up. But one day, on eBay, it did! Like all the Auburn catalogs found so far (1936, 1937, 1940 and now 1941), it's in full color. Twelve pages long, it introduces a number of toys, including eleven soldiers and three ships. Well, it may introduce a twelfth soldier, but more on that later.

Learning the numbers assigned to soldiers is often helpful, as it gives us an idea as to when they were produced. In this case, I knew beforehand they all came out in early 1941, but it's' still fun to see just what the numbers are, and in this case, what they each retailed for.

DIMESTORE UPDATES *by Richard O'Brien* (cont.)
BARCLAY, SOLJERTOYS AND AUBURN

I'll list them in numerical order, with their Auburn description, their price and my coding following: 228 Aircraft Defender, 10 cents (A25); 248 Sound Detector, 10 cents (A30); 272 Plane Shooter, 5 cents (A29); 274 Tank Defender, 5 cents (A33); 284 Firing Line Soldier, 5 cents (A28); 286 Marching Soldier, 5 cents (A27); 288 Motor Scout, 10 cents (A36); 292 Tank Soldier, 5 cents (A34); 294 Color Bearer, 5 cents (A26); 296 Trench Mortar, 5 cents (A32); and 298 Searchlight, 10 cents (A31).

I'd found a couple of those numbers in a Playthings magazine years ago, and couldn't figure out the jump so far from the previously known Auburn number 268. I can explain it now somewhat, but only by including Auburn carelessness. 228 was an open number not used since the 1936 Ethiopian Chief. 248 was also open. 272 and 274 represent a small jump, and then 284 through 298 are missing only #290. Could that be my long-sought-after running "pilot"? Maybe, but I'm betting more on 300, as I suspect it was issued much later in the year, perhaps not until 1942, and perhaps only in a large boxed Aviation set.

1941 Auburn Rubber Catalog page

Also new in the catalog are 1584 Submarine (5 cents); 1588 Dreadnaught (10 cents) and 1592 Freighter (10 cents). A 1500 series, right? And so it should have been, but 1940s 1582 Battleship is numbered (in the two places it's mentioned) 582, another example, I assume, of Auburn sloppiness.

Also new in 1941 was the number 121 Farm Wagon and Team. The "farmer" and his "wife" aren't listed individually, but in a large boxed set they're called "farmer man" and "milkmaid".

It took me two days before I noticed what seems to be a yet undiscovered Auburn soldier (see next page). It's actually shown in my book, on page 208, top left, and also at the bottom of the page, but apparently none of us ever noticed. Ironically, for years I'd been looking for this piece, or something like it. Auburn had made larger versions of its early soldiers, I'd reasoned, so why not the seated machine gunner? And here it is, apparently larger, and very different. It's in several of the boxed sets, including the two (231, 225) I've shown. Frustratingly, it can't be confirmed that this piece was ever produced, as I can't find a single photograph of it in any of the general catalogs on the period, and everything in this catalog is drawn. But the drawings are generally so accurate (and note the earlier machine gunners are also drawn in the 225 set, as they are in another set with both types on a separate catalog page). My guess is that it was made. If so, the biggest clue is to look for an ammo belt that slants toward the front of the gun, rather than back to the soldier. His head is also higher, and the piece in general appears to be larger.

Finally, still with Auburn, recently K. Warren Mitchell has been selling Don Pielin's collection. One piece that turned up seems to be one of a kind. It's the Auburn mounted officer in white, which alone makes it unique. But it's also a smaller size, just like its earliest foot-soldier brothers. I've long looked for another in this size, but with as little luck as I've had searching for a larger machine gunner.

DIMESTORE UPDATES *by Richard O'Brien* (cont.)

BARCLAY, SOLJERTOYS AND AUBURN

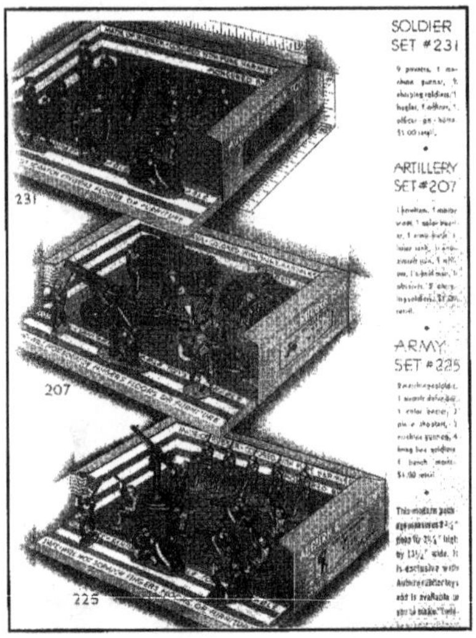

Left: 1941 Auburn Rubber Catalog page showing large size seated machine-gunner.

Above: Auburn Rubber Mounted Officer in White, recently offered by K. Warren Mitchell and formerly part of the Don Pielin collection

Correction Volume 25, #4: Richard O'Brien's Dimestore Update. The statement referring to "Broadway sheet" reproduced in the Barclay catalog book should have read Barclay sheet, not Broadway sheet. Apologies to Richard.

A 'NEW' BARCLAY, RARE BETON BOX, MORE SHACKMANS, AND...1941 GREY IRONS!

by Richard O'Brien

Every once in a while, we need to find out about a "new" dimestore soldier, and this time it's New Jersey collector John Stetson who's found it for us. Years ago, when I was buying pieces from George Fall, longtime head of the shipping department at Barclay, George showed up at my house one day with, among other things, two of the Barclay short-stride cadets painted as wooden soldiers, in mint. As far as I know, it was the first time any of us had seen one. Since then, a few others have turned up, but never the officer. It hadn't even occurred to me that the officer might have been painted that way. But painted that way he is, and John says the fellow who sold him the one I've illustrated has a second one, in much lesser shape.

I'd always assumed the Barclay wooden soldier would have dated back to the middle 1930s, but, oddly, the officer has the number "743" on its underbase, suggesting much-later production. Well, I'm not 100% great at predicting eras, as we shall see later in this article.

Is this Beton box the most interesting and colorful of all toy soldier boxes? I'm no expert, but it seems so to me. In any event, it's as rare as anything in existence can be. When Phil Savino put it up for auction it was wholly new to me, and I've yet to come across another one. Unfortunately, Phil had trouble fitting the whole box into his photo, so I'm also enclosing a picture of the sleeve that contained it. As you'll see, cadets march across the parade ground past a reviewing stand while an assortment of civilians stand outside. At one end, cadets are emerging from a building. The box is rich with various colors, but alas, there's no indication anywhere of when this was offered. Since it says "Carlstadt, N.J." on the sleeve, it's almost certainly pre-war, and since some other Beton box sleeves state "copyright 1941", my guess is that it predates 1941. I'd stab at 1939.

Barclay B35A, West Point Officer painted as a wooden soldier. Courtesy John Stetson

Left end of the Beton Box.

Beton Box (only one known) Courtesy Phil Savino

Sleeve for the Beton Box. This includes a drawing of the actual plastic cadets. Courtesy Phil Savino

I recently picked up several new Shackman catalogs. Shackman, as I've noted in the past, carried Barclay for years, perhaps from its beginning. The 1929-30 page I was sent offers nothing of note, nor does the 1934-35 catalog, so I won't reproduce those here. However, the 1940-41 catalog presents quite a few new items. Among them are a number of civilians. However, since most or all of them were available by 1939 (which I've seen in George Fall's dated Christmas display photos), there's nothing much there. This does suggest that the "Masked Rider on Horse" may not have emerged until 1940. For the record, figures on view in Fall's 1939 photo are: American Legionnaire, walking minister; Santa with holly; Skiing Santa (which is listed under "Santa Claus Figures" in this catalog as "51/160 Santa Claus on Skiis"; it sold at a surprising–to me-fifteen cents, retail); bride and groom; old man; elderly woman; red cap, porter, engineer, man passenger, Boy Scout signaling, postman, and what looked like the little girl with doll.

METAL NOVELTIES SOLDIERS, Etc.
ABOUT 2¼ INCHES EACH.
NICELY PAINTED METAL.

51/148 Soldier with signal flags	51/131 Soldier with gun, assorted
51/147 Soldier with hand grenade	51/151 Soldier with large shell
51/134 Cowboy	51/149 Aviator
51/142 Pirate	51/144 Soldier with machine gun
51/125 West Point Cadet	51/152 Soldier with great coat
51/135 Soldier-with drum, bugle and beton assorted	51/150 Dress Uniform
51/143 Marine Officer	51/126 Marine, blue
51/127 Knight	51/138 Marine, white
51/159 Army Doctor	51/137 Naval Officer
51/167 Boy, Street Clothes	51/133 Indian
51/169 Conductor	51/165 Boy Scout with signal flags
51/173 Engineer	51/157 Traffic Officer
51/166 Girl, Street Clothes	51/171 Man in Street Clothes
51/174 Indian on Horse	51/175 Masked Rider on Horse
51/188 Fireman	51/168 Red Cap with Luggage
51/128 Soldiers with U.S. Flag	51/172 Woman in Street Clothes
51/130 Soldier with gun	51/170 Porter
51/186 American Legion Soldiers, assorted, 3½ Inches.	

FOR PRICES SEE PAGES 129 - 145

60

1940-41 Shackman Catalog No. 86R

40-41

B. SHACKMAN & CO. 34th STREET and MADISON AVE., N.Y.

UNUSUAL BRIDES AND GROOMS

Barclay's Bride and Groom again, in the 1941-42 Shackman Catalog No. 88

UNUSUAL BRIDES AND GROOMS
Our own domestic make, the finest on the market.

Barclay's Bride and Groom as seen in the 1940-41 Shackman Catalog No. 86R

METAL NOVELTIES SOLDIERS, Etc.

1941-42 Shackman Catalog No. 88

As you'll see, the bride and groom are shown in a photograph; the only photograph of Barclays I've seen in a Shackman catalog. They're listed on a separate page and retailed at a nickel apiece. As for the soldiers listed, the Indian on Horse and Masked Rider on Horse both retailed at a dime each. All the rest are priced at a nickel apiece, including, oddly, the American Legion Soldiers". Was this a Shackman mistake, or a closeout price? George Fall thought they were manufactured only during late 1937. Either he was wrong, or Barclay or Shackman were overstocked.

Now to the piece de resistance; the 1941-42 catalog. There are four Barclays I'd particularly like to know the Barclay descriptions of; the ski soldier, the detective, the robber, and the "falling" soldier. Shackman's descriptions don't always match Barclay's, but at least it would have given me some kind of answer. Unfortunately, since Shackman only sold a small portion of the Barclay range, they don't appear here. However, we do get a couple of probables on other pieces; since a 1941 Butler Bros. catalog also lists a "Parachute Jumper" we can assume this was Barclay's designation too. "Soldier with Searchlight" also sounds like a Barclay description.

That does it pretty much for the Barclay soldiers, aside from the curious designation, "Marine, white", especially since "sailor" is listed as well. Was there a white Barclay marine, just as there were white Auburn and Molded Miniatures marines? Not likely, but just remember that Wooden Cadet Officer!

Even more important, look just below the Barclay listings on this page and check out 41/355-41/352. The use of a prefix means these are U.S.-made. At first I assumed they might be Comets, despite the 3-inch size, since Shackman was so inaccurate in this regard (check out the height they show for the Barclays just above). But that 48-cent wholesale price seemed wrong for Comets; too low. Finally, it hit me. This was a catalog appearance I'd been searching for for years: new, 1941 Grey Irons!

Take a gander. "British Soldier with rifle", "British Soldier with gun"; "African Soldier"; 'Greek Soldier". The only item missing from the Grey Irons new in that year is the Ski Soldier (as it's called on its Grey Iron pattern). I think it's time now to ditch the "Italian Soldier" designation forever. There's no indication in any catalogs that Grey Iron ever sold these pieces in their shorts and tropical helmets as anything but British, as the pattern for the soldier with rifle indicates ("British Soldier" is its description). The color Grey Iron catalog that shows the Ethiopians (and NO Italians) indicates their bases are green. The British Soldiers and the "African" (a somewhat different paint job on the "Ethiopian") all have sand-colored bases. My guess is Grey Iron's descriptions for these four pieces were the same as Shackman's, or very close to it.

George Fall once wrote me that Barclay, "in the 1920s" made a set of six (only) pieces for a Japanese Garden. I've been searching catalogs for them for years, without luck. I assumed if I'd find them it would be in the 1920s and at least not much after 1937, because of anti-Japanese feeling that began building about then. So where have I finally found a "Japanese Garden" listed? In the 1941-41 catalog, just a few months before the war began! Are these Barclays? Well, they have a "51" prefix, like other Barclays in the Shackman catalogs, but those all run under 200 in the suffix department, and other companies are listed with 51 prefixes over 200. Still, if Shackman felt it couldn't fit all the Barclay Japanese pieces into the under-200 category (and it's obvious it couldn't), it may have used this ploy. I called Daniel Shackman Jacoby, who was with Shackman from 1935 on. Since it was over sixty years ago, and he's 88, he understandably didn't remember for sure, but he couldn't remember any other company that would have offered something like this. In any event, this section, with its wholesale prices, gives us an idea what Barclay's pieces might have sold for. And by the way, Jacoby remembers having dealt with Grey Iron, though has no specific member of the four soldiers above. He was obviously not one of us.

METAL FIGURES, ANIMALS FOR JAPANESE GARDENS

1941-42 Shackman Catalog No. 88. Was this Barclay's "Japanese Garden"?

DIMESTORE UPDATE
DONZE BEFORE BARCLAY?
by Richard O'Brien

Years ago, during one of my interviews with Louis Picco, who began at Barclay in July 1924, one of the things he told me was that when the company was formed it was Leon Donze who provided "the molds and the set-up" and Michael Levy who furnished the cash. Picco thought Barclay began in 1924, but wasn't positive about this. Later, when I discovered that Donze had been listed in a 1922-23 business directory as a toymaker, I began to wonder if we'd ever find out just when Barclay began and what soldiers, if any, Donze had been producing pre-Barclay. I think we may now have the answer.

As I've mentioned in a number of articles, Shackman, a firm that sold thousands of novelty-type items to shops across the country, regularly listed soldiers made by Barclay. The numbering used

30/415	Colored Metal Limousine. 1¾ inches.....
37/622	Colored Metal Touring Car. "Ford" 3 inches.....
30/496	Colored Metal Automobile Truck. 3 inches.....
30/507	Colored Metal Limousine. 3 inches.....

METAL SOLDIERS AND CANNONS

51/125	Painted Metal Soldier. Khaki uniform. 2¼ inches.....
51/129	Soldier with gun and khaki uniform. Running and kneeling, 2 positions, assorted. 2 inches.....
51/126	Sailor (marine) with blue uniform and gun. 2¼ inches.....
51/128	Indian with tomahawk. 2¼ inches.....
51/127	Indian with gun. 2¼ inches.....
51/130	Soldier in khaki uniform, on black horse. 3 inches.....
51/131	Indian with gun, on black metal horse. 3 inches.....
51/133	Soldier with movable arm and sword in hand. Sitting on black horse. 3 inches.....
20/7131	Gray Metal Cannon on 2 wheels. Pea shooter. 5 inches.....

Shackman 1924-25 catalog

was a prefix of 51 and a suffix that began with 125. Since 1989 I've tried to pry catalogs and, if that failed, photocopies, out of Daniel Shackman Jacoby, who joined the family business in 1935. However, it's been very difficult, and only recently have I been able to get copies of pages that go back as far as 1921. The Shackman catalogs are limited, in that they sold only some of Barclay's pieces, and frequently used generic drawings, instead of illustrations of the actual figures. But they often do provide valuable information, and in this case, these pages seem to indicate that Leon Donze was in business at least as early as 1921, because the same prefix-suffix numbering is used, and the descriptions of the soldiers are similar.

In the 1921-22 catalog (probably printed by early October, 1921), just four items are listed: 51/125 Painted Metal United States Soldier; 51/126 Painted United States Marine; 51/127 Painted United States Marine Officer and 51/128 Painted United States West Point Cadet. Unfortunately, these descriptions are generic, and the illustrations almost certainly don't illustrate these specific soldiers, as much-earlier companies had produced them. So there's no certainty here, but to me it seems likely that this is Leon Donze's firm, and that Shackman simply continued to use the same numbering system when Donze co-founded Barclay, since there was no need to come up with a new coding, as Donze's original firm was now defunct.

B. SHACKMAN & CO. THE LEADING FAVOR AND NOVELTY HOUSE OF AMERICA

1922.23

METAL NOVELTIES
(CONTINUED)

		GROSS
44/676	Painted Metal Soldier, flat. 2 inches.....	$4.00
44/677	Painted Metal Sailor, flat. 2 inches.....	4.00
51/125	Painted Metal Soldier, shaped. 2¼ inches.....	9.00
51/128	Painted Metal Soldier. West Point Cadet, shaped. 2¼ inches.....	9.00
51/132	Painted Metal U. S. Marine, shaped. 2¼ inches.....	9.00
51/126	Painted Metal Sailor, shaped. 2¼ inches.....	9.00
51/127	Painted Metal U. S. Marine Officer, shaped. 2¼ inches.....	9.00
51/130	Painted Metal Indian with tomahawk, shaped. 2¼ inches.....	9.00
51/129	Painted Metal Indian with gun, shaped. 2¼ inches.....	9.00
20/7131	Gray Metal Cannon on wheels. Pea shooter. 5 inches.....	10.50
		DOZEN

Shackman 1922-23 catalog

The 1922-23 issue changes the descriptions and adds three pieces: 51/125 Painted Metal Soldier; 51/126 Painted Metal Sailor; 51/127 Painted Metal U.S. Marine Officer; 51/128 Painted Metal Soldier West Point Cadet; 51/129 Painted Metal Indian with gun; 51/130 Painted Metal Indian with tomahawk and (there is no 51/131) 51/132 Painted Metal U.S Marine. These are all described as "shaped", presumably to indicate they weren't flats.

I now think that Barclay began in 1923, and here's why. Donze needed money, and Levy offered that cash infusion. Suddenly, some significant new soldiers are added, particularly four mounted, and two of them with moving arms. 51/129, formerly Indian with gun (now 5/127), becomes "Soldier with gun and khaki uniform. Running and kneeling, two positions". 51/130, formerly Indian with tomahawk (now 51/128), is listed as "Soldier in khaki uniform, on black horse". 51/131 is listed for the first time, and as "Indian with gun, on black metal horse". 51/133, another new number, is "Soldier with movable arm and sword in hand. Sitting on black horse". Now to back up a number, to 51/132. The U.S. Marine disappears, and here's where dimestore collectors should perk up; is this something new to look for? Because 51/132 reads "Soldier with movable arm and flag in hand. Sitting on black horse". I've never seen a mounted Barclay soldier with a flag in his hand. Have you?

Shackman 1923-24 catalog

1924-25 drops that mounted flag bearer, but that's the only change. And 1925-26? In that issue, 51/134 becomes "Colored Metal Auto with driver. Racing Car". There is no 51/135 but 51/136, the highest number, is "Gray Metal Cannon on 2 wheels. Pea shooter". Picco remembered the cannon as Barclay's best seller in its very early days. Was it new in 1925, or just new on Shackman's lists? Perhaps we'll never find out. Or perhaps one day, a dated Barclay catalog, or two or three or more, will suddenly turn up...Till then, this is what early Barclay - and Donze - looks like to me, and now perhaps to you. Meanwhile, you may have fun looking up Barclay's earliest pieces, and deciding which ones, if any, match up with what was probably produced by Leon Donze. My guess is, you'll find them all. Except, of course, for the mounted flag bearer.

Shackman 1921-22 catalog

CORRECTION
Volume 26 #3 Fall 2002.
Dimestore Article. by Richard O'Brien.
The caption for the Shackman Catalog on Page 78 should have read 1940-41. The caption on first Catalog shown on Page 79 should have read 1941-42. The final Paragraph date should read 1941-42 and the word "Member" should have been "Memory".

DIMESTORE UPDATE:
"GOLDEN" BARCLAYS, 1955 GREY IRON, ETC.
by Richard O'Brien

A few issues back, OTS reported on a boxed set of Barclays that sold on eBay. I'd already got in touch with the winning bidder, Stephen Taylor, and he'd sent me some excellent photos of the contents. What I find interesting is that four of the five pieces in the set have gold trim; apparently an attempt by Barclay to make the pieces distinctive, and thus worth the extra money (the "#50/99 - 5 Piece Masked Rider Set" sold for half a dollar; the pieces bought separately - without the trim - would have cost a kid only 35 cents).

The mounted Indian's rifle is gold, and the horse's eye, oddly, is gold. The standing firing cowboy has two gold pistols (and a black bandanna hiding the lower part of his face). The mounted cowboy has a gold pistol, gold gun belt, and gold saddle. His horse has gold reins and a gold bridle. The cowboy with a tin hat brim has a gold sheriff's badge and two gold slashes on the other side of his vest. I'd always wondered about those slashes, which have turned up on all the known sheriffs, and in Barclay's catalog illustrations. Stephen checked around, and found that cowboy clothing of the dude-ranch type often had these slashes as decorations, so apparently that's all this is.

The sole figure without a bit of gold to his name is the Indian with his rifle across his waist. So my guess is, any time you find a Barclay cowboy or Indian with a touch or so of gold (or a bandanna covering the lower portion of his face), he came from a boxed set.

Barclay cowboy sheriff with star on left and two decorative slashes on the right.
Photo by Stephen Taylor

Another item that turned up on eBay is a 1955 Grey Iron flier. Grey Iron was still using the same numbers for these pre-war figures, but the descriptions occasionally varied a bit; For instance, the first soldier on the page was known pre-WW II as "6 U.S. Doughboy, Shoulder Arms", but in 1955 simply as "No. 6 U.S. Infantry". A gross of the six military figures cost the retailer eight dollars. For some reason, a gross of the three cowboys was a bit more expensive; $9.33. I'd assumed it was

1955 Grey Iron page

because of the wire lasso for one of them, but then noticed the lasso doesn't turn up in the drawing, suggesting it was no longer produced. At any rate, at those prices probably each of these Grey Irons cost kids no more than ten cents.

Back to Barclay for a moment, while remaining with eBay. A Kresge's catalog from 1938 was offered, with "A Tremendous Assortment of Brightly Colored Metal Soldiers" comprising one of the illustrations. Shown are fifteen Barclay soldiers, plus the BC4 cannon. Just common stuff; no surprises. What I did find interesting was that B79a, the seated machine gunner with cast helmet,appears in that photo. Add 1938 to the catalog appearances of 1939, 1940 and I believe, 1941, and this soldier was around for a long time. So, why so relatively hard to find? I asked knowledgeable dealer K. Warren Mitchell and his suggestion was that this piece was vulnerable in the foot area, and so probably was often thrown away after it broke. Adding to the mystery is that this is one of the few Barclay pieces with no known number, and no appearances in all the extant Barclay catalogs.

"GOLDEN" BARCLAYS, 1955 GREY IRON, ETC. *(Cont.)*

Ron Steiner has found a rare Lincoln Logs item; previously unknown both to him and to me. It's "Set No. 30" Lincolnville railroad station. Ron says it's postwar. It came with eight railroad figures. Ron also sent along a scan of his boxed set of Canada's plastic Superior "Fighting Commandos".

The September, 1935 Butler Bros. catalog offered five Barclay "Building and Painting Sets". The one that caught my eye is shown. It's the bottom right compartments that intrigues me. I believe the soldier on the left is the early Barclay 2B10 or maybe

Lincoln Logs "Set No. 30". Photo by Ron Steiner

2B20. But what about the one on the right? It's got to be a doughboy, but I can't figure out which one. Furthermore, I've also tried to determine, without any luck, how they managed to cram all ten listed pieces into that box. It would seem to be one too many. The big mounted cowboy, or "Texas Ranger" at left, is of course BAD.

Boxed set of Superior's "Fighting Commandos", all Beton copies. Photo by Ron Steiner

Finally, I'm occasionally asked if I'll be doing any more editions of my toy-soldier books. I don't know. The first edition of "Collecting Toy Soldiers" sold a bit over 10,000 copies. So did the second. Since there was going to be almost nothing in the way of foreign-made soldiers in "Collecting American-Made Soldiers", I'd have recommended a printing of just 3000. Alas, my publisher didn't ask my opinion and whomped out 12,000. And 10,000 of "Collecting Foreign-Made Toy Soldiers". The American book, as of December 31, had sold 8371 copies. Respectable, but still plenty of copies piled up in the warehouse. The foreign book, as of that date, had sold 7473. My publisher is doing everything it can, via drastically lowered prices, to get rid of the things, but even if it does, I don't know if they'll ask for new editions. eBay may have put a crimp in price guides, as it has in a lot of other areas. But in the meantime I continue to collect prices, photos, and information, just in case, four large boxes full (so far). So if you've anything you'd like to contribute, just get in touch. My email address is grammy3@hargray.com.

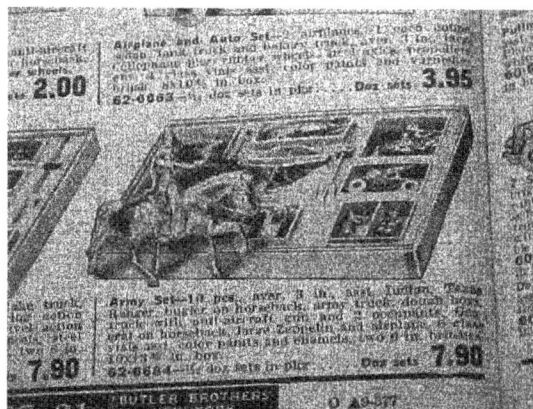

Barclay paint-your-own Army Set in a 1935 Butler Bros. catalog

224

DIMESTORE UPDATE
by Richard O'Brien

Well, it's official. My publisher has decided that, given the current market and the high production cost of my toy-soldier books, they won't be doing any new editions. So from now on I'll confine my toy-soldier writing to articles like this.

The Shackman catalogs are still offering some information. The 1946-47 issue, probably put out about September, 1946, shows Betons being offered (with a mix-up on the listings). Also listed, with the same code given Grey Irons before the war, are almost certainly that company's figures (and without their foreign pieces, which were offered by Shackman just before the war began). Even more interesting is the single listing for 37/383, "Soldier mounted on horse. Made of pulp". This is undoubtedly the Molded Products piece, perhaps a left-over, or a last gasp by Molded Products before it gave up soldier production.

In an undated catalog, probably from 1945, Shackman uses the same prefix, 37, starting from 375. Again, the soldiers are "made of pulp", and presumably from Molded Products, but Shackman, as always, cutting costs, uses two illustrations of Barclay's infantrymen. It's not surprising that Shackman carried Molded Products, as it had the same salesman, Irving Reader, that Barclay had employed, pre-war (and later post-war).

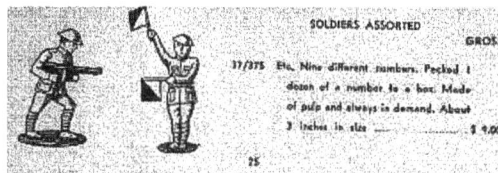

SOLDIERS ASSORTED   GROSS

37/375 Etc. Nine different numbers. Packed 1 dozen of a number to a box. Made of pulp and always in demand. About 3 inches in size .... $ 9.00

B. SHACKMAN & CO. 34th Street and Madison Ave., N. Y.

41/535   41/534

METAL SOLDIERS
Nicely painted, about 3 inches. Dozen, $1.25

41/327	Machine Gunner, kneeling	41/325 Soldier with gun
41/328	Machine Gunner, lying	41/330 Sailor in blue
41/326	Soldier, standing	41/329 Sailor in blue with gun

37/383 Soldier mounted on horse. Made of pulp. 3 inches............Dozen $ .75

DOZEN SETS

41/535 Cowboy Set. Six plastic cowboys mounted on horses. 3". Each set up in box going over hurdle .... $ 7.80

41/534 Cowboys and Indians. Plastic, asst., 3". Six asst. got up in attractive box 7.80

PLASTIC TOYS

BELL RINGER VALUES

6¾ In. Pewter Train Sets
62-6566-2 doz sets in box

80c DOZ SETS

Mold records I have indicate production of Barclay's reindeer began in early 1949, with some turned out that year as Rudolph of the famous red nose. Barclay's George Fall believed the piece was only sold for a year, but Sears catalogs in 1965 and 1967 show it (though not as Rudolph) as part of a winter set.

Ron Steiner recently acquired the illustrated Plastic Toys box of cowboys and Indians. So far there's no indication that the firm made more than the one type of Indian. There seems to have been five cowboys (and a cowgirl), but I'm not sure I've seen two of them; one kneeling with pistols and the other with a pistol raised. Has anyone?

It occurred to me recently that many Barclay collectors haven't seen catalog pages of that company's offerings in the 1930s, so here are three Illustrations, one full-page, from the September, 1935 Butler Brother catalog. Nice stuff, and pretty good prices, too.

62-8131-1 doz in carton.................Doz 2.

Streamlined Pewter Autos—Aver. 5 in., asst. bright colors silver trim, 3 styles, racer, coupe and sedan, 2 cut rhinestones set in black receptacle on front . . . look like headlights, steel spoke wheels, white rubber tires.
62-6588-2 doz in box.....................Doz .8

Army Truck
2⅝ in., dark brown, "U.S. Army" in raised letters, driver.
62-6511—2 doz in box......Doz .39

Tractor
2⅝ in., asst. colors, hook connection on rear, driver.
62-6512—2 doz in box......Doz .39

Fire Department
3 in., 3 asst. models, including fire engine, red, gilt trim.
62-6513—2 doz in box......Doz .42

Wrecker
3 in., white, adjustable steel hook on wrecker arm.
62-6514—2 doz in box......Doz .42

Tootsietoys

All illustrations are actual photographs

An up-to-the-minute line that includes the latest streamline designs! Brilliant enamel finishes! Soft white rubber wheels with steel axles.

Stake Truck
3 in., asst. colors, very realistic miniature.
62-6515—2 doz in box......Doz .42

Anti-Aircraft Gun
3 in., khaki color, on army truck chassis.
62-6516—2 doz in box......Doz .42

Coupe
3¼ in., asst. colors, latest streamline design, large size.
62-6517—2 doz in carton......Doz .42

Racing Car
4⅝ in., silver finish, latest streamline design, large size. We haven't seen anything to equal this number for SIZE and fine FINISH to retail for 5c!
62-6519—2 doz in carton..Doz .42

Racing Car
5¼ in., asst. colors, long streamline body with raised exhaust pipe, driver.
62-6560—2 doz in box......Doz .80

Dump Truck
4½ in., asst. colors, spring action dump, ratchet holds box at any angle.
62-6561—2 doz in box....Doz .80

Coupe
4½ in., asst. colors, dummy lights and bumper, removable spare tire.
62-6562—2 doz in box......Doz .80

Roadster
4½ in. asst. colors, dummy spare tire on either side, trunk rack on rear, driver and steering wheel.
62-6563—2 doz in box......Doz .80

Wrecker
4½ in. asst. colors, rear step and dummy spot light, spring action wrecker arm, ratchet feature for holding arm at any desired angle, large hook.
62-6564—2 doz in box......Doz .80

Stake Truck
4⅝ in. asst. colors, enclosed cab, dummy spare tire under rear end, long stake box.
62-6565—2 doz in box....Doz .80

Sedan
5½ in., asst. enameled colors, enclosed tires, silver finish radiator and front bumper.
62-6576—1 doz in box.Doz .92

Racer
7 in., driver, sprayed silver finish.
62-6573—1 doz in box.Doz .92

Train
7 in., imitation unit, sprayed finish.
62-6577—1 doz in box. Doz

Coupe
5½ in., asst. enameled colors, enclosed tires, silver finish radiator and front bumper.
62-6581—1 doz in box. Doz

4-Car Transport Sets
Overall length 10¾ in., 2½ in. "Mack" design truck with dummy driver, swivel action attachment for hooking to transport carrier, FOUR 2¾ in. autos in asst. colors and styles. Each set in 10⅝x8 in. illustrated box.
62-6632—1 doz sets in pkg.........Doz sets 1.90

Electric Lighted Freight Train
Overall length 15¾ in., 5 pcs. aver. 3¼ in., all with steel axles and couplings, white rubber wheels, locomotive and coal car in black enameled finish, large electric headlight with battery, freight car, oil car and caboose in bright contrasting colors. Each set in 2⅝x18¼ in. illustrated box.
62-6654—½ doz sets in pkg.........Doz sets 4.00

"BARCLAY" BUILDING AND PAINTING SETS

Educational and amusing! Each set contains parts and materials for assembling and painting autos, trucks, airplanes, etc. Attractive partitioned boxes display contents to greatest advantage.

This Set Builds Autos!
3 styles auto chassis, 3¼ in. long, asst. wheels, tires, axles.

Army Set—3½ in., auto with anti-aircraft gun, army truck and soldier on horseback, 3 glass vials paint, brush, asst. color.
62-6638—½ doz sets in pkg.........Doz sets 2.00

Airplane and Auto Set—2 airplanes, 1 each sedan, tank truck and bakery truck, aver. 3 in., Cellophane pkg, rubber wheels, steel axles, prop, etc., 4 glass vials asst. color paints and varnish brush. 8x10½ in. in box.
62-6663—½ doz sets in pkg.....Doz sets 3

Auto Set—Aver. 4½ in., sport coupe, stake truck, roadster, dump truck, wrecker with spring action wrecker arm and "Mack" truck with swivel action

Army Set—10 pcs., aver. 3 in., asst. Indian, Ranger, bugler on horseback, army truck, dough truck with anti-aircraft gun and 2 occupants, seat on horseback, large Zeppelin and airplane.

226

DIMESTORE UPDATE
by Richard O'Brien

For some reason, dating postwar dimestore toy soldiers has been harder than those of the pre-1942 period. The accompanying photo may help a little. This was a news story from February 23, 1951. A mother stood these soldiers in the front window of her home to symbolize her son and his friends who were fighting in Korea. Presumably, she'd recently bought them. The Manoils (I see M177 and M178) had been around for years, but it's surprising to me that they apparently were marketed this late; I'd assumed the smaller 500 series had begun about 1950, supplanting the bigger pieces. In the far left bottom row is Barclay B203. Collector Bill Dunfee bought one of these for ten cents in September, 1947, and here it is, still kicking around. The earliest date I've found for the podfoots that eventually supplanted B203 and its brothers is circa December, 1951, so it's possible both Manoil and Barclay didn't begin manufacturing their smaller series until 1951. This interesting item came from collector Tim O'Callaghan.

Over the years, three different collectors sent me photos of the sailors which bear a copyright mark of DEGAY under their bases (lower right). Oddly, neither Vincent Russo, Don Pielin nor Donald R. Haberman sent me any measurements, so I'd assumed they were about the usual 3-1/4" height. Recently, I wrote Donald and asked. He'd already disposed of the three he owned, but had made a casting (minus the big raised base, shown left) which he sent me, and I found these were in the 54mm range, as shown by Donald's casting next to a Grey Iron. As far as I know, DeGay (or Degay) made only four figures, all sailors; an officer, a seaman, a shore patrol who looks very much like (but not exactly) the seaman, and a deck-swabbing gob. The first three came in both blue and white. When I lived in the New York area, I'd have hied myself to the central Manhattan library, and checked this out in the copyright books on their shelves. Alas, I no longer do, and I can't find out anything via the computer. My guess would be circa 1938-1940. Any New York-area collectors out there willing to check this out? The photo of the four comes from Don Pielin.

When the unpainted soldiers shown below turned up on eBay, my heart skipped a beat; for an instant, they looked as if they might have come from Fichtman & Alexander, whose work we only know from a 1915 drawing in Playthings magazine. But then I read what was posted; found in a warehouse in Patchogue (Long Island, New York). That sounded like George Grampp's soldiers, and that's what they turned out to be. I've already shown the first two on the left as GG20 and GG25. Since the codings in my book ended with GG51, for those who'd like codes for the previous "unknowns", from left to right there's GG52, sailor with rifle; GG53 soldier in campaign hat with rifle; and in a smaller size, GG54 soldier in campaign hat with rifle; GG55 "Marine" with rifle; GG56 Cadet with rifle.

DIMESTORE UPDATE
by Richard O'Brien

In the Depression-pre- WWII era, one WP A project was to photograph every building (even empty lots) in all five boroughs of New York City. Today, an outfit is selling copies of these photos. Unfortunately, my experience is that they're pretty erratic, with some luck on my part, and some no-responses on theirs. Unfortunately, my request for a photo of Manoil's Brooklyn factory resulted in the latter.

Somehow, it had never occurred to me to wonder what that company's Waverly, New York (it moved there in 1940) buildings looked like. Luckily, collector Jan Beck had more curiosity, and has done considerable research in Waverly, plus some good picture-taking. The first factory, which appears to be huge (in the pre-war years, Manoil employed 225 people), was located at 142 Providence. Its size makes the Manoil brothers' hope, mid-war, to turn it into a ware-house and then a poultry farm, look like ideas that had some logical basis, even though neither worked out.

The address for the factory comes from a copy of a 1948 Waverly Directory that Jan sent me. For the record, the Waverly home addresses for Jack and Maurice, respec-

SYNCHRONIZE YOUR WATCHES! It's zero hour as young Billy Brenner of Akron, Ohio lines up two scout cars and a medium tank for an all-out assault! These molded-rubber wheel toys are new Sunruco items developed by The Sun Rubber Co. of Barberton, Ohio; and are made of the same synthetic rubber used by our armed forces in their bullet-sealing gasoline tanks.

tively, were 314 Chemung and 109 Park Place. This seems an appropriate time to point out that the names of the two were inadvertently transposed under their photos in "Collecting American-Made Toy Soldiers". Jack, as I'd shown in previ-ous books, is the tough-looking one with a cigarette hanging out of his mouth, and Maurice (pronounced "Morris") the more sedate-looking bespectacled guy in the tie.

Manoil moved to the smaller brick factory in 1953. The address there, according to a 1957 toy trade magazine, was 533 Broad Street. It was at that address that it expired, probably in 1959.

It occurred to me recently that my books have never listed the Grey Iron animals that seem to have come out about 1941. The Xerox I have of a Greyart Miniatures page is too fuzzy for reproduction. However the listings and sizes should be enough for the experienced Grey Iron collector should he or she stumble over these pieces. The numberings are Grey Iron's.

No 1 Horse. (Trotting) 4 in. high, 5 in. long. No.2 Horse. (Grazing) 3-1/2 in. high, 5 in. long. No. 10 Bull (standing) 2-1/2 in high, 4-1/4 in. long. No. 12 Cow (lying) 2 in. high, 4 in. long. No. 14 Cow (standing) 2-3/4" high, 4-1/2" long. No. 15 Calf (standing) 2-1/4" high, 3" long. No. 20 Sheep (standing) 2 in. high, 3-1/4" long. No. 30 Pig (looks as if he may be feeding) 1-3/4" high, 3-1/2" long. All came in various colors.

The remaining have no sizes given, but presumably are small. 50 Rooster, 54 Hen, 58 Chick, 59 Quail, 60 Duck, 65 Goose, 66 Gander. A 1941 Shackman catalog lists some of these barnyard figures, and doesn't add anything not on Grey Iron's page.

Collector Tim O'Callaghan sent me this news photo of Sun Rubber's tank and scout cars. It's dated May 7, 1946, and the caption mentions the "new Sunroco items developed by the Sun Rubber Co. of Barberton, Ohio". Interestingly, the caption also states that the vehicles were "made of the same synthetic rubber used by our armed forces in their bullet-sealing gasoline tanks".

This may be my last column for a while, or last column, period. Very simply, I've run out of research material. If I turn any up - and I check eBay daily - I'll of course get the news out.

A quick correction: the George Grampp codings in my last article should have read "left to right", not the reverse. My mistake, not the typesetter's.

Maniol's first and last Waverly factory. Photo by Jan Beck

Maniol's second and last Waverly factory. Photo by Jan Beck

DIMESTORE UPDATE
NEW WILLIAM FEIX(?) & 1939 BARCLAY
By Richard O'Brien

Recently, a Fall, 1915 Butler Bros. catalog turned up at auction. I asked the seller to send me a scan of any metal toy soldiers that might be in it. She did, and I promptly bid.

The single scan was very blurry, but what it seemed to show was six sets (five of them previously unknown) by the very early American toy-soldier maker William Feix. Though I couldn't be sure because of the blurriness, one of the headlines under the top set at right seemed to say Soldiers and Indians. This was intriguing in an odd way, as I assumed it would consist of Feix's Indians and its early troops in their helmet-like headgear.

Instead, when the catalog arrived, I was initially disappointed. I'd read the headline correctly, but the illustration showed no Indians. However, that let-down quickly disappeared as I found myself more and more intrigued by what I found on the page. Experts in early American soldiers like Bill Nutting, Will Beierwaltes and Bill O'Brien had used their cultivated eyes to add to likely Feix production based on a 1903 illustrated Feix ad I'd found and similar types they'd run across. After a lapse of several years, it seemed likely that was pretty much all we'd ever find re Feix's soldiers. Instead, with this find, three of the six sets seemed to be showing us a whole new range plus an important addition to an old one. A fourth suggested a paint variation and perhaps a new figure.

One can be pretty certain the top two at left in the illustration shown are from Feix. The soldiers on top are the same types shown in Feix's 1903 ad. The second set, like the one above it, has what seems to be a flag unique to Feix; one with a spear-like tip. However, that lower set has soldiers not previously attributed to the Brooklyn soldiermaker; five Volunteers in the on guard position.

Now for the top two sets at the right: the foot figures all appear to have flat-topped caps, apparel not previously attributed to Feix. There are three types; On Guard, Flag Bearer, Drummer.

Finally, in the bottom set at right the sailors seem to be painted dark blue, unlike those I've shown in my books, and one of them (it's hard to tell by the drawing) may be a flag bearer.

Is this all Feix? Well, the flag-tips in four of the sets are too small to tell if they're Feixlike. However, the cannon which are seen in profile in three of the sets are the types associated so far only with William Feix, the Christies and George Grampp. The Christies weren't making soldiers in 1915 and Grampp's figures bear no resemblance to the ones Feix turned out. The cannon in the two sets at bottom right are seen from overhead, but they bear the same descriptions as those in the other three: "brass finish mounted" .

Okay, collectors. Do any of you have pieces that seem to fit here? And two final notes: this is the first time a Feix set has been seen furnished with a pop gun, like those seen in American Soldier Company boxes. So could this be American Soldier? Absolutely not. No mention of a tray!

A 1939-40 Shackman's catalog has emerged. The former owner of Shackman's has told me his firm would add new Barclays as soon as they were available (not all of them, alas). Thus this catalog helps to confirm that Barclay's large civilian line (the ones mainly in mufti; not the cop, fireman, Scouts) began in 1939. Here are the Boy, the Conductor, the Engineer, the Girl, the Man, the Porter, the Red Cap and the Woman. And, on a separate page devoted to Wedding Favors, the Bride and Groom. Also apparently new that year is a paint variation, the Masked Rider on Horse. As with all but one of Shackman's catalogs, only Barclay's figures appear; Tootsietoy got all of Shackman's attention in the aircraft and vehicles department.

DIMESTORE UPDATE
UNIVERSAL PLASTICS - FINALLY, A TIE TO BETON
By Richard O'Brien

In 1993 I received collector Bill Hanlon's excellent book, "Plastic Toys". Toward the end of it, I got startled. Bill casually mentioned he'd come across a 1939 company called Universal Plastics Corporation that seemed to have some kind of tie to Beton - whether business-wise or because their figures were so similar (some even alike) he didn't know.

In all my years of collecting, I'd never heard of Universal. I quickly got in touch with Bill and in turn he sent me a page from the August 1939 issue of Modern Plastics magazine. There were two photos of Universal's figures. One showed three Indians who looked just like Beton's. The other displayed a trio of soldiers. Those three looked like Betons too, except for one eye-opening detail. Instead of the steel helmets found on Betons, they were wearing soft caps! Already, a question I'd had in my mind for a long time was answered. Some of Beton's soldiers have a normal-looking helmet. Others look as if they're wearing steel derbies. Looking at Universal's military figures, it was obvious that somewhere along the way their molds had been "chased" to change their caps into helmets.

Once I had all this in hand, I quickly got in touch with other collectors, and they in turn sought out others they thought might be helpful. As it turned out, for years some collectors had been aware of "Betons" with rectangular bases (unlike the ovals Beton then employed), and that under the base, there was no mention of Beton, just a symbol that looked like a combined capital U and a small p. As time went on, collectors like Bill Holt, Ron Steiner, John Sicinski and others reported discoveries of still more figures made by Universal. At this moment, we know about six soldiers, three Indians, three cowboys, a fireman and a traffic officer.

What we didn't know was how Beton had got hold of Universal's molds. Had they bought them, or was there no link at all between the two firms; perhaps a third party had provided Beton with them, or Beton on its own had stumbled on the molds.

We now know a bit more. Recently, Bill Hanlon got in touch with me and told me about a Universal ad he'd found in the March, 1940 Modern Plastics. Furthermore, he'd unearthed (via the papers of Islyn Thomas, of Thomas Toys) a 1943 Dun and Bradstreet report that furnished much new information on Universal. I, of course, asked for copies, and Bill soon supplied them.

It took me a few seconds to realize what I was looking at in the ad. I'd expected Universal Plastics soldiers. Instead, they were Betons, both Beton's own early pieces and the "Universals" turned into steel-derby-wearers. What had been Universal's drummer now not only had the new headgear, but his base was a Beton oval. A small bonus was seeing Universal's signalman, till now only known as a lone piece missing both its flags, holding up one of the flags (the lower one hidden behind the back of an infantryman).

Finally, it was obvious. There <u>had</u> been a tie between Universal and Beton. In the ad, there's the suggestion that Universal was now producing for Beton, with the statement "The drummer boy, an example of Universal Custom Molding, is out drumming up business for several Universal customers.. .". The date of the magazine suggests that Universal's own production was short-lived. In August of 1939 they were "experiment-

ing" with a line of figures. Since Modern Plastics was published on the 5th of each month, it seems likely Universal was out of selling its soldiers by February, 1940 at the latest, and presumably earlier.

The Dun & Bradstreet is terrific. It tells us two of its officers in August, 1939 were chairman Julius Loeb, and Hans Meyer the treasurer (succeeded a month later by Dr. Leo West). The company was begun as Superlithe Corp., chartered February 28, 1935. It went bankrupt, and reorganized in 1936 as Universal Plastics Corp.

Importantly, according to the report, Universal, which at this time was located at 235 Jersey Avenue in New Brunswick, NJ, lost money consistently from the time of its founding straight through to the end of 1940. Thus it seems likely it was happy to sell its molds to Beton for hard cash.

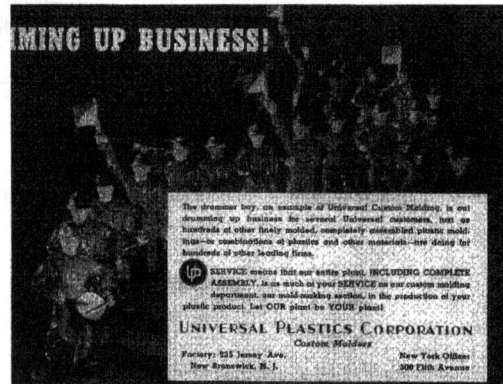

HOORAY FOR EBAY
SOME "NEW" TOY SOLDIERS
By Richard O'Brien

American Mint was a corporation that, sometime in the late 1930s, began selling candy containers whose circular outsides displayed brightly-colored soldiers of the world. There were four types; Troopers, Doughboys, Minute Men and Yanks.

When I reported on them in my book "Collecting American-Made Toy Soldiers", I knew at least one illustration was missing: the soldier who represented Switzerland. Fellow-collector Tom Quinn and I vaguely believed at least one more needed to be added: A Yank in a rakishly-tilted campaign cap. But neither of us was quite sure of this.

Because of that possible Yank and the Swiss, from time to time I've trolled my computer for American Mints. Until this year I'd had no luck. Then, in one day I found not only those two questions answered, but learned about six Yanks I'd never heard of before.

A Yank "Ski-Trooper" was being auctioned off on eBay. And along with his photo was another of what seemed to be every known American Mint. There was "Switzerland"! And there too was the Yank with the askew cap Tom and I had thought we'd remembered! He was a "Military Police". Standing there with him at the bottom row was also the rest of the Yanks, who probably were issued shortly after World War Two began: "Admiral", "Pursuit Pilot", "Parachutist", "Infantry Man", "Nurse", "Marine", "Ski Soldier", "Army Officer" and "Gob". What an unexpected array!

I got in touch with the seller, Patrick Boyer, who told me he'd added all those pieces to the auction site in the hope it would stimulate information on the company. He and his cousin, William Kaiser, are American Mint aficionados. William began buying them in the late 1930s, for a penny apiece. In the 1950s, whenever Patrick had been "a very good boy", he was allowed to play with them. They've obviously researched the subject; Patrick sent me two photos of the building American Mint had been in, both about what it looked like when American Mint was in business, and more recently, after it had been converted to condominiums, with balconies added.

AMERICAN MINTS:
Top, third from left, "Switzerland".
Bottom row, left to right: all Yanks: "Admiral", "Pursuit Pilot", "Parachutist", "Infantry Man", "Nurse", "Military Police", "Marine", "Ski Soldier", a bit of "Army Officer".

The building which housed American Mint, at 114 East 13th Street, Manhattan, NYC

The same building, post-1984, after it had gone condo, with balconies (seen at left) added.

231

Happily, I was able to furnish the two collectors with some new information. They'd never known that "Japan" existed. It looks exactly like "China", even to the same uniform color.

Apparently, like most collectors, Patrick has wound up with some extras. He's offered them on eBay, and told me he'd recently sold the Yank Army Officer for $120, a Minute Man "Sweden" for $70, and that last year he'd sold a few and averaged thirty to sixty dollars apiece, depending on their condition. However, he's never had a Yank sell for less than $100. Wartime shortages may have curtailed their run.

Patrick's not really interested in selling. He lists them in the hopes "that others will see the prices they're bringing and sell theirs. I'm still, buying and upgrading (us old collectors never quit)".

This seems to complete the sets of American Mints. Except that I have a vague memory, far vaguer than my remembrance of the Military Policeman; a rather insane looking Yank general with a white moustache. I've told Patrick that I'm probably wrong, but who knows?

If any readers want to check out American Mints on eBay, I suggest they start with: 1930s American Mint Corp. That's how Patrick begins his headlines.

American Mint, left to right: "Gob", "Army Officer"

Two other "new" soldiers turned up last year, also on eBay. What was being offered was a boxed set of Toy Creations soldiers. The box top was the same as the one shown in my book. But some of the soldiers were different, and unlike any Toy Creations I'd seen. They were four pilots and two soldiers at searchlights. They looked like Metal Casts. I checked my book and there they were: 22A Aviator and 26A Anti-Aircraft Soldier.

Metal Casts produced and sold by Toy Creations

There was a possibility someone had just filled out the box with the Metal Casts. But another possibility was that Toy Creations had made new molds from the Metal Cast pieces. Or simply that Toy Creations had obtained the molds, which of course were sold to the general public.

After the auction was over, I got in touch with the winner (unfortunately I forgot to ask his permission to use his name, so I can't identify him; but the price realized was $ 1025). He confirmed that the two "Metal Casts" had exactly the same paint as the others in the set, so obviously they'd originated with Toy Creations. He also compared them with his own Metal Casts and it was obvious to him they'd come from original Metal Cast molds.

So here's something more to look for, if you've got some American Alloys, whose paint you can compare to seemingly "Metal Cast" soldiers.

1938 Auburn Rubber and 1916 Soldier Sets
by Richard O'Brien

As most collectors know, you can learn a lot about a company's products from catalogs, both general and those from the manufacturers.

We Auburn Rubber fanciers have got pretty lucky. The company dated all of its known pre-WWII catalogs, and they were all in color. 1940 turned up first, then 1937, and after that 1936 and 1941. Recently, I got lucky and wound up with the firm's 1938 eight-pager, plus two extra pages.

I didn't expect too much, what with what we already had in those catalogs, plus the firm's soldiers that were shown in 1939 general catalogs. And I didn't find a lot, but some of it is interesting.

The firm's accompanying April 11, 1938 letter to toy buyers emphasized the toys (not just the soldiers) being in "BRILLIANT NEW COLORS", with an emphasis (their quote) on "silver" hats (their word) on the soldiers. The catalog emphasized it too, as Auburn's printer used a silver dye that actually looks like silver on the original page (Manoil employed this too in their circa 1939 pages). What eventually caught my eye was the fact that the headgear on the Foreign Legion also shows that metallic silver. I've never seen one of the legionnaires with a silver "hat", and when I checked with him, dealer K. Warren Mitchell hadn't either. Has anyone?

A new offering in 1938 was the "Cannon with Tractor" in "army olive green". A mimeographed legal-size sheet that accompanied the catalog states that it sold for $1.60 per dozen. That figures to a bit over thirteen cents. Since this was the Depression, it's possible the tractor only retailed for fifteen.

Back to the Legion. We now know the colors for the foreign legion infantry, as opposed to Auburn's White Guards and Royal Guards. The legion privates could wear a red jacket with blue pants or a white jacket with black trousers. The 1936 catalog shows the Royal Guard officer and trooper both in dark blue with red helmets and the White Guard trooper with white jacket and red pants and helmet. The officers for the White Guard and and Foreign Legion were interchangeable.

As a kid, I'd wondered if the white Auburns were meant as sailors, despite their helmets and uniforms. But white or blue, they're always Marines.

Some oddities; though they're shown in boxed sets, the A22 242 Anti-Aircraft Gun, The A18 216 Observer With Binoculars, the A22 242 Anti-Aircraft Gun, the A23 516 Motorcycle Cop (though 1516 here) are not displayed on the toy-soldier page, nor are they listed in the catalog or the mimeographed sheet. Thus they share the same fate as the seated machine gunner, also shown in boxed sets in 1937 and 1938, but otherwise invisible. Was this a mistake, or at this point were they sold only in sets?

It's nice to have all this information, but I'd love to see a 1935 catalog, if there was one, to find out if Auburn also portrayed its infantry as Italians and Ethiopians. Even more, I'd like to fall upon, if it existed, a 1942 issue, which might perhaps finally show the running "pilot" I know existed. My suspicion is that it would also only appear as part of an illustrated boxed set. Like some of the above.

****

I recently bid on a 1916 Butler Bros. catalog because, from the less than distinct scan I was offered, it looked as if William Feix might have offered some toy soldiers not previously attributed to that company. Alas, when I eyed the actual page, I saw the coding made it obvious that the two sets that were new to me had a manufacturer who wasn't Feix. The pieces looked like homecasts to me, but I didn't remember seeing them before. Accordingly, I fired off a photocopy to homecast expert Ed Poole. Ed, since he doesn't confine his expertise to homecasts, informed me that they were semi-rounds, that he'd seen them before, and were definitely from the hands of a manufacturer, probably in Germany or maybe Austria. Since he was in his second home, he didn't have his reference books handy, so couldn't name just who'd done these interesting-looking pieces.

The catalog is dated November, 1916. Collectors of early soldiers and related toys may enjoy the various sets displayed here. The name of the machine gun attests to a more innocent age.

AUBURN RUBBER CORPORATION

CEMENT APPLIED SOLES
CEMENT APPLIED HEELS
U·FIX·ET CEMENTS
NAIL·ON TAPS
SHORT SOLES AND HEELS

AUBURN Quality

RUBBER KNEELING PADS
RUBBER FLY SWATTERS
RUBBER JAR OPENERS
RUBBER DOOR MATS
RUBBER TOYS

FACTORY AND GENERAL OFFICES

AUBURN, INDIANA

April 11, 1938.

Important Announcement
To the Toy Buyer!

Gentlemen:

HERE'S OUR NEW 1938 CATALOG AND PRICE SHEET - complete with descriptions, packaging and weights.

It's a splendid new and greatly enlarged line that we know you will want to see at the Toy Show -- or we will be glad to send samples. Briefly, the IMPORTANT NEW THINGS we are now offering you are:

1. Exceptionally BRILLIANT NEW COLORS - that you will have to use to appreciate, but that we know you will like. Includes "silver" hats on soldiers, improved new strong, positive-holding box insert trays, etc.

2. MANY NEW ITEMS - which in actual counter sales have already proven big volume sellers; it is Auburn's established policy to feature only Counter-Sales-Tested items - a policy on which you can rely,

For example, in boxed goods, the Farm Implement Set (on face page), Rubber Building Blocks and the Carry Car Trailer Set (page 2), the Sponge Rubber Alphabet Blocks (page 3) and the Artillery Set (page 4) were all made up of NEW items that have proved big sellers since the last Toy Show.

With these new items added to our standard line of soldiers, farm animals, automobiles and airplanes - each offered singly and in boxed sets - we feel confident all previous sales records will be doubled,

Last year's demand taxed us to meet our customers' requirements. With our newer, more complete line, an early order is advisable. Favor us with an early order NOW, that we may serve you better.

Yours very truly,
AUBURN RUBBER CORPORATION,
Sales Mgr.

LAShimer/E

ALL ORDERS, CONTRACTS, OR AGREEMENTS ARE TAKEN SUBJECT TO DELAYS CAUSED BY STRIKES, FIRES, ACCIDENTS, OR OTHER CONDITIONS BEYOND OUR CONTROL. ALL QUOTATIONS ARE MADE BY US SUBJECT TO CHANGE WITHOUT NOTICE.

ORIGINATORS AND LARGEST MANUFACTURERS OF CEMENT APPLIED SOLES (AUBURN PATENTS 1,577,349 AND 1,624,500)

AUBURN RUBBER
1938 AUB-RUB'R TOYS

FREE DISPLAY

A dealer's real help — with initial order.

PLACE ORDERS EARLY. Last year's demand ran beyond our calculation. This year, with the new items, promises to more than double.

BUYERS' INFORMATION

THERE ARE NO OTHER TOYS LIKE THESE. Molded ALL RUBBER, beautifully designed and hand decorated. Superior to other materials, because HARMLESS, UN-BREAKABLE, CANNOT SCRATCH either the child or furniture. LIGHT WEIGHT and WASHABLE. *Small wonder that mothers everywhere are enthusiastic.*

The most complete line on the market with *every item sale tested* and a *proved hot seller.* All wheeled items have our "Spun Lock" axle which prevents either axles or wheels coming off.

MANY NEW ITEMS. NEW SOLDIERS AND ARTIL-LERY ITEMS WITH NEW BRILLIANT COLORS AND "SILVER" HATS; NEW WHEELED ITEMS, NEW TRAC-TOR WITH FARM MACHINERY HITCH-ON; NEW BRICK BUILDING SETS and SPONGE RUBBER BLOCKS.

KEEP A YEAR AROUND DISPLAY. Because small children need to be continually amused and soon de-velop their own growing games of "soldiers," "farms," "autos," etc., our shipment records show *substantial repeat orders every month.*

FARM IMPLEMENT
BOXED SET

A combination of AUB-RUBR's

FASTEST SELLING items

GOOD ALL SEASONS
OF THE YEAR

No. 505 Farm Implement Set—16" x 9" 4 color box—1 red tractor, 1 green tractor, 1 staked trailer, 1 disc, 1 spreader, 1 plow, 1 1938 Olds-mobile.

1 dozen weight 27 lbs. Packed 1 dozen.

236

No. 601

BRICK BUILDING BLOCKS

No. 611

RUBBER
BRICK BUILDING BLOCKS

An EDUCATIONAL TOY with
    YEAR AROUND SALES APPEAL

Includes 46 designs in complete architectural
booklet.

In 4 color 16" x 9" box.

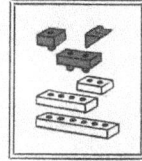

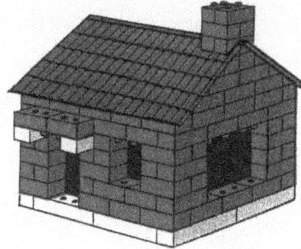

Bricks hold togeth-
er by FIT-TITE con-
struction, Pat. apld.
for.

Rubber pieces
may be boiled
and sterilized.

No. 601 Brick Building Blocks—illustrated—$1.00 retail, consists of 146 rubber pieces, two roofs, and BOOK OF DE-
SIGNS. These are: 80 whole brick, 30 half brick, 20 quarter brick, 6 1" gray blocks, 8 2" gray blocks, 2 3"
gray blocks, Roofs No. 1 and No. 2, and BOOK OF DESIGNS, 1 dozen weight 25½ lbs. Packed two dozen.

No. 603 Brick Building Blocks—double size—$2.00 retail, consists of 292 rubber pieces, three roofs, and BOOK OF
DESIGNS. These are: 160 whole brick, 60 half brick, 40 quarter brick, 12 1" gray blocks, 16 2" gray blocks, 4
3" gray blocks, Roofs No. 1, No. 2, and No. 3, and BOOK OF DESIGNS, 1 dozen weight 45 lbs. Packed 1 dozen.

No. 611 Sack of Blocks. 50¢ retail. Additional or replacement blocks in proper proportion for above sets, 1 dozen
weight 10½ lbs. Packed 1 dozen.

CARRY CAR
TRAILER

Replica of G.M. model

Includes 3 OLDSMOBILES

in NEW 4 COLOR 16" x 9"

DISPLAY CARTON

75¢ retail

No. 511 Carry Car Trailer with 3 Oldsmobiles
—in 4 color 16" x 9" box—12" long, colored red
and blue, 1 green Olds, 1 gray Olds, 1 red Olds.

1 dozen weight 27¾ lbs. Packed 1 dozen.

Medium size—FARM SET—4 color box 16" x 4½".
No. 101—(Illustrated) 1 horse, 1 colt, 1 cow, 1 calf,
1 sheep, 1 pig.
1 dozen weight 12 lbs. Packed 3 dozen.

ANIMAL BOXED SETS

50¢ and $1.00 retail.

MAY BE USED FOR
TEETHING TOYS

Large size—FARM SET—4 color box 16" x 9".
No. 105—(Illustrated) 1 horse, 1 colt, 1 cow, 1
calf, 3 sheep, 1 Collie dog, 2 pigs, 3 fence
panels, 1 fence panel with gate.
1 dozen weight 22½ lbs. Packed 1½ dozen.

Large size—WHEELED SET—4 color box 16" x 9".
No. 503—(Illustrated) 2 large airplanes, 1 small
airplane, 2 Oldsmobiles, 1 Ford Sedan, 2 Ford
Coupes, 1 motorcycle cop, assorted colors.
1 doz. weight 26¼ lbs. Packed 1 doz. $1.00 retail.

WHEEL SETS

New Trays securely hold
Toys in place

All items have one-piece
non-removable axle

NEW HIGH LUSTER
FINISH

BRILLIANT COLORS

Medium Size—WHEELED SET—4 col. box 16"x4½"
No. 501—(Illustrated) 1 large Airplane, 1 small
Airplane, 1 Oldsmobile, 1 Ford Sedan, 1 Ford
Coupe, assorted colors.
1 dozen weight 14¼ lbs. Packed 2 doz. 50¢ retail

SPONGE RUBBER BLOCKS

50¢ retail

GOOD QUALITY
WHITE SPONGE

RUBBER WAGON MADE TO
ATTACH TO NO. 1520
TRACTOR
(See page 8).

7" x 9" Box

No. 609 Dozen Blocks—50¢ retail.
12 - 1¼" Sponge Rubber Blocks
Lettered four sides. Box 7" x 9".
1 dozen weight 9¼ lbs. Packed 3 dozen.

No. 515 Wagon of Blocks—50¢ retail.
Wagon is 6¼" long, colored red.
Eight 1¼" Blocks.
Box 3½" x 6½".
1 dozen weight 9 lbs. Packed 3 dozen.

SOLDIER BOXED SETS

A strip on the tray insert holds
each soldier in place.

NEW INSERT TRAYS
HOLD TOYS
SECURELY IN PLACE

EACH BOX A 4 COLOR
DISPLAY CARTON

ALL SOLDIERS
have NEW high
luster finish.

BRILLIANT
COLORS

SILVER
HELMETS

$1.00 and 50¢ retail.

Non-marring to
furniture.

See page 6 for
description of
individual
soldiers.

No. 207 ARTILLERY SET, as illustrated.
1 dozen weight 22 lbs. Packed 1 dozen.

No. 201 U. S. INFANTRY, as illustrated.
1 dozen weight 7½ lbs. Packed 3 dozen.

No. 209 FOREIGN LEGION, as illustrated.
1 dozen weight 7½ lbs. Packed 3 dozen.

No. 233—FOREIGN LEGION, as illustrated
1 dozen weight 14¼ lbs. Packed 1½ dozen.

No. 231 INFANTRY SET, as illustrated.
1 dozen weight 16 lbs. Packed 1½ dozen.

No. 205 MARINE SET, as illustrated.
1 dozen weight 7½ lbs. Packed 3 dozen.

No. 213 MARINE SET, as illustrated.
1 dozen weight 15 lbs. Packed 1½ dozen.

WEIGHTS and PACKAGING

BOX SETS

Stock No.		Weight 1 dozen	Packed to Carton
207	Artillery Set (asstd. artillery weapons and soldiers, khaki)	22 lbs.	1 dozen
231	Infantry Set (asstd. infantry weapons and soldiers, khaki)	16 lbs.	1½ dozen
213	Marine Set (asstd. blue and white, 2 officers, 2 buglers, 12 marines)	15 lbs.	1½ dozen
233	Foreign Legion Set (red, white, blue, black, 2 officers, 14 privates)	14¼ lbs.	1½ dozen
201	Infantry Set (khaki; 1 officer, 1 bugler, 6 privates)	7½ lbs.	3 dozen
205	Marine Set (blue, white—1 officer, 1 bugler, 6 marines)	7½ lbs.	3 dozen
209	Foreign Legion Set (red, white, blue, 1 officer, 7 privates)	7½ lbs.	3 dozen
105	Farm Animal Set (14 large and small figures, inc. fenced lot)	22½ lbs.	1½ dozen
101	Farm Animal Set (6 large and small figures, assorted)	12 lbs.	3 dozen
505	Farm Implement Set (7 large wheeled implements, assorted)	27 lbs.	1 dozen
503	Wheeled Set (5 large, 4 small assorted wheel toys)	26¼ lbs.	1 dozen
501	Wheeled Set (3 small, 2 large assorted wheel toys)	14¼ lbs.	2 dozen
511	Carry Car Trailer (1 G.M. Trailer, 3 Oldsmobiles, asstd.)	27¾ lbs.	1 dozen
515	Wagon of Blocks (8¼" cube assorted lettered blocks in 6¼" wagon)	9 lbs.	3 dozen
609	Dozen Blocks (sponge 1¼" Alphabet Blocks in 7" x 9" box)	9¼ lbs.	3 dozen
601	Brick Building Blocks (with design books and roofs)	25½ lbs.	2 dozen
603	Brick Building Blocks (with design books and roofs)	45 lbs.	1 dozen
611	Bag of Building Blocks (to supplement No. 601, 603) (not boxed)	10½ lbs.	1 dozen

See pages 1, 2, 3, 4 for descriptions

BULK TOYS

Stock No.		Weight 1 dozen	Packed to Carton
1200	U. S. Infantry Private (khaki, yellow, black, silver)	⅝ lb.	2 dozen
1202	U. S. Infantry Bugler (khaki, red, black, silver)	⅝ lb.	2 dozen
1204	U. S. Infantry Officer (khaki, yellow, black, brown)	⅝ lb.	2 dozen
1210B	Marine Private, blue, (blue, black, yellow, silver)	⅝ lb.	2 dozen
1212B	Marine Bugler, blue (blue, yellow, black, silver)	⅝ lb.	2 dozen
1204B	Marine Officer, blue (blue, yellow, black)	⅝ lb.	2 dozen
1210W	Marine Private, white (white, black, silver)	⅝ lb.	2 dozen
1212W	Marine Bugler, white (white, blue, silver)	⅝ lb.	2 dozen
1204W	Marine Officer, white (white, yellow, black)	⅝ lb.	2 dozen
220	Foreign Legion Officer (white, red, yellow)	½ lb.	2 dozen
214	Foreign Legion Private (red, blue, yellow, silver)	½ lb.	2 dozen
218	Foreign Legion Private (white, black, silver)	½ lb.	2 dozen
232	Officer on Horse (khaki, red, yellow, black)	2¼ lbs.	1 dozen
1236	Signalman (khaki, red, white, black, silver)	½ lb.	2 dozen
1238	Charging Soldier (khaki, black, silver)	½ lb.	2 dozen
1520	Tractor (assorted 8 red, 4 green to dozen)	3¾ lbs.	1 dozen
528	Trailer (red)	6 lbs.	1 dozen
526	Plow (red, silver)	⅞ lb.	1 dozen
504	Ford Coupe (assorted 6 red, 2 green, 2 blue, 2 battleship gray to dozen)	1¾ lbs.	3 dozen
502	Ford Sedan (assorted 6 red, 2 blue, 2 green, 2 battleship gray to dozen)	2 lbs.	3 dozen
1518	1938 Oldsmobile (assorted 6 red, 2 blue, 2 green, 2 battleship gray to dozen)	4½ lbs.	1 dozen
506	Airplane—small (assorted half red, half silver)	⅞ lb.	3 dozen
508	Airplane—large (assorted half red, half silver)	1¼ lbs.	1 dozen
1516	Motorcycle Cop (khaki, trimmed)	2 lbs.	1 dozen
102	Horse (brown and cream)	2⅝ lbs.	1 dozen
108	Cow (black and white)	2½ lbs.	1 dozen
1028	Assorted Horse & Cow	2½ lbs.	1 dozen
104	Colt (brown and cream)	⅞ lb.	2 dozen
106	Pig (black and white)	1 lb.	2 dozen
110	Calf (white and black)	⅞ lb.	2 dozen
114	Sheep (white and black)	1⅛ lbs.	2 dozen
116	Collie Dog (white and tan)	1⅛ lbs.	2 dozen
4046	Assorted Animals (2 colts, 3 calves, 3 sheep, 1 Collie, 3 pigs to dozen)	1 lb.	2 dozen
513	Cannon w/Tractor (army olive green)	7⅞ lbs.	1 dozen
305	Hop Bunnies, 3 piece string (blue, yellow, pink)	5⅜ lbs.	1 dozen
307-9	Scottie Dogs, 3 piece string (black, black-white)	5¾ lbs.	1 dozen
311	Hen and Chicks, 3 piece string (white, yellow, red)	6½ lbs.	1 dozen
322	Sponge Easter Eggs (assorted red, blue, yellow)	1 lb.	3 dozen
611	Bag of Brick Building Blocks (to accompany Boxed Sets No. 601, 603)	10½ lbs.	1 dozen

See pages 6, 7, 8 for description

SOLDIERS

NEW HIGH LUSTER FINISH
SILVER HELMETS
BRILLIANT COLORS

YEAR AROUND SELLERS
QUICK PROFITABLE TURNOVER

(See page 4 for Soldier Box Sets)

No. 1204
Infantry
Officer

No. 1202
Infantry
Bugler

No. 1200
Infantry
Private

No. 1238
Charging
Soldier

U. S. SOLDIERS — 3″ High   1 dozen weight ⅝ lb. Packed 2 dozen to carton.

No. 1204B
Marine
Officer

No. 1212B
Marine
Bugler

No. 1210B
Marine
Private

No. 1204W
Marine
Officer

No. 1212W
Marine
Bugler

No. 1210W
Marine
Private

U. S. SOLDIERS — 3″ High   1 dozen weight ⅝ lb. Packed 2 dozen to carton.

No. 220
Officer

No. 218
Private

No. 214
Private

No. 1236
Signalman

No. 232
Soldier on Horse — 3⅞″ high
1 dozen weight 2¼ lbs. Packed 1 dozen.

FOREIGN LEGION — 3¼″ High
1 dozen weight ½ lb. Packed 2 dozen to carton.

CANNON WITH TRACTOR
Replica of New Army Gun

RETAIL 25¢

A new item of outstanding play value—completing our line of molded rubber SOLDIERS.

No. 513—CANNON WITH TRACTOR
Color army olive green, 11½" long
1 dozen weight 7⅞ lbs. Packed 1 dozen.

STRINGED PULL TOYS

No. 305—HOP BUNNIES—3 piece string—10" long
1 dozen weight 5⅜ lbs. Packed 1 dozen

No. 311—HEN AND CHICKS—3 piece string—9½" long
1 dozen weight 6½ lbs. Packed 1 dozen

Scottie Strings

No. 307-9

No. 307-9 Scottie Strings—11½" long—25¢ retail
Assorted half white, half black
1 dozen weight 5¾ lbs.. Packed 1 dozen

FARM ANIMALS

Stock up the Farm

No. 110 Calf—2½" long
White and black—5¢ retail
1 doz. wt. ⅞ lb. Packed 2 doz.

No. 116 Collie Dog—2¾" long
white and tan—5¢ retail
1 doz. wt. 1⅛ lbs. Packed 2 doz.

No. 106 Pig—2⅜" long
White and black—5¢ retail
1 doz. wt. 1 lb. Packed 2 doz.

No. 108 Cow—3⅝" long
White and black—10¢ retail
1 doz. wt. 2½ lbs. Packed 1 doz.

FARM ANIMALS

WELL DESIGNED
QUALITY RUBBER

MAY BE USED FOR
TEETHING TOYS

Good Year Around Sellers

No. 114 Sheep—2½" long
White and black—5¢ retail
1 doz. wt. 1⅛ lb. Packed 2 doz.

No. 104 Colt—2½" long
Brown and cream—5¢ retail
1 doz. wt. ⅞ lb. Packed 2 doz.

Assortments:

No. 1028—Assorted HORSE and COW—Assorted 6 horses, 6 cows.
1 dozen weight 2½ lbs. Packed 1 dozen

No. 4046—Assorted ANIMALS—2 colts, 3 calves, 3 sheep, 1 Collie, 3 pigs to dozen.
1 dozen weight 1 lb. Packed 2 dozen

No. 102 Horse—4" long
Brown and cream—10¢ retail
1 doz. wt. 2⅜ lbs. Packed 1 doz.

No. 506 Small Airplane
3⅞" wing spread—5¢ retail
Assorted half red and half silver
to 3 dozen container
1 doz. weight ⅞ lb. Packed 3 doz.

No. 508 Large Airplane
6" wing spread—10¢ retail
Assorted half red and half silver
to dozen
1 doz. weight 1¼ lb. Packed 1 doz.

IMPROVED and NEW

WHEEL TOYS

AN EXCLUSIVE FEATURE — *All have one-piece non-removable axle —no nail to get into child's mouth.* NEW high luster finish, brilliant colors.

The NEW 1938 Oldsmobile is a fast selling big 10¢ toy.

MOTORCYCLE COP is a brand new number.

No. 1516 Motorcycle Cop—4" long
Khaki, trimmed—10¢ retail
1 dozen wt. 2 lbs. Packed 1 doz.

No. 1518 1938 Oldsmobile—5⅝" long—10¢ retail
Assorted 6 red, 2 blue, 2 green, 2 grey to dozen
1 dozen weight 4½ lbs. Packed 1 dozen

No. 504 Ford Coupe—4" long—5¢ retail
Assorted 6 red, 2 green, 2 blue,
2 grey to dozen
1 doz. weight 1¾ lbs. Packed 3 doz.

No. 502 Ford Sedan—4" long—5¢ retail
Assorted 6 red, 2 green, 2 blue,
2 grey to dozen
1 doz. weight 2 lbs. Packed 3 doz.

FARM WHEELED IMPLEMENTS

NOTHING ELSE ON THE

MARKET LIKE THEM

No. 1520 Tractor—4¼" long, 2½" high—10¢ retail
Assorted 8 red, 4 green to dozen
1 dozen weight 3¾ lbs. Packed 1 dozen

YEAR AROUND

SALES APPEAL

No. 526 Plow — 4⅞"
long—10¢ retail
Red, with silver
shares

1 dozen weight ⅞ lb.
Packed 1 dozen

Tractor has universal hitch for attaching plow, trailer, cannon (page 7) and Wagon of Blocks (page 3).

No. 528 Trailer — 6"
long—15¢ retail

Red

1 dozen weight 6 lbs.
Packed 1 dozen

243

AUBURN RUBBER CORPORATION
AUBURN, INDIANA

Terms: 2% 10 days net 30
F.O.B. AUBURN, IND.

TOY PRICE LIST
APRIL 1, 1938

STOCK NO.	ITEM	Weight 1 dz.	Pkd. to Carton	Price Dz.
BOXED SETS				
207	Artillery Set	22 Lb.	1	6.75
231	U.S. Infantry Set	16	1½	6.75
213	U.S. Marine Set	15	1½	6.75
233	Foreign Legion Set	14 1/4	1½	6.75
201	U.S. Infantry Set	7 1/2	3	3.40
205	U.S. Marine Set	7 1/2	3	3.40
209	Foreign Legion Set	7 1/2	3	3.40
105	Farm Animal Set	22 1/2	1½	6.75
101	Farm Animal Set	12	3	3.40
505	Farm Implement Set	27	1	6.75
503	Wheeled Set	26 1/4	1	6.75
501	Wheeled Set	14 1/4	2	3.40
511	Carry Car Trailer W/3 Olds (red, silver,green, blue) in individual four color box	27 3/4	1	5.10
515	Wagon of Blocks	9 1/4	3	3.40
609	Dozen Blocks	9 1/4	3	3.40
601	Brick Building Blocks	25 1/2	2	6.75
603	Brick Building Blocks	45	1	13.50
611	Bag of Building Blocks	10 1/2	1	3.40
BULK ITEMS				
1200	U.S. Infantry Private	5/8 Lb	2	.40
1202	U.S. Infantry Bugler	5/8	2	.40
1204	U.S. Infantry Officer	5/8	2	.40
1210B	U.S. Marine Private	5/8	2	.40
1212B	U.S. Marine Bugler	5/8	2	.40
1204B	Marine Officer	5/8	2	.40
1210W	U.S. Marine Private	5/8	2	.40
1212W	U.S. Marine Bugler	5/8	2	.40
1204W	Marine Officer	5/8	2	.40
220	Foreign Legion Officer	1/2	2	.40
214	Foreign Legion Private	1/2	2	.40
218	Foreign Legion Private	1/2	2	.40
232	Officer on Horse	2 1/4	1	.80
1236	Signalman	1/2	2	.40
1238	Charging Soldier	1/2	2	.40
1520	Tractor	3 3/4	1	.80
528	Trailer	6	1	1.20
526	Plow	7/8	1	.80
504	Ford Coupe	1 3/4	3	.40
502	Ford Sedan	2	3	.40
1518	1938 Oldsmobile	4 1/2	1	.80
506	Airplane - Small	7/8	3	.40
508	Airplane - Large	1 1/4	1	.80
1516	Motorcycle Cop	2	1	.80
102	Horse	2 5/8	1	.80
108	Cow	2 1/2	1	.80
1028	Assorted Horse & Cow	2 1/2	1	.80
104	Colt	7/8	2	.40
106	Pig	1	2	.40
110	Calf	7/8	2	.40
114	Sheep	1 1/8	2	.40
116	Collie Dog			
4046	Assorted Animals (2 Colt, 3 calves, 3 sheep, 1 collie, 3 pig to dz.)	1	2	.40
513	Cannon W/Tractor (Army olive green)	7 7/8	1	1.60
305	Hop Bunny (3 pc. string)	5 3/8	1	1.80
307-9	Scotty Dogs (3 pc. string)	5 3/4	1	1.80
311	Hen & Chicks (3 pc. string)	6 1/2	1	1.80
322	Sponge Eggs	1	3	.36

PRICES SUBJECT TO CHANGE WITHOUT NOTICE

F2823 —5¼ x 4½ x 9, chimney with rack, 2 hinged oven doors, 4 holes, 4 covered handled pots, 5 asstd. utensils. ½ doz. in box..Doz. $2.50

F2825 —9¾ x 6¾ x 12, 5 holes, 2 ovens, 1 hot water faucet, 13 utensils—8 dishes, 2 large and 2 small covered stew pans, 1 coffee pot. ⅙ doz. in box..............Doz. $4.75

HIGH GRADE KITCHEN STOVE

With 4 Utensils

STAR VALUE Nickel Plated—8¾x 5x4 nickel plated tin, brick embossed, 2 ovens, hinged doors. 4 in. chimney, 4 holes. coppered utensils—sauce and fry pans, covd. casserole and kettle. Each in box.

F2829—⅙ doz. in pkg. Doz. **$9.00**

and green grounds, playtime scenes, gilt handles. 1 doz. in box..Doz. 45c

F2812 — 7½x6, 3¼ in. handle, 6 in. red stained handled brush..Doz. 95c

LITHO SAND PAILS WITH SHOVELS

6 litho juvenile and seashore designs, lacquered gilt lined, wire bails, turned wood handles; wood handled shovels. Asstd. 1 doz. in carton.

F2875 — 4⅓ x 4¼, painted shovels 8½ in.... ....Doz. 52c

F2876—6¼x6¼, 11 in. litho picture shovels, lacquer back....Doz. $1.00

F2896—Ht. 13 in., heavy wire frame and uprights, lacquered 3¼ in. hopper, 14½ in. incline, 4 in. car, can of sand. ⅙ doz. in box..Doz. $4.50

F2899 — "Dumping Sandy," ht. 13 in., heavy steel frame footed base, 3¾ in. enameled hopper, 3½ in. car, adjustable slide at base dumps car at any point; with 18x14 cardboard tray, metal scoop and box of sand. ⅙ doz. in box............Doz. $4.50

SKY SCRAPER AUTOMATIC ELEVATOR

Marbles dropped in hopper give perpetual motion.

F2895 — Ht. 23 in., litho 10 story sky scraper, elevator inside, heavy steel base, 12½ in. enameled hopper, supply of marbles, red and white electric lights flash alternately when elevator works, wire connections for dry batteries. 1 in box.

Each, $1.25

F2897—Ht. 18 in., heavy wire frame and uprights, 6½ in. lacquered hopper, 19½ in. retinned incline, 5½ in. car, large can of sand. ⅙ doz. in box. Doz. $8.50

F2894 — Crane, ht. 14½ in., base 9x5, enameled heavy steel, litho engineer dumps car; with 12x30¼ cardboard tray, enameled scoop and box of sand ⅙ doz. in box. Doz. $9.00

TANGO TWIRLERS

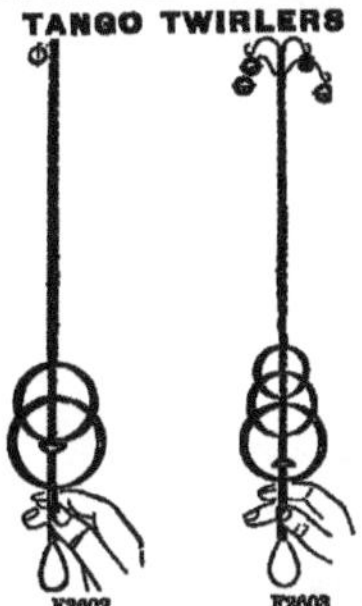

F2602 F2603

Twirlers 21 in.—Heavy twisted copper wire rods with slides, loop handles, brass bell ends, flat colored metal rings, give vari-colored bubble effect when slide is pushed. Doz.

F2602—2 rings. 2 doz. in box..$0.45 (Total 90c)

F2603—3 rings, 4 bells. 1 doz. in box .. .. .89

F2997 — Ht. 11 in., bright enameled in 6 colors, spiral rod, reversible figures on steel bar. 1 doz. in box Doz. 89

F2998—Ht. 16 in., 2 red & blue enameled steel crosspieces, reversible figures and colored pinwheel Each in box. ½ doz. in pkg. Doz. $2

"PANAMA" PILE DRIVI

F2674 — Ht. 17 in., heavy steel enameled incline runway, gilt ing, imitation weight automat operated by 12 large marbles driving action. ⅙ doz. in box. Doz.

PEWTER SOLDIERS

2¼ in. soldiers, 2⅞ in. mounted officers, facsimile U. S. regular and sailors' uniforms. Fine pewter, tinted faces, vari-color painted uniforms large green base, folding white canvas tents; metal tent pole with flag. Each set elastic fastened to glazed card in flat box.

6 Pcs—4 soldiers, mounted officer and tent.

F3491—⅙ doz. sets in pkg. Doz. sets, $2.25

10 Pcs—5 soldiers, captain, 2 mounted officers, brass finish mounted cannon, tent.

F3486—¼ doz. sets in pkg. Doz. sets, $4.50

23 Pcs—Soldiers—running shooting, wounded, etc., red cross nurse, 3 cannon. Box 13 x 10¼.

F5008—¼ doz. sets in pkg Doz. sets, $4.50

17 Pcs and Pop Gun —10 soldiers, captain, drummer, 2 mounted officers, brass finish mounted cannon, 2 tents, 16½ in. lever action pop gun, blued steel barrel, walnut stock, cork and string.

F3487—⅙ doz. sets in pkg. Doz. sets, $9.00

22 Pcs—7 soldiers, captain, 2 mounted officers, 7 Indians and Chief, 2 brass finish brass mounted cannons, 2 tents.

F3488—⅙ doz. sets in pkg. Doz. sets, $9.00

39 Pcs—Soldiers mounted, in groups, etc., 3 trees, 2 cannon, aeroplane cannon in action, red cross corps and nurse, house in flames, etc.

F5009—¼ doz. sets in pkg. Doz. sets, $9.00

35 Pcs — 26 soldiers, flag bearer, captain, 3 mounted officers, 2 brass finish mounted cannons, 2 tents.

F3489—1 set in pkg...... Set, $1.40

53 Pcs — Army and navy outfit, 14 in. khaki color, 14 in. dress uniform, 12 sailors including captain and drummer for each, 6 mounted officers, 3 brass finish mounted cannons, 4 tents.

F3400—1 set in box.........Set, $2.50

BOYS' & GIRLS' TOY WATCH

Printed dials and crystals.

GIRLS' TOY WATCH ASSORTMENT

F5165—1¼ in. gilt finish, asstd. 3 color frosted jewel inlaid enamel effect fronts, moving hands, fleur de lis and scroll brooches. Each on card. Asstd. 1 doz. in box..........Doz. 60c

BOYS' SPRING HUNTING CASE WATCH

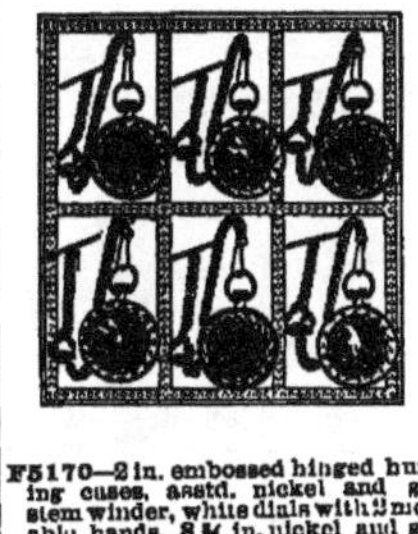

F5170—2 in. embossed hinged hunting cases, asstd. nickel and gilt stem winder, white dials with 2 movable hands, 8¾ in. nickel and gilt chains with crystal charms. ½ doz. on card. 1 doz. in box......Doz. 96c

MECHANICAL TICK WATC

F5171—2 in. gilt bevel cas crystal, printed dial, movin 10 in. heavy chain, when ticks for 2 minutes, lever ping and starting. Each in ered box. ½ doz. in pkg.Dc

TOY WRIST WAT

F3707 — Shaped leather with eyelets, nickel plate imit. watch celluloid dial frame. Asstd. colors. card.............. ....

The good things i world are for the me who hustles. He wh not hustle neither d nor achieves success.

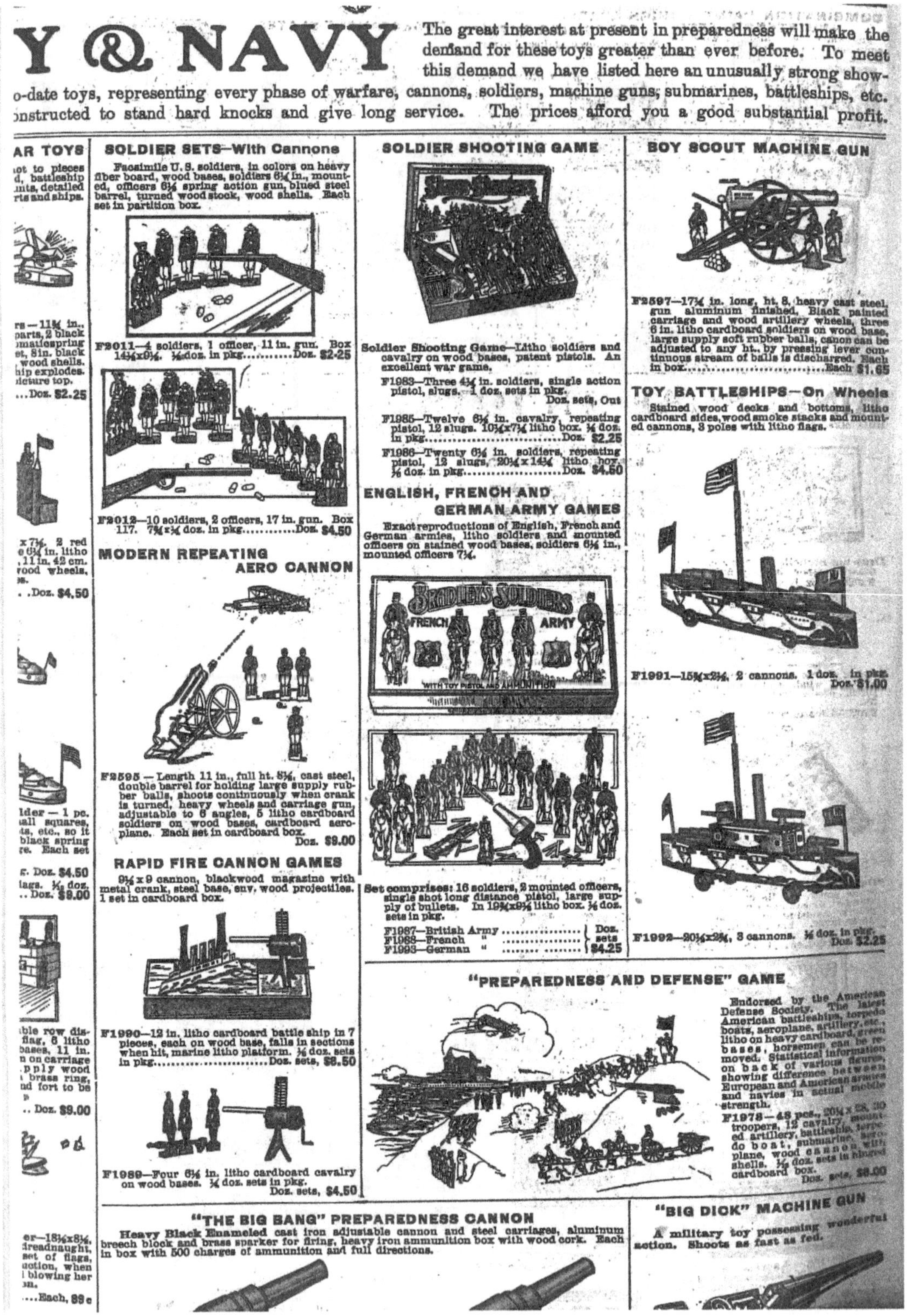

Y & NAVY

The great interest at present in preparedness will make the demand for these toys greater than ever before. To meet this demand we have listed here an unusually strong show- o-date toys, representing every phase of warfare, cannons, soldiers, machine guns, submarines, battleships, etc. onstructed to stand hard knocks and give long service. The prices afford you a good substantial profit.

AR TOYS

ıot to pieces d, battleship ınits, detailed rts and ships.

rs — 11¾ in., parts, 2 black omatic spring et, 8 in. black wood shells. hip explodes. picture top. ...Doz. $2.25

x 7½. 2 red e 6¼ in. litho , 11 in. 42 cm. vood wheels, s. . .Doz. $4.50

lder — 1 pc. all squares, ts, etc., so it black spring re. Each set

g. Doz. $4.50
lags. ⅓ doz. .. Doz. $9.00

ble row dis- flag, 6 litho bases, 11 in. n on carriage pply wood brass ring, nd fort to be ... Doz. $9.00

er—18½x8¼. dreadnaught, set of flags, action, when blowing her m. ...Each, 89c

SOLDIER SETS—With Cannons

Facsimile U. S. soldiers, in colors on heavy fiber board, wood bases, soldiers 6¼ in., mounted, officers 6½ spring action gun, blued steel barrel, turned wood stock, wood shells. Each set in partition box.

F2011—4 soldiers, 1 officer, 11 in. gun. Box 14½x9½. ½ doz. in pkg..........Doz. $2.25

F2012—10 soldiers, 2 officers, 17 in. gun. Box 117. 7¾x¼ doz. in pkg...........Doz. $4.50

MODERN REPEATING AERO CANNON

F2595 — Length 11 in., full ht. 8⅛, cast steel, double barrel for holding large supply rubber balls, shoots continuously when crank is turned, heavy wheels and carriage gun, adjustable to 6 angles, 5 litho cardboard soldiers on wood bases, cardboard aeroplane. Each set in cardboard box. Doz. $9.00

RAPID FIRE CANNON GAMES

9½ x 9 cannon, blackwood magazine with metal crank, steel base, env. wood projectiles. 1 set in cardboard box.

F1990—12 in. litho cardboard battle ship in 7 pieces, each on wood base, falls in sections when hit, marine litho platform. ½ doz. sets in pkg.........................Doz. sets, $8.50

F1989—Four 6½ in. litho cardboard cavalry on wood bases. ¼ doz. sets in pkg. Doz. sets, $4.50

SOLDIER SHOOTING GAME

Soldier Shooting Game—Litho soldiers and cavalry on wood bases, patent pistols. An excellent war game.

F1983—Three 4¼ in. soldiers, single action pistol, slugs. 1 doz. sets in pkg. Doz. sets, Out

F1985—Twelve 6½ in. cavalry, repeating pistol, 12 slugs. 10¼x7¼ litho box. ¼ doz. in pkg..............................Doz. $2.25

F1986—Twenty 6½ in. soldiers, repeating pistol, 12 slugs, 20¼ x 14¼ litho box. ⅙ doz. in pkg......................Doz. $4.50

ENGLISH, FRENCH AND GERMAN ARMY GAMES

Exact reproductions of English, French and German armies, litho soldiers and mounted officers on stained wood bases, soldiers 6½ in., mounted officers 7¼.

Set comprises: 16 soldiers, 2 mounted officers, single shot long distance pistol, large supply of bullets. In 19¾x9½ litho box. ⅙ doz. sets in pkg.

F1987—British Army	Doz.
F1988—French "	sets
F1993—German "	$4.25

BOY SCOUT MACHINE GUN

F2597—17¼ in. long, ht. 8, heavy cast steel, gun aluminum finished, Black painted carriage and wood artillery wheels, three 6 in. litho cardboard soldiers on wood base, large supply soft rubber balls, canon can be adjusted to any ht., by pressing lever continuous stream of balls is discharged. Each in box.................................Each $1.65

TOY BATTLESHIPS—On Wheels

Stained wood decks and bottoms, litho cardboard sides, wood smoke stacks and mounted cannons, 3 poles with litho flags.

F1991—15¾x2¼, 2 cannons. 1 doz. in pkg. Doz. $1.00

F1992—20½x2¾, 3 cannons. ½ doz. in pkg. Doz. $2.25

"PREPAREDNESS AND DEFENSE" GAME

Endorsed by the American Defense Society. The latest American battleships, torpedo boats, aeroplane, artillery, etc., litho on heavy cardboard, green bases, horsemen can be removed. Statistical information on back of various figures, showing difference between European and American armies and navies in actual mobile strength.

F1978—48 pcs., 20¼ x 28, 30 troopers, 12 cavalry, mounted artillery, battleship, torpedo boat, submarine, aeroplane, wood cannon with shells. ½ doz. sets in hinged cardboard box. Doz. sets, $8.00

"THE BIG BANG" PREPAREDNESS CANNON

Heavy Black Enameled cast iron adjustable cannon and steel carriages, aluminum breech block and brass sparker for firing, heavy iron ammunition box with wood cork. Each in box with 500 charges of ammunition and full directions.

"BIG DICK" MACHINE GUN

A military toy possessing wonderful action. Shoots as fast as fed.

POST-WAR PLASTICS COMPANIES

Little is known about post-war American makers of plastic toy soldiers. This is what I've been able to turn up.

The February, 1954 issue of Southern Toy Journal reported the president of MPC was Marvin Ross. The firm's address when the article was written was 303 Fourth Avenue in New York City, but a move was to be made on February lst to 55 West 13th Street, "both offices and factory". In the past, I'd found a 1260 Zerega Avenue, Bronx, address, but I'm not sure when MPC was located there.

The month before, the same publication reported that Multiple Products (MPC) was putting out a Mighty Canoe (13" long) and three Indians. The canoe was made of "high impact plastic" and the braves of "unbreakable polyethylene". The set came in a "full-view, self-display box". MPC also put out Five Indian Warriors – two standing with bow, two kneeling with bow and one standing with rifle – displayed in "crystal clear acetate". They retailed for 29 cents. The canoe alone, with "twin true-to-scale paddles" and "mounting posts for three Indian Warriors" seems to have sold for 29 cents and 49 cents with the figures.

Most of all this research comes from the Southern Toy Journal, which was sent to my by collectors Terry Sells and Dick MacNary. In the February, 1954 issue, ARCHER seems to have introduced its "Complete Space People Family, Style No. 198". There were eleven pieces; five men, three women, three children.

Somewhere along the way, I located an address for ANDY GARD. In 1956 it was located in Leetsdale, Pennsylvania.

REL: An ad in the 1955-56 Toy Yearbook shows a Rel cavalry set with a "U.S. Army" covered wagon, and the note, with logo, that it's "A Plasco Toy". And it's listed as a "Plasco Rel Cavalry Set".

The only address I've found for PAYTON is the usual New York location for so many toy companes: 200 Fifth Avenue. In August, 1955, the Southern Toy Journal stated that Payton's Davy Crockett Giants of the West had passed the two-million mark. The complete set had three frontier figures (including Davy) plus three horses. The figures could be mounted or stood alone. Also mentioned in the same article is that Payton, which began in 1946, was the first to introduce a complete line of polyethylene unbreakable toys. This was in 1953.

GIBBS: In November, 1956, Bob Bard's toy-soldier catalog advertised Gibbs' great Custer's Last Stand set as "New", at $1.95 plus postage.

Two addresses collectors may already know, but which were new to me: PALMER: 31 Stone Avenue, Brooklyn, NY in the April, 1954 Southern Toy Journal and in the 1971 Toys magazine directory issue, at 10720 Avenue D in Brooklyn. A GAY TOYS, INC. is listed at 6432 Cass Avenue, Detroit. Since PFPC reported in its issue 51 (October, 1997) that the soldier-making Gay Toys had an address in Walled Lake Michigan, operating "from the 1950s into the 1970s" this conceivably is the same company, at an early address, perhaps its earliest.

LIDO seems to have begun producing its cowboys and Indians in 1950, and its GIs probably the next year.

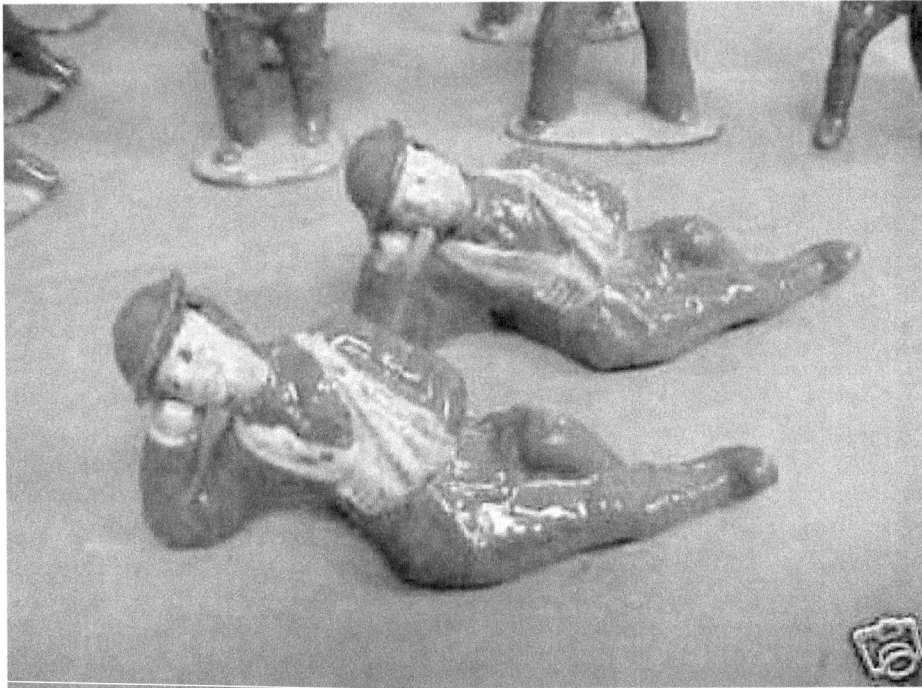

A final note: Here's proof that even the seemingly forever lost can eventually turn up, as this one has in 2009. Collectors, knowing it only from a catalog drawing, have been hunting for this piece for over thirty years. It comes from Metal Cast, and in the company's catalog is described as **28A Wounded**. Metal Cast sold molds to the public, and also manufactured their own soldiers and other products from those molds. After all those decades I was convinced either that Metal Cast had never actually produced the mold, or that absolutely no one had bought it. And suddenly not only did it pop up, but there were two!

In this vein, I'm still looking for three more soldiers: A William Feix Japanese officer. They made a Russian officer for their Russo-Japanese war sets, so a Japanese officer seems likely, but so far none has turned up. An Auburn Rubber larger variation of their seated machine gunner. It appears several times in their 1941 catalog, but only as a very detailed drawing, suggesting it was produced. And finally, an Auburn Rubber piece I know existed, because I played with it. Two other collectors have seen it, but didn't keep it, nor photograph it. It's a running figure, probably a pilot, looking up to his left. If any reader has one or more of these I would naturally appreciate hearing from him or her.

OTHER RAMBLE HOUSE BOOKS BY
RICHARD O'BRIEN

Richard O'Brien is the author of 39 books, including 9 novels. This is the first publication of his 'lost' mystery. It's a modern noir about a private dick who gets into something that just might be tougher than his previous case, the Snelling Affair.

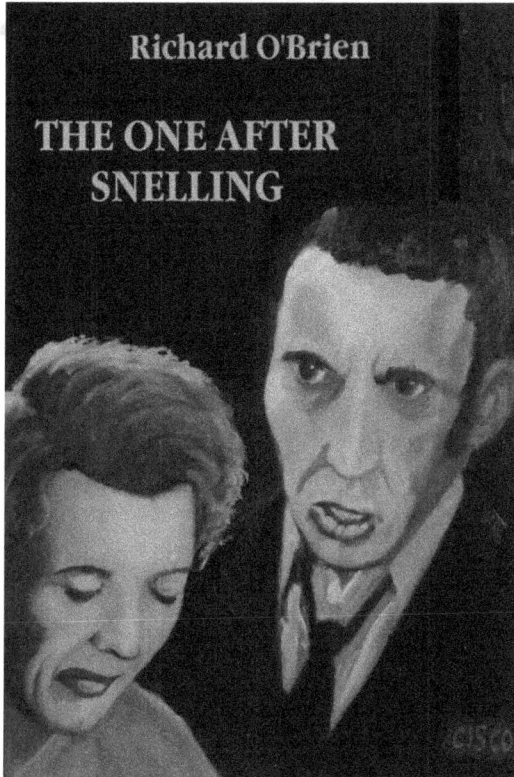

All of Richard O'Brien's Ramble House books are available at www.ramblehouse.com but for the best deal, e-mail, write or call

> **Fender Tucker**
> **10329 Sheephead Drive**
> **Vancleave MS 39565**
> **fender@ramblehouse.com**
> **228-828-1783**

"Hollywood Dreams" is Richard O'Brien's historical novel about the Depression years of the 1930s, as a young girl from the Dust Bowl fights to make her dream of success come true.

"Better than 'The Grapes of Wrath"...
Orville C. Britton

SUZY
BY O'BRIEN & VOJTKO

Richard O'Brien
Bob Vojtko

SUZY is a coffee-table-sized paperback that contains the complete series of comics written by Richard O'Brien and drawn by Bob Vojtko and published back in 1985 -- 216 strips in all. "A remarkable book for a number of reasons. The main one is that the comics themselves are a joy to read. O'Brien's gags are funny, and over the course of just a few weeks of strips, he successfully creates a connection between the characters and his readers. Vojtko's artwork has never been better. This book is a dream come true". Richard Krauss, MIDNIGHT FICTION

250

A collection of all of the Koky Sunday funnies from 1979 to 1981 by Richard O'Brien and artist Mort Gerberg. These 104 B&W comics are reprinted for the first time since they appeared in national syndication.

THE KOKY SUNDAYS 1979 - 1981

The companion piece to THE KOKY SUNDAYS recently published by Ramble House. It's the daily comic strips of the odd family strip by Richard O'Brien and Mort Gerberg from the early 70s.

"The funny side of female" Vogue magazine

"A timely, lifestyle story line about a two-income family". Editor and Publisher

"The funny pages are catching up with real life." Ms. magazine

THE KOKY DAILIES

Richard O'Brien & Mort Gerberg

251

RAMBLE HOUSE's
HARRY STEPHEN KEELER WEBWORK MYSTERIES
Titles in **bold** are available ONLY in the RAMBLE HOUSE edition

The Ace of Spades Murder
The Affair of the Bottled Deuce
The Amazing Web
The Barking Clock
Behind That Mask
The Book with the Orange Leaves
The Bottle with the Green Wax Seal
The Box from Japan
The Case of the Canny Killer
The Case of the Crazy Corpse
The Case of the Flying Hands
The Case of the Ivory Arrow
The Case of the Jeweled Ragpicker
The Case of the Lavender Gripsack
The Case of the Mysterious Moll
The Case of the 16 Beans
The Case of the Transparent Nude
The Case of the Transposed Legs
The Case of the Two-Headed Idiot
The Case of the Two Strange Ladies
The Circus Stealers
Cleopatra's Tears
A Copy of Beowulf
The Crimson Cube
The Face of the Man From Saturn
Find the Clock
The Five Silver Buddhas
The 4th King
The Gallows Waits, My Lord!
The Green Jade Hand
Finger! Finger!
Hangman's Nights
I, Chameleon
I Killed Lincoln at 10:13!
The Iron Ring
The Man Who Changed His Skin
The Man with the Crimson Box
The Man with the Magic Eardrums
The Man with the Wooden Spectacles
The Marceau Case
The Matilda Hunter Murder

The Monocled Monster
The Murder of London Lew
The Murdered Mathematician
The Mysterious Card
The Mysterious Ivory Ball of Wong Shing Li
Mystery of the Fiddling Cracksman
The Peacock Fan
The Photo of Lady X
The Portrait of Jirjohn Cobb
Report on Vanessa Hewstone
Riddle of the Travelling Skull
Riddle of the Wooden Parrakeet
The Scarlet Mummy
The Search for X-Y-Z
The Sharkskin Book
Sing Sing Nights
The Six From Nowhere
The Skull of the Waltzing Clown
The Spectacles of Mr. Cagliostro
Stand By—London Calling!
The Steeltown Strangler
The Stolen Gravestone
Strange Journey
The Strange Will
The Straw Hat Murders
The Street of 1000 Eyes
Thieves' Nights
Three Novellos
The Tiger Snake
The Trap
Vagabond Nights 1 (The Defrauded Yeggman)
Vagabond Nights 2 (10 Hours)
The Vanishing Gold Truck
The Voice of the Seven Sparrows
The Washington Square Enigma
When Thief Meets Thief
The White Circle
The Wonderful Scheme of Mr.
    Christopher Thorne
X. Jones—of Scotland Yard
Y. Cheung, Business Detective

Keeler Related Works

A To Izzard: A Harry Stephen Keeler Companion by Fender Tucker — Articles and stories about Harry, by Harry, and in his style. Included is a compleat bibliography.

Wild About Harry: Reviews of Keeler Novels — Edited by Richard Polt & Fender Tucker — 22 reviews of works by Harry Stephen Keeler from *Keeler News.* A perfect introduction to the author.

The Keeler Keyhole Collection: Annotated newsletter rants from Harry Stephen Keeler, edited by Francis M. Nevins. Over 400 pages of incredibly personal Keeleriana.

Fakealoo — Pastiches of the style of Harry Stephen Keeler by selected demented members of the HSK Society. Updated every year with the new winner.

RAMBLE HOUSE's OTHER LOONS

Strands of the Web: Short Stories of Harry Stephen Keeler — Edited and Introduced by Fred Cleaver

The Sam McCain Novels — Ed Gorman's terrific series includes *The Day the Music Died, Wake Up Little Susie* and *Will You Still Love Me Tomorrow?*

A Shot Rang Out — Three decades of reviews from Jon Breen

Blood Moon — The first of the Robert Payne series by Ed Gorman

The Time Armada — Fox B. Holden's 1953 SF gem.

Black River Falls — Suspense from the master, Ed Gorman

Sideslip — 1968 SF masterpiece by Ted White and Dave Van Arnam

The Triune Man — Mindscrambling science fiction from Richard A. Lupoff

Detective Duff Unravels It — Episodic mysteries by Harvey O'Higgins

Mysterious Martin, the Master of Murder — Two versions of a strange 1912 novel by Tod Robbins about a man who writes books that can kill.

The Master of Mysteries — 1912 novel of supernatural sleuthing by Gelett Burgess

Dago Red — 22 tales of dark suspense by Bill Pronzini

The Night Remembers — A 1991 Jack Walsh mystery from Ed Gorman set in Black River Falls

Rough Cut & New, Improved Murder — Ed Gorman's first two novels

Hollywood Dreams — A novel of the Depression by Richard O'Brien

Six Gelett Burgess Novels — *The Master of Mysteries, The White Cat, Two O'Clock Courage, Ladies in Boxes, Find the Woman, The Heart Line*

The Organ Reader — A huge compilation of just about everything published in the 1971-1972 radical bay-area newspaper, *THE ORGAN*.

A Clear Path to Cross — Sharon Knowles short mystery stories by Ed Lynskey

Old Times' Sake — Short stories by James Reasoner from Mike Shayne Magazine

Freaks and Fantasies — Tales by Tod Robbins, collaborator of Tod Browning on the film FREAKS.

Five Jim Harmon Sleaze Double Novels — *Vixen Hollow/Celluloid Scandal, The Man Who Made Maniacs/-Silent Siren, Ape Rape/Wanton Witch, Sex Burns Like Fire/Twist Session*, and *Sudden Lust/Passion Strip.* More doubles to come!

Marblehead: A Novel of H.P. Lovecraft — A long-lost masterpiece from Richard A. Lupoff. Published for the first time!

The Compleat Ova Hamlet — Parodies of SF authors by Richard A. Lupoff – New edition!

The Secret Adventures of Sherlock Holmes — Three Sherlockian pastiches by the Brooklyn author/-publisher, Gary Lovisi.

The Universal Holmes — Richard A. Lupoff's 2007 collection of five Holmesian pastiches and a recipe for giant rat stew.

Four Joel Townsley Rogers Novels — By the author of *The Red Right Hand: Once In a Red Moon, Lady With the Dice, The Stopped Clock, Never Leave My Bed*

Two Joel Townsley Rogers Story Collections — Night of Horror and Killing Time

All Twenty Norman Berrow Novels — *The Bishop's Sword, Ghost House, Don't Go Out After Dark, Claws of the Cougar, The Smokers of Hashish, The Secret Dancer, Don't Jump Mr. Boland!, The Footprints of Satan, Fingers for Ransom, The Three Tiers of Fantasy, The Spaniard's Thumb, The Eleventh Plague, Words Have Wings, One Thrilling Night, The Lady's in Danger, It Howls at Night, The Terror in the Fog, Oil Under the Window, Murder in the Melody, The Singing Room*

The N. R. De Mexico Novels — Robert Bragg presents *Marijuana Girl, Madman on a Drum, Private Chauffeur* in one volume.

Four Chelsea Quinn Yarbro Novels featuring Charlie Moon — *Ogilvie, Tallant and Moon, Music When the Sweet Voice Dies, Poisonous Fruit* and *Dead Mice*

Four Walter S. Masterman Mysteries — *The Green Toad, The Flying Beast, The Yellow Mistletoe* and *The Wrong Verdict,* fantastic impossible plots. More to come.

Two Hake Talbot Novels — *Rim of the Pit, The Hangman's Handyman.* Classic locked room mysteries.

Two Alexander Laing Novels — *The Motives of Nicholas Holtz* and *Dr. Scarlett*, stories of medical mayhem and intrigue from the 30s.

Four David Hume Novels — *Corpses Never Argue, Cemetery First Stop, Make Way for the Mourners, Eternity Here I Come*, and more to come.

Three Wade Wright Novels — *Echo of Fear, Death At Nostalgia Street* and *It Leads to Murder*, with more to come!

Six Rupert Penny Novels — *Policeman's Holiday, Policeman's Evidence, Lucky Policeman, Sealed Room Murder, Sweet Poison* and *Policeman in Armour*, classic impossible mysteries.

Five Jack Mann Novels — Strange murder in the English countryside. *Gees' First Case, Nightmare Farm, Grey Shapes, The Ninth Life, The Glass Too Many.*

Seven Max Afford Novels — *Owl of Darkness, Death's Mannikins, Blood on His Hands, The Dead Are Blind, The Sheep and the Wolves, Sinners in Paradise* and *Two Locked Room Mysteries and a Ripping Yarn* by one of Australia's finest novelists.

Five Joseph Shallit Novels — *The Case of the Billion Dollar Body, Lady Don't Die on My Doorstep, Kiss the Killer, Yell Bloody Murder* and *Take Your Last Look.* One of the best from the 50s.

Two Crimson Clown Novels — By Johnston McCulley, author of the Zorro novels, *The Crimson Clown* and *The Crimson Clown Again.*

The Best of 10-Story Book — edited by Chris Mikul, over 35 stories from the literary magazine Harry Stephen Keeler edited.

A Young Man's Heart — A forgotten early classic by Cornell Woolrich

The Anthony Boucher Chronicles — edited by Francis M. Nevins
Book reviews by Anthony Boucher written for the *San Francisco Chronicle,* 1942 – 1947. Essential and fascinating reading.

Muddled Mind: Complete Works of Ed Wood, Jr. — David Hayes and Hayden Davis deconstruct the life and works of a mad genius.

Gadsby — A lipogram (a novel without the letter E). Ernest Vincent Wright's last work, published in 1939 right before his death.

My First Time: The One Experience You Never Forget — Michael Birchwood — 64 true first-person narratives of how they lost it.

Automaton — Brilliant treatise on robotics: 1928-style! By H. Stafford Hatfield

The Incredible Adventures of Rowland Hern — Impossible crimes (1928) by Nicholas Olde.

Slammer Days — Two full-length prison memoirs: *Men into Beasts* (1952) by George Sylvester Viereck and *Home Away From Home* (1962) by Jack Woodford

Murder in Black and White — 1931 classic tennis whodunit by Evelyn Elder

Killer's Caress — Cary Moran's 1936 hardboiled thriller

The Golden Dagger — 1951 Scotland Yard yarn by E. R. Punshon

A Smell of Smoke — 1951 English countryside thriller by Miles Burton

Ruled By Radio — 1925 futuristic novel by Robert L. Hadfield & Frank E. Farncombe

Murder in Silk — A 1937 Yellow Peril novel of the silk trade by Ralph Trevor

The Case of the Withered Hand — 1936 potboiler by John G. Brandon

Finger-prints Never Lie — A 1939 classic detective novel by John G. Brandon

Inclination to Murder — 1966 thriller by New Zealand's Harriet Hunter

Invaders from the Dark — Classic werewolf tale from Greye La Spina

Fatal Accident — Murder by automobile, a 1936 mystery by Cecil M. Wills

The Devil Drives — A prison and lost treasure novel by Virgil Markham

Dr. Odin — Douglas Newton's 1933 potboiler comes back to life.

The Chinese Jar Mystery — Murder in the manor by John Stephen Strange, 1934

The Julius Caesar Murder Case — A classic 1935 re-telling of the assassination by Wallace Irwin that's much more fun than the Shakespeare version

West Texas War and Other Western Stories — by Gary Lovisi

The Contested Earth and Other SF Stories — A never-before published space opera and seven short stories by Jim Harmon.

Tales of the Macabre and Ordinary — Modern twisted horror by Chris Mikul, author of the *Bizarrism* series.

The Gold Star Line — Seaboard adventure from L.T. Reade and Robert Eustace.

The Werewolf vs the Vampire Woman — Hard to believe ultraviolence by either Arthur M. Scarm or Arthur M. Scram.

Black Hogan Strikes Again — Australia's Peter Renwick pens a tale of the outback.

Don Diablo: Book of a Lost Film — Two-volume treatment of a western by Paul Landres, with diagrams. Intro by Francis M. Nevins.

The Charlie Chaplin Murder Mystery — Movie hijinks by Wes D. Gehring

The Koky Comics — A collection of all of the 1978-1981 Sunday and daily comic strips by Richard O'Brien and Mort Gerberg, in two volumes.

Suzy — Another collection of comic strips from Richard O'Brien and Bob Vojtko

Dime Novels: Ramble House's 10-Cent Books — *Knife in the Dark* by Robert Leslie Bellem, *Hot Lead* and *Song of Death* by Ed Earl Repp, *A Hashish House in New York* by H.H. Kane, and five more.

Blood in a Snap — The *Finnegan's Wake* of the 21st century, by Jim Weiler and Al Gorithm

Stakeout on Millennium Drive — Award-winning Indianapolis Noir — Ian Woollen.

Dope Tales #1 — Two dope-riddled classics; *Dope Runners* by Gerald Grantham and *Death Takes the Joystick* by Phillip Condé.

Dope Tales #2 — Two more narco-classics; *The Invisible Hand* by Rex Dark and *The Smokers of Hashish* by Norman Berrow.

Dope Tales #3 — Two enchanting novels of opium by the master, Sax Rohmer. *Dope* and *The Yellow Claw.*

Tenebrae — Ernest G. Henham's 1898 horror tale brought back.

The Singular Problem of the Stygian House-Boat — Two classic tales by John Kendrick Bangs about the denizens of Hades.

Tiresias — Psychotic modern horror novel by Jonathan M. Sweet.

The One After Snelling — Kickass modern noir from Richard O'Brien.

The Sign of the Scorpion — 1935 Edmund Snell tale of oriental evil.

The House of the Vampire — 1907 poetic thriller by George S. Viereck.

An Angel in the Street — Modern hardboiled noir by Peter Genovese.

The Devil's Mistress — Scottish gothic tale by J. W. Brodie-Innes.

The Lord of Terror — 1925 mystery with master-criminal, Fantômas.

The Lady of the Terraces — 1925 adventure by E. Charles Vivian.

My Deadly Angel — 1955 Cold War drama by John Chelton

Prose Bowl — Futuristic satire — Bill Pronzini & Barry N. Malzberg .

Satan's Den Exposed — True crime in Truth or Consequences New Mexico — Award-winning journalism by the *Desert Journal.*

The Amorous Intrigues & Adventures of Aaron Burr — by Anonymous — Hot historical action.

I Stole $16,000,000 — A true story by cracksman Herbert E. Wilson.

The Black Dark Murders — Vintage 50s college murder yarn by Milt Ozaki, writing as Robert O. Saber.

Sex Slave — Potboiler of lust in the days of Cleopatra — Dion Leclerq.

You'll Die Laughing — Bruce Elliott's 1945 novel of murder at a practical joker's English countryside manor.

The Private Journal & Diary of John H. Surratt — The memoirs of the man who conspired to assassinate President Lincoln.

Dead Man Talks Too Much — Hollywood boozer by Weed Dickenson

Red Light — History of legal prostitution in Shreveport Louisiana by Eric Brock. Includes wonderful photos of the houses and the ladies.

A Snark Selection — Lewis Carroll's *The Hunting of the Snark* with two Snarkian chapters by Harry Stephen Keeler — Illustrated by Gavin L. O'Keefe.

Ripped from the Headlines! — The Jack the Ripper story as told in the newspaper articles in the *New York* and *London Times.*

Geronimo — S. M. Barrett's 1905 autobiography of a noble American.

The White Peril in the Far East — Sidney Lewis Gulick's 1905 indictment of the West and assurance that Japan would never attack the U.S.

The Compleat Calhoon — All of Fender Tucker's works: Includes *Totah Six-Pack, Weed, Women and Song* and *Tales from the Tower,* plus a CD of all of his songs.

Fender Tucker, Prop.
www.ramblehouse.com   fender@ramblehouse.com
10329 Sheephead Drive, Vancleave MS 39565
228-826-1783

www.ingramcontent.com/pod-product-compliance
Lightning Source LLC
Chambersburg PA
CBHW062038090426
42740CB00016B/2946